The Psychology of Learning

The Psychology of Learning

An Introduction from a Functional-Cognitive Perspective

Jan De Houwer and Sean Hughes

The MIT Press
Cambridge, Massachusetts
London, England

This book was set in Stone Serif and Stone Sans by Westchester Publishing Services. Printed and bound in the United States of America.

Library of Congress Cataloging-in-Publication Data

Names: Houwer, Jan de, author. | Hughes, Sean, author.
Title: The psychology of learning : an introduction from a functional-cognitive perspective / Jan De Houwer and Sean Hughes.
Description: Cambridge, Massachusetts : The MIT Press, 2020. | Includes bibliographical references.
Identifiers: LCCN 2019049224 | ISBN 9780262539234 (paperback)
Subjects: LCSH: Learning, Psychology of--Research. | Cognitive learning. | Functionalism (Psychology)
Classification: LCC LB1060 .H668 2020 | DDC 370.15/23--dc23
LC record available at https://lccn.loc.gov/2019049224

10   9   8   7   6   5   4   3   2   1

Dedicated to the memory of Paul Eelen

Contents

2 Classical Conditioning: Effects of Regularities in the Presence of Multiple Stimuli   57

3 Operant Conditioning: Effects of Regularities in the Presence of Stimuli and Behavior   117

Preface

There may be only two authors listed on its cover, but this book represents the combined effort of many. Its roots stretch back to an earlier textbook on learning that Paul Eelen wrote in the 1980s for a course he taught at the University of Leuven (Belgium). His textbook undoubtedly had its own roots, but it is difficult to discern what they were (some of Paul Eelen's earliest graduate students remember that he was especially fond of Mackintosh, 1983). In 2002, the first author of the current book, Jan De Houwer, who was also a graduate student of Paul Eelen, revised the textbook for his own learning psychology course at Ghent University (Belgium). For that revision, he drew on the textbooks of Domjan (2000) and Schwartz, Wasserman, and Robbins (2002). During subsequent years, Jan Velghe optimized the textbook's layout by adding sections on learning goals and introductory tasks at the beginning of each chapter. A second major revision was undertaken by Jan De Houwer in 2009 when he was on sabbatical leave at the University of New South Wales (Australia). For the first time, the basic tenets of the functional-cognitive framework were added, including the definition of learning as ontogenetic adaptation (i.e., as the impact of environmental regularities on behavior; see the introductory chapter). This revision involved a drastic restructuring of the text, including the systematic separation of functional knowledge about learning (i.e., knowledge about its moderators) from mental theories of learning (i.e., knowledge about its mental mediators). Bouton's (2007) book on learning and behavior provided a welcome source of information for that revision.

The book that you are now reading emerged after a third major revision by both authors, Jan De Houwer and Sean Hughes, in 2018 and 2019. It involved an almost complete rewriting of the introductory chapter, reflecting the conceptual work that both authors were engaged in together with several colleagues (most prominently Dermot Barnes-Holmes and Agnes Moors). The chapter on operant conditioning was also revised substantially, based primarily on the works of Catania (2013) and Michael (2004). The book also grew to include a new chapter on complex learning (to reflect current developments) as well as a chapter on applied learning psychology (to illustrate the power and potential of learning psychology in predicting and influencing real problems facing real people in the real world). Once again, (the second edition of) Bouton's excellent book (2016) served as a benchmark when deciding which topics should be included in our own book.

Because the current book has benefited from the work of many, we were uncomfortable with the thought that we would profit financially from it. Thus, making the pdf version of the book accessible to all seemed like the right thing to do. We hope that the open-access format will also stimulate others to contribute to the future growth and development of this book. We realize that the current version is undoubtedly flawed and limited in many respects given the gaps in our own knowledge and understanding of the literature on learning. We therefore welcome input and suggestions on how we can continue to improve the book in the years to come. To foster such interactions, we created the website www.psychologyoflearning.be through which we can share comments of readers, as well as resources for students and teachers, such as PowerPoint slides.

Although the book certainly has it flaws, many of the limits of our book are the result of carefully considered choices. We use this book for a class of (primarily) second-year psychology bachelor students that involves about thirty hours of teaching. In this setting, it does not make sense to present a complete and detailed overview of the learning literature. Instead, our course (and therefore this book) provides only an introduction to the learning literature. As you will notice when consulting the book, we often refer readers to review papers or to other textbooks after providing only a glimpse of a specific topic in learning research. So let us be clear from the start: if you are looking for a comprehensive and detailed review of the learning literature, this book will not satisfy your appetite. You will be much happier reading other books, particularly the excellent works of Catania (2013) and Bouton (2016).

Nevertheless, as an introduction to the psychology of learning, we believe that our book has several unique strengths. First, to the best of our knowledge, it is the only book on learning that attempts to present and integrate knowledge from both functional psychology (including behavior analysis) and cognitive psychology in a systematic manner. It does so by adopting a functional-cognitive framework that recognizes the fundamental differences between both approaches in psychology while also highlighting the way in which these approaches are mutually supportive. It puzzles and disturbs us that there is so little interaction between functional and cognitive learning researchers despite the huge overlap in the work they are doing. Our aim is not to unite the two approaches but to argue that both approaches have merit and that each can learn from the other. To the best of our knowledge, our book is also the first to integrate aspects from the (functional) literature on relational frame theory in a textbook on learning. We believe that relational frame theory has much to offer with regard to the study of both simple and complex forms of learning.

Second, our book provides a unique perspective on what learning is and on the scope of learning research. Although all definitions have their limitations, our definition of learning (as changes in behavior that are due to environmental regularities) allows us to organize and expand the universe of learning research by highlighting different types of regularities and the different ways that they change behavior. In our opinion, our chapter on complex learning (i.e., changes in behavior that are due to the joint impact of multiple environmental regularities) provides a clear example of the usefulness of our definition. The idea of complex learning not only allows us to reveal similarities and differences between existing learning phenomena, ranging from sensory preconditioning, to Pavlovian-instrumental transfer, and arbitrarily applicable relational responding, but also leads to a new perspective on learning in humans that encompasses seemingly complex phenomena such as relational learning. As such, we look at the past, as is typically done in a textbook, but we also actively explore the future, which is more typical for a monograph. Also because of this mix of old and new ideas, our book is unique within the literature on learning. One downside of this approach is that our own research is featured much more heavily in our book than it is in other textbooks. We realize that this might be frowned upon. However, it is an inevitable consequence of our choice to use the functional-cognitive framework as the organizing principle of this book. Much of the work that we have done over the years either led up to the development of the functional-cognitive framework on which the book is built (e.g., the work on propositional models of learning) or originated from the framework (e.g., our recent work on complex learning). The monograph aspect of our book lies mainly in our aim to demonstrate the heuristic and predictive value of the functional-cognitive framework. We hope to show that the framework (a) provides a coherent means of structuring and integrating the available functional and cognitive literature on learning (which is why the book can also function as a textbook) and (b) highlights new questions and opportunities for future research. We therefore hope that after reading the book, you will share our enthusiasm for the functional-cognitive framework.

In closing, we want to take a moment to explicitly acknowledge many of those who contributed to this book in different ways. Ian Stewart provided exceptionally detailed and insightful comments on a first full draft of the book. Mark Bouton and his collaborators also sent us detailed comments which allowed us to correct many errors. We are also grateful for the feedback of Marc Brysbaert, Mike Dougher, Ralph Miller, and Mikael Molet. Thanks to Rebecca Willems, Ariane Jim, and Inge Van Nieuwerburgh for their help with practical issues (references, table of contents, figures, advice on open access). Thanks also to Philip Laughlin at the MIT Press and to the three anonymous reviewers who provided constructive comments for improving the book. We are grateful for the many discussions about learning that we had over the years with the members of the Learning and Implicit Processes Lab (www.liplab.be) at Ghent University. Finally, we are deeply grateful for the long-term financial support of the Flemish government via Methusalem grant BOF16/MET_V/002 of Ghent University, which was awarded to Jan De Houwer. This support not only allowed us to explore new paths in our research but also made possible the open-access publication of the pdf version of this book.

Jan De Houwer and Sean Hughes

September 2019

Introduction: What Is Learning and How Can We Study It?

After reading this chapter you should be able to:

- State the definitions of the standard three forms of learning, as well as complex learning.
- Identify the differences between learning as a procedure, effect, and mental process.
- Describe the functional and cognitive approaches in learning psychology and the relation between the two.

Introductory Task

- Describe what conditioning means to you.
- Find examples of behavior that you believe can or cannot be changed via conditioning.
- Explain how those changes in behavior come about. Which processes are the basis for those changes in behavior?
- Consider whether conditioning is relevant only for the study of nonhuman organisms. To what extent do you think conditioning also occurs in humans?

At the start of a book on the psychology of learning, it is important to reflect on what exactly the psychology of learning is all about. Like any other scientific discipline, the psychology of learning is defined by its goals. Scientists can have a multitude of goals that differ with regard to not only the object that is studied but also the questions that are asked about that object. Hence, to define an area of research, we need to specify the object of study as well as the questions that are asked about that object.

When applied to the psychology of learning, it seems obvious that the object of study is "learning." But what exactly is "learning"? Although research on learning has a long history in psychology and is still important in the field today, there is surprisingly little consensus about the definition of learning. In reviews of the literature one can find various definitions

Figure 0.1
Let's start!

that differ in important ways (see, e.g., Barron et al., 2015; Burgos, 2018; Lachman, 1997). On second thought, this lack of agreement is to some extent unsurprising, because it is often difficult to reach consensus about definitions. For instance, could you agree with others on the definition of a chair? Must all chairs have four legs? Is anything you can sit on a chair? Nevertheless, in science, it is important to be as explicit as possible about the definitions of core concepts, because those definitions have a huge impact on what researchers do and why they do what they do. In fact, many discussions in science can be traced back to hidden differences between researchers in the way that they define core concepts in their science (Wittgenstein, 1958). In this introductory chapter, we discuss the way we define learning. Our definition deviates somewhat from those used in everyday life and by other scientists. We do not claim that our definition is the best possible definition. Like most other definitions we present in this book, our definition of learning is best thought of as a working definition. However, we do believe that our definition is a very useful one. Compared to other definitions, it has three important qualities: precision (it delineates in a clear manner what does and does not count as an instance of learning), scope (it is broad enough to encompass a wide range of learning phenomena), and depth (it is compatible with research in other areas of science such as biology, genetics, and neuroscience). Rather than enter into unproductive debates about whether our definition captures the "true" essence of learning, we hope that this book will help readers to appreciate how useful our definition can be.

Another advantage of our definition of learning is that it is compatible with two fundamentally different approaches in learning research (and psychology in general). First, the **functional approach** is concerned primarily with describing the factors that moderate learning (*when* does learning occur), and more specifically, with distilling abstract principles of learning from concrete findings. Intellectual traditions such as radical behaviorism, behavior analysis, and more recently, contextual behavioral science, draw heavily on the functional approach; we will return to this later in the book. Second, the **cognitive approach** aims to describe the mental mechanisms that mediate learning (i.e., *how* does learning occur). Although both approaches have been well established for many years, there is little interaction between them. In fact, most textbooks on the psychology of learning focus on just one of these approaches (either a functional or a cognitive approach to learning). In this introductory chapter, we not only try to capture the core of each approach but also—aided by our definition of learning—clarify that both approaches are compatible and mutually supportive. Hence, we provide a unique **functional-cognitive framework** for learning research that reconciles these two main approaches in the psychology of learning.

As the result of addressing these complex issues, this introductory chapter has become quite long, much longer than what is typical in textbooks about learning. Although we illustrate our ideas with concrete examples, some of the points we make remain quite abstract, and some of you may struggle with this introductory chapter. It is, however, our firm belief that a full appreciation of the studies and theories covered in the subsequent chapters requires a coherent perspective on the nature of learning as well as the different questions about learning that psychologists pose and try to answer. We therefore hope you will follow us in this important first step of our journey.

0.1 What Is Learning?

0.1.1 Learning as Ontogenetic Adaptation

Darwin's theory of natural selection is without doubt one of the most important scientific insights that our species has ever achieved. Living creatures are not static entities; they are constantly evolving in response to the world around them. The driver of evolution is adaptation to the environment: the more an organism is able to adapt to the environment in which it lives, the greater its chances of reproducing. This means that those characteristics of the organism that improve its adaptation to the environment are more likely to be passed on to the next generation, compared to characteristics that do not improve adaptation, or even hamper it.

Darwin's theory of evolution via natural selection focuses mainly on *phylogenetic adaptation*—that is, the adaptation of animal species to their environment across generations. In contrast, learning psychology can be seen as the study of *ontogenetic adaptation*, which is the adaptation of individual organisms to the environment during the lifetime of those organisms (De Houwer, Barnes-Holmes, & Moors, 2013; Skinner, 1938, 1984). **Learning** can thus be defined as an observable change in the behavior of a specific organism as a consequence of regularities in the environment of that organism. In order to say that learning has occurred, two conditions must be met:

- An observable change in behavior must occur during the lifetime of the organism.
- The change in behavior must be due to regularities in the environment. Learning is thus seen as an *effect*—that is, as an observable change in behavior that is attributed to an element in the environment (a regularity in the environment).

The above definition clarifies that learning psychology has an essential role to play in understanding the behavior of all organisms—human and nonhuman alike. In much the same way that a species will adapt to the environment across different generations, so too will individual organisms adapt to the environment during the course of their own lives. The goal for **learning psychologists** is to arrive at the best possible understanding of ontogenetic adaptation. Before we consider how this might be achieved, let us first consider in more detail the implications of our definition of learning.

0.1.2 Difficulties in Applying the Definition of Learning

Although the above definition certainly helps clarify what we mean by learning, there are still several issues to consider when determining whether learning has taken place. First, recall that the observed change in behavior (due to regularities in the environment) can occur at any point during the lifetime of an organism. For instance, the impact of a regularity on behavior might be evident immediately, or only after a short delay (e.g., one hour), or even after a long delay (e.g., one year). It is therefore difficult to conclude with certainty that learning has *not* taken place when a regularity is present but there is no change in behavior, because it is possible that a change in behavior will only occur at a future point in time.

Second, there may be disagreement about what is meant by *behavior* and thus what constitutes a change in behavior. We adopt a broad definition that includes any observable response, regardless of whether that response is produced by the somatic nervous system (e.g., pressing a button), the autonomic nervous system (e.g., saliva secretion), or neural processes (e.g., electrical activity in the brain). The concept of behavior also refers to responses that in principle are observable only by the organism itself (e.g., a conscious mental image or thought).[1]

The third and perhaps most important issue is that applying the definition of learning requires that we make a causal attribution. Think back to our definition of learning as an effect (i.e., a change in behavior *due to* regularities in the environment). It is not enough that we merely observe a change in behavior. Rather, a change in behavior qualifies as an instance of learning only when it is caused by a regularity in the environment. There is therefore an assumed causal relation between environment and behavior built into the definition itself. We say "assumed" because causal relations cannot be observed directly. They can only be derived from either logical arguments or empirical evidence.

To illustrate, consider newborn children who initially show a grip reflex during their first six months of life (i.e., they quickly close the palm of their hand whenever it is stimulated) but then stop doing so by their first birthday. This reflex is clearly a behavior (i.e., it is a response to the stimulation of the hand). Moreover, the reflex changes: stimulating the infant's hand (the stimulus) initially leads to a grip reflex (behavior) and this reflex gradually disappears across time. But does the change in behavior qualify as an instance of learning? It would if the change in behavior is due to a regularity in the environment. For instance, the reflex might weaken as the result of repeatedly experiencing stimulation of the palm, like when adults become accustomed to a noise that they frequently hear (e.g., traffic outside your window). Saying that the change in the grip reflex is an instance of learning thus boils down to a hypothesis about the causes of the change in the grip reflex—that it is due to a regularity in the environment (i.e., the repeated presentation of a single stimulus).

An alternative hypothesis is that the grip reflex decreases because of the spontaneous maturation of the infant's brain. This "maturation" hypothesis maintains that during the first months of life, new neural connections are formed as a result of genetic factors that have little to do with the infant's constant interactions with the environment. These spontaneously formed neural connections grow in strength so that, by a certain age, they inhibit the grip reflex entirely. In this case, the change in behavior is due to genetically determined **maturation** instead of regularities in the environment and would therefore not qualify as an instance of learning. But which hypothesis, learning or maturation, is correct? The answer ultimately depends on empirical evidence. The "learning" hypothesis would predict that a decrease in palm gripping will depend on the environmental regularity (i.e., the frequency with which the infant's palm is stimulated). If this prediction is confirmed, then the learning hypothesis would gain support. The "maturation" hypothesis, on the other hand, would predict that the reflex will disappear as a function of time rather than due to the frequency of palm stimulation.

The key point here is that there are causal assumptions at the core of the definition of learning. This is true for other concepts as well. Take the idea of a traffic-related death. Suppose that a driver has a fatal heart attack while driving his car on the motorway. After he dies, the car suddenly comes to a stop and a second car collides with the first, and the second driver also dies. In this situation it is likely that only the second driver will be considered a traffic-related death because the first did not die due to a traffic-related factor. However, if evidence emerges showing that the second driver also suffered a fatal heart attack before he collided with the first car, then a new debate can take place about whether the death of the second driver also qualifies as a traffic-related death. Yet, even then, the classification of what caused the death ultimately depends on what we would consider a direct cause of death (e.g., was the second driver's heart attack due to the sight of the first car)? What this example illustrates is that the ultimate criterion for determining a traffic-related death is not an objective characteristic of the situation (e.g., did the driver have a heart attack; did the death happen in a traffic-related situation). Rather, it is based on how we determine what is a direct cause of death (e.g., did the driver die due to a medical condition that was present prior to the traffic situation, or was the heart attack a consequence of the traffic situation). Sometimes the cause of something is easy to determine (e.g., the fact that flicking a switch turns on a light). But at other times there is a reason for doubt, and more research is needed. The same is true when we want to determine whether a change in behavior is an instance of learning.

0.2   What Are the Different Types of Learning?

0.2.1   Types of Regularity in the Environment

If learning refers to ontogenetic adaptation, then the goal of learning research is to study the impact of environmental regularities on behavior. But what exactly is an **environmental regularity**? In line with De Houwer et al. (2013, p. 634), we define a regularity as "all states in the environment of the organism that entail more than the presence of a single stimulus or behavior" (also see De Houwer & Hughes, 2017). Critically, different kinds of regularities can be distinguished. For instance, we can say that a regularity is present if (a) one particular event is repeated across time or space, (b) different events occur together at one place and

---

Think It Through 0.1: Are Other Definitions of Learning Also Possible?

Given that definitions containing causal attributions are sometimes difficult to apply, the question arises: Are there other definitions of learning that are less problematic? **What do you think?** Try to come up with your own definition of learning and compare its usefulness with that of the definition we offer in this chapter. (For this and all subsequent "Think It Through" questions, some reflections on possible answers can be found at the end of the book.)

moment in time, and (c) different events occur together in multiple places or moments in time (De Houwer et al., 2013).[2] Regularities can also differ from each other with respect to the nature of the events involved. For example, some events involve only stimuli whereas others involve stimuli and responses. We can sometimes even detect regularities in the occurrence of regularities (so-called *metaregularities*). The key point here is that there are many different types of regularities. Yet, strangely, the vast majority of research in learning psychology has tended to focus on one of the following three types:

1. **Regularities in the presence of a single stimulus**: Is a certain stimulus (e.g., food) presented, and if so, in what way (e.g., how much food, how often does it occur, etc.)? This regularity refers to the repeated presentation of a single stimulus in ways that are independent of other events such as the presence of other stimuli or responses.

2. **Regularities in the presence of multiple stimuli**: Is there a regularity in the presence of one stimulus and the presence of another stimulus (e.g., do you find certain foods in certain places)? This type of regularity is most often instantiated by repeatedly presenting two stimuli together in space and time. Note, however, that even the one-time occurrence of two stimuli together qualifies as more than one stimulus at a single moment and can thus be regarded as a regularity. We therefore use the term *regularity* in the broadest sense of the word (for more on this, see De Houwer et al., 2013; De Houwer & Hughes, 2017).[3]

3. **Regularities in the presence of a stimulus and response**: Is there a regularity in the presence of a stimulus and a response (e.g., do you get a specific beverage whenever you press the button of a vending machine)? This regularity is concerned with contingencies between stimuli and behavior.

Think It Through 0.2: The Interaction between Learning and Genetics

Often there is a close interaction between genetic factors and regularities in the environment with regard to their impact on behavior. A good example of this is the phenomenon of *imprinting*. A young bird will develop a singing pattern only if it hears the vocal pattern of a conspecific during a particular period of its life. If the bird does not hear a vocal pattern, or if it hears the song pattern of a different kind of bird, or the song pattern of a conspecific outside the crucial period of its life, then it will never show the pattern later on. It seems clear that both genetic factors (e.g., for determining the crucial period) and regularities in the environment (e.g., repeatedly experiencing a certain song pattern) play a role in this particular behavior. It is as if the animal is genetically predestined to receive a print (imprint) of the song pattern of its kind during a certain period of its life.

What do you think? Is imprinting a form of learning?

0.2.2 Types of Learning

If we define learning as a change in behavior due to regularities in the environment, then we can distinguish between different types of learning based on the regularity that is responsible for that change in behavior.

1. Changes in behavior that are due to a *regularity in the presence of a single stimulus* (regardless of the ways in which that stimulus is potentially related to the presence of other events). To illustrate, imagine that you hear a loud bang. The first time you hear the bang, you may show a strong startle reaction. The second time you hear the bang, your startle reaction will probably be weaker. This response diminishes in magnitude even further with the third bang, and so on. So in this example, there is a change in behavior (the intensity of the startle reaction elicited by the bang declines) that is due to the repeated presentation of a single stimulus (the loud bang).

   In this book we will refer to this type of learning as a change in behavior that is due to **noncontingent stimulus presentations**. The term *noncontingent* refers to the fact that the repeated presentation of a stimulus has an impact on behavior regardless of its links with other events. The example of the reduced startle reaction to the loud bang caused by the repeated presentation of the bang is just one subtype of effects of noncontingent stimulus presentations—specifically, a subtype known as *habituation* (for more on this, see chapter 1).

2. Changes in behavior due to *regularities in the presence of multiple stimuli* (at one moment in time or across several moments in time). Suppose that your computer screen flickers (one stimulus) and a moment later you hear a loud bang coming from the computer's speakers (second stimulus). Afterward, the screen flickers for a second time. The first time your computer screen flickers, you may do no more than look on strangely at what is happening. But the second time the screen flickers, you will probably react very differently (e.g., you may be somewhat irritated or anxious). It is possible that your reaction to the flickering of the screen changes because the flickering was previously accompanied by a loud bang. This is one instance of a type of learning known as **classical conditioning**. This type of learning is sometimes referred to as "Pavlovian conditioning" after Ivan Pavlov, the researcher who first studied it (Pavlov, 1927). Pavlov showed that repeatedly pairing the ringing of a bell and food leads to an increase in salivation when the bell is heard.[4]

3. Changes in behavior that are due to *regularities in the presence of a stimulus and response* (at one moment in time or across several moments in time). Think back to our previous example of the loud bang that comes after your computer screen flickers. Imagine that after the screen flickers (stimulus) for a second time, you (with some trepidation) press the escape key (response) and the loud bang does not follow (consequence). Chances are that when the screen flickers a third time, you will immediately press the escape key. The

probability and speed with which you press the escape key increases because acting in this way reduces the chance of the loud bang occurring. In this case, the change in behavior (increase in button pressing) is due to the relation between that behavior and a certain stimulus (the presence or absence of the loud bang). This is one example of a type of learning known as **operant conditioning**.

The term *operant*, derived from *operation*, refers to the fact that this type of learning is concerned not so much with the relation between stimuli and a specific behavior (e.g., pressing the escape button with your left index finger) as with the relation between stimuli and *a class of behaviors* that all involve the same operation (e.g., pressing a button, regardless of whether this happens with the left index finger, nose, or with a stick). Another frequently used term is **instrumental conditioning**. The term *instrumental* refers to the fact that the operation is an instrument for obtaining a certain result. This type of learning is often related to the work of B. F. Skinner, who showed, for instance, that a rat will press a lever more often if doing so is followed by the delivery of food (see Skinner, 1938).

As we mentioned previously, most work in learning research has focused on changes in behavior that are due to one of these three regularities. These three types of learning can be considered "simple," given that they are due to a single regularity. Critically, however, other more complex forms of learning can also arise. We use the term **complex learning** to refer to changes in behavior that are due to the joint impact of multiple regularities. We distinguish between two types of complex learning: **moderated learning** and **effects of metaregularities**. Moderated learning refers to situations in which behavior changes as the result of multiple **standard regularities**—that is, regularities that have individual stimuli and/or responses as elements. In **metaregularities**, on the other hand, multiple regularities are embedded—that is, one regularity is an element within another regularity. Hence, standard regularities differ from metaregularities in that only the latter have regularities as elements. We will discuss both types of complex learning in detail in chapter 4. However, to give some idea about what complex forms of learning might entail, we briefly discuss a few examples in the following paragraphs.

First, sensory preconditioning (e.g., Seidel, 1959) can be seen as an instance of moderated learning (see figure 0.2). Think back to our previous example of the computer screen flickering and this being followed by a loud bang from the loudspeakers (Time 2). Now imagine that at an earlier point in time (Time 1), the same screen had also flickered and that this initial flickering was not followed by a loud bang (e.g., because the speakers were not switched on). But the flickering of the screen at Time 1 did occur right after a USB stick was plugged into the computer and its light turned on. Now imagine that later that same day (Time 3), the USB stick is reconnected to the computer and suddenly lights up. It may be that the light on the USB stick elicits fear. In the language of learning psychology, this change in behavior

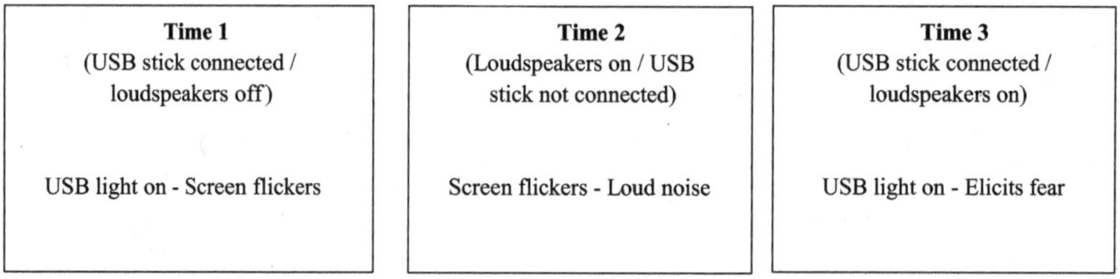

Time 1	Time 2	Time 3
(USB stick connected / loudspeakers off)	(Loudspeakers on / USB stick not connected)	(USB stick connected / loudspeakers on)
USB light on - Screen flickers	Screen flickers - Loud noise	USB light on - Elicits fear

Figure 0.2
Sensory preconditioning: Behavior changes at Time 3 as a result of the joint impact of the standard regularities at Time 1 and Time 2.

(increase in fear) is due to the combined effect of two regularities: (a) the co-occurrence of the illuminated USB stick and the flickering screen at Time 1 and (b) the co-occurrence of the loud noise and flickering screen at Time 2. Both regularities are standard regularities because they involve only individual stimuli as elements. Because the change in behavior is produced by the jointed impact of these standard regularities (i.e., neither regularity alone would produce the change in behavior), it qualifies as an instance of moderated learning.

Second, one way of studying **effects of metaregularities** is by means of a procedure called the *relational matching-to-sample task* (e.g., Ming & Stewart, 2017; see figure 0.3). On each trial of this task, participants encounter three pairs of stimuli on a computer screen. Each pair consists of stimuli that are either identical (e.g., 3–3, 1–1) or different to each other (e.g., 6–7, 5–8). The stimulus pair at the top center in figure 0.3 is called the *sample pair*, whereas the two pairs of stimuli at the bottom are known as the *comparison pairs*. Participants must choose one of the two comparison pairs at the bottom based on whether it matches the sample pair at the top. In the example depicted in figure 0.3, there is a "match" when the relation between the sample pair stimuli (i.e., the two digits are identical or different) corresponds to the relation between the comparison pair stimuli. For instance, in the situations depicted in figure 0.3, one must choose the pair at the bottom left of the left-hand trial (because both 3–3 and 1–1 consist of two identical digits) and the pair on the bottom right of the right-hand trial (because both 5–8 and 6–7 consist of two nonidentical digits).

If you think about it, each of the stimulus pairs in the relational matching-to-sample task can be regarded as a single regularity (i.e., they involve two stimuli being paired with each other). There is also a regularity in the occurrence of these regularities because different pairs co-occur. Moreover, this pairing of pairings is, in its turn, part of another regularity in the way that participants are rewarded for selecting comparison pairs (i.e., the match between the sample and comparison pairs indicates which comparison pair should be selected). The fact that people are able to systematically select the correct response in a relational

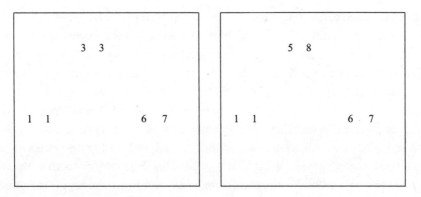

Figure 0.3
Example of two trials during a relational-matching-to-sample task.

matching-to-sample task can thus be seen as one example of an effect of metaregularities. We will return to these and other examples of complex learning chapter 4. For now, it is important only to be aware of the fact that there are complex forms of learning that involve the joint effect of multiple regularities.

0.2.3   Difficulties in Determining Different Types of Learning

Just as it is not always easy to determine whether a change in behavior is caused by a regularity in the environment (and is thus an example of learning), so too, is it not always easy to determine which type of regularity was responsible for a given change in behavior (and thus determine what type of learning has occurred). In daily life, different regularities are often present simultaneously. In such situations, it can be unclear which regularity is responsible for which change in behavior.

To illustrate this, let's return once more to our example of the flickering computer screen. Imagine that we observe a change in a person's reaction to the flickering screen: the first time the screen flickers, their reaction is neutral; the second time, their reaction is more negative than before; the third time, it's even more negative, and so on. Earlier, we assumed that this change in behavior (increased negativity of the reaction to the flickering screen) was due to the regularity involving the flickering of the screen and the loud bang (i.e., stimulus pairings). However, there is another possible explanation. The increase in negativity toward the screen occurs in parallel with the repeated experience of the flickering screen. Thus in principle it is possible that the mere repeated experience of a slightly irritating stimulus such as a flickering screen can result in an increase in the irritation that the stimulus elicits (regardless of that stimulus's relation to other events in the environment, such as the loud bang). In this way, the change in behavior (increased negativity) could be an example of the first type of learning we discussed earlier (i.e., the effect of the repeated presentation of a stimulus) or the second type of learning (i.e., the effect of stimulus pairings). It is also possible that repeatedly experiencing a loud bang causes more negative reactions to the flickering screen, independent of the relation between the loud bang and the flickering screen. So how do we know which type of learning it is? As is often the case, additional research would need to be carried out. For instance, such work could check to see if the negative reaction to the flickering screen still changes if it is experienced repeatedly without the loud bang. If so, then there is support for the idea that it is an instance of the first type of learning (i.e., effects of noncontingent stimulus presentations). If there is an increase in negativity only when the flickering screen is followed by the loud bang, then support grows for the idea that it is an instance of the second form of learning (i.e., classical conditioning).

Although there are ways to identify the causes of behavior in daily life (e.g., by using so-called single case designs), it is often practically difficult to conduct the research that is necessary to discover those causes. Learning researchers therefore often turn to experimental research in the laboratory. After all, in the laboratory they have far more control than in the external world over the regularities that a person experiences. One of the main reasons learning research is an experimental science (i.e., a science that uses the experimental method) is because experimental control is necessary in order to determine whether and what type of learning has occurred. However, it is very important to distinguish between **learning** *effects* and **learning** *procedures*. Procedures are what the researcher does in creating an experimental context in which a certain regularity is present and a certain behavior is observed. Depending on the type of regularity that is being studied, one can therefore refer to different types of procedures, such as procedures with noncontingent stimulus presentations, classical conditioning procedures, and operant conditioning procedures. In contrast to an effect, a procedure is something objective; it is no more than a list of objectively observable actions that the researcher carries out when conducting an experiment. An effect, on the other hand, implies a nonobservable causal relation (e.g., the assumption that a certain regularity was responsible for a change in behavior). What is important to appreciate here is that one cannot determine which form of learning has occurred simply on the basis of the procedure. It is not sufficient to establish that a certain regularity is present in the procedure. To be able to speak of learning as an effect, one must also be able to argue that a regularity is the cause of the observed change in behavior. We will return to this vital distinction between procedures and effects repeatedly throughout the book.

0.3 A Functional-Cognitive Framework for the Psychology of Learning

Now that we have described the topic of learning research, we can discuss its goals. A science is defined not only on the basis of what is studied (e.g., different scientific disciplines may have the same subject) but also on the basis of what one wants to know about that subject. If we look at the history and current state of learning research, we can distinguish between two sets of researchers who have two different but related goals. The first goal is to describe the environmental factors that *moderate* learning. We call this the **functional approach** within learning psychology: learning depends on (and is therefore a function of) elements in the environment. Note that the word *functional* is thus being used in the mathematical sense of function ("X is dependent on Y") and not in the sense of functionality ("X is at the service of Y").[5] The second goal is to describe the mental processes that *mediate* between environmental regularities and behavior. This is the goal of the **cognitive approach** within learning psychology. We first provide more details about each of these approaches and then discuss their relation to one another.

0.3.1 The Functional Approach within Learning Psychology

0.3.1.1 The environment as a moderator of learning The main goal of research for those who adopt the functional approach to studying learning is to understand the environmental conditions under which regularities in the environment influence behavior (i.e., the environmental conditions under which learning occurs). Functional learning psychologists achieve this by carrying out experiments in which they intervene directly in the environment of organisms in a controlled manner in order to determine whether and when regularities result in a change in behavior. In other words, they construct and manipulate different types of learning procedures. Every learning procedure consists of several factors: (a) an environmental regularity brought about by means of stimuli and/or behaviors; (b) a behavior assumed to be causally related to that regularity; (c) an organism that exhibits that behavior; and (d) a broader context in which the regularity occurs and the organism is located. Each of these factors can moderate learning; that is, they can determine whether and to what extent a regularity in the environment has an impact on behavior. We refer to these factors as potential **moderators of learning**[6] and organize them into five groups:

1. *The nature of the stimuli and behaviors that constitute the regularity.* If you want to study the impact of regularities on behavior, then you have to choose certain stimuli or behaviors to create that regularity. In the case of noncontingent stimulus presentations, you must choose a stimulus that you are going to present. In principle, this can be anything from a very simple stimulus (e.g., a noise with a certain duration, frequency, and intensity) to a very complex one (e.g., a complete musical piece). The same is true if you want to study the impact of stimulus pairings on behavior (i.e., one will have to choose certain stimuli that will be paired). These stimuli can also range from the simple (e.g., the ringing of a bell, which is always followed by food) to the more complex (e.g., information about the

food that certain people have eaten and information about the presence of allergic reactions that these individuals exhibit). Likewise, a regularity involving behavior and stimuli can be achieved only if you choose a certain behavior and a certain stimulus. And once again, the possible choices are unlimited, ranging from pressing a lever followed by the delivery of food to obtaining a diploma followed by appreciation from one's parents.

2. *The nature of the behavior used to test the possible effect of a regularity.* Regularities in the environment can, in principle, be used to change any behavior that one can imagine. One can therefore observe any type of behavior to ascertain if a regularity in the environment has had an effect. The only condition on the selection of a behavior is that it is observable. And as we mentioned earlier, behavior comes in many different forms, including controlled behavior (e.g., behavior controlled by the central nervous system, such as speaking or pressing a lever), involuntary behavior (e.g., behavior controlled by the peripheral nervous system, such as salivation), neural behavior (e.g., a certain pattern of electrical activity in the brain), and even reactions that are observable only to the organism that exhibits these reactions (e.g., covert behavior such as thoughts and feelings; see note 1).

3. *The characteristics of the organism whose behavior is observed.* Learning can, in principle, occur in every living organism. The only precondition is that the organism is capable of demonstrating a change in behavior. For instance, an inanimate object such as a stone cannot learn because it is does not behave (i.e., it does not respond to stimuli in the environment) and therefore cannot change its behavior (as the result of either regularities in the environment or any other potential cause of changes in behavior). On the other hand, most living organisms, from the smallest single-celled organism to humans, do behave in ways that change. Hence, living organisms can function as objects in the scientific study of learning (see Roche & Barnes, 1997, for an insightful discussion of the concept of "organism" and its role in the study of learning and behavior). Procedures can differ with respect to the characteristics of the organism being studied. Note that moderation of learning by the nature of the organism is concerned not just with differences between species. It also refers to differences within species such as differences in age, physical condition (e.g., possible damage to the brain), and genetic makeup (e.g., the presence of certain genes or chromosomes).

4. *The nature of the broader context.* The examination of how regularities influence behavior will always take place within a certain context. This **context** always includes specific stimuli (e.g., the room in which an experiment takes place), but may also include other regularities that are also present in that context at the same moment of time. For example, one can study the effect of noncontingent stimulus presentations while the organism is being reinforced for certain actions (e.g., the performance in a burdensome secondary task such as counting back from 1,000 to 1 in steps of three). The point here is that the wider

Box 0.1 Genetic Learning

The majority of work in learning psychology has tended to study learning at the level of the entire organism (e.g., by examining whether and when the behavior of human and nonhuman organisms is influenced by regularities in the environment; see Roche & Barnes, 1997). Yet it is also possible to examine the impact of regularities on specific parts of an organism. Doing so requires only that we can establish that the behavior of specific parts of the organism (e.g., the brain, optical system) changes due to events in the environment. This "micro-" or "suborganis-mic" perspective offers interesting new possibilities for learning psychology. One such possibility is **genetic learning** (i.e., changes in the activity of genetic material as the result of regularities in the environment). Research has shown that our genetic material responds to certain events in the environment. For instance, certain parts of our genetic material will become active when confronted with a stressful event. More recently, it has been established that the activity of the genetic material can change during the life of an organism as a result of certain experiences (see Bjorklund, 2018; González-Pardo & Álvarez, 2013; Masterpasqua, 2009). For example, Weaver et al. (2004) showed that repeated licking and grooming of baby rats by their mother (a regularity in the environment of the baby rats) results in less activation of specific genes in the hippocampus when those rats are confronted with a stressful event as adults (a change in the behavior of those genes). So, one could say that regularities in the environment lead to changes in the behavior of genetic material and thus that genetic material can learn. Once we have taken this perspective, we can start researching the conditions under which genetic learning occurs. In this way, we would be better able to predict when changes occur in the activity of genetic material and how we can control such changes. In other words, we can try to apply all our knowledge about learning in general to the study of genetic learning in particular.

context in which the organism is situated can also moderate the impact of regularities in the environment on behavior.

5. *The nature of the regularity.* As we previously mentioned, there are different types of regularities in the environment (e.g., regularities in the presence of one stimulus, multiple stimuli, behavior and stimuli, or multiple regularities). Yet it is important to realize that there are also differences within each type of regularity. Each regularity has different facets and each of these facets can be manipulated separately from one another (De Houwer, 2009). For instance, when it comes to noncontingent stimulus presentations, the number, duration, interval between, and the intensity of stimulus presentations can be manipulated. Likewise, the relation between stimuli can be manipulated in many ways, including the number of times the stimuli do or do not occur together, or the temporal and spatial ways in which they are presented. The same goes for the regularity involving a behavior and a stimulus: we can vary the number of times that the behavior is or is not followed

by the stimulus, and whether the behavior and stimulus co-occur in different stages of the experiment.

Most experimental studies in learning research include manipulations of at least one potential moderator of learning. In this book, we will organize learning research on the basis of the sort of moderator that is being manipulated.

0.3.1.2 Abstract functional knowledge By conducting studies in which potential moderators of learning are manipulated, researchers generate functional knowledge about learning—that is, knowledge about the environmental factors of which learning is a function. An important point to appreciate is that functional psychologists are not satisfied with only accumulating functional knowledge about individual or specific moderators. Rather, they want to create more *abstract types of functional knowledge* that can be used to predict and influence a wide variety of behaviors across a wide variety of situations (i.e., they engage in the exercise of **abstraction**). Although it might be tempting to view abstraction as referring to an increase in the complexity of our analyses, this would be a mistake. If anything, abstraction refers to the act of simplifying: certain properties of the situation, organism, and context are disregarded and the researcher's focus is centered on one or a limited number of properties that apply across a wide variety of cases. Saying that researchers aim to develop abstract functional knowledge thus means that they attempt to distill out those core aspects of the relation between (regularities in) the environment and behavior that apply across many different situations.

To illustrate, consider the well-known studies by Pavlov (1927) on classical conditioning in dogs (see Todes, 2014, for a more extensive and historically accurate description). In a typical experiment, Pavlov repeatedly gave food to his dogs, and just before he administered that food, he rang a bell. In doing so, he created a regularity in the presence of two stimuli: the bell and the food. After several bell-food repetitions, he set out to determine if there was a change in the dogs' behavior (salivation) when they heard the bell by itself. He indeed found that their salivation systematically increased when they heard the bell, as a function of the number of times that the bell was previously paired with the food. It might be tempting to view this study as being about only salivation and food and to think that the findings might be of interest only to a food expert or physiologist. In fact, Pavlov himself initiated this research based on his interest in digestion and in 1904 was awarded the Nobel Prize for physiology and medicine for this work. But for a learning psychologist, the changes in salivation become really interesting only if we abstract (discard) away from the topographic (superficial) characteristics of the specific stimuli (bell or food) and reactions involved (salivation) and search for the factors that are likely to apply across many different stimuli, behaviors, organisms, and contexts. For instance, we can conceptualize the bell as a conditional stimulus (CS), the food as an unconditional stimulus (US), and the increased salivation due to the bell-food pairings as a conditional response (CR).

When viewed through this lens, we can see that Pavlov's study with dogs, food, and bells is just one example of an abstract functional principle: presenting a CS and US together can lead to a CR. What is really remarkable is that this general principle of learning (classical conditioning) can be applied to all kinds of stimuli, behaviors, and organisms in all kinds of contexts. For instance, imagine that your friend receives a nasty bite from a dog and subsequently develops a fear of dogs. This can also be seen as one example of the general principle of classical conditioning: the dog is the CS, the bite received from the dog is the US, and the increase in fear of dogs is the CR. The key point here is that the broad applicability of functional knowledge is possible only if we can generate abstract concepts such as CS, US, and CR that allow us to describe a situation without referring to superficial characteristics.

The very same type of abstraction yielded the principle of operant conditioning. Imagine that a rat receives a tasty piece of food each time it presses a lever, and that the rat tends to press the lever more in situations where doing so leads to food. Strictly speaking, such a study is only about the influence of food on lever pressing in rats. But if we once again take a step back and abstract away all the superficial characteristics of the behavior (pressing on a handle) and the stimuli (the food chunks), we will see that this specific (lever-food) effect is just one instance of the more general functional principle of operant conditioning (i.e., behavior is influenced by its consequences). In fact, this example involves just one type of operant conditioning known as *reinforcement*, wherein a response increases in frequency due to its consequences. Once again, the remarkable feature of abstract principles of learning (like operant conditioning) is that they can be applied to a vast array of stimuli, behaviors, organisms, and contexts (not just rats pressing levers for food). For example, they allow us to understand why people behave in all kinds of ways, such as their tendency to put money into a vending machine (because it leads to a can of drink), compulsively check their social media accounts (because it leads to new information or validation), study for exams (because it leads to good grades), or study the psychology of learning (because it leads to a better understanding of why humans think, feel, and act in the ways that they do). In other words, the abstract principle of operant conditioning tells us that behavior typically depends on its consequences.

So, one of the main goals for functional learning psychologists is to generate abstract principles (such as classical or operant conditioning) in order to account for specific as well as general classes of behavior. It is important to appreciate that the principles of learning are concerned only with the **function** that stimuli and behaviors have in a given context (i.e., the way in which they are related to other elements in the environment). In classical conditioning, for example, one examines whether a stimulus (CS) elicits a response (CR) following its pairing with another stimulus (US). Whether a stimulus is considered to be a CS or a US does not depend on the superficial characteristics of a stimulus (i.e., whether it is a bell or a buzzer or a dog, or food biscuits or food chunks, or a painful bite of a dog). Rather, we can determine this only by examining the role (or function) that the stimulus has in a given situation (i.e., a stimulus functions as a CS if the reactions to that stimulus change as the result of stimulus pairings; see chapter 2). The very same is true in operant conditioning and reinforcement. Consequences and behaviors are defined in terms of their functions in a given situation. For instance, one would label a consequence a "reinforcer" whenever it leads to an increase in the frequency of a behavior. So in our example of the rat pressing the lever for food, we could describe the food as a reinforcer (i.e., it reinforces the probability of lever pressing). But many different types of stimuli could function in the very same way, whether they involve the delivery of water to a dehydrated rat, warmth to a freezing rat, or access to a running wheel for an exercise-deprived rat. The takeaway message is that for most functional learning researchers, the thing that counts is the function of a stimulus or behavior: what is its role within the relation between environment and behavior.

The approach that focuses on the function of stimuli is also called the *analytic-abstractive functional approach* (see Hayes & Brownstein, 1986; Hughes, De Houwer, & Perugini, 2016).[7] It is worth noting that the overarching goal of this approach (i.e., to develop abstract knowledge or principles that explain many different behaviors) does not come at the cost of explaining individual behaviors. In much the same way that the boiling point of water depends on the local air pressure (and can thus be different on Earth than on the moon), the success of general principles in explaining behavior depends on specific environmental factors. Put another way, the results of individual experiments in the psychology of learning are useful not only for *formulating* general principles of learning (i.e., demonstrating when certain moderators have no influence on behavior) but also for *contextualizing* those principles (i.e., demonstrating when those moderators do have an influence on behavior).

Both are equally important. It is good to know that classical conditioning occurs in almost all animal species but also useful to know that there are important differences in the conditions under which different animal species show conditioning. The same goes for operant conditioning and other forms of learning. The point here is that there is a two-pronged approach to research centered on abstract or general principles of learning: in some cases, the goal is to formulate such principles by abstracting from individual studies, and in other cases, the goal is to contextualize those principles and show when and how they apply to a given situation. Thus, in the functional approach, researchers recognize the importance of the individual but strive for general knowledge through abstraction on the basis of function.

0.3.1.3 Why strive for abstract functional knowledge? Although there are many reasons why researchers might adopt a functional approach to the psychology of learning, an important one is that doing so allows them to influence behavior (Hayes & Brownstein, 1986).[8] The ability to influence behavior not only has practical implications (e.g., for helping people change unwanted behaviors, as in the case of addiction) but is also a vital aspect of explaining behavior. In order to influence a given behavior, one has to intervene on variables that causally produce that behavior. Hence, influencing a behavior implies the ability to explain the behavior in terms of its environmental causes (e.g., regularities in the environment). Explanations of behavior in terms of environmental causes are typically referred to as *functional explanations* of behavior. Functional knowledge about learning (i.e., knowledge about which environmental regularities influence behavior under which conditions) thus provides functional explanations of behavior.

To illustrate, let us return to our example of the rat that receives a tasty piece of food every time it presses a lever. Based on our knowledge of operant conditioning (and more specifically, reinforcement), we could influence in specific ways how the rat will act in the future. That is, we could say with relative certainty that it will press the lever more often whenever doing so is followed by an appetitive consequence such as food. We can also influence how the rat will behave by manipulating the specific type of relation between behavior (lever pressing) and its consequences (food; see chapter 3). Functional knowledge about learning can also help us influence human behavior. For instance, imagine a situation in which posts on a social media site (e.g., Facebook) are socially reinforced by receiving "likes." Facebook knows that users will post messages more often if this leads to appetitive consequences such as "likes." It is therefore a public secret that online companies such as Facebook are only too happy to use knowledge from the psychology of learning to influence the behavior of its users. Such influence will only increase as people become more active in the virtual online world.

Although the general principles of learning can be used for personal or selfish reasons, they can also be used for more prosocial or commendable purposes. For example, many forms of psychotherapy are based on the idea that psychological suffering (e.g., unbearable fear) stems from, and is maintained by, regularities in the environment. Pathological fear of dogs can be the result of previous experiences such as being bitten by a dog. Pathological hand washing can be maintained by the feeling of relief that follows from washing one's hands. Psychotherapy is therefore often set up to bring people into contact with new regularities, or to modify existing ones (e.g., exposure to dogs without negative consequences). This makes (functional) learning psychology one of the most applicable disciplines in psychological science: it produces knowledge about causes of behavior (regularities in the environment) that are directly observable and that are (often) directly manipulable. Throughout this textbook we will pay attention to the many applications of learning psychology and devote an entire chapter to what we call applied learning psychology (chapter 5).

0.3.2   The Cognitive Approach within the Psychology of Learning

0.3.2.1 Mental mechanisms as mediators of learning   As we mentioned previously, there are two different ways that people usually approach the study of learning. In the previous section, we described the functional approach, which sets out to functionally explain *behavior* in terms of the environment. The second approach, known as the cognitive approach, involves a very different goal. Whereas functional learning researchers aim to explain behavior in terms of regularities in the environment, cognitive learning researchers want to explain learning (i.e., the impact of environment on behavior) in terms of mental mechanisms. Cognitive learning researchers assume that regularities in the environment can have an impact on behavior (i.e., that learning can occur) only because those regularities set in motion mental processes that produce mental representations that in turn cause the change in behavior. This mental mechanism therefore *mediates* **learning**: it is a necessary causal step between the environmental regularity and the change in behavior. Note that we use the word *cognitive* as a synonym of *mental*, where *mental* refers to units of information (mental representations) and the processing of information (mental processes; Neisser, 1967). The key message here is that functional learning psychologists search for moderators of learning, whereas cognitive learning psychologists search for mediators of learning.

But what exactly is a mental mechanism? Well, mental mechanisms are metaphorically similar to physical mechanisms (Bechtel, 2008). In both cases, the mechanism involves a sequence of states through which a certain input leads to a certain output. Consider, for example, a car. In a car, there is a physical mechanism whereby turning the ignition key (input) eventually leads to the car's propulsion (output): turning the ignition key leads to the ignition of petrol in an engine, which causes cylinders to be moved, and this leads to the turning of the wheels. The mechanism is thus a sequence of steps in which each link acts on the next link, a bit like how one cog in a machine can act on the next cog. Mental mechanisms are very similar to physical mechanisms except that the parts that act on each other are informational rather than physical. In other words, mental mechanisms are collections of mental representations in which the information contained in these representations is processed step-by-step (Bechtel, 2008). To illustrate these ideas, let's return to the example of Pavlov's dog. Whereas functional researchers would attribute the change in behavior (salivation) to the prior pairing of a bell and food, cognitive researchers want to (a) explain why pairing a bell and food leads to a change in salivation, and (b) do so by searching for some mental mechanism that might mediate the relation between the environment and behavior. There are many possible mechanistic explanations for this environment-behavior relation. One is that the pairing of the bell and food leads to the formation of associations between the representation of the bell and representation of the food in memory. More specifically, each time the bell and food are presented in memory, their representations in memory are co-activated,

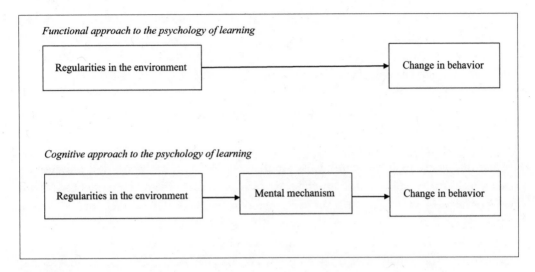

Figure 0.4
Schematic representation of the functional and cognitive approaches to the study of learning.

which results in a gradual strengthening of the association between the two representations (see Hebb, 1949, for a neural analogue of this idea). Once the association is strong enough, the presentation of the bell on its own will result not only in the activation of the representation of the bell but also, via the newly formed associations, in the activation of the representation of the food, which in turn results in salivation.

A strength of cognitive theories is that they also deal with abstract types of knowledge. For instance, mechanisms such as the formation and activation of associations between mental representations apply to all kinds of situations, regardless of the stimuli or behaviors involved. Note, however, that this knowledge (about mental mechanisms that mediate learning) is of a different kind than the knowledge acquired by functional learning researchers (who focus on abstract knowledge about the environmental moderators of learning).

0.3.2.2 Why strive for cognitive knowledge?   So why exactly do certain researchers adopt a cognitive approach to learning research? Or put another way, why do they have the goal to explain learning in terms of mental mechanisms? Two reasons stand out. First, cognitive researchers are often driven by the urge to understand the "underlying substance" of a phenomenon. Especially in the Western world there is a tendency to view a phenomenon as being "really" understood only when the underlying mechanism is known. Learning psychologists who share this tendency will never be satisfied with purely (even abstract) functional knowledge because, for them, this provides only a description of the relation between environmental regularities and observed changes in behavior. A cognitive learning psychologist also wants to understand *how* regularities lead to changes in behavior. The difference between cognitive and functional learning psychologists therefore has much to do with their **philosophical assumptions**, **scientific goals**, and what they ultimately consider a satisfactory explanation to be (Bechtel, 2008; Hayes & Brownstein, 1986).

Second, cognitive researchers also tend to believe that knowledge of underlying mental mechanisms is useful because it leads to new questions that increase the chances that we can predict and influence behavior. Understanding a mechanism requires that we not only observe (to predict) or change (to influence) the input but also know all of the different steps in the mechanistic chain. To illustrate, think back to the example of the car. If we know that turning the key leads to the ignition of fuel in the engine, we can predict the movement of the car not only on the basis of the position of the key, but also on the basis of the amount of fuel present in the fuel tank. We can also use our knowledge of the physical mechanism to make new predictions about driving the car (e.g., that the car will not run when the engine is disconnected from the wheels). Even Skinner, a key proponent of the functional approach, recognized that knowledge about mental mechanisms can provide important added value in predicting and influencing behavior (Skinner, 1953, p. 34).

Although there are good reasons why cognitive psychologists are attracted to (mental) mechanistic explanations, there are important limitations to explanations in terms of such mechanisms. Unlike physical mechanisms (such as the car key and engine), mental mechanisms cannot be observed directly. As Wiener (1961, p. 132) said, "Information is information, not matter or energy." Consequently, the presence or absence of mental processes and contents can only ever be inferred on the basis of behavior (irrespective of whether that behavior is controlled, involuntary, verbal, or neural). This presents an unavoidable problem to the researcher. The problem is that in order to make such an inference, you already need to know how mental processes and representations influence behavior. If you are not 100 percent sure what the mental causes of a particular behavior are, then you cannot be certain what that behavior says about the presence of certain mental processes and contents. Yet, in order to find out what the mental causes of behavior are, you have to observe behavior that you know is 100 percent due to the assumed mental causes. This often leads to a catch-22 where you are never really sure whether and how you can study certain mental processes and contents (see De Houwer, 2011b; Hughes et al., 2016). Although we can certainly gain insight into the mental mechanisms that are assumed to mediate between environment and behavior (Bechtel, 2008; De Houwer & Moors, 2015), the question arises whether the search for mental mechanisms is a good way to achieve prediction and influence over behavior. Debate continues, but one thing is certain: when you conduct cognitive research with the aim of improving your ability to predict or influence behavior, it is always good to check on a regular basis whether the cognitive theories you are working on actually bring you closer to this goal of prediction or influence (De Houwer, Hughes, & Barnes-Holmes, 2017).

Box 0.2 Latent Learning

The distinction between the functional and cognitive approaches can be nicely illustrated by a phenomenon known as **latent learning** (Chiesa, 1992; De Houwer et al., 2013; see Jensen, 2006, for a detailed treatment from the perspective of functional psychology). Tolman and Honzik (1930) placed a rat in a maze at Time 1. They allowed the rat to explore the maze and then later returned it to the starting position. The researchers did so a number of times and observed little change in the behavior of the rat. Later on (Time 2), the rat was brought back to the same maze. The researchers now placed food at a certain place in that maze. After the rat found the food the first time, it was once again returned to the starting position. Immediately thereafter, the rat returned to the place where it had previously found the food *via the shortest route*. Other rats that had not been given the opportunity to explore the maze at Time 1 took much longer to find the food the second time. This work indicates that the rat had indeed acquired knowledge about the structure of the maze at Time 1 despite the fact that (a) its behavior did not change at Time 1 and (b) no reinforcers were present in the maze at Time 1. The knowledge that the rat had acquired at Time 1 therefore remained latent (invisible) until it could use this knowledge to find the food at Time 2.

On the one hand, the phenomenon of latent learning is nothing special for a functional learning psychologist. The change in behavior at Time 2 is, after all, a function of the regularities that the rat experienced when it explored the maze at Time 1. The only unique thing about latent learning is that there is a period of time between experiencing the regularities (experience with the layout of the maze at Time 1) and the observed change in behavior (quickly finding the food again at Time 2). This, however, does not fundamentally change the fact that the change in behavior is due to regularities in the environment. Hence, from a functional perspective, the term *latent* does not explain anything. It does not refer to some hidden or mental level that mediates between environment and behavior. It is merely a descriptive label that orientates the researcher toward the fact that there was a temporal gap between the occurrence of a regularity and the observation of a change in behavior.

On the other hand, the phenomenon of latent learning is very important and special for cognitive psychologists. These researchers are searching for the mechanism via which the environment can influence behavior. The fact that an experience at Time 1 can have an influence on a later Time 2 proves to them that there must be a mechanism by which the experience at Time 1 can be preserved in some way so that at Time 2 it can lead to a change in behavior. After all, from a mechanistic viewpoint, there must be an immediate cause behind every change in behavior that triggers this change, just as one cog must be set in motion by another cog in a machine (Chiesa, 1992, 1994). In latent learning, the regularities that are present at Time 1 cannot be the immediate cause because the change in behavior takes place when these regularities are no longer present. So there must be a mental representation that is formed at Time 1, which then remains in memory, and it is this representation at Time 2 that is the immediate cause of the change in behavior. This mental representation remains latent (i.e., hidden) until it influences behavior at Time 2. Hence, for cognitive learning psychologists, latent learning offers proof of the existence of mental representations.[9]

(continued)

Box 0.2 (continued)

Note that latent learning is often used as an argument for the conclusion that a cognitive approach to learning is superior to a functional approach: it shows that one has to assume mental representations in order to explain how regularities in the environment can influence behavior. However, this conclusion is wrong because it loses sight of the fact that cognitive and functional learning psychologists have fundamentally different scientific objectives. As we previously outlined, functional psychologists are looking not for immediate (mechanistic) causes of behavior but rather for functional causes (i.e., environmental regularities that drive changes in behavior). For them, it is enough to know that a behavior is a function of a certain regularity in the environment, because this information allows behavior to be predicted and influenced. Latent learning is crucial only for learning psychologists who have the goal of explaining how regularities in the environment lead to changes in behavior. For them, latent learning offers proof that mental representations must be part of the mediating mechanism.

One final point. According to our definition, learning cannot occur without a change in behavior (regardless of whether this change occurs at the motor, physiological, or neural level; see our definition of behavior). Hence, in the experiment of Tolman and Honzik (1930), the conclusion that the rat has learned makes sense only after the experimenter observes that the rat took the shortest route at Time 2. Once this change in behavior has been observed at Time 2, and provided that it can attributed to the regularities at Time 1, it is justifiable to conclude that learning has taken place.

We realize that our perspective on this issue is unusual. For many, learning is defined as the storage of knowledge rather than as a change in behavior due to regularities. From such a perspective, it is self-evident that learning can occur without a change in behavior so long as knowledge has been stored. Thus, one can define learning in different ways. As we mentioned before, we adopt a pragmatic approach to definitions, one that is less interested in whether a definition is "true" or "correct" in some absolute sense and more interested in whether a definition helps us to better predict and influence behavior. We believe that, in general, the definition we offer throughout this book is useful in this latter sense. Also note that if there is no impact of regularities on behavior, then there is nothing to explain at the cognitive level. Hence, even if one were to define learning as the storage of knowledge, it can be studied only by examining learning as a behavioral phenomenon (see also our reflections on "Think It Through 0.1").

Box 0.3 Behaviorism and the Myth of the Cognitive Revolution

The functional approach has close ties with a tradition in psychology known as **behaviorism**. Importantly, however, there have historically been several branches of behaviorism. Perhaps the most well-known is **methodological behaviorism**, as proposed by John B. Watson (1913). Watson's perspective was very close to logical positivism, a movement within the philosophy of science that stated that "true" knowledge can be obtained only on the basis of objective observation. This led Watson to question the scientific validity of the introspective method, which was dominant in psychology at that time. Introspection requires that people report their subjective sensations

Box 0.3 (continued)

and feelings. Watson argued that introspection can never be part of a scientific psychology given that the accuracy of these introspections can never be objectively determined. He instead proposed that only objectively observable stimuli and behaviors should make up the matter of psychological science. He argued that behavior should be explained only in terms of links between stimuli and responses ("behavioral chains"), in which a stimulus leads to a first reaction, which then elicits a second reaction, which then elicits a third, and so on until the behavior of interest eventually takes place. This perspective fits perfectly within a mechanistic approach to science. Indeed, the only difference with the cognitive approach outlined previously is that Watson did not accept that mental representations are part of the mechanism that leads to behavior. The phenomenon of latent learning (see box 0.2) was therefore very problematic for Watson's perspective.

What should be clear from this section is that Watson's version of behaviorism is not part of the contemporary functional approach to psychology. Actually, the functional approach to the psychology of learning that we have described in this handbook is very similar to the **radical behaviorism** of Skinner (1938, 1953). Unlike Watson, Skinner was not interested in mechanisms but rather in functional relations between the environment and behavior. And unlike Watson, Skinner also accepted that subjective thoughts and feelings can also be studied scientifically, provided that thoughts and feelings are considered to be covert behaviors (i.e., behavior that is observable only to the person emitting that thought or feeling).

Today, functional and cognitive psychologists largely go their separate ways, with theories and findings in one approach rarely informing or driving progress in the other. One of the reasons for this problematic relation is that often no distinction is made between the methodological behaviorism of Watson and the radical behaviorism of Skinner. Cognitive psychologists assume that findings such as latent learning (see box 0.2) prove conclusively that behaviorism (as a whole) is wrong and must be replaced by the cognitive approach. This idea is part of the **myth of the cognitive revolution** (Watrin & Darwich, 2012), which states that cognitive psychology has replaced behaviorism as the dominant approach in psychology, a bit like when one animal species supplants another during natural evolution. This myth propagates the idea that cognitive psychology and behaviorism are *competitors* in a contest in which cognitive psychology has emerged superior and behaviorism, like the dinosaur, has gone extinct.

As Watrin and Darwich (2012) rightly point out, many questions can be asked about where this myth comes from and why it persists. First, many of the critiques of behaviorism apply only to methodological behaviorism and not to Skinner's radical behaviorism (e.g., think back on the phenomenon of latent learning). Likewise, the criticism of Skinner's work as formulated by Chomsky (1959) is also unjustified in many ways (for reasons why, see MacCorquodale, 1970; Palmer, 2006; Watrin & Darwich, 2012) and applies only to Skinner's theories and not to other theories in functional psychology (Hayes, Barnes-Holmes, & Roche, 2001). Second, it is a misconception to think that behaviorism is extinct. Contrary to popular belief, many functional psychologists still consider Skinner's work, as well as more recent work in this area, as a source of inspiration for their own research and theorizing. They unite in associations such as the Association for Behavioral Analysis International (ABAI) and the Association for Contextual Behavioral Science (ACBS),

(continued)

Box 0.3 (continued)

both of which have thousands of members worldwide who are influential in applied and clinical psychology. Finally, theories within functional psychology continue to emerge and evolve, as evidenced by, among other things, the development of relational frame theory (Hayes et al., 2001) as an alternative to Skinner's own theory (1957) of language and cognition.

Nevertheless, the poor relation between these two approaches in psychology is not just the result of misunderstandings on the part of cognitive psychologists. Functional psychologists such as Skinner (1990) are also partly responsible for the poor relation between these two approaches. Instead of seeing both approaches as complementary, Skinner and other functional psychologists continued to ask questions about the scientific character of cognitive psychology, particularly with regard to the use of concepts that refer to unconscious mental processes such as inhibition and spreading or activation. In doing so, they lost sight of the fact that such concepts are unavoidable when the goal is to describe the mental mechanisms that underlie behavior (such as latent learning, see box 0.2). Thus, the poor relation between functional and cognitive psychology can in large part be reduced to a mutual lack of insight in and respect for the nature and objectives of the other approach.

0.3.3   The Relation between the Functional and Cognitive Approaches in Learning Psychology

The relation between the functional and cognitive approaches is currently less than ideal. Both traditions have their own scientific associations, conferences, journals, and textbooks, and supporters of one approach have little or no contact with supporters of the other. Although there are historical reasons why the relation between the two approaches is so problematic (see box 0.3), there is in principle no reason why this must be the case. Indeed, from the perspective of our functional-cognitive framework, these two approaches are not competing for scientific legitimacy but are simply playing two different scientific games (De Houwer, 2011b; Hughes et al., 2016). On the one hand, the functional approach in learning research wants to explain *behavior* by first examining which environmental regularities influence behavior under which environmental conditions and then abstracting out general principles that can account for classes of behavior that differ across time and situations. On the other hand, the cognitive approach wants to explain *learning* (the impact of regularities on behavior) in terms of mental mechanisms. The two approaches are thus situated at different levels of explanation, each with their own **explanandum** (i.e., the concept that has to be explained) and **explanans** (i.e., the concept used to explain; see table 0.1).[10]

What is clear is that both levels of explanation have their respective merits. Therefore, it is difficult, if not impossible, to decide which approach is the "best" or "most important" (questions about what is "best" are prescientific and are decided on the basis of one's philosophical

Table 0.1

The concepts that need to be explained (explanandum) and the concepts used to explain (explanans) in the functional and cognitive approaches to the psychology of learning

	Explanandum (*Concept that must be explained*)	Explanans (*Concept used to explain*)
Functional	Behavior (e.g., salivation)	Regularities in the environment (e.g., pairings of bell and food)
Cognitive	Learning (e.g., classical conditioning)	Mental processes (e.g., association formation)

assumptions; Hayes & Brownstein, 1986). Instead of pitting the two approaches against each other, we believe a more productive strategy would be one in which people accept that (a) the two approaches have very different scientific objectives, and that (b) the objectives important to one approach can be used to evaluate only the products that emerge from that approach and not others, in much the same way that the rules that make sense in one sport (e.g., soccer) cannot be used to govern the activity of others (e.g., basketball; see Hughes, 2018). In other words, neither approach is strengthened by showing the weakness of the other.

Once one accepts that these two approaches are not in competition, it quickly becomes clear that the functional approach can reinforce progress within the cognitive, and vice versa. Take the functional approach: functional knowledge about learning can provide new insights into the mental mechanisms that are assumed to mediate learning. For instance, one can compare existing cognitive theories and evaluate the extent to which they are able to account for the existing body of functional knowledge. After all, a good mental process theory is a theory that can explain why a certain regularity in the environment has an impact on behavior only under certain conditions (i.e., a good mental process theory has a high **heuristic value** insofar as it can explain existing functional knowledge). The more functional knowledge we accumulate, the better we are able to evaluate and compare mental process theories with one another. This explains why cognitive learning psychologists also carry out experiments in which they manipulate environmental factors and check whether this has an influence on learning (i.e., because doing so allows them to test their mental process theories; see Hughes et al., 2016, for a more nuanced view). What is important to appreciate here is that cognitive learning psychologists do not have to restrict themselves to accumulating their own functional knowledge by conducting experiments. Rather, they can also use the wealth of experimental data already collected by functional learning psychologists. But functional learning psychologists have more to offer than just their data. As we noted earlier, functional psychologists strive to formulate abstract principles on the basis of individual findings. The abstract concepts that they develop when formulating these principles can also be useful for cognitive psychologists. This is because cognitive psychologists tend to describe their data either in very superficial terms or in terms of their cognitive theories, which has all sorts of disadvantages that we will not discuss here. Describing data in terms of abstract functional concepts overcomes these disadvantages and can thus be useful for cognitive psychologists (see De Houwer, 2011b; De Houwer et al., 2017; Hughes et al., 2016).

Cognitive learning research can also help functional psychologists to discover the moderators of learning. This is because a good mental process theory has, in addition to a high **heuristic value**, a high **predictive value** (i.e., the ability to make novel predictions about the conditions under which learning occurs). Therefore, testing predictions derived from mental process theories leads to new functional knowledge about the conditions under which learning occurs. This functional knowledge can be used by functionally oriented researchers to refine their own analytic-abstractive concepts, theories, and procedures (see Barnes-Holmes & Hussey, 2016, for a discussion about the possibilities and limitations of what functional psychologists can learn from cognitive psychologists).

The key point here is that there is a natural interaction between observation, functional knowledge about learning (knowledge about the moderators of the impact of regularities in the environment on behavior), and mental process theories about learning (hypotheses about the mental mechanisms responsible for the impact of environmental regularities on behavior), and this interaction can be useful for functional and cognitive learning psychologists alike. Both conduct experiments in which they manipulate environmental factors and observe behavior. Provided there are sufficient controls, they both can arrive at functional knowledge. Because functional knowledge provides insight into the causes of behavior, one can use this knowledge to predict new observations (which behavior will occur under which conditions), which can in turn lead to new functional knowledge. Thus, an interaction between the level of observation and functional knowledge is possible.

But there can also be an interaction between the functional and cognitive level of explanation. Based on existing functional knowledge, cognitive psychologists can try to design theories about the mental causes of learning. These theories can in turn lead to new predictions about functional relations (i.e., about moderators of learning), which are tested in new experiments, leading to observations that in turn can result in new functional knowledge. This interaction between observation, functional knowledge, and mental process theories is depicted in figure 0.5 (for more on this idea, see box 0.4).

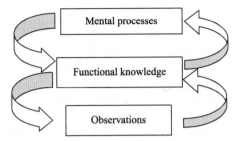

Figure 0.5
The interaction between observation, functional knowledge, and theories about mental processes.

Box 0.4 Distinguishing Two Levels of Functional Knowledge

If researchers stick to the results of individual experiments, they will be able to say something only about the specific effects that occur in those experiments—that is, the impact of those specific aspects of the environment (e.g., the pairing of bell and food) on those specific types of behavior (e.g., salivation). The functional knowledge that is generated by individual experiments has some merit (i.e., it allows for prediction and influence within that particular setting), but its merit is restricted to the effect that is being studied. Hughes et al. (2016) therefore referred to the functional level of the individual experiment as **the effect-centric functional level**. Scientists, however, also want to use the data of individual experiments to arrive at more abstract knowledge that can be applied to a wider range of situations, including situations never encountered before. As noted earlier, functional psychologists achieve this by formulating abstract principles that refer to the function of events. For instance, the principle of reinforcement states that behavior increases in frequency if it is followed by a reinforcer; this principle can be applied not only to rats pressing a lever for food but also to any other organism that emits behaviors that have consequences. This type of knowledge is functional in nature (it is about environment-behavior relations) but it is formulated in abstract functional terms rather than in terms that refer to the stimuli and behavior involved in a specific experimental setup. Hughes et al. (2016) referred to this level of functional knowledge as the **analytic-abstractive functional level**. Developments at the analytic-abstractive functional level are driven by developments at the effect-centric functional level. Likewise, developments at the analytic-abstractive functional level give rise to new predictions that produce new effect-centric functional knowledge. In sum, the two functional levels interact in mutually supportive ways.

Cognitive psychologists also aim to develop abstract knowledge that can be applied in a wide range of situations. They also formulate this knowledge on the basis of individual experiments and thus also draw on effect-centric functional knowledge. However, cognitive psychologists typically formulate their abstract knowledge in terms of mental constructs (e.g., association formation, inhibition, working memory) that (ideally) can be applied across a range of situations.

(continued)

Box 0.4 (continued)

Figure 0.6 provides a schematic representation of this extended analysis of levels of explanation in psychological research. The increase in complexity of this analysis is counterbalanced by a more fine-grained view on ways in which functional and cognitive researchers can interact. First, both approaches can feed into the effect-centric functional level and thus into developments at both the cognitive level and the analytic-abstractive functional level. Second, cognitive psychologists can benefit from knowledge and concepts developed at the analytic-abstractive functional level, just like functional psychologists can find inspiration in cognitive theories when formulating abstract functional principles.

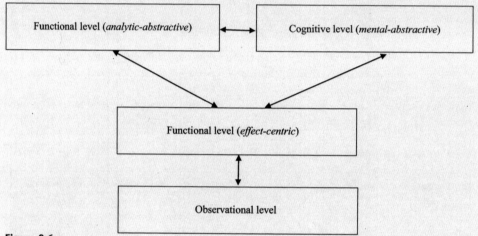

Figure 0.6
An extended analysis of levels of explanation in psychology.

Critically, this interaction between the two approaches can succeed only if they are clearly distinguished from each other. Take the interaction between functional knowledge and mental process theories. Separating these two levels implies that elements of functional knowledge (i.e., behavioral effects) are not treated as interchangeable with elements of mental process theories. Mixing the functional and mental levels occurs whenever one starts to define behavioral effects in terms of mental processes. Unfortunately, this tendency is all too common in the psychology of learning and elsewhere in psychological science. To illustrate, take classical conditioning. Many researchers mistakenly believe that classical conditioning effects are synonymous with the formation of associations between mental representations in memory. Conflating the thing that needs to be explained (effect) with the thing that is used to explain (mental process) has many disadvantages (see De Houwer, 2007, 2011b; De Houwer et al., 2017).

One major disadvantage is that it quickly becomes difficult to actually study classical conditioning. After all, from this perspective, it is not enough to establish that a regularity in the presence of multiple stimuli leads to a change in behavior. Researchers also have to show that

Box 0.4 (continued)

the impact of stimulus pairings is mediated by the formation of associations in memory. Yet, as we noted earlier, it is very difficult to establish that mental representations are present (especially given the nonobservable nature of information; Wiener, 1961). This makes it very hard to establish that classical conditioning has actually occurred, and thus difficult to study the phenomenon. A second disadvantage is that theories about mental causes often change. For example, new theories have emerged that question the very idea that learning is due to the association formation and activation (Mitchell, De Houwer, & Lovibond, 2009). Now if one were to define classical conditioning mentally (in terms of association formation) and to decide that associations do not actually exist, then one should conclude that classical conditioning does not exist either.

Critically, however, the fact that a theory about a phenomenon is wrong does not necessarily mean that the phenomenon itself does not exist. Quite the opposite: classical conditioning as an effect (i.e., the impact of stimulus pairings on behavior) exists irrespective of whether the mental explanation of that effect (in terms of association formation) is correct or not (Eelen, 1980/2018). It is therefore essential that a strict distinction be made between what the mental process theory sets out to explain (e.g., classical conditioning effects) and elements of the mental process theory itself (e.g., the formation of associations in memory). In the case of learning, this means a distinction must be made between the impact of environmental regularities on behavior (i.e., learning as an effect) and the mental processes that are assumed to mediate between these regularities and behavior (i.e., learning as a mental process). In combination with the distinction between procedures and effects that we discussed earlier (see section 0.2.3), we can therefore conclude that we define learning (both in general and the different types of learning) as an *effect* and not as a procedure or a mental process. It is this distinction between procedure, effect, and mental process that allows us to create an interaction between the functional and cognitive approaches to learning.

0.4   Structure of the Book

We have organized our book in the following manner. The first three chapters are devoted to the three forms of learning that have traditionally been studied in this field: the effects of noncontingent stimulus presentations (chapter 1), classical conditioning (chapter 2), and operant conditioning (chapter 3). In chapter 4 we discuss more complex forms of learning in which multiple regularities are involved. Each of these chapters begins with an overview of the most important functional knowledge we currently have on each type of learning—that is, the factors that are known to moderate the type of learning that is addressed in that chapter (e.g., the nature of stimuli and/or behaviors, the nature of the observed behavior)—and then we turn our attention to the mental process theories that currently dominate our thinking on each type of learning. Finally, chapter 5 provides an overview of how the psychology of learning has contributed to solving real-world problems such as psychological suffering.

Think It Through 0.3: What Is the Relation between Functional and Mental Process Explanations?

Which of the following statements is correct?

- If you have a functional explanation, then by definition you also have a mental process explanation.
- If you have a mental process explanation, then by definition you also have a functional explanation.

Think It Through 0.4: What Is the Relation between Cognitive and Neural Explanations of Learning?

The cognitive approach offers an explanation for learning in terms of mental processes and content. However, learning can also be explained on the basis of other processes such as neural processes in the brain. For example, it can be said that learning is the result of the formation of new connections in the brain.

What do you think? What are the differences and similarities between a statement of learning in terms of the brain and a statement of learning in terms of mental processes?

The book you are now reading differs considerably from other textbooks on the psychology of learning, especially in the way it organizes knowledge on learning. For instance, in many cognitively inspired textbooks, no clear distinction is made between functional knowledge and mental process theories (e.g., Bouton, 2007, 2016; Domjan, 2000; Schwartz, Wasserman, & Robbins, 2002), which often leads readers to confuse learning phenomena (e.g., classical conditioning) and mental process theories (e.g., association formation). Likewise, in textbooks written by functional psychologists, little or no attention is paid to the mental process theories of learning (e.g., Catania, 2013; Michael, 2004; Pierce & Cheney, 2008). This is regrettable, given the heuristic and predictive value of those theories. The functional-cognitive framework that lies at the heart of this book celebrates and embraces both approaches to learning psychology. This book is unique because it combines insights from both approaches.

Another important difference between this and other books on learning research is that we explicitly limit ourselves to the psychology of learning. The titles of many other books contain the phrase "learning and behavior." They discuss not only learning (changes in behavior that are caused by regularities in the environment) but also other causes of behavior (e.g., a single stimulus at one point in time, genetic factors). As we noted at the start of this chapter, we believe that behavior that is a function of a single stimulus (e.g., fear response to a loud bang) does not qualify as learning. A discussion of genetic factors does fit in a book on the psychology of learning insofar as it concerns the moderating impact of genetic factors on learning (see Think It Through 0.2). However, behavior that is determined *only* by genetic factors and not by regularities in the environment does not qualify as learned behavior, and thus falls outside the scope of a book on learning.

Before we delve into the first chapter, we should make several things clear. First, we cannot discuss every study or insight relevant to learning. That would be impossible, given that the discipline has existed for more than one hundred years and was for a long time the dominant topic of research in all of psychological science. A wealth of theories, procedures, and findings have accumulated over the decades, and we can cover only a thin slice of that knowledge in this book. For this reason, we focus on those insights that have had a major impact on our understanding of learning and, where possible, we consider potential applications of these findings for domains elsewhere in psychology and society. Nevertheless, we hope to provide a representative and cutting-edge picture of this research area.

Second, we pay little or no attention to the growing literature on the role of neural processes and states within learning. This research fits within the so-called behavioral and cognitive neurosciences. Although neural processes and states certainly fit within the functional-cognitive framework outlined in this introductory chapter (see box 0.5), it would require considerable space to provide even a limited overview of this research area. For readers interested in acquiring information on behavioral and cognitive neuroscience, we recommend Breedlove and Watson (2016) and Gluck, Mercado, and Myers (2016). Third, connectionist models also will not be described. These models can be regarded as simulated neuronal systems and thus as belonging to neuroscience (see Clark, 1990; De Houwer, 2009).

Box 0.5 What Is the Role of the Brain in Learning Research?

Neural structures (parts of the brain) and processes (brain activity) can be involved in the study of learning in different ways. In contrast to mental processes and contents, neuronal structures and processes are observable and directly manipulable because they are part of the physical universe. Therefore, these structures and processes can be included in a functional approach to learning research, either as an independent or dependent variable (see also Vahey & Whelan, 2016). For instance, one can treat neuronal structures and processes as independent variables that are manipulated (e.g., through brain surgery or administering chemical substances that influence the activity of the brain) and examine how doing so impacts learning (i.e., the impact of environmental regularities on behavior). In this way, neuronal structures and processes can be seen as elements of the environment (in a broad sense, the organism is also part of the environment) that potentially moderate learning. One can also treat neuronal processes as a dependent variable (i.e., as a form of behavior) and examine the conditions under which environmental regularities lead to changes in

(continued)

Box 0.5 (continued)

these neuronal processes. This would constitute a functional study of neuronal learning: how does the behavior of the brain change as a result of regularities in the environment? (see also box 0.1 about a comparable study of genetic learning). Both approaches can be found in a research domain called *behavioral neuroscience* (see Breedlove & Watson, 2016, for an overview).

In addition to a functional approach of the brain in learning research, one can also adopt a neural mechanistic approach. This involves looking for the neural mechanisms that mediate learning. This assumes that neural structures and processes are necessary links in a neural mechanism through which environmental regularities can influence behavior. This approach differs from a functional approach to learning psychology because attention is centered on the search for *neural mechanisms* instead of functional knowledge (i.e., environment-behavior relations). Certain functional psychologists are also interested in neural mechanisms, given that they help them achieve prediction and influence over behavior. After all, neural mechanisms consist of physical components (such as parts of the brain and chemicals) that are directly observable and manipulable (see also Skinner, 1953, p. 34, who acknowledged the importance of physical mechanisms). But for a functional psychologist, knowledge about mechanisms is at best only a means and never an end in itself; the main goal will remain one's capacity to influence behavior. Once again, we see that the scientific approach of a researcher is determined by his or her goals, not by what type of research he or she engages in.

Finally, one can also examine the brain from a cognitive approach to the psychology of learning. Both functional knowledge about the role of neural structures and processes in learning as well as knowledge about the neural mechanisms that mediate learning can be used as input for cognitive theories of learning. This becomes possible as soon as we make assumptions about which mental processes are carried out by which neural structures and processes. If we then see, for example, that a certain neural structure is involved in a certain form of learning, and we know that this structure is responsible for storing certain information, then we can decide that storing that information is crucial in that form of learning. It is, however, important to realize that there are risks in making inferences about mental processes on the basis of activity at the neural level. Even if we look at the brain, we can never directly observe mental representations or processes. We can only ever make assumptions about what information is processed in the brain by examining how the brain responds to stimuli in the environment (the brain as a dependent variable) and how interventions in the brain change behavior (the brain as an independent variable). And so long as there is uncertainty about the assumptions underlying the relation between brain and mental mechanism, there will be uncertainty about what we can learn about mental processes based on neural research (see also Poldrack & Yarkoni, 2016). Consequently, it seems easier to evaluate theories about neural rather than mental mechanisms.

We hope that once you finish reading this book you come to see that the psychology of learning is concerned with (and thus can help you better understand) the very "source code" that underpins the behavior of human and nonhuman animals. Equipped with an understanding of the behavioral principles, theories, and findings discussed in this book, you will be better able to examine many behaviors in daily life and ask questions about the regularities that give rise to and sustain them. Those interested in clinical psychology can ask whether arachnophobes are afraid of spiders because they previously had a negative experience with spiders (e.g., a painful bite) or their phobia is based on complex learning (e.g., negative verbal information about spiders). Those interested in marketing research can better identify whether people buy a certain product because earlier purchases were followed by positive consequences (e.g., social reinforcement from others) or merely because the product was paired with other positive stimuli (e.g., a nice advertisement). Readers interested in public policy can better understand the factors that influence pressing problems created by human behavior, such as climate change, conflict, overeating, overpopulation, and resource depletion. Once you can read the source code that drives human behavior, you will be better positioned to predict and influence that behavior yourself. Learning research is an essential part of psychology. It is this vision that we aim to convey throughout this book.

1 Effects of Regularities in the Presence of a Single Stimulus

After reading this chapter, you should be able to:

- Summarize the available functional knowledge about different effects of noncontingent stimulus presentations.
- Describe the mental process theories of Sokolov, Bradley, and the opponent-process theories of Solomon.

Introductory Task

Sometimes the repeated presentation of a stimulus can lead to changes in reactions to that stimulus. Can you think of three reactions or behaviors that can change as a result of repeated stimulus presentations? Also, think about possible explanations of those effects: how can repeated stimulus presentations result in such effects?

1.1 Functional Knowledge

In this section we provide an overview of what is currently known about the conditions under which regularities in the presence of a single stimulus (i.e., noncontingent stimulus presentations) lead to changes in behavior. Most of the research we discuss concerns a phenomenon known as **habituation**, which is one of several effects of noncontingent stimulus presentations. It differs from those other effects with regard to the nature of the change in the behavior (i.e., a decrease in the intensity of a response). For example, a loud bang will elicit a strong startle response the first time you hear it. The second time you hear the bang, the reaction will be less strong, the third time even less so, and so on. This effect (the decrease in intensity of the original reaction as a result of the repeated presentations of a stimulus) is called *habituation* (see http://www.youtube.com/watch?v=Kfu0FAAu-10). Note

Figure 1.1
A baby rat becoming acquainted with human contact.

that habituation is an effect and not a mental process, so it is pointless and circular to say that the intensity of a reaction decreases because habituation occurs. Although this form of learning was first described thousands of years ago, a systematic study was carried out only in the middle of the last century (see Thompson, 2009, for a historical overview). After a period of lesser interest in this phenomenon, there has been an increase in interest in recent years, mostly outside of traditional learning psychology, and especially in neuroscience and biology (but see De Paepe, Williams, & Crombez, 2019, and Rankin et al., 2009, for recent reviews of behavioral research). Below, we provide a brief overview of what is known about the way effects of noncontingent stimulus presentations are moderated by the type of stimulus that is used (section 1.1.1), the type of behavior that is observed (section 1.1.2), the organism that is studied (section 1.1.3), the broader context in which the stimulus is presented (section 1.1.4), and the way the stimulus is presented (section 1.1.5). Taken together, this constitutes a summary of the available functional knowledge about the effects of noncontingent stimulus presentations on behavior.

1.1.1 The Nature of the Stimuli

Although habituation effects have been found with a wide variety of stimuli, these effects occur more quickly for some stimuli than for others. Consider studies on the habituation of skin conductance responses. In response to the first presentation of a particular image (e.g., the picture of a cute puppy), there is a slight increase in the extent to which electricity is conducted across the skin (as measured by, for instance, electrodes attached to the hand of a person). This increase is referred to as the skin conductance response. When that image is presented a second time it will again result in a skin conductance response, but the magnitude of the response is smaller, and even smaller the third time, and so on (see figure 1.2). Interestingly, the rate of habituation (i.e., the extent to which the skin conductance response weakens as the result of the repeated presentation of the image) depends on the content of the image. Specifically, habituation of skin conductance is slower for affective (positive and negative) images (e.g., a picture of a cute puppy or a snarling dog) than for neutral images (e.g., a picture of a table; see Bradley, 2009, for an overview).

The biological relevance of stimuli also seems to be important. Evans and Hammond (1983a, 1983b) found that rats habituated as quickly to the distress call of a conspecific

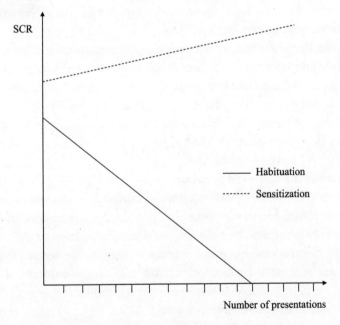

Figure 1.2

A fictitious example of habituation (a decrease in the strength of skin conductance responses as the number of stimulus presentations increases) and sensitization (an increase in the strength of skin conductance responses as the number of stimulus presentations increases).

(arguably, a biological significant stimulus) as to a control stimulus. However, habituation of the response to the distress call was less long-lasting and more context-specific than habituation of the response to the control stimulus. This effect of the biological significance of stimuli on habituation could have important evolutionary benefits.

With certain very important or intense stimuli (e.g., a painful shock or loud noise), **sensitization** can occur. Sensitization is an effect in the opposite direction from habituation; that is, it is an *increase* in the intensity of a reaction as a result of repeated stimulus presentations (see figure 1.2). Habituation and sensitization are therefore two possible effects of noncontingent stimulus presentations. As a real-life example, consider people who move to a house near a busy road. Whereas some people get used to the noise (i.e., habituation), other people become more and more annoyed by the sound of cars (i.e., sensitization). Whether sensitization or habituation occurs depends on various factors (see Groves & Thompson, 1970, for a review). Influential theories of addiction attribute a very important role to sensitization (e.g., Robinson & Berridge, 1993, 2008). For example, it has been established in nonhuman animals that the repeated administration of drugs leads to an intensification of certain motor reactions to the drug. This finding led to the idea that repeated use of a drug results in an increase in the urge to use the drug (more wanting), even if you experience less pleasure in using the drug (less liking; but see Tibboel, De Houwer, & Van Bockstaele, 2015, for a critical discussion of the concepts "wanting" and "liking").

Finally, we note that the effects of noncontingent stimulus presentations are not limited to the stimulus that is presented in a noncontingent way. Habituation responses can be generalized from one stimulus to another: if one repeatedly presents a certain stimulus (e.g., a loud tone with a frequency of 1000 Hz), the reaction to other stimuli will also be influenced if these other stimuli resemble the stimulus that was repeatedly presented (e.g., a loud tone with a frequency of 900 Hz; Rankin et al., 2009).

1.1.2 The Nature of the Observed Behavior

Noncontingent stimulus presentations can have an influence on different aspects of different types of behavior, ranging from very simple to very complex behaviors. In the nineteenth century, Fechner (1876) wondered how the aesthetic appreciation of certain stimuli (e.g., paintings, musical works) changes when they are repeatedly presented. He formulated the following law: due to constant repetition, what is originally considered pleasant will first become more pleasant but ultimately unpleasant. This constitutes the first reference to what later became known as the **mere exposure effect**, which typically refers to the observation that novel, neutral stimuli become positive as a result of the repeated presentation of that stimulus (Moreland & Topolinski, 2010; Zajonc, 1968). Also in the nineteenth century, Peckham and Peckham (1887) published an article titled "Some Observations on the Mental Powers of Spiders." It describes how the researchers repeatedly presented the sound of a tuning fork next to the web of a spider. The first time, this triggered a pronounced response from the spider, which moved on its web. This response diminished with each additional presentation. These old studies not only illustrate the range of behaviors that can be influenced by noncontingent stimulus presentations, they also show that interest in this form of learning has long existed (see Thompson, 2009, for a historical overview).

Finally, the effects of noncontingent stimulus presentations are not limited to the initial reactions elicited by these stimuli; they also involve reactions that come about only after those presentations. For example, a change in behavior due to a regularity in the presence of two stimuli (classical conditioning; e.g., the impact of bell-food pairings on salivation) can be reduced by first presenting one of these two stimuli by itself (e.g., repeatedly presenting the bell on its own before the bell-food pairings; see section 2.2.2).

Although many types of behaviors can be influenced by noncontingent stimulus presentations, laboratory research often focuses on changes in one type of response: the **orientation response** (OR). Interestingly, it was Pavlov (1927) who described this response, when he noticed how difficult it was to demonstrate classical conditioning to guests visiting his laboratory. After all, the dogs oriented their attention to those new people instead of the sounds that accompanied the food. The OR is now considered to consist of a set of different reactions that all seem to be aimed at the investigation of new and potentially important stimuli in the environment (which is why the OR is sometimes also called the *investigatory reaction* or *what-is-it response*). These components include orienting the head toward the stimulus, an increase in skin conductance, a decrease in heart rate, and neuronal responses such as certain changes in electrical activity in the brain (as measured by an electroencephalogram, or EEG). Importantly, research has shown that repeated stimulus presentations can have different effects on different components of the OR. For example, the decrease in heart rate seems to be the effect that most quickly disappears as a result of the repeated presentation of the trigger stimulus. On the other hand, there is almost no habituation of certain changes in EEG (see Barry, 2006, and Bradley, 2009, for an overview). Hence, there is growing doubt about the usefulness of viewing the OR as one unitary response (see Barry, 2009).

Habituation studies also reveal intriguing interactions between the nature of the stimulus and the nature of the response (Bradley, 2009). As we mentioned earlier, habituation of the skin conductance response is faster for neutral images than for affective images. However, habituation of changes in heart rate is as fast for neutral as for affective images. Such findings suggest that the different components of the OR are determined by different aspects of the environment.

Finally, the effect of repeated stimulus presentations can be opposite for reactions compared to counterreactions. Certain stimuli (e.g., drugs) elicit not only a reaction (e.g., a "high") but also a counterreaction (e.g., a hangover). This also applies to certain activities (e.g., jogging can lead to discomfort initially, and later to a buzz). This sequence of observable reactions and counterreactions is called the **dynamics of affect** because it refers to the dynamic development of affective reactions over time. However, research has shown that the dynamic changes as the result of repeatedly presenting a stimulus. The initial reaction to a stimulus will become increasingly weaker, while the counterreaction will become increasingly stronger as a result of the repeated presentations of a stimulus. For example, a drug user will feel less of a "high" the more often she takes a certain fixed amount of the drug. She will therefore have to use increasingly larger quantities to reach the same state of high. The counterreaction (withdrawal symptoms) when using a certain amount of the drug, however, becomes stronger with repeated use. We see something similar in activities where the reaction is unpleasant and the counterreaction pleasant. Take the example of jogging. Initially, one has strong negative experiences during jogging and few positive experiences afterward. However, as people jog more often, the negative reactions during jogging become weaker and the positive reactions after jogging become stronger. Some seasoned joggers seem addicted to the buzz they experience after jogging. More generally, it seems that repeated presentations have opposite effects on reactions and counterreactions: reactions become weaker and counterreactions become stronger with the repeated experience of stimuli. In section 1.2.2 we discuss the **opponent-process theory of Solomon**, which provides an explanation for this intriguing phenomenon.

1.1.3   Properties of the Organism

Effects of noncontingent stimulus presentations have been demonstrated in humans (see Bonetti & Turatto, 2019, for a recent example), nonhuman animals (e.g., spiders), and even single-celled organisms and plants (box 1.2). Nevertheless, certain characteristics of the organism do moderate the effects of noncontingent stimulus presentations; that is, they determine whether and how those presentations influence behavior. The fact that biological significance moderates habituation (see section 1.1.1) shows that the type of organism involved is important: whether a stimulus is biologically significant (and thus how quickly habituation takes place for that stimulus) varies from species to species (e.g., distress calls by rats are relevant mainly to rats).

1.1.4   The Impact of the Broader Context

There is very little research on the influence of the broader context on the effects of noncontingent stimulus presentations. One such study was carried out by Iacono and Lykken (1983). They repeatedly presented a loud tone (110 dB) and examined the extent to which this led to a decrease in the skin conductance response that was triggered by the tone. Importantly, they also manipulated the instructions given to the subjects. Certain subjects were instructed to ignore the tones as much as possible. Others were asked to count the tones and see if each tone was the same. Habituation was more pronounced in the first group. The focus away from stimuli thus seems to accelerate habituation.

Box 1.1 Habituation as a Research Tool

Both nonhuman animals and young human babies cannot say what they see, hear, and feel. Yet we can form an idea of their subjective experience by using habituation as a research tool. After all, if habituation is different for different stimuli, then it seems likely that the organism can perceive the difference between these two stimuli. For example, a baby will look at figure 1.3B for a longer period than figure 1.3A, and the habituation of this fixation time will occur more quickly for figure 1.3A than for figure 1.3B (see Colombo & Mitchell, 2009, for an overview of research into habituation in children).

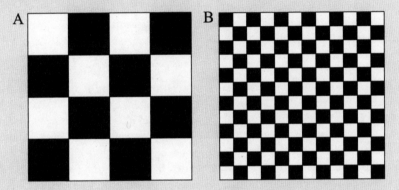

Figure 1.3
An example of stimuli used with babies in order to study habituation of the fixation time (based on the description provided by Bashinski, Werner, & Rudy, 1985, p. 585).

Recently, habituation of neuronal responses (as measured by fMRI) has been used to investigate the functioning of brain parts. For example, imagine that a drawing of a bicycle is presented repeatedly. During a subsequent test phase, the presentation of that drawing is followed by the presentation of either the same drawing or a drawing that differs in a single respect (e.g., the bicycle is slightly larger or a different color). If in a certain part of the brain there is a different reaction to the altered image than to the identical image, this would indicate that this part of the brain is involved in the processing of the deviating characteristic (e.g., size or color; see Kumaran & Maguire, 2009, for an overview).

Box 1.2 Habituation in Single-Celled Organisms and Plants

It is often thought that only organisms with a central nervous system are able to learn (but see Burgos, 2018, for a conceptual analysis, and Adelman, 2018, for a review of the available evidence). This misconception is reinforced by a definition of learning as a mental process responsible for storing information (because it seems natural to assume that living organisms need brains to store information), and even more so by the idea that learning is accomplished through the formation of connections between neurons in the brain (because by definition, you would need a system of neurons to learn). One important advantage of our functional definition of learning is that it does not make any a priori assumption about mediating mechanisms; it requires only an organism whose behavior might change as the result of regularities in the environment. Hence, our definition of learning is perfectly compatible with the idea that organisms without a central nervous system can learn, too. It is therefore interesting to see more and more evidence for learning in organisms that do not have a central nervous system (such as plants) and even organisms that consist of only one cell.

Take the example of habituation in slime mould, a creature that consists of just one enormous cell (Boisseau, Vogel, & Dussutour, 2016; see also https://www.youtube.com/watch?v=2UxGrde1NDA for an interesting TED talk about this organism). Slime mould can move via pulsating movements, and in this way it actively searches for food in its surrounding environment. In recent studies on the habituation of slime mould, researchers have made use of the finding that mould does not like to move across quinine (a bitter but harmless substance). In figure 1.4 the right panel (EXP) shows that the mould initially does not move over the quinine, but after repeated exposure to the quinine (images with the letter Q) it eventually moves over the quinine. This is an example of habituation: an original avoidance reaction to quinine (hesitation to move over this substance) disappears after repeated exposure to that substance.

Habituation also has been observed in plants. Consider *Mimosa pudica*, the "shy" plant. This particular plant closes its leaves whenever they are stimulated (see figure 1.5). In a study by Gagliano, Renton, Depczynski, and Mancuso (2014), this reaction was repeatedly elicited by dropping the plant (which is in a pot) from a certain height. After a while, the response disappeared: the plant did not close its leaves after it had fallen.

The fact that habituation can be found in single-celled creatures and plants shows that learning is not always dependent on a central nervous system. Partly on the basis of these findings, it has become clear that learning is not always due to the formation of connections between neurons; it can also be achieved by chemical processes within one cell, including changes in genetic material (i.e., genetic learning; see box 0.1). Even a single phenomenon such a habituation could in principle be mediated by different mechanisms in different species or even within one species.

These examples of habituation in single-celled creatures and plants allow us to further clarify the definition of learning in general and habituation in particular. For example, it is possible that the disappearance of the leaf-folding response of the *Mimosa* plant is a consequence of exhaustion. In other words, it is quite possible that the plant has only enough energy to close its leaves two or three times.

Box 1.2 (continued)

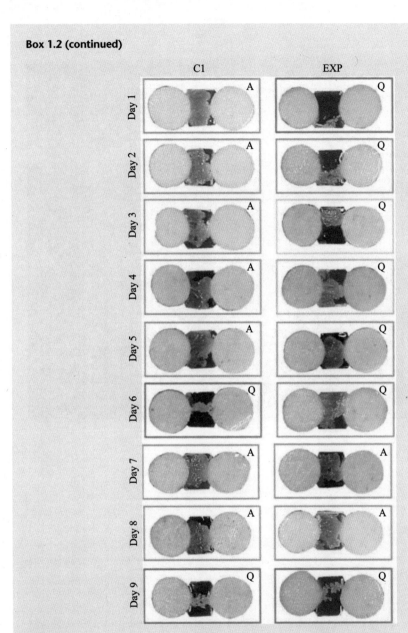

Figure 1.4
Habituation in slime mould (retrieved from Boisseau et al., 2016; figure 5)

(continued)

Box 1.2 (continued)

Figure 1.5
Leaf-folding response of the *Mimosa* plant. The image above shows the leafs when open; the opposite image shows the leafs when closed. Transition from the open to closed state occurs when the
leaves are stimulated, for instance by touching or shaking them.

In that case, it seems pointless to say that the plant has learned something when we find that it no
longer closes its leaves on the fourth presentation of a stimulus. The plant simply is no longer able
to perform the behavior, and at that moment, the closing of the leaves no longer belongs to the
behavioral repertoire of the plant (i.e., the collection of all behaviors that the plant can make).
Imagine, for example, that someone repeatedly eats poisonous food and then dies. There can be no
doubt that the behavior of the person changes when he or she dies, but this can hardly be called
learning because someone who is dead is no longer able to emit any behavior; the repertoire of
possible behaviors has been reduced to zero. A distinction can therefore be made between learning
on the one hand and changes in the behavioral repertoire on the other hand. More specifically,
changes in behavior that are due to changes in the behavioral repertoire could be excluded from
the realm of learning.[1]

Box 1.2 (continued)

Figure 1.5
(continued)

Fortunately, it is relatively easy to exclude the possibility that there is a change in the behavioral repertoire: one simply has to demonstrate that the organism is still capable of performing the old behavior. Let us return to the example of habituation in the *Mimosa* plant. After the leaf-folding response has disappeared as a result of the plant repeatedly falling, you can elicit the same response by stimulating the plant in another way—for example, by shaking the plant back and forth (Gagliano et al., 2014). This shows that the leaf-folding response is still part of the plant's behavioral repertoire and that the disappearance of this response is thus a real change in behavior due to the repeated stimulation of the plant. In other words, by showing that habituation does not generalize to other stimuli (e.g., the shaking of the plant), one can conclude with more certainty that habituation has occurred. Changes in the behavioral repertoire can also be excluded by demonstrating that **dishabituation** occurs. Dishabituation refers to the finding that a habituated response to a first stimulus is restored after a second stimulus is presented. Take our previous example of habituation in the slime mould. On the right-hand side of figure 1.4 you see that after

(continued)

Box 1.2 (continued)

a successful habituation of the avoidance response during the first six days, a neutral stimulus (A) is presented on the seventh and eighth days. This stimulus, too, is not avoided. On Day 9 the quinine is presented again and a renewal of the avoidance response occurs. This restoration of the original response as a result of presenting a different stimulus is an example of dishabituation (see section 1.1.5.2). Based on this observation, we can conclude that the avoidance response still belongs to the behavioral repertoire of the slime mould, which supports the hypothesis that the disappearance of the avoidance response on Days 1–6 is an example of habituation.

In short, research into habituation in plants and single-celled beings is interesting not only because it shows that habituation (and therefore learning) is a very general phenomenon that occurs in all kinds of organisms, but also because it provides new insights into the biological basis of learning and allows us to further refine the definition of learning.

However, many questions remain unanswered about this class of moderators. For example, researchers have not yet investigated whether habituation is also influenced by the presence of other tasks. We know that the original response to a stimulus will usually decrease in intensity if the stimulus is repeatedly presented. But what happens if test subjects have to perform another task while the stimuli are presented (e.g., count backwards from one thousand)? Does habituation become stronger or weaker? Further research is needed to answer this and other such questions.

1.1.5 Characteristics of Noncontingent Stimulus Presentations

When one repeatedly presents a stimulus, different aspects of those presentations can be varied. In what follows we discuss those aspects of the presentations that have an influence on habituation (a decrease in the intensity of the reaction as a result of repeated stimulus presentations) or sensitization (an increase in the intensity of the reaction as a result of repeated stimulus presentations; see Rankin et al., 2009, for a more complete overview).

1.1.5.1 The nature of the noncontingent stimulus presentation   What appears to be particularly important is the frequency with which the stimulus is presented. With each presentation of the stimulus, the intensity of the reaction gradually decreases to a certain minimal level. It is therefore not the case that only the first presentation has an effect on behavior.

1.1.5.2 Changes in the nature of the noncontingent stimulus presentations   The effect of repeatedly presenting a stimulus (e.g., habituation) can be nullified by presenting another stimulus unexpectedly. This nullification of the habituation effect is called *dishabituation* (see http://www.youtube.com/watch?v=4x-2WoyXPSM; see also box 1.2). Suppose that an intense light is repeatedly presented. The response to the light will decrease across repeated presentations of the light (i.e., habituation as an effect). If, afterward, a loud bang is unexpectedly presented, and later the light is presented again during a test phase, then the reaction to the light will be more intense than the reaction to the previous presentation of the light. Dishabituation is an important phenomenon because it shows that the original decrease in the intensity of the reaction is not due to a change in the behavioral repertoire (i.e., the collection of all responses that an organism can make at a certain point in time; see box 1.2).

Epstein, Temple, Roemmich, and Bouton (2009) developed a very nice analysis of eating behavior in terms of habituation and dishabituation. You can see the eating of a certain food (e.g., potatoes) as repeated presentations of that food, where every bite is a new presentation. As a result of these repeated presentations, the pleasure elicited by the food decreases (habituation) and you stop eating after a while. However, if you take a bite of another food (e.g., white cabbage) and then a bite of the first food (potatoes), then the first food will once again elicit more pleasure and satisfaction (dishabituation). This analysis provides a functional explanation for why people eat varied meals with many different types of food. It also explains why there is always room for a dessert, because the dessert is a completely different type of food than the starter and main course. There will therefore be little generalization of the habituation: the habituation that has occurred in relation to the food you have eaten during the starter or main course will have little or no effect on the pleasure that the eating of the dessert elicits. You eat more of a dessert than a kind of food that is similar to the starter or main course. Finally, it has also been established that there is a relation between habituation to food and obesity. The speed of habituation to food in the lab was a predictor of an increase in body weight in the following year (Epstein, Robinson, Roemmich, & Marusewski, 2011).

1.1.5.3 Temporal aspects of the noncontingent stimulus presentation Temporal aspects of the stimulus presentation seem to strongly influence the course of the habituation. The stimulus can be repeatedly presented in short succession (short interstimulus interval) or repeatedly with longer intervals. In the first case, one speaks of massed practice; in the second case, of distributed practice. In case of massed practice, habituation is faster (i.e., fewer presentations are needed to eliminate the response) but is less sustainable (i.e., the reaction will quickly reemerge as the result of the mere passage of time), whereas with distributed practice, habituation is relatively slower but more sustainable (see Rankin et al., 2009).

1.2 Process Theories

There is no overarching theory that provides an adequate explanation for all effects of noncontingent stimulus presentations. That is why the following section is limited to a discussion of two sets of theories, each of which attempts to explain a subset of effects of noncontingent stimulus presentations. First, we discuss the **theories of Sokolov** (1975) and **Bradley** (2009) on habituation of the orientation reflex (OR). Then we discuss **Solomon's theory** about the effect of repeated stimulus presentations on reactions and counterreactions (i.e., on the dynamics of affect).

1.2.1 The Model of Sokolov and the Model of Bradley

The model of Sokolov (1960, 1963, 1975) is concerned with the habituation of the OR. Following numerous tests, Sokolov came to formulate a kind of **discrepancy model**. The basic idea in his model is that each organism constantly builds up a model of the environment in which it is located. When a stimulus is subsequently administered that is not part of this model, an OR is triggered, and at the same time, this new stimulus is included in the model. After repeated presentations of the same stimulus in the same context, there is no longer a discrepancy between the input and the stimulus representation, and as a result, the OR mechanism will be inhibited (see figure 1.6).

However, as soon as there is any change in the stimulus, the OR will be retriggered. In other words, as soon as something changes, this is immediately recorded. From this perspective, it is also understandable that an OR can also occur when an expected stimulus does not occur. An everyday example is the ticking of a clock. Over time, the ticking of a clock is not consciously attended to, but one usually becomes alert as soon as the ticking stops.

Although Sokolov's theory was groundbreaking, it also had shortcomings. First of all, doubts have arisen about the finding that the unexpected absence of a stimulus can elicit

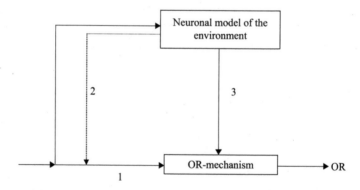

Figure 1.6
The model of Sokolov. The input (1) activates the OR mechanism (by which an OR is elicited) and is gradually included in the model of the environment. As the difference between the environment and the model becomes smaller, the inhibitory activity is triggered via (2), which blocks the impact of the stimulus on the OR mechanism. If, after habituation, the stimulus is no longer presented, then the OR mechanism is triggered by the difference between the actual environment and the model of the environment (3), as a result of which the absence of the stimulus will elicit an OR.

Box 1.3 Sokolov and Predictive Coding Models

The Sokolov model can be considered a precursor to **predictive coding models** that are currently very popular in cognitive psychology and neuroscience (e.g., Clark, 2013; Friston, 2009). The idea of predictive coding is also based on the assumption that organisms build a model of their environment and, on the basis of this model, make predictions about what should happen in the world. When there is a mismatch between a prediction and the actual situation in the environment, this will lead to an adjustment of the model. Predictive coding models have further crystallized this basic idea and applied it to various aspects of perception, thinking, and behavior (e.g., Clark, 2013). However, it is remarkable to see that in the extensive literature on predictive coding, there is seldom or never a reference to the work of Sokolov (see Bridgeman, 2013, for an exception). This is a good example of how ideas in science are sometimes reinvented without making the link with relevant earlier work. It is not surprising that the same idea can arise at different places or moments in time, but it is regrettable that often there is too little effort made to check whether similar ideas have already been formulated and, above all, what can be learned from earlier research. After all, one can learn a lot from both the successes and the problems of previous research. We therefore endorse Pavlov's statement, "If you want new ideas, read old books."[2]

an OR. At best, this phenomenon seems to be limited to certain reactions such as skin conductance (see Thompson, 2009, for a historical overview). Because this finding is the raison d'être of the Sokolov model (it is a crucial finding that is generally regarded as the origin of the idea that organisms build a model of the environment; Barry, 2009), these doubts have led to doubts about the model itself.

Furthermore, it has become clear that the heuristic value of the model is limited. For example, based on Sokolov's theory, one cannot explain why habituation is influenced by the nature of the stimuli or the observed behavior. For example, we mentioned earlier that habituation of the skin conductance response is faster for neutral stimuli than for affective stimuli. Habituation of heart rate deceleration (i.e., the slowing down of the heartbeat upon presentation of a salient stimulus), on the other hand, appears to be as fast for affective as for neutral stimuli. Bradley (2009) has proposed an alternative theory for such findings (see also Bernstein, 1981; Gati & Ben-Shakhar, 1990). It is based on the assumption that every stimulus that is motivationally relevant will elicit an OR. New, unexpected stimuli are motivationally relevant because new stimuli can indicate a danger or an opportunity. Other stimuli can be motivationally relevant because people learn that they are important for certain goals—biological goals such as survival and reproduction as well as cognitive goals such as tasks that people have in a given context. In other words, stimuli can elicit an OR, either on the basis of the extent to which they are new (novelty) or on the basis of their motivational meaning (significance; Gati & Ben-Shakhar, 1990). New neutral stimuli will therefore initially trigger an

OR weaker than that triggered by new affective stimuli. The neutral stimuli elicit an OR only on the basis of their novelty, whereas affective stimuli elicit an OR on the basis of both novelty and significance. Repeatedly presenting a stimulus very quickly makes the novelty disappear, but only very slowly changes the meaning (and therefore significance) of a stimulus. As a result, the repeated presentation of a neutral stimulus will lead to the rapid disappearance of the OR in relation to that stimulus (because the OR is elicited on the basis of novelty only, and novelty disappears very quickly), whereas the repeated presentation of affective stimuli leads to the slow disappearance of the OR (because the OR is elicited by novelty and significance, and novelty quickly disappears but significance disappears very slowly). Bradley's model can therefore better explain the influence of the nature of the stimuli on the habituation of the OR by assuming that different elements of a stimulus can lead to an OR and that these different elements are influenced in a different way by repeatedly presenting a stimulus.

Bradley (2009) also accounts for the fact that the nature of the observed behavior has an influence on habituation, by assuming that different components of the OR are determined to varying degrees by novelty and significance. The delay in heart rate is determined mainly by novelty, whereas skin conductance is determined mainly by significance. Through repeated stimulus presentations, the novelty decreases and therefore the strength of those OR components that are determined by novelty also decreases. Habituation therefore quickly occurs for those components. However, the repeated presentation of a stimulus adds little to the significance of the stimulus and thus also little to those components of the OR that are determined by it. Habituation is therefore slower for those components (see also Barry, 2006).

The interaction between the influence of the nature of the stimulus and the influence of the nature of the observed behavior is explained as follows: habituation of a component of the OR that is determined by novelty only (e.g., the delay of heartbeat) will occur equally quickly for neutral stimuli and affective stimuli. After all, only novelty counts for such components, and both types of stimuli are initially new or unexpected. Habituation of components that are determined also by significance, however, will show a slower habituation for affective stimuli than for neutral stimuli, because the significance of the affective stimuli disappears slowly. The mental process theory of Bradley (2009) is therefore able to explain more functional knowledge than the original theory of Sokolov (1975) can, and in that sense is a better theory. It does this by making additional assumptions about mental processes, namely (1) that the OR is determined not only by the novelty but also by the significance of a stimulus (where novelty and significance are hypothetical mental constructs), (2) that repeatedly presenting a stimulus has a different effect on novelty than on significance, and (3) that different components of the OR are influenced differently by novelty and significance.

1.2.2 The Opponent-Process Model of Solomon

Whereas the theories of Sokolov and Bradley try to explain habituation of the OR to all possible stimuli, Solomon (Solomon & Corbit, 1973, 1974; Solomon, 1980) formulated an **opponent-process theory** that is aimed specifically at habituation of reactions and sensitization of counterreactions (i.e., on changes in the dynamics of affect). Examples from daily life (e.g., use of drugs, jogging) suggest that repeatedly presenting a stimulus results in the weakening of the reaction and the strengthening of the counterreaction. Solomon studied the dynamics of affect in the laboratory by repeatedly administering electric shocks to dogs. He observed the heartbeat frequency of the dogs during the presentation of the shock (the reaction) and after stopping the shock (the counterreaction). Figure 1.7 shows what happens when the shock (lasting ten seconds) is administered (left figure) and when the shock ceases (right figure).

The left graph shows a clear acceleration of the heartbeat, which is greater for more intense shocks. Note that while the shock is still being delivered, a slight decrease in heart rate is already visible. The right graph shows what happens immediately after the shock has stopped. Heart rate does not immediately return to the baseline (the heart rate level before the shock was presented); there is a clear delay before returning to the baseline.

These observations of the dynamics of affect are based on the first administration of such shocks. But what is the effect of repeated electric shocks on the dynamics of affect (i.e., on the occurrence of the reaction and counterreaction)? The answer can be found in figure 1.8. The results come from what Solomon calls veteran laboratory dogs (i.e., dogs that have often been exposed to electric shocks). On the left, we see the heartbeat during the shock—there is

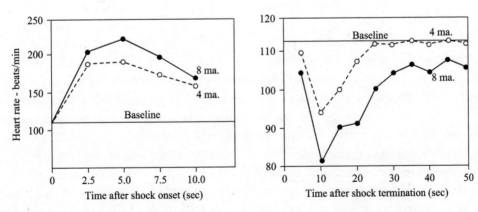

Figure 1.7
Heart rate during (left) and after (right) shocking dogs that had never experienced a shock before, measured in milliamperes, where 8 ma is more intense than 4 ma (retrieved from Solomon, 1980, figure 1).

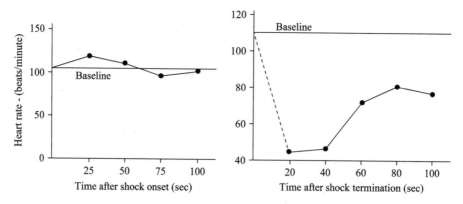

Figure 1.8

Heart rate during (left) and after (right) the shock in dogs that have already been exposed many times (retrieved from Solomon, 1980, figure 3).

no acceleration at all (compare with the left side of figure 1.7). On the right is the heartbeat after the shock. We see that the delay in heart rate is much more pronounced than after the first administration (compare with the right side of figure 1.7).

According to Solomon, these findings reflect a fundamental principle with regard to the reactions and counterreactions of humans and animals to emotionally charged stimuli. Initially, emotional stimuli provoke strong primary reactions that are positively or negatively valenced. The cessation of the stimulus brings the organism into an opposite state. As the result of the repeated presentation of the emotional stimulus, the primary reactions reduce in intensity (habituation) but the opponent state (the counterreaction) becomes even stronger (sensitization).

To explain these changes in dynamics of affect, Solomon (1980) developed the opponent-process theory (see Koob & Le Moal, 2008, for a variant of the model). Every emotional stimulus evokes a primary process that Solomon conveniently calls an **a-process**. This a-process is constant as long as the stimulus lasts. The a-process also does not change as a result of the repeated experience of the stimulus. It is determined only by the presence and intensity of the stimulus (the more intense the stimulus, the stronger the a-process). The organism reacts to the a-process with an opposite process, the **b-process**. In other words, the b-process is evoked by the a-process and its intensity depends on the intensity of the a-process. Initially, it takes some time for the b-process to get going, it is rather weak, and it lasts only a little while. After repeated presentations of the emotional stimulus, the b-process gets a shorter latency time (it is thus provoked more quickly), grows in strength, and lasts longer after the stimulation stops.

Importantly, the a- and b-processes are not directly observable; they are hypothetical constructs that researchers have come up with in the hope of explaining learning effects (in this case, the influence of repeated stimulus presentations on reactions and counterreactions).

Solomon assumes that the observable emotional state of the organism is the result of the sum of the states of the a- and b-processes (see figure 1.9). Note that the a- and b-processes have opposite directions. Hence, the b-process can counteract the effect that the a-process has on behavior.

Another important idea that was added to the opponent-process model is that the b-process can be provoked not only by the a-process but also by stimuli that repeatedly co-occur with the b-process (see Schull, 1979, for a detailed explanation). The importance of this assumption is best illustrated in the context of drug abuse (see Drummond, Tiffany, Glautier, & Remington, 1995, and Siegel, 1989, 2008 for overviews). Researchers have found that the desire for a drug (i.e., drug craving) and the risk of relapse depend on context. More specifically, the desire for a drug and the risk of relapse increase in contexts in which a person often used drugs in the past. Suppose someone smokes a lot at work, but not at home. This person, if he or she stops smoking, will experience a stronger desire (craving) to smoke at work than at home. Often, drug users who successfully kick a heroin habit in a clinic will relapse if they are in situations similar to those in which they formerly used drugs. In the opponent-process theory, these context effects have been explained by assuming that stimuli that co-occur with drug use can trigger the b-process. This triggering of the b-process causes a "craving," which could lead to using the drug in order to satisfy the "craving." Not only external stimuli such as certain rooms but also internal stimuli such as feelings can be associated with the

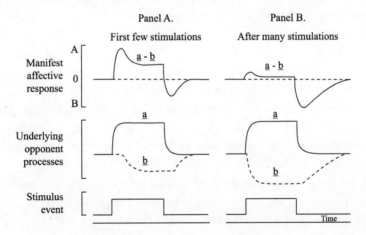

Figure 1.9
Schematic depiction of the opponent-process theory. Panel A shows what happens when the stimulus is presented for the first few times; panel B, what happens after repeated presentations. The top graphs depict the course of the manifest affective response, which is seen as resulting from the underlying opponent processes a and b (retrieved from Solomon, 1980, figure 7).

b-process. For persons who used drugs when they felt depressed or anxious, there will be a stronger craving for the drug when feelings of depression or anxiety return. Also, the context dependency of drug tolerance can be understood from this perspective (e.g., Remington, Roberts, & Steven, 1997). In situations where a person uses drugs regularly, the b-process is enhanced by environmental stimuli. This compensates for the direct effects of the drug, including dangerous physiological effects (e.g., increased blood pressure as part of a-process). If the same person uses the same amount in another situation, the b-process will be weaker (less tolerance), and this can lead to an overdose.

These insights are also important for designing treatments (see Drummond et al., 1995). For example, abstaining from drugs while being in a clinic may result in a reduction of the b-process ("cold turkey"), but it will not change the ability of external stimuli to trigger the b-process. Even after all withdrawal symptoms are gone, returning to situations that co-occurred with drug use in the past will trigger the b-process and hence increase the chance of relapse. A better approach is to expose the patient during the withdrawal to stimuli that were related to drug use. However, as we will see in the next chapter, such extinction procedures seem to have only a temporary effect (see the phenomenon of **spontaneous recovery**). Perhaps the best thing is to also teach the patient how he or she can cope with "craving" without returning to drug use.

The idea that the b-process can be elicited by stimuli that frequently accompany the process has proven very influential (e.g., Ramsay & Woods, 2014; Siegel, 2008). However, it raises questions about one of the key assumptions of the opponent-process model—namely, the idea that repeated presentations of a stimulus will lead to the strengthening of the b-process. Whenever a drug is presented, there will also be other stimuli that are present (e.g., the room in which the drug is used). The more you administer a drug, the more other stimuli will co-occur with the b-process, and thus the more the b-process can be enhanced by the presence of those other stimuli. It is therefore perhaps unnecessary to assume more than that the b-process strengthens as a result of the repeated administration of a drug. According to this view, changes in reactions and counterreactions with the use of drugs are not an example of noncontingent stimulus presentation effects (i.e., it is not the repeated use of the drug itself that is responsible for the change in the reactions and counterreactions), but rather an example of classical conditioning (the change in the reaction and counterreaction to the drug caused by stimuli that repeatedly occur with the drug). This is a good illustration of the fact that learning can never be observed directly. When one says that a certain type of learning has occurred (e.g., an effect of noncontingent stimulus presentations), this implies only a hypothesis about the cause of a change in behavior. Often, a similar change in behavior can be the result of several regularities in the area. The various hypotheses (types of learning) can then be distinguished by very carefully and separately manipulating the various regularities in the environment.

2 Classical Conditioning: Effects of Regularities in the Presence of Multiple Stimuli

After reading this chapter, you should be able to:

- Indicate under what conditions classical conditioning (as an effect) will occur.
- Give an overview of the core assumptions of the most important mental process theories of classical conditioning.

Introductory Task

Pairing two stimuli together will sometimes lead to changes in behavior—but sometimes not. Make a list of factors that you think might influence whether classical conditioning (as an effect) will occur. Do you think that the same factors always have the same impact regardless of the nature of the behavior that changes?

2.1 Some Basic Terms and Procedures

2.1.1 Basic Terms

In this chapter we discuss classical conditioning, or the impact of regularities between stimuli on behavior (see http://www.youtube.com/watch?v=Eo7jcI8fAuI for a real-life example). The prototypical example of classical conditioning is Pavlov's dog salivating whenever it hears a bell because the bell was always followed by food. The bell is called the **conditional stimulus** (CS). The food is called the **unconditional stimulus** (US). The increased salivation after hearing the bell is called the **conditional response** (CR). Research into classical conditioning aims to understand *when* (functional approach) and *how* (cognitive approach) the regularity in the presence of the CS and the US leads to a CR toward the CS.

First, we must note that it is not always clear whether a stimulus is functioning as a CS or a US. We choose to make the distinction by defining a stimulus as a CS if one checks whether

Figure 2.1
Ivan Pavlov.

reactions to this stimulus are *conditional* (i.e., dependent on the relation between that stimulus and other stimuli). The US is the stimulus that is presented together with the CS and that, through its relation with the CS, comes to influence reactions to the CS. If a certain reaction to the CS depends on the relation between the CS and the US, we call that reaction a CR. The response to the US is called the **unconditional response** (UR). The advantage of these definitions is that they are not dependent on mental process theories about conditioning and do not exclude any type of stimulus or reaction from the realm of classical conditioning research (De Houwer, 2011a).

One last terminological point. If there are different CSs present in a given situation, they are often referred to by different letters of the alphabet (e.g., A, B, X, Y). The presence of a US is often expressed by the + sign and its absence by the – sign. Therefore, the notation A+, for example, refers to a situation where CS(A) and the US are both present, and the notation AX- refers to a situation where both CS(A) and CS(X) are present but the US is absent.

2.1.2 Procedures

Although Pavlov's procedure for conditioning a salivation response is perhaps the most famous example of classical conditioning, it is worth noting that it is rarely used in contemporary conditioning research (see Van Gucht et al., 2008, for one of the few studies on conditioning of salivation responses in humans), mainly because it is highly impractical to measure how much an organism salivates. To do so we would have to surgically operate on the person (as in Pavlov's research) or work with cotton balls in the mouth to catch the saliva and weigh it afterward (as in Van Gucht et al.'s research). Researchers have therefore developed procedures that are much more practical. To illustrate, let's consider two types of classical conditioning procedures: conditioning of the **eyeblink reflex** and **fear conditioning** (see Bouton, 2016, pp. 85–90, for a more extensive overview).

In studies on the conditioning of an eyeblink reflex, a device is used in humans or non-human animals that administers a short pulse of air to the eye. Such an air blast causes an eyeblink reflex. In this case, the air blast is the US and the blink reflex is the UR. Now imagine that prior to each blast of air we present a CS such as a tone or light. As a result of the joint presentation of the CS and US, the CS will also elicit a blink reflex over time (e.g., Gormezano, Kehoe, & Marshall, 1983; Thompson & Steinmetz, 2009). One can record the blinking of the eyelid automatically via electrodes placed on the eyelids, and the presentation of the CS and US can be controlled by a computer.

In studies on fear conditioning, researchers are concerned with changes in a variety of reactions that are assumed to index fear or anxiety (see Lonsdorf et al., 2017, for a methodological overview). For example, sweating (e.g., moist palm) may be an indication of arousal that is part of an anxiety reaction. The moister the skin (e.g., through sweating), the greater the skin conductance (i.e., conductance of electricity over the skin). Hence, skin conductance is often used as an index of fear in fear conditioning. In studies on skin conductance conditioning, aversive stimuli such as unpleasant electric shocks (US) and neutral stimuli (CS) such as shapes (e.g., a triangle), sounds, or lights are used. Following the joint presentation of the CS and US, skin conductance will increase upon presentation of the CS.

In yet other studies on fear conditioning, *behavioral suppression* is used as an index of anxiety. The first step is to ensure that the organism has a stable rate of behavior. For example, rats can be taught to regularly press a lever to obtain food (see figure 2.2). When an aversive US is presented (e.g., an electrical shock), the animal will stop pressing the lever. The behavior is thus suppressed (hence the term *behavioral suppression*). When the presentation of the US is preceded by a CS (e.g., a light), the presentation of the CS will also suppress that behavior over time. This is called **conditioned suppression**. It is usually seen as an index of the degree to which the animal experiences fear of the upcoming US (see Arcediano, Ortega, & Mature, 1996, and Meulders, Vervliet, Vansteenwegen, Hermans, & Baeyens, 2011, for a conditioned suppression procedure in humans).

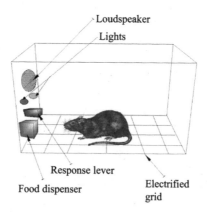

Loudspeaker

Lights

Response lever

Food dispenser

Electrified grid

Figure 2.2

A rat in a Skinner box, where pressing a handle is followed by the delivery of food. An electric shock can be delivered via the rods in the floor (US). Because of that shock, the rat will temporarily stop pressing the lever (suppression). Stimuli that repeatedly precede the shock (e.g., a light) will also result in a temporary reduction of the frequency with which the rat presses the lever (conditioned suppression).

Box 2.1 On the Relation between Anxiety Disorders and Classical Conditioning

Research on the classical conditioning of fear and anxiety reactions contributed to the rise of behavior therapy, one of the most important traditions in psychotherapy (see Craske, Hermans, & Vansteenwegen, 2006). The starting point was a functional analysis of anxiety disorders in clinical practice. Such functional analyses refer to the possibility that anxiety disorders are an example of classical conditioning (i.e., fear that results from regularities in the occurrence of two or more stimuli). For example, a man's phobia of dogs may be due to the fact that he was bitten by a dog during childhood. Likewise, a woman's fear of elevators may be due to the fact that she experienced a hyperventilation attack when riding an elevator. Based on this functional analysis, we can investigate whether procedures that influence conditioned anxiety reactions in the lab also have an impact on anxiety reactions in clinical practice. This approach has led to various treatment techniques such as exposure therapy and systematic desensitization (see also box 2.6). Although it is generally accepted that at least certain anxiety disorders are examples of classical conditioning, it has also become clear that fears are not always the result of regularities in the occurrence of stimuli in the environment. For example, research shows that many people develop phobias even though they have never had a negative experience with the object they fear. Likewise, many people experience panic attacks when confronted with objects they have rarely or never been directly confronted with (e.g., snakes) or situations they are already afraid of when they are confronted with them for the first time (e.g., traveling in an airplane). It seems that anxiety disorders are often the result of observing others and/or hearing stories from others (Poulton & Menzies, 2002; Rachman, 1977). Note, however, that learning through observation and instructions can also be studied within learning psychology. We will return to this issue in section 2.2.1 and in chapter 4.

2.2   Functional Knowledge

In this section we discuss the most important functional knowledge about classical conditioning (i.e., the most important knowledge about the conditions under which regularities in the presence of two or more stimuli have an influence on behavior). Again, we organize our overview according to the type of moderator that influences conditioning.

2.2.1   The Nature of the Stimuli

2.2.1.1 Classical conditioning is a general phenomenon   Research shows that classical conditioning is a very general phenomenon in that it can occur with all kinds of stimuli. The CS can be very simple (e.g., the ringing of a bell), but even a very complex event can be a CS (e.g., receiving information about the food that someone else has eaten; see studies on human contingency learning discussed in section 2.2.2.2). The US can also vary from something very simple (e.g., a piece of food) to something very complex (e.g., information about the occurrence of a particular allergic reaction in a patient). In each case, the pairing of two stimuli can lead to a change in behavior. It is precisely because of this broad applicability that classical conditioning is such an interesting phenomenon.

As we noted in the introductory chapter, some researchers talk about classical conditioning only if the US is a biologically relevant stimulus (e.g., food or a painful shock). They then use terms such as *associative learning* to refer to other situations in which the combination of (non-biologically relevant) stimuli leads to changes in behavior. However, we do not see any substantive reasons for restricting classical conditioning to situations with biologically relevant USs (De Houwer, 2011a). Moreover, such a distinction is difficult to make because it is not always clear a priori which stimuli for which organisms are biologically relevant in which situations. Because our definition of the different types of learning is based on different types of environmental regularities, there is no need for us to restrict classical conditioning to certain types of stimuli.

There are two types of conditioning in which two special types of stimuli are used: *observational conditioning* using social stimuli and *conditioning through instructions* using verbal stimuli. In observational conditioning research, an observer looks at a model that shows a reaction to a stimulus. For example, a young monkey (observer) is shown a video in which an older conspecific (model) shows a fearful reaction to a snake (e.g., Mineka, 1987). The young monkey does not show any fear toward the snake prior to watching the video but does show fear toward the snake after watching it. In this instance, the snake can be seen as the CS, the fear reaction of the older monkey is the US, and the learned fear reaction of the young animal is the CR that is the result of the co-occurrence of the CS and US. Many studies support the idea that emotional reactions in humans are often based on observational conditioning (e.g., Dunne & Askew, 2018; see Debiec & Olsson, 2017, for an overview).

Observational conditioning is just one instance of a much bigger class of social learning phenomena (see Heyes, 1994; Olsson & Phelps, 2007). Starting from our definition of learning, social learning can be defined as the impact of a particular type of regularity on the behavior of an observer—namely, those regularities that (a) involve the behavior of a model as one of its elements (which is why the learning qualifies as being "social") and (b) do not involve the observer's behavior as one of the elements (which disqualifies learning *about* others, such as how to influence others, and restricts social learning to learning *from* others). For instance, in observational conditioning there is a regularity between two events, one of which is the behavior of a model (e.g., a fearful response) and the other is the presence of a stimulus (e.g., a snake). One could also imagine situations in which one element of the regularity is the behavior of a model (e.g., a rat pushing a lever) and the other element is the outcome of the behavior of the model (e.g., a food pellet that is presented to the model after pressing the lever). If the behavior of an observer changes as the result of being exposed to such a regularity (e.g., the observer starts pressing the lever), one could describe this as an instance of observational operant conditioning. Hence, just as different types of learning can be distinguished on the basis of the type of regularity that causes the change in behavior, so too can different types of social learning be distinguished on the basis of the type of regularity that changes behavior, though our focus is now on changes in the behavior of an observer, and all regularities involved in social learning must involve a model but not the observer. Just as classifying changes in behavior as instances of particular types of learning involves a hypothesis on the part of the researcher about the causes of the change in behavior, so too do different types of social learning involve different hypotheses about the causes of changes in behavior, with the difference that the research now seeks to explain the behavior of an observer on the basis of the behavior of others. The study of social learning can thus provide unique insights into the social origins of behavior.

Conditioning through instructions is also an important source of behavior (Rachman, 1977). From the work of Cook and Harris (1937), we know that instructions about a CS-US relation are sufficient to establish a CR. For example, if subjects are told that the presentation of a triangle (CS1) may be followed by an electric shock and that a circle (CS2) will never be followed by an electric shock, then during a subsequent test phase we will observe more fear after the presentation of the triangle than the circle. This effect occurs even when the triangle and shock have never been presented together. More recent research shows that the moderators of conditioning through instructions are very similar to the moderators of standard conditioning that involves actual pairings of the CS and US (for an overview, see Mertens, Boddez, Sevenster, Engelhard, & De Houwer, 2018). Just as social learning can involve different types of regularities, so too can instructions relate to several types of regularities (e.g., regularities in the presence of one stimulus or in the presence of stimuli and responses; see Van Dessel et al., 2015, 2017). As we will argue in chapter 4, however, we believe that the effects of observed regularities and instructions about regularities are not simple effects of the regularities themselves but instead are instances of a complex form of learning involving many different regularities.

2.2.1.2 The influence of the properties of the CS or US, and the relation between CS and US on classical conditioning effects

Although classical conditioning can occur with many different stimuli, properties of the CS and US can still have an influence on the strength of the behavioral change that occurs as a result of the pairing of stimuli. An obvious factor is the *intensity* of the stimuli. Few readers will be surpised to learn that regularities involving more salient, intense, or biologically relevant stimuli are learned more quickly (i.e., they require fewer presentations of the CS and US in order to produce a fixed level of behavioral change) and will have more impact on behavior than less intense stimuli. For example, a regularity involving the ringing of a bell and food will impact behavior more quickly if the ringing of the bell is clearly audible than if one can barely hear it. It also seems logical that a regularity involving the ringing of a bell and a biologically relevant stimulus such as food will have a greater impact on behavior than a regularity involving the ringing of a bell and a biologically irrelevant stimulus such as the appearance of a light.

What is less obvious is that in addition to the influence of CS and US properties, there is also an influence of the *intrinsic relation* between those stimuli. By intrinsic relation we mean the combination of or "match" between the two stimuli. In other words, effects of the intrinsic relation between stimuli are concerned not with the properties of the CS or the US (e.g., how intense the CS is or how important the US is), but rather with the interaction between the properties of those two stimuli. Observing these interactions shows that learning can be selective in the sense that certain relations are learned more quickly than other relations. The importance of the intrinsic relation between the CS and US was demonstrated for the first time by Garcia, in the context of research on conditioned food aversion (see Freeman & Riley, 2009, for a historical analysis of Garcia's research). Garcia studied a phenomenon called *aversion learning*. What we mean by aversion learning is probably best explained using the following anecdote by Seligman (see Seligman & Hager, 1972). After eating "filet mignon and béarnaise sauce," Seligman became ill later that same night. It subsequently turned out that this nausea was actually the beginning of a bout of the flu. But Seligman had already attributed it to the béarnaise sauce, and since then, he cannot tolerate the sight, let alone the taste, of this sauce. This anecdote raises several questions (see Bouton, 2016, pp. 206–220, for an overview), one of which is related to the selectivity in learning. Why did his reaction to the béarnaise sauce change? And why did he not show an aversive reaction to the steak, the dessert, the drink, the restaurant, or even the waiter?

Similar questions emerge from the work of Garcia and colleagues. Garcia and Koelling (1966) placed rats in a cage, and during a learning phase, they could drink from a tube of water that was infused with sugar. Each time the tube was touched, a light and a noise were also automatically presented. So in this case, there were two CSs: the sweet taste of the water and the light-sound stimulus. The nature of the US was manipulated between groups. In a first group, lithium chloride was delivered after drinking, which led to nausea; in a second group, an electric shock was delivered two seconds after drinking. This was followed by the test phase, in which the two CSs were presented separately: either the light + sound stimulus was delivered during the drinking of pure water (no taste), or the water had the sugar taste but the light-sound stimulus was not presented. In the lithium group, the animals drank very little of the water with the sugar taste; it was as if that taste had become aversive for them. However, the light-sound stimulus did not affect drinking the tasteless water (see figure 2.3). In the group with electric shocks during the learning phase, the animals drank little of the water that coincided with the light-sound stimulus but much of the water with the sugar taste (see figure 2.3). The key point here is that there is an interaction between the nature

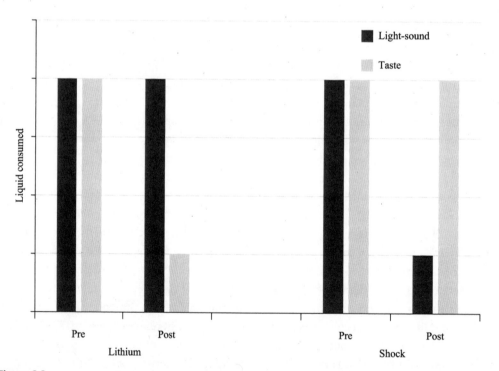

Figure 2.3
Idealized results from Garcia and Koelling (1966). With lithium as a US (left), the taste stimulus but not the light-sound stimulus reduces the amount of liquid consumed after the conditioning phase (post). With shock as a US (right), less liquid is consumed after conditioning in the presence of the light-sound stimulus, whereas the taste does not reduce drinking.

of the CS (taste or light-sound) and the nature of the US (lithium or shock): when the US is lithium (a poison that leads to nausea), the taste of the water during test has more impact on drinking than the presence of the light-sound stimulus; when the US is an electric shock (which leads to pain), the light-sound stimulus has more influence on drinking than the taste of the water. Note that these differences did not occur during a pretest that took place before the learning phase. It is therefore the learning phase that was responsible for the observed interaction (see Domjan, 2015, for a discussion of the limitations of Garcia's research and of subsequent research that has circumvented these limitations).

2.2.1.3   The impact of the nature of the US on the nature of the CR

Sometimes a distinction is made between **appetitive** and **aversive** USs. Both types of USs are stimuli that elicit an (unconditional) response. With appetitive USs, this unconditional response (UR) is positive and often related to the fulfilment of a particular biological need (e.g., hunger or thirst). The prototypical example of an appetitive US is food. Salivation is an example of an appetitive UR because it is directed at consuming food. Aversive USs elicit negative URs (e.g., fear responses). The prototypical example of an aversive US is an electric shock, whereas freezing is a common example of an aversive UR. *Freezing* refers to the finding that because of the presentation of an aversive stimulus, the animal will not move for a period of time (i.e., it "freezes"; Hagenaars, Oitzl, & Roelofs, 2014). Although both types of USs can lead to changes in responses to the CSs with which they are paired, there seems to be a difference between appetitive and aversive conditional responses (CRs). A CS coupled with an appetitive US often provokes positive (appetitive) responses, whereas a CS accompanied by an aversive US usually provokes a negative (aversive) reaction. This demonstrates that the properties of the US can determine the properties of the CR.

That said, there is still a great deal of uncertainty about the relation between the US (and more specifically, the UR that the US evokes) and the CR. For example, it was long thought that the CR was identical to the UR that is elicited by the US. This is indeed the case in the example of Pavlov's dog: initially, only food elicits salivation (salivation is therefore a UR that is elicited by the food), and later, as a result of pairing the bell and food, the bell also comes to elicit salivation (salivation is therefore a CR to the bell). To this day, classical conditioning is often defined as a transfer of reactions as a result of pairing stimuli. This idea is depicted in figure 2.4.

However, research shows that the relation between the CR and US is far more nuanced than initially thought. Recent work shows that the CR can in some cases be opposite to the UR; for example, whereas morphine causes a reduction in pain, stimuli that occur repeatedly with morphine administration seem to evoke more sensitivity to pain (Siegel, 1975; see Bouton, 2016, pp. 187–193, for a discussion).

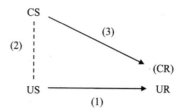

Figure 2.4
The traditional representation of classical conditioning. (1) The US initially elicits a UR. By pairing the CS and US (2), the CS will also trigger the UR (3). The UR therefore becomes a CR.

Importantly, classical conditioning not only is sensitive to the properties of the US during conditioning but also to changes in the US after conditioning. This phenomenon is called *US revaluation*. In a typical US revaluation study, a tone is repeatedly presented with food and this leads to the tone eliciting an appetitive CR (e.g., salivation). Thereafter, the appetitive nature of the food is changed (e.g., by pairing it with nausea). The US is thus "revaluated" and becomes negative instead of positive. Now, presentations of the tone will no longer elicit appetitive responses and sometimes even elicit aversive responses (e.g., Holland & Rescorla, 1975). As we shall see in section 2.3, this finding has important implications for mental process theories of learning.

Finally, it is worth mentioning one last phenomenon known as **counterconditioning** (e.g., Pearce & Dickinson, 1975). In studies on counterconditioning, the nature of the US changes during CS+ presentations. During an initial learning phase, a tone is repeatedly followed by an aversive electric shock (causing the tone to elicit fear). Next, the same tone is followed by an appetitive stimulus such as food. This change in the nature of the US that a CS is paired with also leads to a change in the nature of the CR (e.g., fear responses to the tone will weaken and gradually be replaced by appetitive reactions).

2.2.2 The Nature of the Observed Behavior

2.2.2.1 Influences on involuntary behavior It is a common misconception that regularities involving multiple stimuli can have an impact only on autonomic reactions (i.e., behavior driven by the autonomous nervous system). This misconception may be due to the fact that Pavlov's dog is regarded as the prototypical example of classical conditioning. In Pavlov's procedure, an autonomic reaction (i.e., salivation) was indeed measured to investigate learning. Research on the conditioning of anxiety responses (which has been very influential, see box 2.1) has also made use of autonomic (physiological) reactions.

However, it is clear that not only autonomic reactions but also controlled behavior can be influenced by stimulus pairings. A good example of this is the phenomenon of

autoshaping. Brown and Jenkins (1968) placed pigeons in a Skinner box and let a key light up just before the grain appeared in the food dispenser. After several presentations of the stimuli (light and food) the pigeon began to peck at the key (see http://www.youtube.com /watch?v=cacwAvgg8EA). So there is a change in controlled behavior (i.e., the pigeon starts to peck at the key) as a result of a regularity in the presence of two stimuli (light and food). This behavior is apparently formed in an "automatic" way (i.e., without the behavior being related with a certain result); hence the name *autoshaping*.

This change in behavior counts as an example of classical conditioning only if we are certain that the change is due to the relation between two stimuli and not to some other factor. A possible alternative cause of the pigeon's pecking on the metal plate is that this behavior somehow leads to the presence of an appetitive stimulus (e.g., food). In that case, the behavior would be an example of operant conditioning (a change in behavior due to the relation between that behavior and a stimulus in the environment). The results of a study by Hearst and Jenkins (1974) suggest that such an alternative explanation in terms of operant conditioning is probably not correct. The setup can best be explained with reference to figure 2.5. A pigeon is placed in a long cage. On one side of the cage there is a light that always lights up before food appears in a dispenser that is on the other side of the cage. When the food appeared, it was accessible for only four seconds. In other words, the pigeon had to be at the dispenser within four seconds. An extremely strange behavior developed in their study. After a while, the pigeon spontaneously ran to the light that was paired with food, pecked on it, and then hurried to the dispenser. Given the distance, the bird often came too late—the food had already disappeared. And yet, the pigeons seemed to persevere in this completely useless and even counterproductive behavior. Because pecking on the key apparently has no appetitive consequences and even leads to a negative result (arriving at the dispenser too late to eat the food), it seems unlikely that the behavior is under the control of the stimuli that follow that behavior (food). A more likely explanation involves the relation between the light and the food. Moore (1973) showed that in an autoshaping trial, the behavior of the pigeon (CR)

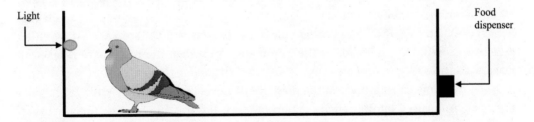

Figure 2.5
Longbox autoshaping with pigeons. When the light (left side) always precedes availability of the food in the food dispenser (right side), the pigeon will approach and peck on the light.

differs depending on whether food or water is used as the US. In both cases an illuminated image is presented, but in one case this image leads to behavior that shows the topography of "eating behavior," and in the other case "drinking behavior" (see https://www.youtube.com/watch?v=50EmqiYC9Xw). The nature of the reaction with regard to the lighting of the key (pecking as if it is eating vs. pecking as if it is drinking) is thus determined by the nature of the stimulus that accompanies the illumination of the key, which suggests that the change in behavior is indeed a consequence of the CS-US relation (i.e., it is an instance of classical conditioning).

2.2.2.2 Three types of behavior   Although a large variety of behaviors can be influenced by stimulus pairings, past research has largely concentrated on changes in three categories of behavior. First, in most experiments, changes in *preparatory responses* are examined (see Mackintosh, 1983, and Bouton, 2016, for an overview). This concerns responses that prepare the organism in a certain way for the arrival of a certain stimulus. Both appetitive and aversive responses can be seen as preparatory responses. For example, one can assume that an appetitive response such as salivation prepares the organism for the arrival of food and enables it to consume the food more efficiently (which is why such responses are sometimes also called *consummatory responses*). An aversive response such as freezing can facilitate the detection of aversive stimuli and thereby reduce the impact of those stimuli. Note, however, that preparatory responses are not always adaptive (in the sense of being useful for fulfilling the goals of the organism). In autoshaping (see previous section), for example, we see that a pigeon will peck at a key when the lighting of that key is followed by the delivery of food. This behavior does not actually help the bird get food and therefore it is not adaptive (if anything, it is sometimes counterproductive). Nevertheless, because the topography of the behavior depends on the nature of the US (food or water), one could argue that the behavior is preparatory in that it is an attempt to prepare the organism for the ingestion of food or water, albeit a misguided attempt.

Second, studies on human contingency learning examine changes in judgments that are due to regularities involving stimuli (see De Houwer & Beckers, 2002, and Shanks, 2010, for an overview). In these studies, participants are shown situations in which certain cues (which could be seen as CSs) and certain outcomes (which could be seen as USs) are either present or absent.[1] On the basis of the information provided, the participant is asked to make a **contingency judgment**—that is, a judgment about the strength of the relation between the presence of a cue and the presence of an outcome. If such contingency judgments are influenced by the actual relation between the two stimuli, this qualifies as an instance of classical conditioning because behavior (contingency judgments) changes as the result of stimulus pairings (the regularity involving the presence of the cue and the presence of the outcome). The food allergy paradigm is one specific task that is often used in studies on human contingency learning. Participants are told that they will receive information about a patient who is allergic to certain types of food. During each trial, participants are told what the patient ate during a certain meal and whether the patient showed an allergic reaction after the meal. Each trial therefore corresponds to a separate meal. On the basis of that information, participants indicate the extent to which a food will lead to an allergic reaction in that patient. Results show that judgments about the (causal) link between foods and allergic reactions are influenced by the information about the co-occurrence of those foods and allergies.

Box 2.2 Why Does Classical Conditioning Receive Less Attention from Functional Psychologists?

One of the striking differences between handbooks on learning research concerns the extent to which attention is paid to classical versus operant conditioning. In the handbooks on learning written by functional psychologists (e.g., Catania, 2013; Pierce & Cheney, 2018), often there is only one short chapter devoted to classical conditioning, whereas it is covered extensively in textbooks written from a cognitive approach (e.g., Bouton, 2016; Schwartz et al., 2002). One reason for this difference is that only the cognitive approach devotes attention to theories about the mental mechanisms that mediate classical conditioning. A second is that classical conditioning is conceptualized in a more restrictive manner in the functional approach. In this box, we focus on the difference in conceptualization.

In the functional approach, the term *respondent conditioning* is often used instead of *classical conditioning*. The term *respondent* refers to "respondent behavior"—that is, behavior elicited by a stimulus. In contrast to operant behavior, which is a function of its consequences (e.g., whether an animal presses a lever depends on whether food follows that behavior or not), respondent behavior is dependent only on the antecedents of the behavior (e.g., seeing a lemon elicits salivation). Thus, you can change operant behavior by changing the consequences of behavior, but respondent behavior can be changed only by manipulating the stimulus that elicits that behavior. In functional psychology, classical conditioning is sometimes seen as learning respondent behavior, while operant conditioning is seen as learning operant behavior (e.g., Pierce & Cheney, 2018). The type of conditioning (classical vs. operant) is thus defined in terms of the type of behavior that changes (respondent vs. operant). Once it has been determined that a behavior is dependent on a certain outcome of that behavior, it can be concluded that the behavior is an operant and therefore that it falls outside the scope of classical conditioning. For functional psychologists, most behavior that humans and nonhumans emit is operant in nature (dependent on its consequences). This may explain why classical conditioning is not so interesting for functional psychologists: it only tells us something about the less interesting and less prevalent class of respondent behavior.

For cognitive psychologists, research on classical conditioning is important because it can provide them with insights into how organisms learn to anticipate events in the environment and how they manage to adapt to that environment (e.g., Bouton, 2016, p. 28). For them, it is not so important whether the organisms learn relations between stimuli or relations between their

(continued)

Box 2.2 (continued)

behavior and outcome stimuli. In both cases, a mental mechanism is needed that detects the relation between elements in the environment and allows the organism to adjust its behavior. When cognitive psychologists choose to study classical conditioning it is a largely pragmatic choice: the researcher has complete control over the stimuli presented during a study on classical conditioning. It is much more difficult for them to exercise control over operant conditioning because the presence or absence of stimuli is dependent on the behavior of the organism (e.g., the rat receives food only when it presses the lever, so the presentation of food depends on the behavior of the rat). The study of classical conditioning is therefore the most convenient way for a cognitive psychologist to investigate mental mechanisms of learning.

In this book, we also give classical conditioning greater weight than what is typical in functional learning psychology handbooks. The reason for this is that we define classical conditioning only in terms of regularities in the environment and not in terms of types of behavior. Take our previous example of changes in contingency judgments. Strictly speaking, contingency judgments are not respondent behavior, because making judgments clearly depends on the consequences of that behavior. For example, participants will provide judgments only because doing so is required by the task (e.g., the task can be terminated only if judgments are given). Contingency judgments are therefore an operant behavior because they depend on the outcomes of that behavior (e.g., the fact that they bring the end of the task closer). Nevertheless, the change in the *content* of the judgments (e.g., whether people believe that there is a positive or negative contingency between a certain food and allergic reactions) can be influenced by a regularity in the occurrence of two stimuli (e.g., the co-occurrence of the food and an allergic reaction). For us, this impact of a regularity on the judgment is sufficient to view the change in the judgment as an example of classical conditioning. In other words, if one aspect of the behavior is influenced by a regularity in the co-occurrence of stimuli (e.g., the judgment about the strength of a contingency), the change in that aspect of the behavior can be considered an example of classical conditioning. For our definition of classical conditioning, it is not important that there are other aspects of the behavior that are dependent on the consequences of the behavior (e.g., why the participant provides a judgment). Some instances of classical conditioning might even depend on (extensive training that leads to) verbal capacities (see chapter 4). From this broad perspective, classical conditioning is very important because many changes in behavior are determined by the co-occurrence of two stimuli. All of this does not mean that each instance of classical conditioning is necessarily moderated by the same variables or mediated by the same mental processes. Yet, there is merit in unifying a wide range of phenomena under the umbrella of classical conditioning because it allows one to describe them using the same concepts (e.g., CS, US) and thus to compare them in terms of the role of moderators (e.g., impact of CS-only trials) and mediators (e.g., associations, propositions).

A third type of behavior examined in classical conditioning research is evaluative behavior. Although it is difficult to pinpoint the exact difference between evaluative and nonevaluative behavior, at least intuitively it makes sense to classify certain behaviors as evaluative in the sense that they imply a certain liking or disliking of a particular stimulus. Most often, explicit ratings are used to measure changes in liking (e.g., selecting a number on a scale ranging from -100 to +100 to express one's liking of a stimulus, with -100 being the rating for extremely negative stimuli and +100 the rating for extremely positive stimuli). The term **evaluative conditioning** is typically used to refer to changes in liking that are the result of stimulus pairings (see De Houwer, Thomas, & Baeyens, 2001, and Hofmann, De Houwer, Perugini, Baeyens, & Crombez, 2010).[2]

The prototypical way of studying evaluative conditioning is a picture-picture procedure originally developed by Levey and Martin (1975) and elaborated by Baeyens (e.g., Baeyens, Eelen, Crombez, & Van den Bergh, 1992). During a first phase, participants encounter a series of images (e.g., faces of unknown individuals or abstract geometrical shapes). For each of these images, the participant must indicate how pleasant or unpleasant he or she finds the image (e.g., by rating it on a scale of -100 [very unpleasant] to +100 [very pleasant]). On the basis of these ratings the researcher selects images that are considered neutral (e.g., a rating of 0, +10, or -10), positive (e.g., a rating of +80 or more), or negative (e.g., a rating of -80 or less). The experimenter then creates a series of stimulus pairs consisting of a neutral (CS1) and positive image (USpos) and another set of pairs of neutral (CS2) and negative images (USneg). In the second phase, participants see a pair of images on each trial. The neutral picture usually appears first, followed by a brief pause, and then the positive or negative image. The next trial starts several seconds later. In this way, certain neutral images are repeatedly paired with a positive image, whereas other neutral images are paired with negative images. Afterward, participants have to reassess the valence of the images on the same scale as before. In most evaluative conditioning studies, the neutral images that were paired with positive images are subsequently evaluated more positively than the neutral images paired with negative images. In other words, the valence of the neutral images changes in the direction of the valence of the images with which they were paired. It should be clear that the procedure used in evaluative conditioning studies corresponds to a classical conditioning procedure: the neutral stimuli can be regarded as CSs, the positive and negative stimuli as USs, and the change in valence as the CR. The only unique procedural element of evaluative conditioning is that it focuses on changes in evaluative responses to the CSs instead of preparatory responses or contingency judgments (De Houwer, 2007).

2.2.2.3 Unconscious learning: The relation between different conditioned changes in behavior

Earlier in this chapter we argued that changes in contingency judgments about the relation between stimuli can be regarded as an instance of classical conditioning (i.e., a change

Box 2.3 Applications of Evaluative Conditioning to Social and Consumer Psychology

Our likes and dislikes determine many aspects of our behavior. For example, we tend to avoid the things we do not like and approach things we do like. This applies to objects, products, places, and people. Hence, a better understanding of how our likes and dislikes come about can lead to better prediction and control of other types of behavior. Research on evaluative conditioning has important implications for other research domains in and outside psychology. Take social and consumer psychology. In those domains, people want to learn more about how attitudes toward persons and products are created and how these can be changed. Research on evaluative conditioning can easily be applied to the domain of advertisements (e.g., Hütter & Sweldens, 2018). For example, in advertisements, a product (e.g., Coca-Cola) will often be presented together with positive stimuli (e.g., a smiling person). The product can be considered the CS and the smiling person the US. The aim is to transfer the positive valence of the US to the CS as a result of the joint presentations of the CS and US; this is a classically conditioned change in evaluative responding.

in behavior that is due to the pairing of stimuli). This functional perspective differs from the typical cognitive view in which verbal judgments are seen as providing a direct index of knowledge (i.e., of mental representations). From a cognitive perspective, judgments about relations can tell us if the knowledge that mediates conditioning is consciously accessible. The answer to this question is not just interesting as such but also relevant for the much broader question of whether there are unconscious influences on behavior.

However, when we look at this research from a purely functional point of view, we must abandon the idea that a contingency judgment or any other behavior is a direct reflection of underlying knowledge. A judgment is also a behavior that is a function of certain factors in the environment, including regularities such as the pairing of stimuli. From a functional perspective, instances of **unconscious learning** illustrate that regularities can influence different types of behavior (e.g., judgments, skin conductance) in different ways (e.g., no impact on judgments, impact on skin conductance). This functional perspective does not exclude the possibility that this research may have implications for cognitive theories about the mental mechanisms that mediate conditioning, but as with other research, it is important to keep the effects (changes in judgments or skin conductance as a result of regularities in the presence of stimuli) separate from the mental processes (whether the mediating knowledge has to be consciously accessible).

Empirical research on unconscious conditioning strongly suggests that relations between stimuli in the environment must have an influence on judgments about that relation in order to influence other behavior. To illustrate this more clearly, let's consider the work of Dawson and Schell (see Dawson & Schell, 1987, for an overview, and Mertens & Engelhard, 2020, for a review of related evidence). Their participants were exposed to a regularity involving the presentation of a light (CS) and an electric shock (US). Dawson and Schell investigated the conditions under which these stimulus pairings resulted in a change in skin conductance during CS presentations. They also asked participants to judge during each CS presentation the extent to which they expected the US to occur. They found that a change in skin conductance occurred only after a change in US expectancy had occurred. In other studies, Dawson and Schell found that factors that prevent changes in expectancies from occurring (e.g., making the CS less conspicuous and thus making the relation between the CS and the US less conspicuous) also prevented changes in skin conductance from occurring. Research into evaluative conditioning has also shown that the strength of changes in evaluative responding (how positive or negative you consider the CS to be) are to a large extent dependent on judgments about which CS went together with which US (contingency awareness). For example, a meta-analysis (Hofmann et al., 2010) showed that differences in contingency awareness was by far the most important determinant of the strength of the changes in valence (i.e., the better one's conscious knowledge about the CS-US pairings, the stronger the evaluative conditioning effect). From a cognitive perspective, this implies that conscious knowledge is very important for classical conditioning effects.

Although it is clear that contingency awareness is an important factor in classical conditioning, there is still a debate about whether there are certain instances of conditioning that occur in the absence of contingency awareness. In other words, are there certain conditions under which conditioning can occur unconsciously? Whereas the existence of unconscious conditioning is self-evident for certain researchers (e.g., Clark, Manns, & Squire, 2002), others continue to question the evidence for unconscious learning (e.g., Lovibond & Shanks, 2002; Mertens & Engelhard, 2020; Mitchell et al., 2009; Vadillo, Konstantinidis, & Shanks, 2016). Although we do not exclude the possibility that conditioning can occur unconsciously under certain conditions (e.g., Greenwald & De Houwer, 2017), it seems to us that conditioning most often requires contingency awareness. In functional terms, it will usually be possible to observe changes in contingency judgments before one can observe other effects of stimulus pairings. The big question for future research is, what are the conditions that determine whether conditioning can take place unconsciously? To answer this question, however, we first need procedures that allow us to demonstrate unconscious conditioning in a reliable and unambiguous way. There is still no consensus about which procedures are suitable for achieving that aim.

2.2.3 The Properties of the Organism

Effects that result from stimulus pairings seem to occur in almost all animal species. For example, classical conditioning has been demonstrated in worms, fruit flies (see https://www .youtube.com/watch?v=-dPfZE5adYg), snails, bees, fish, birds, rats, and people. Given the large differences between these species, it seems unlikely that, at the cognitive level, classical conditioning is always based on a single (cognitive or neuronal) mediating mechanism. It also highlights the need for caution when we generalize knowledge about conditioning in one animal species to another species. Even if there are major similarities between the moderators of classical conditioning in, for example, bees and humans (e.g., Bitterman, 1996), this does not mean that the same mental mechanism is responsible for conditioning in both animal species. The presence of classical conditioning effects in so many species is probably due to the fact that different animal species are confronted with similar problems in their world; the principle of convergent evolution holds that animal species evolve independently of each other but still display similar characteristics because of similarities in their interactions with the environment (Van Horik, Clayton, & Emery, 2012). Every animal has a greater chance of survival and reproduction if it can adapt to environmental regularities (e.g., if it can predict where food can be found or when dangerous situations will occur). Almost all animals will thus show classical conditioning when doing so increases their chances of survival and reproduction. However, these similarities do not imply that the underlying mechanisms (at either the mental or neuronal levels) are always the same.

Moreover, there are also clear differences in the conditions under which classical conditioning occurs in different animal species. For example, research on the influence of intrinsic relations shows that one animal species can be more strongly influenced by certain regularities than another animal species. For example, mammals will learn more quickly about relations between the taste of food and nausea than about relations between the color of food and nausea (whereas there is no such difference in learning the taste-shock relation and the color-shock relation). Birds, on the other hand, seem to learn a relation between color and nausea more quickly than a relation between taste and nausea (whereas there is no such difference in learning the taste-shock relation and color-shock relation). This could be due to the fact that the selection of food in mammals is determined mainly by the taste of the food, whereas in birds this is determined mainly by the visual characteristics of food. It also seems that certain instances of selectivity in learning are already present from birth, indicating a genetically determined influence on learning (e.g., Gemberling & Domjan, 1982).

In light of these differences, it is therefore useful to also view conditioning from the perspective of the specific organism being studied (for an overview, see Domjan, 2005, and Bouton, 2016, pp. 193–200). From this perspective, conditioning is primarily a function of the survival and reproduction of the organism. Conditioning (as an effect) is thus seen as an adaptive phenomenon that occurs in natural situations. This perspective has two important implications for how conditioning research will be carried out. If you want to learn more about conditioning in natural situations, then you need to take stimuli that can occur together in the natural environment of an organism. There is little point in using CSs that normally do not occur with USs in the environment of an organism (e.g., a light flash followed by an electric shock), as is the case in the majority of the existing conditioning experiments. Instead, it is better to use CSs that often occur together with the US in the organism's environment, because they are potential causes of the US (e.g., food with a certain taste [CS] and nausea [US]) or because the CS is an integral part of the US (e.g., the visual characteristics of a sexual partner [CS] preceding copulation with that partner [US]). Domjan (2005) calls such CSs **ecologically valid.**

Domjan (2005; Domjan, Cusato, & Krause, 2004) reviewed research that indicates that conditioning with ecologically valid CSs has different characteristics than conditioning with arbitrary CSs. He did research into sexual conditioning with quails (small birds that live predominantly in grasslands, see figure 2.6). Domjan and his colleagues repeatedly showed male quails a fake (i.e., taxidermic) female quail (CS) just before they were given access to a real female quail and had sexual contact with it (US). As a result of these "pairings" (i.e., the joint presentation of the CS and the US), the number of times the males attempted to mate with the fake female (the CS) increased. Domjan (2005) also discusses aversion learning (see section

Figure 2.6
A Japanese quail.

2.2.1.2) as an example of conditioning with ecologically valid CSs. One can say that there is a "natural relation" between the taste of food and gastrointestinal sensations (including nausea).

A second consequence of an ecological perspective on classical conditioning is that extra attention is given to adaptive conditioning effects (i.e., conditioning effects that help the organism to survive and reproduce; also see note 5 in the introduction). An important adaptive effect may be that the organism deals with the US in a more efficient way. The emphasis here is not on how conditioning as a procedure changes reactions to the CS (i.e., changes in the CR), but how conditioning influences reactions with respect to the US (i.e., changes in the UR). Domjan (2005) provides an overview of various findings that show that conditioning as a procedure can lead to changes in the UR. Perhaps the most imaginative is his own research into sexual conditioning in quails (see Domjan & Gutiérrez, 2019, for a recent review on sexual learning).

Again, Domjan showed a fake female quail to male quails (CS) just before they had access to a real female quail with which they could have sexual contact (US). During a subsequent test phase, the researchers evaluated not responses to the fake quail (CS) but rather actual sexual contact with the real female (US). They checked whether prior presentations of the CS had an effect on the efficiency of sexual contact and found that after the presentation of the fake quail (CS), sexual contact with the live quail was more efficient. For instance, the male needed less time to initiate sexual contact, semen contained more sperm, and the chance of conception of the egg was greater. These effects were obtained only when the fake quail was presented prior to the real female quail during the test phase (i.e., prior to sexual contact with a female) and when during a previous learning phase, the fake quail was paired with the presentation of a real female. The changes in the UR (the response to the sexually available female) were therefore the result of prior pairing of the CS and the US. Another example is conditioned drug tolerance (see section 1.2.2). Stimuli (CSs) associated with the use of a drug (US) will reduce the response to the drug (UR) and thus reduce the likelihood of death by overdose. In sum, conditioning plays an important adaptive role in dealing with many important events.[3]

2.2.4   The Influence of the Broader Context

Most studies that are relevant to the impact of the broader context on classical conditioning deal with the effect of secondary (additional) tasks. The results of these studies can be summarized as follows: a secondary task that draws the attention away from the relation between the CS and the US will weaken classical conditioning effects. For example, McKell Carter, Hofstötter, Tsuchiya, and Koch (2003) presented numbers as a tone was systematically followed by an electric shock. When subjects were given the task of repeating the numbers presented to them in a sequence, the tone subsequently elicited a smaller CR than when no (or a simpler) secondary task was given. In short, the presence of a secondary task that directs attention away from the CS-US relation seems to interfere with classical conditioning.

2.2.5 Characteristics of the CS-US Relation and Changes in Those Characteristics

A regularity involving two stimuli encompasses several aspects: the number of times they occur together, the number of times they do not occur together, the time between stimulus presentations, and so on. In this section we discuss the importance of these different aspects for classical conditioning effects. Here we mainly discuss studies on changes in preparatory responses, because research on those responses was popular from the very start of learning research and provided the inspiration for research into the classical conditioning of other behaviors. First, we discuss the influence of the nature of the spatiotemporal relation: how exactly is the spatiotemporal presence of the stimuli related? Next, we look at the impact of changes in the spatiotemporal relation itself.

2.2.5.1 The nature of the spatiotemporal relation We have defined classical conditioning as an effect of regularities in the spatiotemporal occurrence of stimuli. In this section we discuss whether the properties of the regularity are important. A key point to appreciate is that stimuli can occur together in time and space in different ways. There is a *contiguous* relation when stimuli are presented together in time and space at least once (e.g., they are presented next to each other on a computer screen at the same moment in time). There is a *contingent* relation when there is a reliable statistical relation in the presence of the two stimuli: the probability that one stimulus is present depends on the presence of the other stimulus. In this section, we investigate what kind of relation needs to exist in order for classical conditioning to occur.

a) Contingency is more important than contiguity Early in the psychology of learning, as outlined by Pavlov and the associationist tradition in philosophy (philosophers such as Locke and Hume), the coexistence of two events or "ideas" in time and space (i.e., the spatiotemporal contiguity) was often regarded as necessary and sufficient for organisms to learn a relation ("association") between stimuli. Later, however, it was argued that a contingency between stimuli is more important than mere contiguity. **Contingency** refers to a logical or statistical relation between the presence of the stimuli. This depends not only on the co-occurrence of stimuli but also on situations in which the stimuli do not occur together. Logically speaking, there is a relation between the presence of two stimuli if the probability of the presence of one stimulus depends on the presence of the other stimulus. If the presence of the US is more likely in situations where the CS is present than in situations where the CS is absent, one speaks of a positive relation, or a *positive contingency*. If the presence of the US is less likely in the presence (than in the absence) of the CS, one speaks of a negative relation or a *negative*

Figure 2.7
The four-field contingency table.

contingency. Statistically, the probability of the US given the presence of the CS is expressed as p(US/CS), and the probability of the US in the absence of the CS is expressed as p(US/~CS). Both probabilities depend on the frequency of four possible events: (a) both the CS and the US are present, (b) the CS is present but the US is absent, (c) the CS is absent but the US is present, and (d) both the CS and the US are absent. These four events correspond to the four cells of the four-field table shown in figure 2.7.

The p(US/CS) is equal to the frequency of cell (a) divided by the summed frequency of cells (a) and (b). The p(US/~CS) is equal to the frequency of cell (c) divided by the summed frequency of cells (c) and (d). The strength of the relation (indicated by the notation ΔP or delta P) is thus determined as follows:

$$\Delta P = p(US/CS) - p(US/\sim CS) = (a/(a+b)) - (c/(c+d))$$

Therefore, all other things being equal, when the CS and the US co-occur more often (the value of cell a increases) or are both absent more often (the value of cell d increases), the contingency between the two will become more positive. The more often that only the CS (cell b) or only the US (cell c) occurs, the more negative the contingency becomes. ΔP thus reflects the extent to which the presence or absence of the US is correlated with the presence or absence of the CS. A positive contingency indicates that the stimuli tend to be present together or absent together. A negative contingency indicates that the presence of one of them signals the absence of the other, and vice versa.

Rescorla (1966) was one of the first to systematically study the role of contingency in classical conditioning. In various experiments, he showed that CRs are dependent not only on the value of cell a, but also on the value of the other cells in the four-field table. He determined that *excitatory conditioning* occurs as soon as there is a positive contingency, or when p(US/CS) > p(US/~CS). The term *excitatory* refers to the finding that there is an excitation (i.e., an increase or intensification) of a certain behavior (e.g., an increase in anxiety). *Inhibitory conditioning* occurs as soon as there is a negative contingency. In this case, presenting the CS will lead to an inhibition (i.e., decrease or weakening) of a certain behavior (e.g., decrease of anxiety; see Sosa & Ramírez, 2019). Rescorla thus showed that there is a clear relation between the value of ΔP and the nature of the change in behavior (see figure 2.8). When ΔP = 0 and there was therefore no contingency between the occurrence of the CS and the US, there was no change in the behavior, even if the CS and US sometimes co-occur (i.e., even if cell (a) is greater than zero). This suggests that contiguity (CS and US sometimes occur together) is not a sufficient condition for conditioning (but see Papini & Bitterman, 1990, for a criticism of this conclusion).

Although contingency therefore plays an important role in conditioning, it should be noted that it is not easy to determine the degree of contingency between two stimuli in an unambiguous way. Take the example shown in figure 2.9:

If the time intervals are broadly defined as in figure 2.9A, one will conclude that there is a perfect contingency between the CS and the US (in each time interval they occur together

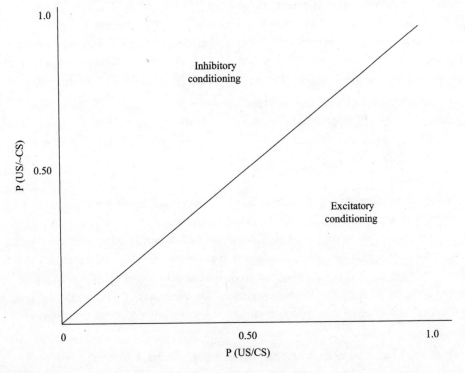

Figure 2.8
The X-axis represents the conditional probability that the US occurs together with the CS. The Y-axis represents the probability that the US occurs without CS. On the diagonal where both probabilities are equal, there is no contingency between the stimuli (after Seligman, Maier, & Solomon, 1971).

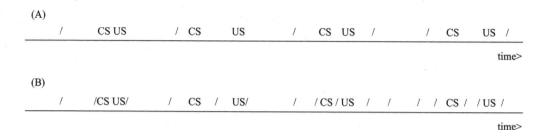

Figure 2.9
The influence of the way in which time intervals are defined on the calculation of contingency. The slash (/) represents the beginning or end of a time interval.

or are absent together). If one works with short time intervals as in figure 2.9B, however, one must conclude that the relation is not perfect because there are six time intervals in which only the CS or the US occurs. The calculation of the contingency between two stimuli is possible only if an artificial unit is created in an artificial way—when does a situation start and when does that situation end? But defining situations is always arbitrary, so one can never be absolutely certain how to determine the start and end of a situation. Different time formats lead to a different interpretation of the four-field table and thus to different statements about contingency (see Gallistel, Craig, & Shahan, 2019, for a recent discussion of this issue).

b) Conditional contingencies are more important than simple contingencies   There are a number of findings that show that even the presence of a statistical contingency between two stimuli is not sufficient to observe classical conditioning. The two most important findings are overshadowing and blocking.

– Overshadowing

In studies on **overshadowing**, two conditions are compared. In one condition, X is always the only CS on a trial and it is always followed by the US (X+). In the other condition, X is always presented together with another CS—namely, CS A—and both are followed by the US (AX+). When at the end of both conditions X is presented on its own during a test trial, X evokes a stronger CS in the first condition (X+) than in the second condition (AX+). It seems that the presence of A in the second condition "overshadows" the effect of the (perfectly contingent) X-US relation. This phenomenon was extensively described by Pavlov (1927).

– Blocking

The **blocking** effect is without doubt one of the most important findings in cognitive learning psychology (but see Maes, Vanderoost, D'Hooge, De Houwer, & Beckers, 2017, for a number of critical considerations). Kamin (1968) was the first to bring the phenomenon to light. One stimulus A (e.g., a visual signal) is always followed in the first phase by an electric shock

(A+). In a second phase, stimulus A is presented along with stimulus X (e.g., a sound). This compound of both stimuli is also followed by shock (AX+). In a subsequent test phase, only X is presented. In a well-designed blocking experiment, there are also control conditions in which the first phase is omitted or a third stimulus is presented during the first phase (B+). So the design can look like this:

	Phase 1	Phase 2	Test
Experimental condition:	A+	AX+	X?
Control condition 1		AX+	X?
Control condition 2	B+	AX+	X?

Blocking refers to when the CR elicited by X during the test phase is weaker in the experimental condition than in the control conditions. There is complete blocking if X does not elicit any CR in the experimental condition (but does do so in the control conditions). Blocking is interesting because X is always followed by the US in all conditions. The only thing that is manipulated across conditions is the relation between A and the US (but see Think It Through 2.1).

Blocking shows that the existence of a positive contingency between X and the US is not a sufficient condition for conditioning effects to occur. The name *blocking* is poorly chosen because it refers to a possible explanation for the effect: it seems that the existence of the A-US relation "blocks" (prevents) the learning of the X-US relation. But this is not entirely correct, as indicated by the fact that *backward blocking* can also occur. Here, the CR to X is weakened by presenting A+ trials after the AX+ trials (i.e., AX+ followed by A+). With backward blocking, it is not possible for a strong A-US relation to block the learning of the X-US relation because the A-US relation is only strengthened after the AX+ trials (but see Miller & Matute, 1996, for evidence that backward blocking occurs only under certain conditions).

Findings such as overshadowing and blocking suggest that the influence of a spatiotemporal relation between stimuli on behavior (i.e., classical conditioning) depends on the extent to which there is a *conditional contingency* between two stimuli. Conditional contingency refers to the contingency between two stimuli in situations where a certain condition is met:

Think It Through 2.1: Control Conditions for Determining Blocking

In your opinion, what is the use of the second control condition (i.e., those in which B+ trials are presented in the first phase?)

Box 2.4 Blocking in Real Life

When developing their products, companies sometimes use a technique called *rebranding*. A new brand name will be related to an existing product. For instance, in Europe, the famous snack Twix used to be called Raider (see figure 2.10).

Figure 2.10
Rebranding: in some countries, Twix used to be called Raider.

Although the name changed, the packaging remained largely the same. In many cases, companies hope that during rebranding, the relation between the old product and the new name will be learned quickly. But research on blocking suggests that learning this new name-product relation will be more difficult if the packaging remains unchanged. Prior to the rebranding, there was already a contingency between the golden packaging of Raider and the product. If we consider the packaging as CS (A), the old name as CS (B), and the product itself as the US, then we can consider consuming the product in its original packaging as AB+ trials. After the rebranding, the golden color of the packaging remains constant, but the name changes. If we use the letter X to refer to

Box 2.4 (continued)

the new name, then we can describe the new situation as AX+. The golden package (A) can delay the learning of the relation between the new name and the product (X-US) because the package was previously presented together with the product. The fact that people did indeed require a lot of time to learn the new name of the product can thus be seen as an example of blocking. It is worth noting, however, that blocking does not occur under certain conditions, and even the opposite effect can occur: the CR for X can, under very specific conditions, be stronger after A+ and AX+ trials than after only AX+ trials (e.g., Liljeholm & Balleine, 2009). Thus, learning research can provide inspiration to optimize the effects of rebranding (see Van Osselaer, 2008, for an overview of various implications of conditioning research for marketing and product development).

the situations differ only with regard to the presence of the CS. Take the example of blocking. In a blocking experiment A is always present when X is present (AX+). There is a perfect contingency between X and the US: the probability of the US if X is present [p(US/X)] is equal to 1, while the probability of the US if X is absent [p(US/~X)] equals 0. However, the calculation of this contingency is based on a comparison of situations where both A and X are present (the AX + trials) and situations where no CS is present. The difference in the probability of the presence of the US in those situations could be an indication not only of the strength of the relation between X and the US but also of the strength of the relation between A and the US. A correct estimate of the strength of the relation between X and the US can only be made by comparing the probability of the US between situations that differ only with regard to the presence or absence of X. In a blocking experiment this can be done by comparing situations where A and X are present (AX+ trials) to situations where only A is present (A+ trials). If we take into account only those situations (and not situations where both A and X are absent), then we can conclude that the probability of the US in both situations is equal. The US is always present, regardless of whether X is present (AX+ trials) or absent (A+). The conditional contingency is therefore zero, so the relation between X and the US will not affect the response to X. Conditional probability can therefore be represented as follows (see Cheng & Novick, 1990, 1992; Cheng & Holyoak, 1995):

$$\Delta Pc = p(O/A.X) - p(O/A.\sim X)$$

In this equation, p(O/A.X) stands for the probability of the US when both A and X are present and p(O/A.~X) represents the probability of the US when only A is present. You can calculate ΔPc via the four-field table if you take into account only the trials in which A is present (i.e., determining the number of AX+, AX-, A+ and A- trials; see figure 2.11). In other words, you calculate the contingency between X and the US conditional on the presence of A.

	US	
	Present	Absent
X Present	#AX+	#AX−
X Absent	#A+	#A−

Figure 2.11
The four-field table for situations where X always occurs with A.

At the functional level (i.e., purely in terms of factors in the environment or behavior), one can describe blocking as an example of the impact of conditional contingencies on behavior: it shows that in situations where X always occurs together with other CSs, the CR for X is determined by the degree of conditional contingency and thus not the degree of contingency per se. Note that conditional contingency is important only when X always occurs together with A. If there are situations where X occurs without A, then the strength of the relation between X and the US can be determined by comparing situations in which only X is present and situations where no CS is present $[\Delta P = p(O/X) - p(O/\sim X)]$.

c) Indirect stimulus relations Neither contingency nor conditional contingency is absolutely necessary for the occurrence of classical conditioning. Even when there is no (conditional) contingency or even contiguity between stimuli, conditioning can still take place. After all, stimuli can also be indirectly related. To illustrate, imagine that a tone (CS1) is always followed by a light (CS2) and that the light (CS2) is always followed by an electric shock (US) (i.e., CS1-CS2; CS2-US). In this case, there is no direct (first-order) relation between the tone and the electric shock (i.e., between CS1-US): they never co-occur in space and time. There is, however, a second-order relation between the two: both the tone and the shock are related to the light. Studies in *sensory preconditioning* and *higher-order conditioning* have shown that such an indirect relation between the tone and the shock can lead to changes in the response to the tone. Sensory preconditioning refers to the procedure in which the two neutral stimuli (e.g., tone and light) are first presented together during a first phase and the

Think It Through 2.2: Overshadowing and Conditional Contingencies

Problem: How can you explain overshadowing based on the assumption that conditioning is determined by conditional contingency?

second neutral stimulus is presented with the US only during a subsequent second phase (e.g., light and shock in Phase 2; see also figure 0.2). In higher-order conditioning, the order of the two phases is reversed (e.g., first light-shock and only then tone-light). Note, however, that sensory preconditioning and higher-order conditioning depend on the (conditional) contingency of the underlying (first-order) relations. If there is no (conditionally) contingent relation between the tone and the light or between the light and the electric shock, the indirect relation between the tone and the shock has no influence on the reaction to the tone. Thus (conditional) contingencies are necessary for the effect of indirect relations. Also note that the effects of indirect relations can be seen as examples of complex forms of learning in which different regularities together determine the behavior. We will therefore return to sensory preconditioning and higher-order conditioning in chapter 4 on complex learning.

2.2.5.2 Changes in the nature of the spatiotemporal relation The spatiotemporal relation between stimuli (i.e., the way in which they occur in space and time) is not necessarily fixed or unchanging. Sometimes there is no relation between two stimuli at first, but later there is. At other times there is initially a relation and then it disappears. In yet other situations two relations can be present simultaneously in different contexts. We will discuss each of these three situations separately.

a) No relation followed by a relation: CS pre-exposure, US pre-exposure, and the absence of contingency There are three ways in which a CS and US can occur in an unrelated manner: the CS always occurs alone, the US always occurs alone, or both CS and US are presented in a noncontingent way. When these events occur before the pairing of the CS and US, they all reduce and delay the effect of the relation between the CS and US on behavior.

– Effects of CS pre-exposure
The term **CS pre-exposure** refers to procedures in which the CS is repeatedly presented before a relation is established between the CS and US (see Byrom, Msetfi, & Murphy, 2018, for a recent review). For example, in the first phase of an experiment, a tone is repeatedly presented (CS pre-exposure phase) to an organism; in a second phase, the tone always precedes an electric shock (CS-US conditioning phase). Findings show that the organism will find it much more difficult to learn the relation between the tone and shock than another organism that did not receive CS pre-exposure trials. This effect due to pre-exposure to the CS is often called the *CS pre-exposure effect*. In some cases, the term *latent inhibition* is used. The problem with the latter term is that it refers to a possible (but not necessarily correct) mental explanation of the CS pre-exposure effect. Because we choose to strictly separate the description of effects from possibly explanatory mental processes, we will refer to it as the CS pre-exposure effect. The pre-presentation of the CS is thus a way to weaken future learning about that CS.

At the functional level, we might also wonder why pre-exposure to the CS has a detrimental effect on classical conditioning effects. As we already know, when conducting a functional analysis, one does not search for mediating mental processes; instead, we want to identify other known environmental moderators of conditioning to which the CS pre-exposure effect could be related. Therefore, the question to ask in a functional analysis is the following: can I describe a particular phenomenon (e.g., the CS pre-exposure effect) in terms of another known phenomenon (e.g., the impact of other moderators on classical conditioning)? There are two potential moderators that may play a role here: (1) the intensity or conspicuousness of the CS and (2) the statistical contingency between the CS and the US. First, it is possible that a CS that is presented frequently is experienced as being less intense or important than one that is not presented frequently. This will reduce the effect of the CS-US relation simply because the CS is less conspicuous (see the section on the effects of CS properties). Second, each CS pre-exposure is a CS-only trial. These trials will therefore reduce the contingency between the CS and US. In other words, the CS pre-exposure effect might also be an example of the impact of statistical contingency on classical conditioning.

The CS pre-exposure procedure can be used to study situations where conditioning can have negative effects on people's well-being. In the Surwit study (1972) on fear of dentists in young children, the fear can be seen as a CR that results from a pairing of the dentist (CS) with a painful treatment (US). Hence, fear of the dentist can be reduced by allowing the child to meet and interact with the dentist before the first treatment (CS pre-exposure). Similarly, some findings on the occurrence of conditioned nausea in cancer patients undergoing chemotherapy point to the role of CS pre-exposure in preventing or at least attenuating such conditioning (Bernstein, Webster, & Bernstein, 1982). Cancer treatment involves the administration of drugs that evoke nausea (US). Because the drug is administered in a hospital setting, the nausea co-occurs with many hospital-related stimuli such as the sight of nurses in white uniforms and the taste of food eaten while in the hospital (CSs), which might lead to an aversion (CR) to those stimuli (e.g., white uniforms, certain foods). Allowing a patient to visit the hospital ward before the start of the treatment (CS pre-exposure) can weaken conditioned aversion.

– Effects of US pre-exposure

Based on the previous section, it may already be clear what a US **pre-exposure** procedure involves: the US is repeatedly presented on its own before the CS is paired with that US. US

Think It Through 2.3: The CS Pre-exposure Effect and Habituation

What do you think is the link between the effect of CS pre-exposure and habituation?

pre-exposure also leads to a slowdown and weakening of the effect of the CS-US relation. For example, in a first phase, an organism receives an electric shock repeatedly (US). In the second phase, the shock is always given after a tone (CS). The question is whether the conditioning effect for the tone now differs from what we see in a second organism that was not pre-exposed to the US. Results show that this is indeed the case: the tone elicits less fear if the shock was previously presented alone compared to when the shock was not presented alone.

As in the case with the CS pre-exposure effect, when performing a functional analysis of the US pre-exposure effect, two potential explanations of the effect in terms of other moderators of conditioning present themselves (see Randich & LoLordo, 1979). First, it is possible that the US-only presentations reduce the intensity of the US (habituation), which will weaken the effect of the CS-US relation (because the CR is weaker when the US is weaker). On the other hand, the effect of the US-only presentations can also be attributed to the reduction in the statistical contingency between the CS and the US. Additional research is needed to distinguish these two possibilities.

–Effects of the absence of a relation

A period during which there is a statistical relation between a CS and US can be preceded by a period in which both the CS and the US occur in a noncontingent way (i.e., in the absence of a statistical link between the two stimuli). For example, during a first phase you can present both a tone and a shock in such a way that the chances of encountering the US do not depend on the presence of the tone [$p(US/CS) = p(US/\sim CS)$]. If there is then a (conditional) contingency between the CS and the US [$p(US/CS) > p(US/\sim CS)$ or $p(US/CS) < p(US/\sim CS)$] this contingency will have less influence on the CR. This finding suggests that it is not only the *presence* of a relation that can have an influence on the behavior—so too can the *absence* of a relation. In other words, it seems that organisms can also learn that there is no relation between stimuli (which makes them learn more slowly that there is a relation; Mackintosh, 1975). We will return to this issue later in chapter 3 in the context of a phenomenon known as **learned helplessness.**

b) A relation followed by no relation: CS postexposure, US postexposure, and the absence of a contingency

– Effects of CS postexposure

Many studies in learning psychology use **CS postexposure** procedures (i.e., present the CS alone after the [contingent] pairing of that CS with a US). Researchers do so because they want to know not only how behavior can be established as a result of stimulus pairings but also how it can be modified after it has been established. At first sight, it is very easy to modify conditioned behavior: it is enough to repeatedly present the CS by itself. Imagine that we first pair a tone with an electric shock. As a result of this contingent relation, the tone will come to elicit a conditioned anxiety response (CR). If the tone is then repeatedly presented without the shock, the fear response to the tone will become weaker each time the tone is presented by itself. This effect (the weakening of a CR as a result of CS-only presentations) is called *extinction*.

Interestingly, however, research has shown that extinction is not permanent and sometimes does not occur at all. Pavlov (1927) showed that an extinguished CR can sometimes spontaneously return after a period of time. This phenomenon is called the *spontaneous recovery* of the CR (see figure 2.12). Another finding is that CS postexposure does not lead to extinction when it takes place in a context different from that in which the CS-US relation was initially learned and ultimately tested (e.g., Bouton, 1993, 1998). Suppose, for example, that an animal is exposed to the pairing of a tone (CS) and a shock (US) (i.e., CS+ trials) in a blue room. Across trials, the CR gradually becomes stronger. The animal is then transferred to another (green) room, where the CS is presented without the US (CS trials). This leads to the disappearance of the CR. If, however, the animal is then returned to the original learning context (i.e., the blue room) or to a new context (e.g., a yellow room), presenting the CS will immediately provoke a CR again, as if extinction in the green room never happened. This phenomenon is known as *renewal* (see figure 2.12).[4]

There are also studies in which CS postexposure does not lead to extinction, even when CS-only trials take place in the same context as the CS+ trials. For example, evidence suggests that extinction is less rapid or even does not occur with biologically relevant CSs. In studies by Öhman (e.g., Öhman, Fredrikson, Hugdahl, & Rimmö, 1976; also see Neumann & Longbottom, 2008), images of biologically relevant CSs (e.g., spiders and snakes) or biologically less relevant CSs (e.g., flowers) were first repeatedly paired with electric shocks. Thereafter, all CSs elicited an anxiety reaction. During the second phase, the CSs were presented without any electric shocks. The decrease in the CR was less pronounced for the biologically relevant compared to biologically less relevant CSs.

The nature of the observed behavior also seems to have an influence on the extent to which extinction occurs. For example, conditioned changes in valence (evaluative conditioning) seem much less sensitive to the effects of CS postexposure (e.g., Baeyens, Crombez, Van den Bergh, & Eelen, 1988; see De Houwer et al., 2001, for an overview, but Hofmann et al., 2010, for a meta-analysis that suggests that extinction does occur in evaluative conditioning, albeit only to a small extent). When a photo X has become negative because it was paired with a negative photo, X will retain that negative valence even if it is no longer followed by a negative photo.

– Effects of US postexposure

Although effects of US postexposure have been identified (e.g., Hammerl, Bloch, & Silverthorne, 1997), they often do not occur (e.g., Miller, Hallam, & Grahame, 1990). If, after pairing a tone and a shock, only the shock is presented, then the CR to the tone will sometimes

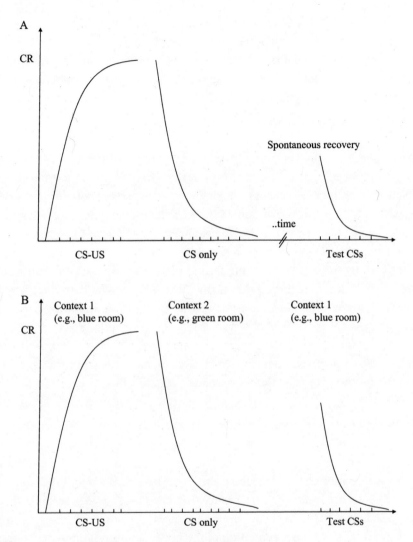

Figure 2.12
A schematic overview of spontaneous recovery (A) and renewal (B).

weaken. As with other effects of CS or US (pre- or post-) exposure, one may ask whether the effects of US postexposure are due to changes in the characteristics of the US in itself (e.g., the shock is less negative after it is presented repeatedly; see US revaluation) or to changes in the relation between the CS and US (the contingency between the two decreases when the US is presented repeatedly on its own).

– Effects of the absence and reversal of a relation

We do not know of studies in which the presence of a contingency between a CS and US is followed by a phase in which both the CS and the US are presented but in a noncontingent manner (i.e., contingency equals zero). However, there have been many studies designed to reverse relations (contingency reversal). During the first phase of those studies, a certain CS (A) is followed by a US, whereas a second CS (B) is not followed by the US. During the second phase, A is no longer followed by the US, whereas B is followed by the US. Afterward, researchers check whether the CR with respect to A and B is determined mainly by the regularity in the first phase or by the regularity in the second phase. One speaks of a **primacy** effect if the first regularity is more important (i.e., if the CR to A is stronger than the CR to B) and a **recency** effect if the second (most recent) regularity has more of an influence (i.e., CR to B is stronger than the CR to A). Several factors determine whether primacy or recency effects occur. For example, in human contingency learning (see section 2.2.2.2), evidence shows that recency effects become stronger as participants are more frequently asked to judge the strength of the contingency (e.g., Collins & Shanks, 2002; Matute, Vegas, & De Marez, 2002).

c) The presence or absence of relations depends on the context   Often, a regularity between two stimuli will exist only under certain conditions. For example, seeing a clock that indicates twelve o'clock will go together with hearing twelve strokes of the bell only if the clock is equipped with a (correctly working) mechanism for producing clock strokes. The effect of these conditional relations has been studied also in the lab (see Holland, 1992, and Schmajuk & Holland, 1998, for an overview). For instance, Rescorla (1987) used procedures that lead to autoshaping. In half of the trials, a background noise was presented for fifteen seconds. During the last five seconds of the presentation of the noise, a button illuminated. Immediately after the end of the presentation of the noise and the illuminated button, food was delivered. In the other half of the trials, the illuminated button was presented without any sound or food. Over time, the pigeon came to peck at the illuminated button (which is an example of autoshaping), but only if the noise was also present.

There are two functional analyses that can potentially explain this effect, which are based on a different description of the same objective situation. First, you can say that there is one CS-US relation—namely, the regularity between the illumination of the button and the delivery of food. However, this relation is valid in only one particular situation (i.e., after the background noise has been presented). The background noise, then, is an *occasion setter*: a signal that indicates when a regularity involving a CS and a US is present. In this case, the noise is a *positive occasion setter* because the presence of the sound indicates the presence of the CS-US relation. *Negative occasion setters* are stimuli that indicate that the CS-US relation is absent in the presence of that stimulus. The fact that the CS (e.g., the illumination of the button) elicits a CR only if the occasion setter (e.g., background noise) is present can be seen as a consequence of the fact that the regularity involving the CS and US is present only when the occasion setter is present. The effect of occasion setters on CRs is called *occasion setting*.

However, a second functional analysis is also possible. One can say that there are two different relations, each involving a unique CS. The background noise and the lighting of the button can be viewed as a *compound CS* that is more than the sum of its two elements (just as the letter *T* is more than the sum of a horizontal and a vertical line). In that case, there are two different relations with two different CSs: CS (A) (the compound stimulus) is followed by the US, while CS (B) (only the illumination of the button) is not followed by the US. The fact that CS (A) does elicit a CR can be explained by the presence of a relation between CS (A) and the US. The fact that CS (B) does not elicit a CR can be explained by the absence of a relation between CS (B) and the US (see Pearce, 2002, for a discussion of how many phenomena in conditioning can be explained by the idea that learning is about compound stimuli instead of individual stimuli).

It is very difficult, if not impossible, to determine which of these two functional analyses is most useful. After all, the statements refer to the same aspects of the procedure (characteristics of situations in which the US occurs and situations in which the US does not occur) but describe them in a different way (but see Bonardi, Robinson, & Jennings, 2017, for arguments in support of the view that not all findings on occasion setting can be explained in terms of compound stimuli). Despite this difficulty in studying occasion setting, there has been much research on this topic (see Leising & Bonardi, 2017, for a brief history of this research, and Trask, Thrailkill, & Bouton, 2017, for a review). The interest in occasion setting is partly due to the parallel between occasion setting and the context sensitivity of extinction (e.g., Bouton, 1993).

Think It Through 2.4: The Relation between Renewal and Occasion Setting

Question: What do you think is the connection between the phenomenon of renewal in extinction and the phenomenon of occasion setting? Moreover, what is the relation between spontaneous recovery to occasion setting?

2.2.5.3. The way that the CS-US relation is presented   The same regularity involving two stimuli can be presented in different ways. First, one can vary the time when the CS and US are presented. For instance, the presentation of the CS can begin before, together with, or after the initial presentation of the US. Procedures in which the CS comes before the US are called **forward conditioning procedures**. When CS and US are presented at the same time, this is called **simultaneous conditioning**. When the US comes before the CS, this is called **backward conditioning**. Researchers have observed that backward conditioning effects are usually smaller than forward conditioning effects (but see Prével, Rivière, Darcheville, & Urcelay, 2016, and Prével, Rivière, Darcheville, Urcelay, & Miller, 2019, for evidence that reliable backward conditioning effects can be found). Another general finding is that conditioning effects become smaller as more time passes between the end of the presentation of the CS and the start of the presentation of the US. When, however, there is an intrinsic relation between the CS and US (e.g., food and nausea), the duration of this interstimulus interval will have less impact, and conditioning effects can be observed even with very long intervals (Etscorn & Stephens, 1973).

2.3   Mental Process Theories

In the second part of this chapter we will investigate which mental processes mediate the impact of regularities in the presence of stimuli on behavior (i.e., classical conditioning effects). Specifically, we will investigate the heuristic and predictive value of several mental process theories—that is, the extent to which they are able to explain existing functional knowledge (*heuristic value*) and predict new functional knowledge (*predictive value*). We focus on two classes of theories. The first class is defined by the assumption that the effect of stimulus pairings on behavior (classical conditioning) is mediated by the formation of associations between representations in memory. We call this class of theories *associative models*. A second, more recent class of *propositional models* assumes that classical conditioning is mediated by the formation and evaluation of propositions about stimulus relations in the environment.

2.3.1   Associative Models

This broad class of models has dominated the study of learning since the emergence of the discipline (see Pearce & Bouton, 2001, and Bouton, 2016, for an overview). A common feature of all associative models is the assumption that stimulus pairings under certain conditions lead to the formation of associations in memory. Associative models differ with regard to their assumptions about the conditions under which associations are formed (figure 2.13, Step 1), the elements involved in the association (figure 2.13, Step 2), and the conditions under which associations influence behavior (figure 2.13, Step 3).

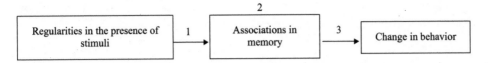

Figure 2.13
Schematic representation of associative models of conditioning. All associative models are based on the assumption that classical conditioning is mediated by the formation of associations in memory, but they differ with regard to assumptions about: (1) the conditions under which associations are formed, (2) the elements involved in the associations, and (3) the conditions under which associations in memory affect behavior.

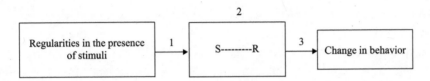

Figure 2.14
Schematic representation of S-R models. (1) The co-occurrence of CS and UR is sufficient to form an association between the representation of the CS (S) and the UR (R) in the memory (2). After forming the S-R association, presenting the CS is a sufficient condition for the change in behavior: the CS then elicits a CR that is identical to the UR (3).

With regard to the first point, we make a distinction between S-R (**stimulus-response**) models that assume that learning is based on the formation of associations between stimuli and responses and S-S (**stimulus-stimulus**) models that postulate the formation of associations between the representations of stimuli. Within the S-R and S-S models, there are several models that each make unique assumptions about the conditions under which associations are formed and under which they influence behavior.

2.3.1.1 S-R models

a) The core of S-R models According to S-R models, an association is formed between the representations of the CS and the UR (see figure 2.14). As a result, presentation of the CS can also trigger the UR, and the UR thus becomes a CR. Let us apply this idea to the case of Pavlov's dog. Initially, the dog salivates only when presented with food (UR). By pairing the bell and food (and thus also the occurrence of the bell and the salivation that is elicited by the food), the bell will also trigger salivation (the UR becomes a CR). A prototypical S-R model therefore starts from the assumption that contiguity between CS and UR is a sufficient and necessary condition for forming S-R associations. Once the S-R association is formed, the CS can activate the UR via this association, leading to the CR. This assumption states that the US is important only in order to elicit the UR and thus ensure that the CS and UR occur together. So there is no learning *about* the US but only learning *through* the US.[5]

b) General evaluation of S-R models   Although S-R models are able to explain that presenting two stimuli together can lead to changes in behavior, the prototypical S-R model is contradicted by several findings. Some of these findings go against the basic assumption that the combination of CS and UR is a necessary and sufficient condition for conditioning to occur. Other findings show that conditioning is effectively mediated by knowledge about the US. Next, we review some of the failures of S-R models (also see Rescorla, 1988).

– Not contiguity but (conditional) contingency determines whether classical conditioning will occur (see section 2.2.5.1)

Most S-R models are based on the assumption that the formation of S-R associations is determined by contiguity (i.e., by the degree to which and number of times that the CS and UR occur together in space and time; e.g., Guthrie, 1946). Yet this idea conflicts with the finding that it is not contiguity but rather (conditional) contingency that seems to be the most important determinant of classical conditioning effects. In other words, research clearly shows that contiguity is not a sufficient condition for conditioning, contrary to what is assumed in a prototypical S-R model.

– Sensory preconditioning (see section 2.2.5.1)

The influence of indirect stimulus relations on behavior also cannot be explained by S-R models, because the CS then elicits a CR despite the fact that the CS and UR have never occurred together. Take the example of sensory preconditioning: in a first phase, two neutral stimuli (e.g., a tone and a light) are presented together; in a second phase, one of the two stimuli (e.g., the light stimulus) is followed by a US until a CR is established; in a third phase, the other neutral stimulus from the first phase also provokes a CR (e.g., the tone). Such a finding shows that the coexistence of a CS and UR is not a necessary condition for the occurrence of conditioning: the crucial CS (in our example, the tone) was paired only with another neutral stimulus that did not elicit a response at the time of those pairings.

– US revaluation (see section 2.2.1.3)

Studies on US revaluation have shown that changes in the US after conditioning can influence behavior. For example, if you first pair a bell with food and then make the food negative (e.g., by pairing it with nausea), the bell will no longer trigger salivation. This cannot be explained on the basis of S-R models. According to an S-R model, an association between the bell (CS) and salivation (UR) is learned during the bell-food trials. Nothing is learned about the US. The US serves only to establish the UR so that an association can grow between the CS and UR representations. Changing the US after forming the CS-UR association should therefore have no influence.

– The CR may differ from the UR (see section 2.2.1.3)

Because S-R models assume that classical conditioning is the result of an association between the CS and UR, these models cannot explain why the CR can be different from the UR. After all, according to S-R models, the only difference between the CR and the UR is that one speaks of an UR if the reaction is elicited by a US, while the term *CR* is used to refer to the same reaction when it is elicited by the CS. Research shows, however, that usually the CR seems to be a reaction that prepares the organism for the arrival of the US. This preparatory response (e.g., fearful anticipation of a shock) can be very different from the UR (e.g., the pain evoked by the shock). This therefore suggests that knowledge about the US is very important in the creation of classical conditioning.

– Conclusion

It seems that S-R models cannot explain many aspects of functional knowledge about classical conditioning. We must admit, however, that we have assumed a caricature of S-R models, especially with regard to the assumption that the co-occurrence of the CS and US is a sufficient condition for forming associations. After all, it is easy to make variants of S-R models that state that factors other than contiguity are also important (e.g., attention). Nevertheless, it is not an accident that we focused on a model in which contiguity is seen as a sufficient and necessary condition. This model remains the prototypical S-R model of conditioning, which we see discussed in many psychology textbooks and which many people have in mind when they think of conditioning (e.g., Byrne & Bates, 2006). As Rescorla (1988; also see Eelen, 1980/2018) remarked a long time ago, it is high time we realize that these types of simplistic S-R models are highly problematic.

That said, we cannot exclude the possibility that S-R associations could mediate conditioning effects under very specific conditions. For example, Rescorla (1982) conducted experiments in which CS1 was first paired with a US. Then CS2 was repeatedly followed by CS1. After that phase, it was determined that CS2 also triggers a CR. This is an example of *second-order conditioning* (see section 2.2.5.1). If a US revaluation procedure was then applied (e.g., the food is now coupled with nausea), this did not appear to affect the extent to which CS2 provokes a CR. The CR with respect to CS2 thus seems to be based on S-R associations. It is indeed quite possible that different conditioning effects are mediated by different mechanisms and that some effects (e.g., second-order conditioning) rely on an S-R mechanism. Note, however, that if one accepts this view, then one must also try to find out the specific conditions under which the mechanism operates. This is not an easy task because it is already difficult to determine which mental mechanism is effective in a given situation (one cannot directly observe mental processes; see De Houwer, 2011b).

2.3.1.2   S-S models

a) The core of S-S models   According to S-S models, the pairing of the CS and US results in an association between the representations of the CS and US in memory (see figure 2.15). Presenting the CS will lead to an activation of the CS representation. This activation spreads via the CS-US association to the US representation and thus elicits the UR (which is part of the US representation or associated with the US representation). For example, you could say that Pavlov's dog salivates when he hears the bell because the bell reminds him of food, and thinking of food leads to salivation.

A crucial difference between S-S and S-R models is that S-S models view conditioning as being dependent on knowledge about the US. Another crucial difference is that most S-S models assume that the pairing of the CS and US is not a necessary and sufficient condition for the occurrence of conditioning. Usually it is assumed that certain "cognitive conditions" must be met so that the pairing of the CS and US leads to the formation of associations (e.g., attention to the CS and/or US; see De Houwer, 2018b). Because of these differences, S-S models can explain certain findings that are problematic for S-R models. Below, we first provide an overview of how S-S models (in general) can explain some important functional properties of classical conditioning, then we discuss a number of specific S-S models in greater detail.

b) General evaluation of S-S models

– US revaluation (see section 2.2.1.3)
According to S-S models, a CR can occur only after the US representation is activated. Changes in the US representation can therefore lead to changes in the CR. Let's return to the example of Pavlov's dog. The repeated pairing of the bell and food leads to salivation because the bell is reminiscent of the tasty food. Thinking about the food elicits salivation. After US revaluation (e.g., food is accompanied by nausea) the dog will still think of food, but the food is no longer tasty, so thinking of that food will not elicit salivation. Hence, US revaluation will eliminate the conditioned salivation response to the bell.

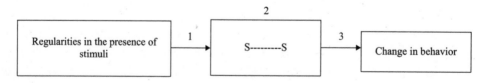

Figure 2.15
Schematic representation of S-S models. (1) The pairing of CS and US leads, under certain conditions (e.g., if attention is paid to the CS and US), to (2) the formation of an association between the representation of the CS (S) and the representation of the US (S) in memory. After forming S-S associations, CS presentations will lead, under certain conditions, to the CR (3).

– The impact of secondary tasks on conditioning (see section 2.2.4)

In S-S models, contiguity is not a sufficient condition. For example, most S-S models start from the assumption that S-S associations are formed only if attention is paid to the CS and US (e.g., Wagner, 1981; see below). Such models are consistent with the finding that secondary tasks have a detrimental effect on classical conditioning because these secondary tasks divert attention from (the pairing of) the CS and US. In box 2.5, we discuss how one can also explain other findings such as blocking based on the assumption that attention is important for forming associations.

– Sensory preconditioning (see section 2.2.5.1)

For S-S models, contiguity is not a necessary condition. For example, one can explain sensory preconditioning based on S-S models. It is possible that during the first phase, an association is formed between the representations of the two neutral stimuli. During the second phase, an association is formed between the second neutral stimulus and the US. When the first neutral stimulus is subsequently presented, this leads to activation of the representation of that stimulus. This activation spreads to the representation of the second neutral stimulus and then to the representation of the US through which the UR/CR occurs (see figure 2.16).

– Conclusion

In sum, S-S models can explain a range of findings. Despite these successes, one could also ask questions about the basic idea underpinning S-S models. For instance, take the idea that the CR is the result of activation that spreads through a CS-US association in memory. This

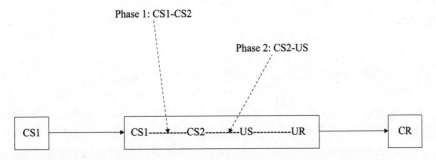

Figure 2.16

Schematic representation of how S-S models provide an explanation for sensory preconditioning. The co-occurrence of CS1 and CS2 during the first phase results in the formation of an association between the representations of CS1 and CS2 in memory. The joint presentation of CS2 and the US in the second phase creates an association between the representation of CS2 and the US. When CS1 is presented during the test phase, this will lead to activation of the CS1 representation. This activation can then spread via the CS1-CS2 association to CS2 and so on, via the CS2-US association and the US-UR association up to the representation of the UR. Once the representation of the UR has been activated, this will lead to a CR.

idea implies that the CR must always be identical to the UR because the CS activates the UR components that are connected to the US. It is therefore not entirely clear how S-S models explain how the CR and UR may differ from each other (see Bouton, 2016, p. 187, for a more in-depth discussion of the relation between the CR and the UR).

Instead of supposing that the activation of the CS ultimately leads to the activation of the UR, one could also assume that the activation of the CS leads only to the activation of the US representation. This, in turn, would lead to the expectation that the US will occur. According to this version of S-S models, the CS is a signal for the arrival of the US. The expectation of the US can then give rise to (controlled and involuntary) preparatory responses (i.e., responses that help the organism prepare for the arrival of the US; e.g., salivation that allows it to consume food better; see Kirsch, Lynn, Vigorito, & Miller, 2004, for a discussion). This could then explain why the CR (e.g., fear that an electric shock will occur) can differ from the UR (e.g., pain in response to the actual presence of an electric shock). But even that statement leaves a number of questions unanswered. It is especially unclear how the activation of a US representation can give rise to an *expectation* of the US. The mere activation of the US may lead to thinking about the US (e.g., the bell is reminiscent of food), but this is not the same as an expectation that the US will be effectively presented. After all, there are many situations in which one thinks of a stimulus without expecting that this stimulus will occur (Baeyens et al., 1992; Jozefowiez, 2018). It is not clear how one and the same process of US activation through S-S associations can lead to such fundamentally different cognitive states (i.e., thinking of something and expecting the presence of something).

Also, the importance of conscious knowledge about the CS-US relation in classical conditioning cannot be explained by S-S models in a straightforward manner. According to some S-S models, the S-S association must first give rise to a conscious expectation of the US before a CR can occur. The conscious expectation of the US is thus a "necessary gate"—that is, a necessary intermediate step that must be present before the S-S association can lead to a CR (Dawson & Schell, 1987). However, this does not explain why, in many situations, awareness of the CS-US relation seems necessary for conditioning to occur (see Mitchell et al., 2009). After all, a conscious expectation of the US is not the same as conscious knowledge of the CS-US relation.

c) The Rescorla-Wagner model as a prototypical S-S model The **Rescorla-Wagner model** (Rescorla & Wagner, 1972) is often considered a prototypical example of S-S models. It differs from other associative S-S models with regard to the assumptions about the conditions under which associations are formed and influence behavior. The core assumption in the Rescorla-Wagner model is that the extent to which CS-US associations are modified (see Step 1 in figure 2.15) depends on the extent to which the presence or absence of a US is expected or unexpected. If the presence or absence of the US is expected, no new associations will be formed and the strength of existing associations will not change. If the presence or absence of the US is unexpected or surprising, new associations will be formed and the strength of existing associations will change. One can also say that according to the model, "learning" (i.e., forming and changing associations) is dependent on **expectation discrepancy**. The second crucial assumption is that the strength of the CR to the CS is more or less a direct consequence of the strength of the association between the representation of the CS and US (see Step 3 in figure 2.15). In other words, the translation of associations to the behavior is simple. Initially, little attention was paid to this second assumption; researchers focused on testing the first assumption. Nevertheless, it will become apparent that this second assumption is crucial and also can be questioned.

The assumption that the formation of associations is driven by expectations was captured by Rescorla and Wagner (1972) in the following mathematical formula:

$$\Delta V_A = \alpha_A \, \beta \, (\lambda - V_A)$$

The symbols used represent the following:

ΔV_A = the change that occurs in the **associative strength** of CS (A); that is, the strength of the association between the representation of CS (A) and the US. Associative strength is often seen as the degree to which the CS leads to expectations that the US will occur.

α_A = a parameter that reflects the salience or intensity of the CS.

β = a parameter for the salience or intensity of the US.

λ = the asymptote of conditioning; this is the maximum associative strength that is possible for a particular US with a certain intensity.

V_A = the existing associative strength of stimulus A.

From the formula, it can be concluded that conditioning will increase in strength as the discrepancy between λ and V_A becomes larger. Let's demonstrate this point with an example in which we assign the following values: $\alpha_A \beta$ equals .50; λ equals 10; and V_A initially equals 0.

Trial 1: $\Delta V_A = .50 \, (10-0)$	=	5
Trial 2: $\Delta V_A = .50 \, (10-5)$	=	2,5
Trial 3: $\Delta V_A = .50 \, (10-7,5)$	=	1,25
Trial 4: $\Delta V_A = .50 \, (10-8,75)$	=	0,625
V_A after four A+ trials	=	9,375

In this example, after four trials the associative strength has become 9.375; with further pairings it approaches the asymptotic (i.e., maximum) value 10. We also see that the associative strength changes more during the first than during later trials. This is because the presence of the US is more surprising (ΔV_A is greater) at the beginning than at the end of the learning phase.

If after the acquisition phase (CS-US trials) an extinction procedure is implemented (repeatedly presenting the CS without the US), the CR will systematically decrease in intensity. As we noted earlier, this effect is called **extinction**. According to the Rescorla-Wagner model, extinction as an effect is due to a decrease in the associative strength of the CS. After all, during the first trials of the extinction procedure, the presentation of the CS leads to a pronounced expectation that the US will follow ($V_{CS} > 0$). Because the US is not presented during an extinction trial, λ will have a value of 0 on that trial. As a result, (λ-V_{CS}) is less than zero and the associative strength of the CS decreases ($\Delta V_{CS} = \alpha_{CS} \beta (\lambda - V_{CS})$). Therefore, according to the Rescorla-Wagner model, extinction (as an effect) is due to the "unlearning" or forgetting of a CS-US association. To illustrate, let's continue the numerical example listed above, and add four trials with only CS A:

Trial 5: $\Delta V_A = .50 \ (0 - 9.375)$	$=$	-4.69
Trial 6: $\Delta V_A = .50 \ (0 - 4.69)$	$=$	-2.34
Trial 7: $\Delta V_A = .50 \ (0 - 2.34)$	$=$	-1.17
Trial 8: $\Delta V_A = .50 \ (0 - 1.17)$	$=$	-0.58
V_A after four A+ and four A-trials		0.58

Another important assumption of the Rescorla-Wagner model is that the expectation of the US is determined by all CSs present at that time (see Witnauer, Urcelay, & Miller, 2014, for a critical discussion of this assumption). This is presented as follows:

$$\Delta V_A = \alpha_A \beta (\lambda - V_{AX})$$

$$\Delta V_X = \alpha_X \beta (\lambda - V_{AX})$$

V_{AX} stands for the sum of the existing associative strength of A and X (i.e., $V_{AX} = V_A + V_X$). Therefore, the change in associative strength for CS X on an AX+ trial (both A and X will be presented and followed by the US) will depend on not only the expectation elicited by X but also the expectation elicited by A. This assumption allows the Rescorla-Wagner model to explain phenomena such as **blocking**. Blocking refers to the finding that the CR for X after AX+ trials is weaker when these trials are preceded by A+ trials. According to the Rescorla-Wagner model, this is because an A-US association is formed during the A+ trials, as a result of which A already elicits the expectation that the US will be presented on the first AX+ trial. Consequently, there is little expectation discrepancy (difference between what is expected and what actually occurs) and the X-US association will not be formed, or will be weak. In more formal terms, we can say that V_A has a high value as a result of the A+ trials. As a result, V_{AX} will also have a high value (because it is equal to the sum of V_A and V_X) and the difference between λ and V_{AX} is also small, as a result of which the associative strength of X changes little (ΔV_X is small). Note that according to the Rescorla-Wagner model, blocking occurs because the association between the blocked stimulus X and the US is not formed. Blocking thus points to the failure of learning (in the cognitive sense of acquiring knowledge).

Interestingly, because the expectation of the US is determined by all CSs present at a certain point in time, associative strength can sometimes become negative. Imagine that you present Y+ trials intermixed with YA- trials. As a result of the Y+ trials, Y will get a positive associative strength. Hence, the US will be expected also on the YA- trials. However, because the US is always absent on YA- trials, the change in associative strength on those trials will always be negative, which means that the associative strength of A will drop below zero. If this happens, then the presence of A will lead to the inhibition of the US representation, which is assumed to result in the expectancy that the US will *not* occur (which is not the same as having no expectancy of the US, as would be the case when the associative strength is zero). Hence, the Rescorla-Wagner model captures the idea that organisms can also actively learn to predict the absence of stimuli.

The Rescorla-Wagner model has both high heuristic and high predictive value. It has led to the discovery of a number of phenomena, such as **superconditioning**, whereby you can make conditioning extra strong by pairing a CS together with a CS that has a negative associative strength. Again imagine that you first present Y+ and YA- trials. As noted in the previous paragraph, this will result in inhibitory learning about A; that is, A will develop a negative associative strength. If you subsequently present AX+ trials, the associative strength of X will be greater than if you only present AX+ trials (i.e., no Y+ and YA- trials).

Because of its high heuristic and predictive value, the Rescorla-Wagner model has been very influential both in and outside of learning psychology. For example, it has been important in the development of so-called **connectionist models** (Rumelhart & McClelland, 1986), research into reinforcement learning as it is now conducted in computer science (e.g., Lee, Seo, & Jung, 2012; Sutton & Barto, 1998), and related theories of **predictive coding** (e.g.,

Think It Through 2.5: Rescorla-Wagner (Example 1)

Create a numerical example showing how the Rescorla-Wagner model explains superconditioning.

Think It Through 2.6: Rescorla-Wagner (Example 2)

Create a numerical example in which you show how the Rescorla-Wagner model explains the effect of contingency— that is, the fact that conditioning depends not only on the co-occurrence of CS and US (cell (a) in the four-field table) but also on the occurrence of the CS or US on its own (cell (b) and cell (c) in the four-field table).

Clark, 2013; Friston, 2009). Yet it was clear very quickly that the Rescorla-Wagner model also had important limitations. A critical analysis of the theory was published by Miller, Barnet, and Grahame (1995), who described no fewer than twenty-three "failures" of the model (i.e., findings that cannot be explained by the Rescorla-Wagner model). That is why researchers have looked for alternative associative models that make other assumptions about the way in which associations are formed and influence behavior. We discuss a number of these models, always drawing on findings that the Rescorla-Wagner model cannot explain.

d) Extinction is not due to the removal of associations: The models of Wagner and Bouton As we noted above, the Rescorla-Wagner model explains extinction in terms of reduction in associative strength. Therefore, according to the Rescorla-Wagner model, extinction (as an effect) is due to the "unlearning" or forgetting of a CS-US association. In section 2.2.5.2, however, we discussed evidence that shows that extinction is not due to unlearning or forgetting. For example, CS postexposure trials (CS-only trials after acquisition) have no influence when presented in a separate context (renewal). Extinguished CRs can also reappear spontaneously over time (spontaneous recovery). These effects should be impossible if CS postexposure trials lead to the disappearance of an association.

Wagner (1981; see also Wagner & Brandon, 2001, and Vogel, Ponce, & Wagner, 2019, for a recent review) presented the **sometimes opponent processes** (SOP) model, which was an important first step in explaining phenomena such as renewal. In line with earlier proposals (e.g., Konorski, 1967; Pavlov, 1927), Wagner's SOP model postulated that two types of S-S associations can be formed: *excitatory associations* and *inhibitory associations*. Excitatory associations will increase in strength when a CS is followed by the unexpected presence of a US, while inhibitory associations will increase in strength when a CS is followed by the unexpected absence of the US. So you could say that the strength of an excitatory association is a reflection of the extent to which the CS helps predict the presence of the US, while the strength of an inhibitory association is a reflection of the extent to which the CS helps predict the absence of the US. When a CS and US representation are connected by an excitatory association, the delivery of the CS will lead to an increase in the activation of the US representation. When an inhibitory CS-US association is formed, the CS presentation will lead to a reduction in the activation of the US representation. The same CS and US can be connected by both an excitatory and an inhibitory association. The strength of both determines the effect that CS presentations will have on the activation of the US representation and thus on the strength of the CR.

We will not go into the precise way in which inhibitory and excitatory relations come about (see Bouton, 2016, pp. 144–150), but we do want to note that Wagner's SOP model is still one of the most elegant and influential models in cognitive learning psychology. In contrast to the Rescorla-Wagner model, which is essentially no more than a mathematical formula and can be considered cognitive only because the different elements in the formula can be interpreted as mental states (e.g., ΔV as expectation discrepancy), the SOP model is firmly entrenched in the cognitive approach to learning psychology. Although the idea of inhibitory associations was not well received by everyone (e.g., Miller & Matzel, 1988), it continues to be very influential. For instance, it has had a big impact on the development of techniques for the treatment of anxiety disorders (e.g., Craske, Treanor, Conway, Zbozinek, & Vervliet, 2014) and obesity (Epstein et al., 2009). In addition, the SOP model makes interesting predictions about the interaction between habituation and conditioning (see also section 1.2.2 on the role of conditioning of opponent processes). It is not for nothing that Bouton (2016, p. 144) describes Wagner's SOP model as "the single most complete account of conditioning and associative learning that is available."

Box 2.5 The Role of Attention in Classical Conditioning

In various S-S models, we see that a major role is reserved for attention. Pairing CS and US together is not a sufficient condition for forming associations; sufficient attention must also be paid to the US (and the CS) so that associations can be formed. We can already recognize the role of attention in the Rescorla-Wagner model and Wagner's SOP model (1981). After all, it can be assumed that the degree of expectation discrepancy determines how much attention is paid to the presence or absence of a stimulus (see Dickinson, 1980, chapter 4, for an excellent discussion). If the US is unexpected, much attention will be paid to the US, and much is "learned" (in the cognitive sense of knowledge acquisition). In the Wagner model (1981) we see that the formation of associations depends on the extent to which the CS presentation is expected. If the presentation of the CS is unexpected, much attention is paid to the CS and associations can be formed. The idea that attention to the CS is important provides an elegant explanation for the effects of CS pre-exposure on classical conditioning. When the CS is repeatedly presented on its own (CS-only trials) and only afterward the CS is presented together with the US (CS-US trials), classical conditioning will be less pronounced than when there are only CS-US trials. Wagner's model attributes this to the fact that, as a result of the CS-only trials, the presence of the CS is expected in that context and therefore receives little attention. Thus, context-CS associations are formed that determine the extent to which the CS presentation is expected, which in turn determines how much attention is given to the CS, and thus how well the CS-US relation is "learned."

There are many other S-S models in which attention also plays an important role. These models often differ with regard to the factors that determine how much attention is paid to the CS and US. As we have seen earlier, attention is determined by the degree of expectation discrepancy in the Rescorla-Wagner and Wagner models. Yet, in the model of Mackintosh (1975), attention to the CS is determined by the extent to which the CS is a good predictor of the US. It indeed seems worthwhile to pay more attention to stimuli that help you predict important events than to stimuli that give little (additional) information about events in the environment. One can

(continued)

Box 2.5 (continued)

explain many findings about classical conditioning on the basis of this idea. The effects of CS pre-exposure, for instance, fit perfectly within the Mackintosh model. If you repeatedly present only a CS, this implies that the CS is not a predictor of important events, which will reduce attention to that CS. As a result, the CS-US relation is not noticed as quickly afterward. Note that both Wagner (1981) and Mackintosh (1975) offer an explanation for CS pre-exposure effects in terms of attention to the CS, but that they differ in the way that CS pre-exposure leads to lower attention to the CS (for Wagner, this is because of context-CS associations, whereas for Mackintosh, this is because the CS does not predict anything). Blocking can also be explained on the basis of the Mackintosh model. As we discussed previously, blocking refers to the finding that CS X elicits a weaker CR when AX+ trials are preceded by A+ trials than when there are only AX+ trials. Mackintosh explains this by assuming that as a result of the A+ trials, a lot of attention is paid to CS A. During the AX+ trials, the organism will determine that A remains a perfect predictor of the US, while X does not provide any additional information. This will reduce the attention for X, and the X-US association will be weaker after A+ and AX+ trials than after only AX+ trials.

On the other hand, one could also argue that there is no need to continue to pay a lot of attention to CSs that you already know are important. It indeed seems more important to pay attention to stimuli that you are uncertain about, compared to stimuli that you have certainty about with regard to how they act or what they predict. If you notice a CS and you know that the CS is a predictor of the US, then you can direct your attention away from that CS. However, if you see a new, unprecedented CS in an environment in which unpredictable USs occur, it is important to pay a lot of attention to the new CS because the CS could help you in predicting these USs. This idea lies at the core of the Pearce and Hall model (1980): if you are confronted with unpredictable USs, it is better to pay attention to the stimuli that you do not yet know the meaning of than to those you already know the meaning of. This model also offers an explanation for the effects of both CS pre-exposure and blocking. For instance, after CS-only trials, the meaning of the CS becomes clear: it does not predict anything. That is why less attention is paid to this CS and the CS-US relation will be noticed less quickly. In blocking, the A+ trials ensure that the organism learns that the USs are predictable (by A). As a result, the US is also expected on the AX+ trials (i.e., there are not unpredictable USs) and there is therefore no need to pay attention to new (X) or old (A) CSs.

The fact that models with diametrically opposed assumptions can explain the same phenomena can be very confusing. It shows how careful we must be when drawing conclusions about mediating mental processes on the basis of functional knowledge. As Bouton (2007, p. 123) points out, both the Mackintosh (1975) and Pearce and Hall (1980) models have contributed to understanding the role of attention in classical conditioning (see Le Pelley, Mitchell, Beesley, George, & Wills, 2016, for an overview). The core assumption of both models (and also the models of Rescorla-Wagner, 1972, and Wagner, 1981) is that attention is a crucial determinant of classical conditioning. On the other hand, research into the role of attention in conditioning also shows that conditioning is important in determining attention: attention to the CS varies depending on whether it is a predictor of other events. In this way, conditioning research has also contributed to a better understanding of the determinants of attention (see Le Pelley et al.,

Because excitatory and inhibitory associations can exist simultaneously, the meaning of a CS can be ambiguous: it can be at the same time a signal for the presence of the US and a signal for the absence of the US. Bouton (1993, 2004; see also Rosas, García-Gutiérrez, & Callejas-Aguilera, 2006) noted that this ambiguity can be solved by taking the context into account. It is indeed possible that a CS in a given context is a signal for the presence of the US and in a different context, a signal for the absence of the US. This assumption is in line with effects such as renewal (see section 2.2.5.2). In studies on renewal, the CS is followed by the US in a certain context (e.g., a blue room). According to Bouton, this leads to the formation of an excitatory association between the CS and the US (see figure 2.17, solid line). This association would be context-independent because at that moment in time, the meaning of the CS is not yet ambiguous (see Rosas et al., 2006). Afterward, the CS is presented alone in a different context (e.g., a green room). This leads to the formation of an inhibitory association (see figure 2.17, dashed line) that is context-dependent (see figure 2.17, dash-and-dot line). In other words, the organism first learns that the CS is a predictor of the US (which is reflected in the strength of the excitatory association) and then learns an exception to that rule—namely, that the CS is sometimes (e.g., only in the green room) followed by the

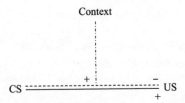

Figure 2.17
How the model of Bouton (1993) explains extinction. During CS-US presentations an excitatory association is formed (full line; +). During the extinction procedure, an inhibitory association (dashed line, –) is formed. The inhibitory association is modulated by the context so that the inhibitory association is active only when the context is present (dash-point line, +).

absence of the US. Because the inhibitory association is context dependent, it will only play a role in the context in which it is formed (i.e., in the context in which extinction took place; the green room). Based on this model we can explain why the CS does not elicit a CR in the extinction context (e.g., green room; both associations have an influence on the US representation and therefore on behavior) but does subsequently do so in the original context (e.g., blue room; only the excitatory association has an influence on the US representation).

The essence of **Bouton's model** is that extinction as a procedure does not lead to the unlearning or forgetting of an association, but to the acquisition of new knowledge about the CS-US relation (namely, the inhibitory association). Extinction does not involve "unlearning" but "learning" (in the cognitive sense of changing knowledge). Spontaneous recovery can also be explained in this way if one considers time as a kind of context. During extinction, the animal "learns" that the CS is no longer followed by the US at that moment in time. If time passes, the animal is in a different time context and it can therefore no longer be certain that the CS will still not be followed by the US. It still knows that at some point in the past the CS was not followed by the US, but it is possible that this period is over.

Box 2.6 Implications of Bouton's Model

Bouton's (1993) model has important clinical implications (Vervliet, Craske, & Hermans, 2013). As mentioned earlier (box 2.1), behavior therapy is derived directly from research on classical conditioning. The basic idea here is that psychological complaints such as anxiety disorders are examples of classical conditioning (i.e., changes in behavior that result from stimulus pairings). This functional analysis implies that anxiety disorders can be treated in the same way that conditioned anxiety is modified in the laboratory. This has led to the development of exposure therapies where patients are repeatedly exposed to the stimulus that elicits fear (e.g., a spider). These exposure treatments are equivalent to the extinction procedures developed in the laboratory. Although exposure therapy is very effective in the short term, it appears that the original complaint can sometimes reemerge even after treatment (e.g., the client becomes frightened by spiders once more). This relapse can be understood from the literature on extinction. The work of Bouton (1993) implies that exposure to spiders will not lead to the disappearance of the associations that initially led to the phobia. Instead, during exposure, the patient will "learn" that under certain circumstances (e.g., in the therapist's treatment room, in the presence of the therapist, during that particular period) seeing or touching spiders does not lead to unpleasant consequences. This additional knowledge is inherently context dependent. It is therefore possible that the patient will still have a fear of spiders when he or she comes home (renewal) or that the fear will return spontaneously after a certain period of time (spontaneous recovery). To reduce the probability of relapse after successful treatment, the therapist can apply the exposure treatment in different environments, including environments in which the patient is often confronted with the phobic object (see Craske et al.,

Box 2.6 (continued)

2014). From the above it can also be understood why relapse occurs so often in drug use (also see discussion of the opponent-process theory of Solomon in chapter 1, section 1.2.2).

The idea of context-dependent learning has also played an important role in research on our first impressions of other people. When we meet another person, we often immediately feel good or bad about this person. Research shows that this spontaneous impression can be an example of evaluative conditioning. This means that this first impression is the result of an earlier event in which the person co-occurred with something positive or negative (e.g., the person did or said something good or bad). Further research suggests that the first experience with a certain person is extremely important in the long term. Imagine seeing a new colleague at work for the first time in the hallway on the way to your desk. You greet him but he does not respond, or he looks angrily at you. As a result of that first experience, you probably develop a negative impression of your new colleague. Afterward, your boss presents the new colleague to you. At that moment, the new colleague is very friendly. Probably that second experience will do little to change your negative impression of the colleague and you will only learn that the colleague is friendly when your boss is present. One possible way to explain this is that the first experience with someone results in context-independent knowledge: you assume that your new colleague is unfriendly. A second experience that contradicts the first experience will only result in context-dependent knowledge: your new colleague is friendly when your boss is there. This idea is very similar to that of Bouton: the first thing you learn (the CS is followed by the US) is context-independent, but the second thing you learn (the CS is no longer followed by the US) is context-dependent (see Rosas et al., 2006). Because your original impression is based on context independent knowledge, it will be applied to all new contexts (e.g., when you meet your new colleague at a party) while the second experience will only have an impact in one context (i.e., when your boss is present). The context independence of initial learning might thus explain why first impressions can be so important (see Gawronski, Rydell, De Houwer, Brannon, Ye, Vervliet, & Hu, 2018, for an overview of this research).

Box 2.7 Can Emotional Memories Be Erased?

Over the past decade much attention has been focused on the idea that emotional memories can be erased from memory (see Beckers & Kindt, 2017, for a review). The starting point of this research is that memories of emotional events in the brain must be "consolidated" (strengthened) before they can have a long-lasting effect. Furthermore, it is assumed that even old, already consolidated memory tracks have to be consolidated again (reconsolidation) each time they are activated (e.g., every time the memory of a traumatic event comes up). Finally, it is assumed that both consolidation and reconsolidation can be weakened by administering certain chemical substances (e.g., propranolol). If these assumptions are correct, then one could make memory traces unstable and even erase them if one administers these chemicals at times when (re)consolidation

(continued)

Box 2.7 (continued)

is necessary, for example, when people think back to a traumatic event. This prediction has been tested in the context of classical conditioning (e.g., Nader, Schafe, & LeDoux, 2000). A CS (e.g., a tone) was presented together with an aversive US (e.g., an electric shock). The next day only the tone was presented. The idea was that this would activate the memory trace of the CS-US pairing. A chemical was then used in a first condition to prevent the reconsolidation of that memory trace while in a second condition an inactive substance was administered. On the third day it was found that the CS elicited less fear in the first condition than in the second condition. However, later research has shown that such effects only occur (at best) under very specific conditions. Even if the effects do occur, it is unclear whether these are due to the deletion of memory traces or to other, already known processes such as context-dependent learning as described by Bouton (1993, for example, renewal where the drug provides a special feeling and thus a unique context that differs from the context during acquisition and test). It would of course be very useful therapeutically if one could erase a traumatic memory from a patient's memory, but as is often the case with sensational ideas, this idea might be "too good to be true." The problem with such "too good to be true" ideas is that scientists also seem to fall prey to a confirmation bias (i.e., the tendency to see their own ideas as true). One consequence is that they publish research data more quickly when they confirm their ideas than when they contradict their ideas (see Simmons, Nelson, & Simonsohn, 2011, for an overview of various reasons why research can lead to false conclusions). Even if scientists act in good conscience, false conclusions can still be drawn. It therefore remains important to be critical when you consult the literature, especially if research results seem too good to be true.

e) Blocking is not due to the failure to "learn": The comparator model of Miller   We previously clarified that blocking—according to the Rescorla-Wagner model—is due to a "failure to learn": because the presence of the US is expected on A+ and AX + trials the X-US association is not formed. Backward blocking, however, cannot be explained by the Rescorla-Wagner model. In studies on backward blocking, the organism is first confronted with AX+ trials and only then with A+ trials. According to the Rescorla-Wagner model, the X-US association should be formed on the AX+ trials. The subsequent A+ trials should have no effect on the strength of the X-US association simply because X is not present on those trials. However, several studies show that the CR triggered by X is smaller if the AX+ trials are followed by A+ trials than if only AX+ trials are presented. Such backward blocking effects indicate a fundamental error within the Rescorla-Wagner model. Within this model, it is assumed that all information about a CS-US association is abstracted (summarized) in a single parameter (i.e., the strength of the CS-US association [V_{CS}]). Once information (e.g., a CS-US pairing) has had its influence, this information is forgotten. One can only learn about a stimulus at the moment at which it is presented. The fact that backward blocking can occur, however, suggests that the organism retrospectively revises the implications of the AX+ trials in the light of the A+ trials (see Miller & Witnauer, 2016, for an overview of research into backward blocking and other forms of retrospective revaluation).

Backward blocking is consistent with an alternative associative model which is called the **comparator model** (Miller & Matzel, 1988; Ghirlanda & Ibadullayev, 2015; Stout & Miller, 2007). According to this model, expectation discrepancy plays no role in establishing or changing associations. The only thing that has an influence on the strength of the CS-US association is the number of times that two stimuli occur together in time and space (i.e., contiguity is the driving force behind associations). Also essential to this model is the assumption that CRs with respect to a CS are not a direct reflection of the strength of the CS-US association. According to the comparator model, CRs depend on a comparison of the strength of different associations. Take the example of blocking. Because of the AX+ trials, an A-US and an X-US association are formed, regardless of whether there are additional A+ trials and regardless of whether the A+ trials come before or after the AX+ trials. If additional A+ trials are delivered, this results in a strengthening of the A-US association, but the X-US relation remains unaffected. Because X always occurred together with A, the CR with respect to X will not only be determined by the strength of the X-US association, but also by the strength of the A-US association. The CR with respect to X is in fact a function of the X-US association strength *relative to* the strength of A-US association. If A+ trials are presented in addition to the AX+ trials, the strength of the X-US association will be weak in comparison to the strength of the A-US association. When there are only AX+ trials, the X-US association will be as strong as the A-US association (all other things being equal). Because the CR is dependent on the X-US association strength relative to the A-US association strength, the CR for X will be weaker when both A+ and AX+ trials have been presented than when only AX+ trials were delivered. This prediction holds irrespective of whether the A+ trials precede or follow the AX+ trials.

Given that our book is designed to be an introduction to learning psychology, it is not so important to know the details of the comparator model but it is important to understand its essence: (a) "learning" (i.e., association formation) takes place in a fairly simple and unconditional way (the only thing that counts is the extent to which two stimuli occur together in time and space), and (b) associations are not directly translated into behavior but only indirectly after a comparison is made with other associations. Blocking in the comparator model is due to the fact that the learned X-US association is not reflected in behavior because it is counteracted by a stronger A-US association.

Note, therefore, that blocking according to the comparator model is not due to a failure to form X-US associations but to the fact that the formed X-US association has no impact on behavior. The model therefore makes a clear distinction between the formation of associations and behavior: the fact that no CR occurs does not necessarily mean that no association has been formed. In this respect, the comparator model is much more realistic than the

Rescorla-Wagner model, which makes virtually no distinction between the formation of associations and performance (i.e., CRs in the Rescorla-Wagner model are a direct reflection of associative strength). Although the comparator model cannot explain all existing evidence, it has led to new findings and offers an interesting alternative perspective on classical conditioning (see Miller & Witnauer, 2016, and Stout & Miller, 2007, for reviews).

2.3.2 Propositional Models

2.3.2.1 The core of propositional models Associative models have dominated learning research for more than one hundred years now, basically right from the start. As a result, for some, classical conditioning as an effect is almost synonymous to association formation as a mechanism (see De Houwer, 2018b, for an historical review). It is only by clearly separating the functional level of explanation (including classical conditioning as an effect) from the cognitive level of explanation (including association formation as a mechanism) that one can take seriously the idea that classical conditioning might be mediated by processes other than association formation.

It is only recently that a second class of mental process theories on classical conditioning has been proposed (e.g., De Houwer, 2009, 2018c; Mitchell et al., 2009; Waldmann & Holyoak, 1992). What they have in common is the assumption that the effect of stimulus pairings on behavior is mediated by the (typically nonautomatic) formation of propositions about relations in the environment. **Propositions** are units of information that specify assumptions about the nature of events in the world. For instance, a proposition could specify that the ringing of a bell is always followed by food. Propositions have two unique characteristics: (1) A proposition has a truth value: it is possible, at least in principle, to evaluate whether the assumptions about events in the world are right or wrong (Strack & Deutsch, 2004). (2) Propositions contain relational information, that is, information about how events are related (e.g., bell *predicts* food, smoking *causes* cancer; Lagnado, Waldmann, Hagmayer, & Sloman, 2007; Waldmann & Holyoak, 1992). Suppose you establish that people with a certain disease always have a certain chemical in their blood and that this substance is not present in people who do not have the disease. One possible proposition about this relation is that the chemical in the blood *causes* the disease. Another possible proposition is that the disease *causes* the chemical in the blood. According to both propositions, there is a relation between the chemical and the disease. The propositions differ, however, with regard to the nature of the relation between the two (Waldmann & Holyoak, 1992). Note that propositions are not necessarily verbal (i.e., expressed in words). It seems fair to assume that nonverbal organisms also have knowledge about how events in the world are related. Nevertheless, the exact nature of and the flexibility in using propositions might vary greatly depending on whether an organism is verbal or not (see De Houwer, Hughes, & Barnes-Holmes, 2016, for a discussion). We will revisit this issue in chapters 3 and 4.

Associations in memory are not propositions because they do not have the two characteristics of propositions: (1) An association in memory does not specify any assumption about events in the world. It is a hypothetical state in memory that is assumed to have been created as the result of a spatiotemporal relation in the environment. It is pointless to say that an association is right or wrong. (2) An association does not encode relational information, that is, information about how events are related.[6]

What do we mean when we say that learning is the result of nonautomatic formation of propositions about relations in the environment? First of all, this means that people (and certain nonhuman animals) form hypotheses about relations in the environment and try to determine which hypothesis is correct. When doing so, they deploy all information that can be useful to discover and evaluate a relation. This is not only information about when stimuli occur, but also knowledge that people already have in memory and knowledge that they acquire through observations and instructions. They can deploy this knowledge not only when they experience the events that constitute the regularity (e.g., when a tone and a shock are paired) but also when changes in behavior are assessed (e.g., when the conditioned fear for the tone is measured). Secondly, they often do this in a nonautomatic way, that is to say (among other things) that they are aware of the propositions they form and that they have to make an effort to form those propositions. The effect that a relation in the environment will have on behavior is determined by what the person consciously thinks about that relation (i.e., what proposition about the relation people perceive as being true).

How does all of this relate to classical conditioning? Let's return to the example of Pavlov's dog. According to propositional models, presenting an important stimulus such as food will encourage the dog to actively (purposefully) search for predictors or causes of the food. Because the bell is a salient stimulus, the dog will soon consider the possibility that there is a relation between the bell and the food. The fact that the bell is indeed always followed by food offers support for the hypothesis that the arrival of the food can be predicted on the basis of the bell. Behavior can be influenced by the bell-food relation only after the dog has formed a proposition about that relation. More specifically, the proposition specifying that the bell is followed by food will lead to the expectation that food will be delivered after hearing the bell. That expectation results in salivation when hearing the bell.

2.3.2.2 General evaluation of propositional models Can propositional models offer an explanation for available functional knowledge on classical conditioning? We will now discuss a number of important findings.

– *Influence of stimulus characteristics and intrinsic relations (see section 2.2.1.2)* How fast one discovers a particular relation depends on the properties of the CS, US, and the intrinsic relation between the two. People will be more motivated to discover relations with important

USs. One will detect relations that contain striking CSs more quickly. A relation is also easier to detect if there are pre-existing reasons to suspect that such a relation would exist. For example, when people become nauseated, they will tend to think of food as a cause of that nausea because they know from experience that you can become nauseous from food (see Testa, 1974, for a precursor to this idea). Organisms therefore use available and past knowledge to discover new relations in the environment.

– Classical conditioning can also influence involuntary behavior (see section 2.2.2.1) In principle, propositions can influence all kinds of behavior. Contrary to what is sometimes thought (e.g., Shanks, 1990), behavior does not have to be a rational, logical consequence of a proposition about the relation between stimuli. Let us consider the fact that in autoshaping studies, pigeons move toward and peck on the illuminated key when doing so reduces their chance of contacting food. From the perspective of propositional models, it is possible that the propositional belief that the illumination of the key is followed by food, creates a tendency to walk toward the key. Propositional models of learning do not in themselves say anything about why certain propositions have certain effects on behavior. That is, they do not provide a full specified theory of behavior. What they do say is that relations in the environment can have an effect on behavior only after a proposition has been formed about that relation. It is, however, not possible to predict behavior perfectly on the basis of propositional knowledge unless one has a perfect theory of behavior (see Mitchell et al., 2009).

– Contingency awareness is important (see section 2.2.2.3) In contrast to associative models, propositional models can explain why learning usually occurs only after people are aware of the relation. At least in humans, forming and evaluating propositions happens in a nonautomatic and therefore conscious manner. The existence of conditioning without awareness of the CS-US relations would, however, be difficult to explain on the basis of propositional models (but see De Houwer, 2018c).

– Classical conditioning is a general phenomenon that occurs in different organisms (see section 2.2.3) At first sight, this observation seems to contradict propositional models. If all learning is based on propositional processes, then one would have to assume that all animal species are capable of forming and evaluating propositions in a conscious, nonautomatic way. This criticism is correct in the sense that it is unlikely that learning in simple animal species such as snails and bees is based on propositional processes. Yet, there are indications that learning in certain nonhuman animals such as rats is indeed based on the formation and evaluation of propositions (e.g., Blaisdell, Sawa, Leising, & Waldmann, 2006; Beckers, Miller, De Houwer, & Urushihara, 2006; see also Mitchell et al., 2009).

– Secondary tasks have an important impact on classical conditioning (see section 2.2.4) This conclusion fits well with the idea that learning is determined by propositional processes. After

all, it takes a lot of effort to formulate and test hypotheses. If you have to invest energy in performing secondary tasks, there is less energy left for forming and evaluating propositions. If, however, attention is focused on the relation between the CS and the US (see Baeyens, Eelen, & Van den Bergh, 1990), then one will more quickly form hypotheses about that relation and evaluate them as being present.

– Conclusion   In sum, from the above it appears that propositional models are capable of explaining many aspects of the existing functional knowledge about classical conditioning. They therefore have a high heuristic value. Nevertheless, there are also findings that seem to challenge a propositional account of classical conditioning. Perhaps the most intriguing challenge comes from research on the so-called Perruchet effect. Perruchet (1985) presented a series of trials in which a tone could be followed by an air puff delivered to the eye of the participant. He registered eye blink responses after presentation of the tone and asked participants to rate the extent to which they expected that an air puff would be delivered after hearing the tone. As the number of consecutive trials on which the tone was followed by the air puff increased, the likelihood of an eye blink response increased whereas the expectancy of the air puff after the tone decreased. The expectancy results are in line with the so-called gambler's fallacy, which refers to the fact that gamblers believe that a loss is more likely after a series of wins, even when the chance of winning is equally high with each gamble. This clear dissociation between conscious expectancies and conditioned eye blink responses seems to suggest that the latter are not based on propositional knowledge of the tone-air puff relation but that they might reflect the operation of a separate, nonpropositional learning system. Although this conclusion is still being debated (e.g., Weidemann, McAndrew, Livesey, & McLaren, 2016), the Perruchet effect is widely regarded as a problem for the idea that all conditioning effects are mediated by propositions.

The predictive value of propositional models is also high. Propositional models have led to a better understanding of the conditions under which conditional contingency is important. More specifically, these models have led to a number of important studies on blocking (see Mitchell et al., 2009, and Boddez, De Houwer, & Beckers, 2017, for an overview). As indicated earlier, blocking refers to the finding that a cue X elicits a less strong CR when AX+ trials are presented together with A+ trials than when only AX+ trials are offered. According to propositional models, this result can be the consequence of causal reasoning. Suppose A and X are seen as two possible causes of the US. The fact that the US is just the same when only A is present than when both A and X are present, suggests that X has no causal influence on the US. After all, causes normally have additive effects. The effect of two causes should therefore be stronger than the effect of one cause in itself. However, we note that A and X together have just the same effect as A alone. We can therefore conclude that X is not a cause of the US. If blocking is indeed the result of this reasoning, then it should only occur if A and

X are presented as possible causes of the US. Waldmann and Holyoak (1992) confirmed this prediction. In human contingency learning studies in which participants had to assess the strength of the relation between X and the US, blocking was only established when A and X were described as chemical substances in the blood and the US as a disease that could be caused by A and X. However, they found no blocking if A and X were described as chemical substances in the blood and the US as a disease that can cause A and X. So blocking only occurred if A and X were possible causes of the US but not if the US was a possible cause of A and X.

Even if A and X are considered as possible causes of the US, blocking should only occur if one assumes that the effects of two causes are additive. De Houwer, Beckers, and Glautier (2002) investigated the role of this assumption by providing test subjects with information about the maximum intensity of the US. In the submaximal condition, the subjects were told that the US had an intensity of 10 out of 20 on both the A+ trials and the AX+ trials. Given this information, one can be pretty sure that X is not a cause of the US because the US is just as intense on the A+ trials as on the AX+ trials. If X was a cause, the US should have been stronger on the AX+ trials than on the A+ trials. In this condition blocking was observed: test subjects believed that there was no causal relation between X and the US. In the maximal condition, participants were told that the intensity of the US on the A+ and AX+ trials had a value of 10 out of 10. Because A alone has the maximum effect, it is no longer possible for X to strengthen this effect. The fact that the US is the same on the A+ trials than on the AX+ trials therefore does not say anything about the effect of X on the US. It is possible that X does have an effect on the US, but that this extra effect does not show up because A alone already has the maximum effect. In other words, there is a "ceiling effect" that makes it impossible to draw conclusions about the relation between X and the US. No blocking was found in this condition. Beckers et al. (2006) showed that blocking in rats also depends on how likely it is that the effects of different causes are additive.

On the basis of such findings, most researchers now agree that at least some of the conditioning effects in humans are due to propositional processes (e.g., McLaren et al., 2014). Most researchers, however, continue to assume that associations can also lead to conditioning. Such **dual-process models** are currently very popular because they can explain more data than single-process models. But if there is more than one learning system, the question arises as to how these different learning processes relate to each other (e.g., when do the different processes guide behavior). Attention is increasingly being paid to this difficult question by proponents of dual-process models (see Mitchell et al., 2009, for a critique of dual-process models).

Despite the successes of propositional models of classical conditioning, their impact on learning research has been relatively limited. In part this can be attributed to the lack of precision in formulating these models. Whereas associative models are often formulated in very precise mathematical terms (e.g., Rescorla & Wagner, 1972; Stout & Miller, 2007), propositional models are often not more than a few verbally formulated ideas about the nature of the mental processes and representations that mediate learning. This lack of precision not only renders it difficult to derive precise predictions from propositional models but also to falsify those models on the basis of empirical evidence. Although these criticisms are valid, it is important to realize that propositional models as they are currently described in the literature, are a class of models that share the core idea that learning is mediated by propositional knowledge. It is indeed difficult to falsify a whole class of models. What is often forgotten, however, is that it is also impossible to falsify the class of all possible associative models of learning (Miller & Escobar, 2001). For every result in the learning literature, it is possible to find an associative model that can explain that result. At the same time, it would also be possible to find another (version of an) associative model that predicts the opposite result. More generally, we believe that the possibility to formalize or refute a theoretical model is not an essential criterion for the quality of the model (De Houwer, 2018c). What is more important is the ability of the model to explain existing functional knowledge (i.e., its heuristic value) and to predict new functional knowledge (i.e., its predictive value). From that perspective, we continue to believe in the value of propositional models of classical conditioning.

3   Operant Conditioning: Effects of Regularities in the Presence of Stimuli and Behavior

After reading this chapter, you should be able to:

- Indicate under which conditions operant conditioning (as an effect) will occur.
- Provide an overview of the core assumptions of the main mental process theories of operant conditioning.

Introductory Task

Try to find five examples from daily life that show that behavior can be influenced by the consequences of that behavior. Which factors determine whether operant conditioning will occur? What does this say about the mental processes that mediate operant conditioning effects?

3.1   Some Basic Terms and Procedures

3.1.1   Basic Terms

Operant conditioning (sometimes also referred to as *instrumental conditioning*) is, like classical conditioning, an effect of regularities in the presence of events in the environment. However, operant and classical conditioning differ with regard to the nature of events that occur. Whereas classical conditioning refers to regularities in the presence of stimuli, operant conditioning refers to the effect of regularities in the presence of behavior and stimuli. By describing operant conditioning in such broad terms from the outset, we reject the stereotype that it has to do only with the rats that press levers in Skinner boxes. It is more than that, just as classical conditioning is more than the prototypical example of Pavlov's dog; these are just two of many possible procedures that may be used to study (operant or classic) conditioning. Indeed, Skinner knew that by placing a rat in a noise-free room containing only a food box and a lever to push, he was creating a fairly artificial situation. He did so purposefully because

Figure 3.1
B. F. Skinner.

this allowed him to study (in a controlled manner) the conditions under which the regularity involving behavior and stimuli leads to changes in behavior, which in turn allowed him to develop general principles that would also apply outside of the lab.

3.1.1.1 The three terms of the three-term contingency In an operant conditioning procedure, three elements play a crucial role (thus learning psychologists often talk about a **three-term contingency**). These three elements are the discriminative stimulus, or Sd; the behavior, or R (response); and the result of the behavior, or Sr (resultant stimulus, or consequence). Their relation is typically formalized in the following manner:

Sd: R – Sr

This relation is often also called the **A-B-C contingency**, where A stands for antecedent (that which precedes the behavior; more specifically the Sd), B stands for behavior, and C stands for consequence (the result of the behavior, or more specifically, the Sr). Each of these three terms can be used at the descriptive level of the procedure (the objective situation as created by a researcher) and at the functional level of the effect (the causal impact of environment on behavior and behavior on the environment). Let us start with the concept of the **discriminative stimulus**. At the **descriptive level**, an Sd is simply an event that indicates whether an R will be followed by a certain Sr. For example, assume that pressing a lever is followed by food when a light is turned on but not when that light is off. In this example, the light is an Sd—that is, a stimulus that can be used to discriminate (distinguish) between situations where the R-Sr relation holds and situations where it does not hold.[1] Note that Sds are not limited to clearly defined, individual stimuli such as lights or sounds. Events that include multiple stimuli (e.g., a piece of music or a specific sequence of lights) can also be Sds. Another important point is that the Sd can also refer to a collection or class of stimuli (often referred to as a **stimulus class**). Suppose that pressing a lever is followed by food only when an object with a red color appears on a screen (and not if an object with a different color appears). In that case, the Sd corresponds to the class of *all* red objects. The characteristic "red" is the "unit" that is used to distinguish the Sd class from other stimuli (or classes of stimuli). At the **functional level**, we refer to a stimulus as an Sd when this stimulus actually has an impact on the behavior because of its Sd role in the procedure (i.e., when it functions as an Sd). For example, when a rat presses the lever more often when the light is on than when it is off, then the light functions as an Sd (i.e., the light influences the rat's behavior because it indicates when the relation between R and Sr holds). It is therefore possible that a stimulus is descriptively an Sd but does not function as an Sd for the organism under investigation (e.g., if the researcher makes the relation between lever pressing and food contingent on the presence of the light, but the presence of the light does not influence the rat's lever pressing). If a certain class of stimuli procedurally plays the role of an Sd and effectively also functions as an Sd, then we speak of a functional stimulus class (i.e., a class of stimuli that function as Sds).

We can also distinguish between the descriptive and functional levels when it comes to the **Sr**. For instance, at a descriptive level, every event that depends on a behavior is an Sr. For example, if a food pellet is delivered each time the rat presses the lever, then the food pellet is descriptively an Sr that is related to lever pressing. Again, it is important to appreciate that the Sr is also (conceptually speaking) broader than an individual stimulus such as a food pellet. For example, an Sr may consist of multiple stimuli (e.g., pressing the lever may result in the delivery of ten food chunks over a period of one minute), the absence of a stimulus (e.g., when pressing a lever results in the termination of an impending shock), or a class of stimuli (e.g., red food chunks). That is why it is better to think of the Sr as an event, or more specifically, something that results from performing a behavior. On a functional level, one speaks of an Sr when the stimulus influences the behavior because of the R-Sr relation. For example, when the rat presses the lever more often because doing so is followed by the delivery of food, then the food functions as an Sr. Once again, it is possible that a stimulus is descriptively but not functionally an Sr (e.g., if the researcher makes the relation between lever pressing and food dependent on lever pressing but the delivery of food after lever pressing does not influence the rate of the rat's lever pressing).[2]

Finally, one can also conceptualize **behavior** or the response (R) in descriptive or functional terms. At the descriptive level, operant conditioning procedures are always concerned with behavior that has a certain impact (i.e., responses that "operate") on the environment. Note that when we refer to behavior, we are not necessarily referring to a singular, individual event. It can also be a certain sequence of behaviors (e.g., typing a code to open a door). And more often than not, it is a class of behaviors (or "response class") that is delineated on the basis of the consequences of these behaviors. For example, the behavior "pressing a lever" is a class of many different behaviors that all result in a downward movement of the lever. Such a response class can include many different motor movements, such as pressing with the left leg, with the right leg, with the chin, and so on. Moreover, the unit with which a response class is delineated can be very abstract. For example, an animal can be given a food pellet each time it imitates a conspecific. In this case, the crucial unit of behavior is the degree of overlap between the observers and the model's behaviors. The resulting response class is huge in this case because it includes all behaviors of the same species that the animal is capable of imitating.

At the functional level, we speak of an operant behavior when the behavior is influenced by a certain outcome related to that behavior. For instance, pressing a lever is functionally an operant behavior when lever pressing occurs because it is followed by food. The existence of this causal relation can be investigated by manipulating the elements in that relation (e.g., comparing a condition in which lever pressing is followed by food and a condition in which the lever pressing is not followed by food, to see if the presence of the food influences the rate of lever pressing). If the manipulation has an impact, one can say that the behavior is a function of the Sr and therefore that the behavior is an operant behavior. A distinction is often made between the term **response class** and the term **operant class** (see Catania, 2013, 117–127). While the term *response class* is always defined descriptively (i.e., as a certain set of behaviors), the term *operant class* is used at the functional level only to refer to a set of behaviors that are due to a particular outcome (e.g., pressing a lever to gain access to food). Again, a key point here is that an operant behavior is much more than one particular motor movement: it is always a class of behaviors. Let's return to the lever pressing example. All motoric movements that result in a downward movement of the lever belong to the class "lever pressing" (e.g., pressing a lever with the left leg, with the right leg, and so on). This response class functions as an operant class whenever the behaviors in the class are effectively influenced by their outcomes. Note that even two seemingly identical behaviors (e.g., two subsequent instances of pressing a lever with the left leg) will never be exactly the same (e.g., the force applied to the lever will always be slightly different). Hence it is best to always think about a class of behaviors when you use the term **operant behavior**. Also remember that operant behavior can involve very complex behaviors with various components that can extend over time (e.g., typing a code to open a door, or even studying to obtain a diploma). This means that research into operant conditioning can provide us with insight into very complex behaviors.

3.1.1.2 Types of operant conditioning   Often, a distinction is made between two differ-ent types of operant conditioning: *reinforcement* and *punishment*. Reinforcement is a behav-ioral effect whereby the relation between an R and Sr leads to an *increase* in the frequency of behavior. Punishment is a behavioral effect whereby the relation between an R and Sr leads to a *decrease* in the frequency of behavior. Reinforcement and punishment are there-fore distinguished on the basis of the direction of the effect of the R-Sr relation on behavior (i.e., an increase or decrease). Within reinforcement and punishment there are also different subtypes of behavior that can be distinguished. For example, a distinction is often made between positive and negative reinforcement. Both are instances of reinforcement (i.e., they involve an increase in the frequency of behavior), but with **positive reinforcement**, the increase is due to the fact that the behavior results in the presence of a stimulus (i.e., there is a positive contingency between the behavior and the stimulus), whereas with **negative reinforcement**, the increase occurs because the behavior results in the absence of a stimulus (i.e., there is a negative contingency between the behavior and the stimulus). Within the class of negative reinforcement, a further distinction can be made between avoidance learn-ing and escape learning. **Avoidance learning** is an effect in which the response reduces the probability of Sr presentation, and this R-Sr relation results in an increase in the frequency of avoidance behavior. **Escape learning** is also a form of reinforcement where a negative contingency between R and Sr leads to an increase in frequency of certain types of behavior. In escape learning, the performance of R coincides with the termination or disappearance of the Sr (the Sr is therefore present before R occurs), whereas in avoidance learning, R leads to the continuing absence of the Sr (the Sr is not present before a R). The relation between these different classes of reinforced behavior is depicted in figure 3.2.

Again, (a subtype of) operant learning cannot simply be observed. Classifying a behavioral change as an example of a certain type of (operant) learning always implies a hypothesis about the causes of that change in behavior. One must therefore always have arguments to support that hypothesis. It is not enough to observe a change in behavior and a regularity in the environment; you must also show that the change in behavior is due to that regular-ity. Take, for example, punishment. There are many situations in everyday life in which the frequency of a behavior decreases when it is followed by an aversive stimulus. Think of a child who is naughty, receives a scolding from a parent, and then stops acting naughty (see Michael, 2004, pp. 36–37). On the surface, this seems to be an instance of punishment. How-ever, there are several possible reasons why a behavior changes. For example, it may be that simply receiving a reprimand is sufficient to induce a change in behavior; it is not illogical

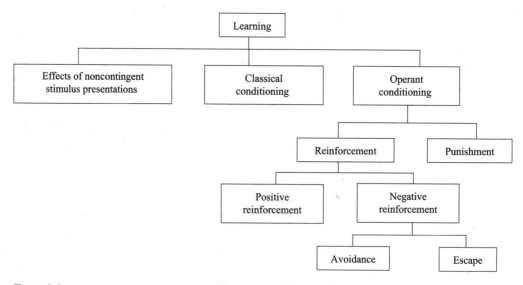

Figure 3.2
Schematic overview of the relation between different forms of learning.

to think that such an intense, aversive stimulus ensures that the child stops what it does and sets the stage for a different behavior (e.g., crying). This explanation implies that the change in behavior (stopping the problem behavior) does not constitute an instance of learning—according to our definition—because it is the result not of a regularity in the environment (i.e., the combination of being naughty and a scolding) but of one stimulus at one moment (the scolding).

3.1.2 Procedures

There are many methods for studying operant conditioning experimentally. Most can be categorized into one of two categories: *discrete trials methods* and *free-operant methods*.

3.1.2.1 Discrete trials methods   Thorndike's puzzle box method is the prototypical example of a discrete trials method. In Thorndike's experiments, a hungry cat was placed in a wooden box. By pulling a loop (R), the cat could open the door of the box and eat a tasty fish (Sr). At the start of this procedure, the cat engages in a whole series of behaviors, one of which (pulling the loop) is followed by access to the fish. Thorndike found that over time, the large variety of behaviors is reduced until finally only one behavior remains: as soon as the cat is placed in the cage, it pulls the loop and can eat. This is an example of the discrete trials method, because each trial is clearly distinguishable from the next. Each time the cat emits the correct behavior, it is freed from the cage and has to be put back into it before the next trial can begin (see http://www.youtube.com/watch?v=Vk6H7Ukp6To). Another class of discrete trials methods is maze methods. The organism (e.g., a rat) is placed in a maze where food has been placed at a certain location. The rat is set down at the starting position and is then free to look for the food. After it has found the food, the researcher must put the rat back at the starting position before the next trial can begin. Results show that the rat needs less time to find the food in each successive trial. The disadvantage of a discrete trials method is that the researcher must be constantly present and restart each trial. An advantage is that the time between two trials can be manipulated precisely.

3.1.2.2 Free-operant methods It was the time-consuming nature of discrete trials methods that motivated Skinner to develop an alternative task. His original goal was to construct a maze in which the rat was automatically brought to the starting position after finding the food. This would not only ease the workload of the research but also allow the researcher to study both the speed (e.g., how quickly the rat finds the food) and frequency of this behavior (how often the rat goes looking). Skinner tried different approaches and eventually developed what is now known as the *Skinner box*. A Skinner box is a small chamber, usually with a lever the rat can press, one or more lights that can light up, and an opening through which food can be delivered (see figure 2.2). All responses are recorded automatically and the delivery of the food can also be pre-arranged (e.g., one food pellet each time the rat presses the lever). As mentioned above, in a discrete trials method, the animal can emit the behavior of interest (e.g., pulling a loop in the puzzle box) only when the researcher starts the next trial by placing the animal in the correct position (e.g., back in the puzzle box). In a Skinner box, however, the animal is free to determine when it emits a response (e.g., to press the lever). That is why the Skinner box method is called a **free-operant method**: the organism is free to operate on the environment. The big advantage of this task is that the frequency of behavior can be registered as a dependent variable.

3.2 Functional Knowledge

3.2.1 The Nature of the Stimuli

3.2.1.1 Operant conditioning is a general phenomenon Like the other forms of learning we have encountered so far, operant conditioning is a general phenomenon that occurs with all kinds of stimuli. This applies both to the nature of the Sd (which can vary from a simple discrete stimulus such as a light to a complex context such as a classroom) and to the nature of the Sr (which can vary from simple biologically relevant stimuli such as food to complex social stimuli such as receiving parental approval). As we noted in the discussion of the three-term contingency (section 3.1.1.1), it is often also more meaningful to consider the Sd and Sr as (classes of) events rather than as well-defined individual stimuli.

To illustrate the generality of operant conditioning, consider an unusual, type of operant conditioning: **sensory reinforcement** (Kish, 1966). This term refers to the observation that the mere presentation of sensory stimuli can be reinforcing in itself. Research shows, for example, that rats who are housed in a dark room will learn to press a lever in order to turn on the light. The Sr is therefore not a specific stimulus (e.g., the light), but the fact that some stimulus is presented, regardless of what that stimulus might be.

3.2.1.2   The influence of the properties of the Sd and Sr on the degree of operant conditioning

a) (Changes in) the intensity of the Sd and Sr   The properties of the Sd and Sr influence the strength of an operant conditioning effect. An obvious factor is the intensity of the stimuli involved. For instance, a more intense Sd or Sr will have a larger impact on behavior than a less intense Sd or Sr would. Also, changes in the intensity of stimuli play an important role in operant conditioning. For example, research shows that punishment is especially effective if an intense aversive stimulus is used as the very first punisher. The initial use of mild-aversive stimuli can even have a detrimental effect. Consider the experiment by Azrin and Holz (1966) in which rats initially learned to press a lever in order to obtain food. During a subsequent phase, this behavior continued to be emitted even when it was followed by a mild electric shock administered via the floor of the cage. If the intensity of the shock gradually increased, the rat learned to adapt to it and continued to press the lever. However, if an intense shock was delivered from the outset (i.e., immediately after the first phase in which the rats learn to press the lever), this resulted in an immediate and almost permanent suppression of the operant behavior of lever pressing. Hence, the same outcome (an intense shock) had a different impact depending on whether its delivery was preceded by the delivery of less intense outcomes.

b) Intrinsic relations   The way in which the nature of the stimuli influences the strength of operant conditioning can depend on the nature of the behavior of interest. Put another way, operant conditioning is moderated by the intrinsic relation between stimuli and behavior. We will first discuss the impact of **intrinsic R-Sr** relations and then the impact of **intrinsic Sd-R relations.**

A nice illustration of the importance of the intrinsic relation between the nature of the response and consequence (Sr) can be seen in Sevenster's (1973) study of male sticklebacks (a type of small thin fish). There are two types of responses that need to be learned in this experiment: swimming through a ring (R_1) and biting on a stick (R_2), both of which hang in the aquarium. There are also two types of stimuli that can follow from a behavior: the appearance of a male rival (Sr_1) or a female stickleback (Sr_2). It appears that swimming through a ring (R_1) will increase in frequency if it leads to the presentation of a female stickleback (Sr_2) but not when it is followed by presentation of a male rival (Sr_1). The opposite is true for R_2:

biting on a stick will increase in frequency if it leads to presentation of a male rival (Sr_1) but not when it leads to presentation of a female (Sr_2). This pattern of results constitutes an interaction between the impact of the nature of the Sr (male vs. female stickleback) and the nature of the R (biting vs. swimming). It is the instrinsic relation between the two that influences the resulting operant conditioning effect. Research shows that it is especially relevant whether R belongs to the class of behavior that is spontaneously elicited by the Sr (Bolles, 1972; see box 3.5 for a related phenomenon). For example, biting on a stick is compatible with the aggression typically provoked by male rivals but not with the ritual provoked by a female stickleback. Operant conditioning is more likely to occur or occurs more quickly when R belongs to those behaviors spontaneously elicited by the Sr. The Sr therefore largely determines what R may or may not be learned.

Another example of selectivity in learning R-Sr relations can be found in research on avoidance learning. As previously mentioned, avoidance learning is a form of operant conditioning in which a behavior increases in frequency because it reduces the chance of an aversive stimulus. Imagine that you put a rat in a shuttle box (i.e., a space consisting of two rooms). When the animal is placed in the first room (for the first time), it receives an electric shock, which will cause it to run to the other room. When it is in the second room, the shock stops. The movement from the first to the second room during the delivery of the shock is called an **escape response** because it ends the presence of the shock. After several repetitions of escaping the shock by running from the first to the second room, the animal will run to the second room immediately after it has been placed in the first room (and thus before the shock is delivered). We call this an **avoidance response** because it prevents the future presence of a shock that is currently absent. Often, one presentation of the shock (US) in the first room is sufficient to make the animal move immediately from the dangerous to the safe side of the cage on a second trial, even before the shock is presented on that second trial (Maatsch, 1959; Theios, 1963). Not all behaviors, however, are learned as quickly as this type of avoidance behavior. For example, it is very difficult to teach a rat to press a lever to avoid a shock, but it is fairly easy to teach a rat to press a lever to receive food. What is important here is not the nature of the R itself (pressing the lever or running away) or the nature of the Sr (absence of shock or presence of food), but the interaction between the two.[3]

In addition to these limitations in learning R-Sr relations, there also are limitations in learning Sd-R relations. Let's switch to humans and take the example of a coffee thermos that has a button on its top that you need to press to access the beverage. Now imagine that this button can be set to two positions, indicated by the colors red and blue, and pressing is possible in only one of the two positions. Thus, the color is an Sd that indicates whether pressing the button (R) will be followed by the delivery of coffee (Sr). If blue indicates that pressing (and therefore coffee) is possible and red indicates that pressing is not possible, we might see that people quickly learn when they should and should not press the button. If the positions are reversed (pressing is not possible in the blue position but is in the red), we might see that people make a lot of mistakes and therefore find it difficult to learn when they should and should not press. One possibility is that this hypothetical difference in learning Sd-R relations is due to the person's past experiences (e.g., a red traffic light indicates that one should stop or remain stationary). Regardless of the reasons for differences in Sd-R learning, it is clear that such differences do exist. Recognizing these differences has important applied implications in many areas, such as ergonomics, the science of how the environment (e.g., products such as thermoses) can be adapted to better fit the characteristics of people.

3.2.1.3 The impact of the nature of the Sr on the nature of change in R Properties of the Sr not only have an impact on the strength of operant conditioning effects but also determine how an R will change as a result of its relation with that Sr. A relation between an R and Sr can have an impact on different aspects of the R (see below, section 3.2.2.2). In past work much attention was focused on changes in the frequency of a response. As mentioned earlier, reinforcement refers to the fact that an R-Sr relation leads to an increase in the frequency of R. If the R-Sr relation results in a decrease in the frequency of R, then we speak of punishment. Reinforcement and punishment are two different effects of relations between behavior and stimuli in the environment. Much research on operant conditioning is aimed at trying to understand the properties of the Sr that determine when reinforcement occurs (i.e., whether and when an R-Sr relation leads to an increase in frequency of R; Domjan, 2000). Below, we first discuss which stimuli can be used to reinforce or punish behavior. Then we briefly discuss the finding that changes in the characteristics of the Sr have a large influence on whether reinforcement or punishment occurs.

a) Which stimuli lead to reinforcement or punishment when used as Sr? The question of which stimuli function as reinforcers or punishers has received much attention in learning research. The reason for this is obvious: if we know in advance which stimuli will function as a reinforcer or a punisher, then we know which stimuli we should use to make a behavior more frequent (i.e., by relating the execution of the behavior to the availability of a stimulus known to function as a reinforcer) and which we should use to make a behavior less frequent (i.e., by relating the execution of the behavior to the availability of a stimulus known to function as a punisher). Unfortunately, it is not easy to answer this crucial question. Some have appealed to concepts such as feelings and needs, but it is also difficult to assess those concepts, in part because they refer to mental constructs. Others have tried to answer the question in functional terms. In this section, we evaluate the different attempts to solve this issue.

– Thorndike's "law of effect": Preferences
At first sight, you might think the answer to this question is simple: behavior that has appetitive (positive) outcomes will increase in frequency (reinforcement), whereas behavior that

results in aversive (negative) outcomes will decrease in frequency (punishment). Thorndike (1911) came to a similar conclusion long ago in his famous **law of effect**. In everyday life, this law of effect is indeed a useful rule of thumb: if you look closely, you will usually see that the frequency of behavior does increase whenever it leads to an appetitive outcome for the organism. Hence, when the aim is to change existing behavior, the behavior can be increased in frequency by linking it to an appetitive outcome (e.g., governments can encourage environmentally friendly building practices by giving people discounts or tax breaks for using them) and reduced in frequency by linking it to an aversive outcome (e.g., fining people when they drive too fast). However, it is not always easy to know a priori whether a certain outcome (Sr) is functioning as an appetitive or aversive stimulus for an organism. To illustrate, consider masochism. Some people engage in certain behaviors (e.g., visiting an S&M club) to experience painful stimuli (e.g., whipping). For most people, painful stimulation is an aversive stimulus, but in this case, those same stimuli are functioning as reinforcers. We could say that the behavior (frequenting the club) increases in frequency because it is followed by whiplashes and then deduce that the whiplashes must be appetitive. But that is a circular argument: whipping is appetitive because it reinforces the behavior; the behavior is reinforced because the whiplashes are appetitive. As Catania (2013, p. 95) rightly points out, "Masochism is just a name we use when a stimulus that should be a punisher serves as a reinforcer; it does not explain anything." In summary, Thorndike's law of effect offers no conclusive answer to the question of which stimuli will act as reinforcers or punishers because it is difficult to determine in advance which stimuli will be appetitive or aversive, and there is little explanatory value in determining it after the effect is observed.[4]

– Hull: Drives

Defining appetitive and aversive in mental terms (such as *motivation*) also does not solve the problem. For instance, Hull (1943, 1952) attempted to explain why certain stimuli serve to reinforce or punish behavior better than others, by assuming that each organism has certain **drives** or **needs** and will strive to achieve an optimal level of satisfaction of those needs. He assumed that stimuli that satisfy a certain need are appetitive and can be used as reinforcers (e.g., food, drink, heat). More recently, Dickinson and Balleine (1995) argued that it is insufficient that the stimuli meet a need; one must also learn that they meet a need (see box 3.1). But in the end, the concept of "need" does not help us to describe which stimuli will lead to reinforcement as an effect. After all, it is also difficult to determine in advance with 100 percent certainty which stimuli will satisfy which needs. Although Hull tried to define needs in terms of the observable environment, his concept of "drives" still has a theoretical edge that goes beyond what is present in the environment (see MacCorquodale & Meehl, 1948). Arguably, it is because of this mental nature of the concept "needs" that it is difficult to determine on an a priori basis which stimuli meet which needs. Hence, it also does not offer a definite answer to the question of which stimuli will function as a reinforcer or a punisher.

– Neural processes: Dopamine

Instead of determining the reinforcing value of stimuli in terms of mental processes such as the gratification of needs or drives, one might be tempted to determine it on the basis of neural processes. In the case of masochism, for example, we could look at the presence of dopamine in the brain (the so-called reward hormone). If we see that being whipped leads to an increase in dopamine in the recipient's brain, we might conclude that the lashes are appetitive and thus reinforcing (see Izuma, Kennedy, Fitzjohn, Sedikides, & Shibata, 2018, for an example of such an approach). The problem with this approach is that it assumes that the release of dopamine provides a perfect and exclusive indicator of how appetitive a stimulus is (such an indicator is also called a proxy). From experience, we know that indicators of a certain mental state or process are seldom perfect, if only because nearly all indicators are influenced by multiple mental processes (De Houwer, 2011b). For example, what would you conclude if research shows that a behavior decreases in frequency when it is followed by a stimulus that elicits dopamine? Does this mean that the law of effect is wrong, or that dopamine is not a

---

Box 3.1 Incentive Learning: Learning the Reinforcing Value of Stimuli

According to Dickinson and Balleine (1995), organisms can learn about the extent to which stimuli meet certain needs. Imagine that a group of rats is first deprived of food. In this deprived state, half of them are given access to a new food, which allows them to experience that this food can alleviate their hunger. Next, both groups of rats are given access to food. In this undeprived state, they learn to press a lever in order to gain the new food. For the crucial test, the rats are again food-deprived. During this test, the rats that initially had access to the food while being hungry more vigorously pressed the lever than the group that did not have prior experience with the food while being hungry (Balleine, 1992). Hence, it seems as if the food has a higher value for the first group of rats, most likely because they had learned that the new food can alleviate their hunger; that is, they learned that it meets a need.

This is a very important finding because it can explain why the reinforcing value of the same stimulus can vary greatly from individual to individual. For example, for some people, alcohol is a very strong reinforcer; they will do all kinds of things if it helps them to get an alcoholic drink. It may be that these people have learned that alcohol can have positive effects (e.g., that it can trigger a pleasant intoxication or that it can reduce stress), whereas people who are not attracted by alcohol have previously experienced mainly the negative effects of alcohol (e.g., nausea). For this reason, the idea of **incentive learning** has had a lot of influence in research on addiction. However, because of the reliance on (semi-) mental concepts such as needs, the ideas of Dickinson and Balleine (1995)—like those of Hull (1943, 1952)—are situated at the mental level of explanation rather the functional level, and therefore add little to a functional description of (the stimuli that give rise to) reinforcement.

perfect indicator of the appetitive nature of a stimulus? It is important to dwell on questions such as these because many contemporary psychologists seem to regard neural processes as more important than how an organism behaves (see Schwartz, Lilienfeld, Meca, & Sauvigné, 2016, for an excellent discussion of the relation between neuroscience and psychology).

– Premack: Natural frequency of behavior

Premack (1962) introduced a completely new perspective on the nature of the Sr, which readily fits within a functional approach. The radically new aspect to Premack's perspective was that he saw reinforcers as responses and not as stimuli. Take the typical example of a rat pressing a lever and receiving food. Traditionally, the food or the administration of the food is seen as the reinforcer. Premack, however, saw eating the food as the reinforcing element. The reinforcer is therefore a response—an act, such as eating food. From this perspective, one particular behavior (e.g., pressing a lever) makes possible another behavior (e.g., eating). A second insight is that behaviors differ in the frequency with which they are performed in situations where there are no restrictions on these behaviors. Suppose an animal is placed in a room where it can press a lever and where it has unlimited access to food. One will find that it will spend more time eating than pressing the lever. Eating is thus a behavior with a higher frequency than lever pressing. On the basis of both insights, Premack formulated a principle that is now known as the **Premack principle**: if performing behavior (A) creates the possibility of performing a higher frequency behavior (B), then the frequency of behavior (A) will increase. In other words, the opportunity to perform a high frequency behavior (e.g., eating) serves to reinforce behavior with a lower natural frequency (e.g., pressing a lever).

– Timberlake and Allison (1974): The response deprivation model

Later, Premack's principle was adapted by Timberlake and Allison (1974) to create the **response deprivation model** (see Timberlake, 1984, and Timberlake & Farmer-Dougan, 1991, for an extension). The response deprivation model adds a new element to the equation: situational frequency—that is, the frequency of behavior in a specific situation. Imagine that an animal presses the lever and suddenly receives enough food for a whole week. According to Premack's principle, eating food is a very frequent behavior and will therefore be a strong reinforcer for lever pressing. Yet according to the response deprivation model, when food is readily available, in that situation the food loses its reinforcing value because the frequency with which the "eating" behavior can occur is equal to the natural frequency of this behavior; the animal now has so much food that it can eat as often as it likes. Therefore, a behavior will function as a Sr only if the situational frequency of that behavior differs from the natural frequency. Research provides support for the response deprivation model: the frequency of lever pressing does not rise when lever pressing is followed by a lot of food. You can also understand punishment from this same perspective: the compulsory performance of behavior (e.g., forced labor) can be seen as behavior whose situational frequency is higher than the natural frequency. If you link a behavior to the compulsory performance of another behavior, the first behavior will decrease in frequency (Premack, 1971).

Note that neither Premack's principle nor the response deprivation model make any assumptions about mental processes. The impact of an Sr is defined only in terms of environment and behavior—namely, how often this behavior is performed when there are no restrictions on behavior (i.e., the natural frequency of behavior) and how often the behavior is performed in the current situation (i.e., situational frequency of behavior). Despite the elegance of these ideas, both have been criticized. They stand or fall with guidelines on how to assess the natural frequency of behavior, which is not always so simple. Bouton (2016, p. 280) gives the following example: suppose you want to check the natural frequency of sex and coffee drinking for a certain person. When assessed over a twenty-four-hour period, it is likely that a person will spend more time drinking coffee than having sex, even when both coffee and a sexual partner are constantly available. Hence, based on a twenty-four-hour test, you would decide that drinking coffee has a higher natural frequency than sex. The result will probably be different if you do the same test during a more limited thirty-minute period in which both coffee and the partner of the person is available in a private context. So the estimate of natural frequency will depend heavily on the design of the test. This is problematic because it is not always clear what the most appropriate design of the test should be.

– Conclusion: The function of an Sr cannot be reduced to its physical characteristics
Taken together, it should be clear that the function of an Sr (i.e., the extent to which it functions as a reinforcer or punisher) cannot be deduced from just the physical characteristics of the stimulus itself. First, Premack's principle draws attention to the fact that the function of a Sr is highly dependent on the behavior that the Sr is related to. The same Sr (for example, the chance for a rat to run in an exercise wheel) will lead to reinforcement if it is related to an R that has a lower natural frequency (e.g., the pressing a lever will increase if it leads to the chance to run in the wheel) but not if R has an even higher natural frequency than Sr (e.g., eating food pellets will not increase in frequency if it leads to the chance of running in an exercise wheel). This brings us to a first important conclusion: *you cannot predict the effect of an Sr without taking into account the behavior to which it is linked* (Catania, 2013, p. 78). Second, the response deprivation model implies that the broader context in which the organism is located is also crucial. Even if you keep R constant, the effect of an Sr will be highly dependent on the specific situation. For instance, food will not cause an increase in lever pressing if the animal already has sufficient food.

In short, the functioning of an Sr (i.e., the effect that this stimulus has on the behavior to which it is related) can never be determined solely on the basis of the physical characteristics of the stimulus. On the one hand, this is a sobering conclusion because it implies that one can never be completely certain whether a certain Sr (e.g., food) will lead to reinforcement (increase in frequency of R) or punishment (decrease in frequency of R). On the other hand, this conclusion encourages us to pay even more attention to the moderators of operant conditioning. Operant conditioning is not a simple process in which stimuli such as food or money always function as reinforcers (see box 3.6). We can try to predict the effect of an Sr on the basis of the effect that Sr had in the past and on what we know about the current situation. But the question of whether an Sr functions as a reinforcer or a punisher can be answered with certainty only after the fact, by examining the influence it had on the behavior with which it was linked.

b) Changes in the characteristics of the Sr Even though we do not know exactly which characteristics of the Sr will determine the nature of the change in behavior, it is clear that changes in the properties of the Sr can have an influence on operant behavior. This can be inferred from an experiment by Colwill and Rescorla (1985; see also Adams & Dickinson, 1981). In rats, two different behaviors were learned in a first phase, each of which was linked to a specific outcome. For instance, when they pressed a lever, they received food, and when they pulled a chain, they received a sucrose solution to drink. In a second phase, both the lever and the chain are removed from the cage and either the food or the drink is subjected to an aversion procedure: in one condition, lithium is given after drinking but not after eating; in a second condition, lithium follows eating but not drinking. In both cases, the rat feels nauseous due to the lithium. At the end of this second phase, you see that the animals from the first condition no longer drink but still eat, while the animals from the second group no longer eat but still drink. That is, one of the reinforcers has been devalued. In a third phase, the handle and the chain are placed back in the cage. The behavior that used to lead to the aversive Sr (pulling the chain for the first condition and pressing the lever for the second condition) is, from the outset, less frequent than the behavior that used to lead to the other Sr.[5] We can therefore conclude that the reinforcing effect of an R-Sr relation can be nullified by subsequently making the Sr aversive. This effect is often referred to as the *reinforcer (Sr) devaluation effect.*

Think It Through 3.1: Devaluation Effects

When reading about the study of Colwill and Rescorla (1985), what kind of findings in classical conditioning are you reminded of? What do you think the implications are for theories about the representations important in operant conditioning?

3.2.2 The Nature of the Observed Behavior

3.2.2.1 Influences on voluntary and involuntary behavior? It is often thought that only controlled (voluntary) behavior (e.g., pressing a lever) can be influenced by the relation between behavior and stimuli in the environment. However, there are indications that autonomic reactions (involuntary behavior; e.g., heart rate, electrical activity in the brain) may also depend on R-Sr relations. A distinction can be made between **direct and indirect operant conditioning** of such autonomic reactions. The indirect form is quite obvious. Many autonomic reactions can be influenced via controlled behavior. For example, it is possible to influence electrical activity in the brain (as measured by EEG) by closing one's eyes, or to increase one's heart rate by breathing in and out several times. If someone gives you money every time your heart rate goes above a hundred beats per minute, then you can indirectly try to produce that rate by repeatedly walking up and down stairs.

In order to conclude that direct operant conditioning of autonomic reactions has occurred, one has to be sure that the observed effect is not an instance of indirect operant conditioning. In other words, one has to be sure that the observed impact of the R-Sr relation on the autonomic reaction is not mediated by a change in a controlled behavior. To this end, Miller and DiCara (1967; Miller, 1969) worked out the following procedure. Rats were injected with a drug (curare), which resulted in total muscle paralysis. An oxygen device was used to control their breathing. During this paralysis, the researchers installed a contingency between the animal's heart rate and the administration of electrical stimulation to a pleasure center in the brain. In the original studies, this relation had an impact on the heart rate of the animal. However, this effect could not be reproduced in subsequent replications of this study. Hence, it remains an unresolved question to what extent one can directly influence autonomic reactions via reinforcement or punishment (see Taub, 2010, for an overview of the available research).

In the meantime, however, the studies of Miller (Miller & DiCara, 1967; Miller, 1969) stimulated applied research on the benefits of biofeedback in clinical settings (see Binnun, Golland, Davidovitch, & Rolnick, 2010, for a review). In biofeedback procedures, information is provided about biological functions (e.g., heart rate, patterns of brain activity) and people are given the task to try to influence these functions (e.g., to lower heart rate). Researchers have repeatedly observed that people can succeed in this task, usually by forming mental images (e.g., thinking of a relaxing situation such as resting on a beach can result in a decrease in heart rate). It is not clear whether these effects should be regarded as direct or indirect forms of operant conditioning of autonomic reactions, but they have huge applied value and are indeed used in many kinds of contexts (see Gaume, Vialatte, Mora-Sanchez, Ramdani, & Vialatte, 2016, for an analysis).

3.2.2.2 The nature of the change in behavior

a) Different aspects of behavior and why they matter   Regularities involving behavior and stimuli in the environment not only have an influence on different types of behaviors, they can also influence different aspects of the same behavior. Earlier, we saw that an R-Sr relation can lead to an increase (reinforcement) or decrease in the frequency of a behavior (punishment). Yet, behavior has many other characteristics in addition to frequency. For example, pressing a lever can be described not only in terms of how often the lever is pressed but also in terms of the force with which the lever is pressed, the way it is pressed (e.g., with which body parts), and the speed with which it is pressed (e.g., number of times per minute). The point here is that many different characteristics of behavior can be influenced by operant conditioning procedures. For instance, the force with which an animal presses the handle can be influenced by feeding the animal as soon as it presses with the desired force. One can also slow down the speed at which the animal presses the handle by giving it food only if it waits a certain amount of time between one lever press and the next. Another good example is the variability of behavior: suppose that a piece of food is given to a rat every time it presses the handle in a way it has not pressed the lever before. For instance, the first time, it might press with the right paw and receive food. If it presses again with the right paw, it will not get food. But if it presses with the left paw, it will receive food. The third time, it will not receive food if it presses with the right or the left paw, but it will if it presses in a different way (e.g., with both paws simultaneously), and so on. When the operant contingencies are arranged in this way, one will see an increase in the variability with which the rat presses the lever (e.g., Neuringer, 2002). In other words, when creative behavior is reinforced, organisms will exhibit more creative behavior. This conclusion goes against the preconception that operant conditioning always leads to simple, rigid, and stereotyped behavior; that is the case only if simple, rigid, and stereotypical behavior is reinforced. More generally, it is important to realize that different aspects of behavior can be changed depending on what characteristics of behavior determine the delivery of the Sr.

Once again, the concept of a "unit of behavior" is very important. As we previously mentioned, the unit of behavior is the criterion used to delineate the class of behaviors that is related to a certain outcome (i.e., the response class). In principle, a researcher can focus on and define any property of behavior as the unit of behavior they are interested in, from very specific characteristics such as the degree to which a lever is moved downward (as with the lever-pressing behavior) to very abstract features such as the extent to which behavior is new (as in studies on creativity). Which unit of behavior you use to delineate the response class will determine what kind of change in behavior you will get. For example, if you allow each new (i.e., never before emitted) behavior to be followed by the delivery of food, this will lead to an increase in the number of new behaviors. The operant behavior is then "performing a new behavior." If you provide food only when the animal waits for a period after pressing the lever and before pressing it again, then the animal will start pressing that lever less quickly. The operant behavior is then "pressing the lever at long intervals."

The above examples provide us with crucial information about how best to think of operant conditioning. First, it becomes clear that operant behavior is never an individual behavior but always a class of behaviors (i.e., a response class). For example, if food is presented after each new behavior is emitted, then by definition, the response class consists of many different behaviors (e.g., pressing the lever with the left leg, with the right leg, with the snout). But if you think about it, no behavior is ever performed twice in exactly the same way (e.g., one time you will press the lever a bit harder than another time). So we always need to think in terms of response classes (i.e., sets of behaviors that have something in common with each other). The element that the behaviors within a class have in common is the unit of behavior. Secondly, it becomes clear that we need to take the unit of behavior into account if we truly want to understand operant conditioning effects. To illustrate why, let's return to the example of reinforcing novel behavior.

If you look at each individual behavior (e.g., pressing the lever with the left paw), you would mistakenly decide that the relation between that behavior and receiving food leads to a decrease in the frequency of that specific behavior. After all, once this specific behavior has been emitted once, it will never be emitted again, because it is no longer new. However, when we shift our thinking and define our unit in terms of "novel behavior," then we see that novel behavior becomes more frequent if every novel behavior is followed by food. So what is reinforced is not the individual behavior but the class of behavior as it was delineated on the basis of the chosen unit of behavior (in this case, the fact that the behavior is novel). We come to a similar conclusion based on the example in which rats receive food only when they wait for a certain period of time before they press the lever again (Catania, 2013, p. 126). As a result of this procedure, the frequency of lever pressing decreases. If we see "lever pressing" as the unit of behavior (i.e., bringing about a downward movement of the lever), we come to the strange conclusion that the frequency of lever pressing decreases because it is sometimes followed by food. However, if we see "slow lever pressing" as the unit of behavior (i.e., a pattern of lever presses where a certain period of time is expected between each response), then we see that this pattern increases in frequency when it is always followed by food. In short, we need to take the properties of behavior into consideration when we think about operant conditioning, and without this insight, it is impossible to fully appreciate the richness of operant conditioning itself.

b) Shaping: Creating new behavior   So far, we have considered only situations in which the unit of behavior (and thus the class of responses that is followed by an Sr) remains constant. However, the unit of behavior can also change over time. In this way, behavior can be

systematically **shaped** to the point that completely new behavior arises. Indeed, even prototypical operant behaviors such as pressing a lever are often new behaviors that have been
established via shaping procedures. For instance, a rat will seldom or never press a lever the
first time it is placed in a Skinner box. However, it will already be familiar with the different
behavioral components involved in pressing a lever (e.g., standing on its hind legs, bringing one or more legs forward, pressing the legs down on an object). What is new, then, is
the sequence in which these behaviors have to be made, and this sequence forms the **molar
behavior** "pressing a lever" (see http://www.youtube.com/watch?v=0tYUS5ljGhI).

Shaping as an effect (i.e., systematic changes in behavior through a gradual change in the
unit of behavior) can be achieved only because there are always differences between the
specific behaviors within each class of behavior. To illustrate why, let's return to the idea of
lever pressing (see figure 3.3). During a first phase, a reinforcer is delivered each time the rat
presses a lever, regardless of how hard it presses. Initially, the rat presses the lever with an
average force of 52, but the force of pressing varies between 16 and 88 (distribution on the
left). During a second phase, a reinforcer is delivered only if the rat presses with a force of
64 or more. As a result, the rat starts pressing the lever harder, with a force ranging from 40
to 112, averaging 76 (distribution on the right). Hence, behavior that never occurred before
(e.g., pressing with a force of 112) has been shaped. This shaping procedure can be continued
step-by-step. For instance, during a third phase, one could deliver a reinforcer only if the rat
presses the lever with a force of 88 or more. This will again shift the distribution of responses
to the right, as the rat presses the lever even harder than before.

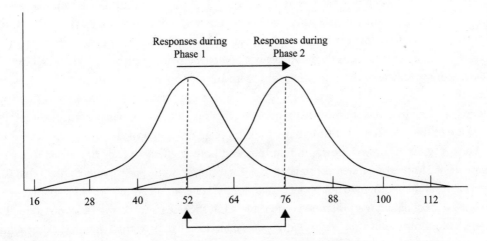

Figure 3.3
An example of shifting distributions of behavior that result from the application of a shaping procedure.

Domjan (2000, pp. 90–91) gives the following example of how shaping is important also for understanding human behavior:

> Riding a bicycle, for example, involves three rather large response components, steering, pedaling, and maintaining balance. Children learning to ride usually start by learning to pedal. Pedaling is a new response. It is unlike anything a child is likely to have done before getting on a bicycle. To enable the child to learn to pedal without having to balance, parents usually start by giving a child a tricycle or a bicycle with training wheels. While learning to pedal, the child is not likely to pay much attention to steering and will need help to make sure she does not drive into a bush or off the side walk.
>
> Once the child has learned to pedal, she is ready to combine this with steering. Only after the child has learned to combine pedaling with steering is she ready to add the balance component. Adding the balance component is the hardest part of the task. That is why parents often wait until a child is proficient riding a bicycle with training wheels before letting her ride without them.

Note that shaping can be viewed as the ontological evolution of a new behavior (i.e., the development of a new behavior during the lifetime of an organism). Like the phylogenetic evolution of new characteristics and behaviors of a species, shaping, too, is dependent on variability (Skinner, 1984). There must be variability in behavior for the desired behavior to be reinforced. It is thanks to variability in behavior that one can shape (step-by-step) a completely new behavior.

c) The relation between different conditioned changes in behavior Like classical conditioning with humans, operant conditioning with humans appears to arise only after a change occurs in the judgment about the relation between the behavior and the stimulus (e.g., Lovibond & Shanks, 2002; Vadillo et al., 2016). In cognitive terms, one would say that humans need to be aware of the relation between R and Sr in order for this relation to influence behavior. Since the mid-twentieth century, attempts have been made to show that operant conditioning can occur without awareness of the contingency between R and Sr. In one of these studies, researchers tried to influence the language use of a participant by providing verbal reinforcement. More specifically, the researcher said "Mm-hmm" in a positive, affirmative way every time the participant used a plural (e.g., "chairs" instead of "chair"). Results showed that this indeed resulted in an increase in the frequency of using plurals. Yet, participants were totally unaware of the rule that the researcher was using (e.g., Greenspoon, 1955).

Further research showed, however, that the conditioning effect was due to the fact that participants had learned a different, correlated rule. For example, some participants thought that the researcher would like them to talk about certain topics. For example, when they talk about jewels, they use a lot of plurals (e.g., diamonds and rubies) and the researcher showed a lot of interest by saying "Mm-hmm" quite frequently. Participants consciously noticed this relation (talking about jewelry [R] leads to interest from the researcher [Sr]). They therefore continued to talk about that topic and therefore used many plurals (see Dulany, 1961; Shanks & St. John, 1994).

This example clarifies a more general problem with studies on unconscious learning. If one measures conscious knowledge about contingencies in the environment, one should check not only whether the participant is aware of the rule used by the researcher but also whether the participant is aware of other, correlated rules that could also lead to a change in behavior.[6] The rule "talk about jewels because the researcher likes that" differs from the rule used by the researcher ("give a positive reaction when the participant uses a plural"), but the application of either of these rules leads to the same result (e.g., using plurals more often). The rules are therefore correlated. To be certain that the rule of the researcher had an impact on behavior even though the participant is unaware of this rule, one must be certain not only that the participant is unaware of that rule but also that the participant did not consciously detect and follow another rule that is correlated with the rule of the researcher. When examining the evidence for unconscious learning in more detail, a lot of effects appear to be actually the result of conscious learning of a correlated rule (see Shanks & St. John, 1994, Lovibond & Shanks, 2002, Mitchell et al., 2009, and Vadillo et al., 2016, for reviews).

Other research shows that behavior is a function of "conscious" (in the sense that they can be verbally reported) knowledge about the relations between behavior and stimuli in the environment, even when this knowledge is not in accordance with the actual relations in the environment. For instance, if participants think that the researcher would like them to use singulars, they will use singulars even if the researcher reinforces the use of plurals. In this context, Skinner made a distinction between rule-governed and contingency-governed behavior in humans (Skinner, 1966, 1969). The distinction refers to the unique role that language can play in regulating the behavior of people. Language rules or instructions can be formulated so that they influence operant behavior—often, regardless of the nature of the actual reinforcement schedule. These rules or instructions can be communicated via verbal messages given by others, but they can also be developed by the person who shows the learning effect, based on his or her own experiences. Regardless of the source of the rule, once the rule has been formulated, it regulates subsequent behavior. We will return to this point later in the chapter (and in chapter 4) when we consider the role that rules and language play in learning.

3.2.3 The Properties of the Organism
Like classical conditioning, operant conditioning can be found in all kinds of living organisms, ranging from very simple ones such as snails and fruit flies to very complex organisms such as humans. For example, fruit flies will spend more time in a room where they often come into contact with food than in a room where they never access food. Because the genetic code of fruit flies is relatively simple, it is possible to find out which genes are important for the occurrence of operant conditioning (see Brembs, 2003, for an overview). The fact that operant conditioning is influenced by **intrinsic relations** (i.e., between the R and the

Sr and between the Sd and the R) suggests that genetic makeup may be important for other organisms as well.

3.2.4 The Influence of the Broader Context

The impact of a certain Sd: R-Sr relation on behavior is moderated by events in the broader context in which other stimuli and behaviors are involved, without these events being part of or having an influence on the nature of the Sd: R-Sr relation. In this section, we discuss the moderating impact of two types of contextual events: Other S:R-Sr relations and establishing operations.

3.2.4.1 Other Sd: R-Sr relations

The influence of a certain Sd: R-Sr relation is always dependent on the presence of other Sd: R-Sr relations in the environment. First, it is important to look at all the options that an organism has in a given situation. Suppose that pressing a lever is followed by food. The extent to which this will influence behavior depends on whether there are other behaviors that can also lead to food or other (perhaps more important) outcomes. As we shall see in section 3.2.5.3, each behavior implies a choice: if one performs behavior A (e.g., press a lever), one cannot simultaneously perform behavior B (e.g., rest). What behavior one carries out is dependent not only on the consequences of that behavior, but also on the consequences of other behavior that can be emitted in the broader context in which one is present. This offers an interesting (additional) tool for changing behavior: differential reinforcement of other behavior (DRO). Catania (2013, p. 74) gives the following example of DRO. Suppose you are confronted with a developmentally delayed child who shows self-injurious behavior (e.g., constantly banging his head against a wall). One might try to punish the behavior, but as we will later discuss, this may have negative side effects (see box 3.4). One could also try to remove the regularity that maintains the problem behavior. But sometimes it is not clear what actually sustains this behavior. Even if it is clear which regularity in the environment is crucial (e.g., the child emits this behavior because it leads to attention from caregivers), often it is not easy to change that regularity (e.g., not paying attention to a child who injures himself is unethical to do). An alternative solution is to reinforce a different behavior, preferably a behavior that cannot be performed together with self-injurious behavior (e.g., pay more attention to the child when he is still well-behaved). DRO can therefore be a useful technique for changing behavior.

Second, the impact of one Sd: R-Sr relation seems to depend on how *unique* that relation is in a given context. Suppose you want to teach a pigeon to peck a left button when a green light is lit and a right button when a red light is lit. In one condition, every time the pigeon responds correctly, it receives the same type of food, regardless of whether it pecks the left or right button. In the second condition, it also gets food for each correct answer, but now that food has a different shape or flavor after pecking the left button (e.g., round shape) than after pecking the right button (e.g., square shape). Research shows that more correct answers are given in the second than in the first condition. This shows that you can facilitate learning by making a difference in the outcomes of different behaviors. This effect is called the *differential outcomes effect* (DOE). It has very important pedagogical implications. For example, when working with people who have learning difficulties, one can facilitate learning by making the outcomes of different behaviors more distinctive (see Mok, Estevez, & Overmier, 2010).

3.2.4.2 Establishing operations   All sorts of aspects of the broader context will determine to what extent an Sr will function as a reinforcer or punisher. Think back to the example of the rat pressing a lever (R) and receiving a food pellet (Sr). This R-Sr relation will have much more impact (a faster increase in the frequency of lever pressing) when the rat has not eaten for a long time before the experiment. Such an intervention is called *food deprivation*: a delay between the current delivery of food and the last time the rat ate. In mental process terms, one would say that this intervention ensures that the rat is "motivated" to eat and therefore quickly learns that it can get food by pressing the lever. In the functional approach, however, one goes no further than (relations between) environment and behavior and speaks of interventions that influence the reinforcing value of the Sr. We refer to such procedures that alter the reinforcing or punitive value of a Sr as *establishing operations*; in the above example, food deprivation increases the reinforcing value of the Sr. Just as the functional approach provides the input for theories about the mental processes that mediate learned behavior, so too can the study of established operations provide insights into the mental processes that mediate motivational behavior (e.g., Bouton, 2016, chapter 9). However, we limit ourselves here to the functional level.

We can assume that certain events function as an establishing operation (i.e., have an establishing function) from birth onward (e.g., food deprivation; see Michael, 2004, p. 50, for an overview). Other events have an establishing function that has been learned at some point during the lifetime of the organism. Often these are events that occurred together in the past with the presence of certain outcomes. Consider, for example, the smell of freshly brewed coffee. The mere presence of the smell often ensures that the reinforcing value of coffee increases (e.g., people may make more of an effort to get coffee after they have been exposed to the smell of coffee than when they have not smelled coffee). This example also makes clear that not only complex interventions (e.g., deprivation) but also single stimuli (e.g., an odor or sound) can have an establishing function. Moreover, it allows us to distinguish two subtly different effects of establishing events (see also Michael, 2004, pp. 45–47). First of all, there is a *retrospective* effect (also referred to as an *evocative effect*): the establishing event influences the impact of old R-Sr relations on current behavior. Suppose you learned in the past that you can buy nice coffee in a certain store. The smell of fresh coffee increases the chance that you will go to that store to buy coffee. The relation between that store and coffee was already present in the past; the smell of coffee only strengthens the effect of that old R-Sr relation on current behavior. Second, there is a *prospective* effect (also called a *reinforcer-establishing effect*): the establishing event determines the extent to which new R-Sr experiences have an influence on behavior. Imagine that you are walking in a shopping mall and you smell freshly brewed coffee. A few moments later, you enter a new coffee bar that you have never been to before and you drink coffee in that bar. After that experience, you find yourself repeatedly returning to that specific coffee bar more than to other coffee bars. From a functional perspective, one could say that going to the new coffee bar is a new behavior (R) that increases in frequency because of the relation between that behavior and drinking a nice cup of coffee (Sr). Importantly, the impact of this novel R-Sr relation on behavior was amplified by the smell of fresh coffee that you experience just before entering the coffee bar. In other words, the smell functioned as an establishing operation in that it increased the reinforcing value of drinking coffee. Without that smell, the novel R-Sr relation would have a smaller effect on future behavior (i.e., you would not have returned so often to that specific coffee shop).

Finally, we should point out a subtle but important distinction between stimuli that function as Sds and stimuli that function as establishing operations. Both types of stimuli moderate the impact of R-Sr relations on behavior. The difference between the two is the reason why they have this moderating effect. When it comes to stimuli with an Sd function, these stimuli have this function because, at the descriptive (procedural) level, they indicate when the R-Sr relation holds (i.e., when a response will lead to a certain consequence). Take the example of a light that indicates that pressing a lever will be followed by food. The light is a stimulus that influences behavior because it indicates what consequences will follow that behavior. In contrast to Sds, the presence of an establishing operation can be completely unrelated to the presence of the R-Sr relation. For instance, at the descriptive (procedural) level, lever pressing will be followed by food regardless of whether the animal has been deprived beforehand.

This distinction may become clearer if we take the example of a torch that works using batteries (see Catania, 2013, p. 25). Imagine that on the torch there is a small red light that indicates whether the batteries are still charged. This light is an Sd: pressing the power button on the flashlight (R) will result only in the flashlight (Sr) shining when the red indicator is on. However, the chance that you press the "on" button also depends on the broader context. It is more likely that you will turn the flashlight on when you are in a dark room than when you are in a well-lit room. The lighting of the room functions as an establishing operation: the shining of the flashlight has a higher reinforcing value when you are in a dark than well-lit room. However, the brightness of the room has no influence whatsoever on the chance that pressing the button (R) will be followed by the illumination of the flashlight (Sr). Thus, both the indicator light and the brightness of the room have an impact on behavior, but for different reasons.

Nevertheless, we should also note that stimuli can function simultaneously as an Sd and as an establishing operation. For instance, a light indicating that lever pressing will be followed by food will itself often occur together with the food: whenever the rat presses the lever after seeing the light, the food will be presented shortly after the presentation of the light. The light can therefore increase the frequency of lever pressing for two reasons: (1) because it indicates that lever pressing is followed by food (which is the Sd function of the light), and (2) because it increases the reinforcing value of food as the result of the light-food pairings (which is the establishing function of the light). The fact that one stimulus can have multiple functions also demonstrates the need to always make a distinction between procedures and functions (see also section 3.1.1.1). A stimulus that is descriptively an Sd (i.e., that signals when an R-Sr relation holds) can function not only as an Sd (influence R because it signals the R-Sr relation) but also as an establishing operation (influence R because it determines the reinforcing value of Sr) or in many other ways. The function of a stimulus cannot be determined by simply looking at the topography of a procedure (i.e., what it looks like or how we assume it works).

3.2.5   The Nature of the Relation

3.2.5.1 Contingency is more important than contiguity   Just as the contingency between a CS and a US is determined by the difference between the probability of the US given the CS [p(US/CS)] and the probability of the US given the absence of the CS [p(US/~CS)], the contingency between an R and Sr is determined by the difference between the probability of the Sr

---

Box 3.2 Imprinting as an Establishing Operation

Many people are familiar with the image of Lorenz (1937) being followed by a row of little ducks because he was the first moving object they saw after they hatched from their eggs. Normally, the first moving object they see is the mother duck, and they will follow her. But Lorenz showed that they will follow any moving object (including Lorenz himself) as long as it is the first moving object they see. Based on what we have just learned, what is the function of the first object that ducks see? A first possibility is that the object reflexively elicits a tracking behavior: when they see the object, they walk behind it. A second possibility is that the proximity of the object is a reinforcer: any behavior that leads to the proximity of the object will increase in frequency. Research supports the second option (Peterson, 1960; see Catania, 2013, p. 53). Research shows that ducks learn to peck on a key or even to stand still if this behavior results in their ability to see their mother duck. But the proximity of the mother duck had a reinforcing function only if the mother duck was the first moving object they saw after they came out of the egg. We can therefore conclude that the closeness of the mother duck has the function of a reinforcer because they saw the mother duck immediately after birth. In other words, seeing the mother duck immediately after birth is an establishing operation: it increases the reinforcing value of closeness of the mother duck.

given the R [p(Sr/R)] and the probability of the Sr in the absence of R [p(Sr/~R)]. In other words, operant conditioning is highly dependent on the degree to which p(Sr/R) differs from p(Sr/~R).

The fact that animals are sensitive to the degree of contingency between an R and Sr was nicely shown by Hammond (1980) in rats. She artificially divided the experiment into periods of one second. Within each period, the rat could either press the lever, which resulted in delivery of food (Sr) with a probability of 0.05 (i.e., only one in twenty lever presses was reinforced), or not press the lever, in which case food was not administered; hence, p(Sr/R) = 0.05 and p(Sr/~R) = 0.00. In this way, there was a positive contingency, albeit minimal, between lever pressing and the delivery of food. Under these conditions, the frequency of R increased. However, once Hammond changed the task so that the probability of food in the absence of a response was equal to 0.05—in other words, once p(Sr/R) = p(Sr/~R)—the rats stopped pressing the lever altogether. It was as if they understood that regardless of what they did, food was delivered equally often. When Hammond introduced this latter contingency at the beginning of the experiment, the rats did not show any evidence of operant behavior.

So contingency matters. Not only is the presence of a contingency important, but the type of contingency (positive or negative) matters too. As with classical conditioning, the effect of positive contingencies between an R and Sr is opposite to the effect of negative contingencies between an R and the same Sr. For some Srs, a positive contingency between R and Sr will lead to an increase in frequency of the behavior (i.e., reinforcement as an effect; e.g., more likely to press a lever when doing so increases the chance that food will be delivered), while a negative contingency between R and Sr will lead to a decrease in the frequency of behavior (i.e., punishment as an effect; e.g., less likely to press a lever when doing so reduces the chances of food). For other Srs, the opposite is true: a positive R-Sr contingency leads to punishment as an effect (e.g., lower chances of pressing the lever if doing so increases the risk of an electric shock), whereas a negative R-Sr contingency leads to reinforcement (e.g., higher chance of pressing the lever if this reduces the risk of electric shock).

As previously mentioned, it is difficult to be completely certain a priori which Sr will function as a reinforcer or punisher (see section 3.2.1.3.a). But the law of effect remains a useful rule of thumb: behavior that leads to seemingly positive outcomes will increase in frequency, while behavior that leads to seemingly negative outcomes will decrease in frequency. Note once more that we speak of "outcomes" (consequences) instead of "stimuli" because not only the presence of a stimulus but also other events can function as an Sr. More specifically, if we start from the position that there is a difference between positive and negative contingencies and a difference between "positive" and "negative" stimuli (although we know that it is difficult to determine a priori whether a stimulus is positive/appetitive or negative/aversive; see section 3.2.1.3.a), then we can make a distinction between four possible outcomes of a behavior: (1) an increase in the chance of a positive outcome; (2) an increase in the chance of a negative outcome; (3) a decrease in the chance of a positive outcome; and (4) a decrease in the chance of a negative outcome. Outcomes (1) and (4) can be regarded as positive outcomes that will usually result in an increase in the frequency of the behavior (i.e., reinforcement as an effect). Outcomes (2) and (3), on the other hand, are negative and will usually lead to a decrease in the frequency of behavior (i.e., punishment as an effect). This idea is schematically shown in table 3.1.

When there is a negative contingency between a R and Sr, there are two ways R can reduce the probability of the Sr. The first is when the Sr is already present and an R leads to the removal of the Sr. As noted earlier, an R that increases in frequency because it causes an Sr to stop or disappear is called an *escape behavior*. For instance, when someone is nagging you incessantly (Sr), you can get up and leave (R). A second way is that an R effectively reduces the chance of the occurrence of the Sr in the first place. As noted earlier, an R that increases in frequency because it leads to a reduction in the probability that a Sr will occur is called *avoidance behavior*. For instance, when you know that talking with a certain person will inevitably lead them to nag you (Sr), you can reduce the chance of that negative event by dodging that person before they come close to you (R).

3.2.5.2 Conditional contingency is more important than contingency

Some findings suggest that *conditional contingencies* are equally important for operant conditioning and classical conditioning. St. Claire-Smith (1979), for example, examined rats that had already learned to press a lever in order to receive food. At a certain point, lever pressing was no longer followed by food, but instead by a mild electric shock. This reduced the frequency of lever pressing. A second group of rats received exactly the same procedure but they also learned (in a previous part of the experiment) that the presence of a light was always followed by a mild electrical shock. The researchers presented this light between the rat's lever pressing and the delivery of the electric shock. In the second group of rats, the reduction in the frequency of lever pressing was much less pronounced. It seems that the contingency between the light and the shock interfered with the learning of the R-shock relation. In functional terms, there was a *conditional contingency effect*: pressing the lever did not influence the probability of shock in

Table 3.1
The effect of operant learning procedures as a function of the type of R-Sr contingency (positive vs. negative) and properties of the Sr (positive vs. negative)

R-Sr contingency	Properties of the Sr	
	Positive	Negative
Positive	Reinforcement effect	Punishment effect
Negative	Punishment effect	Reinforcement effect

those situations where there was a light. Put another way, the chance of receiving a shock was just as great when only the light was present (A+) as when the light was present and lever was pressed (AX+, where A = light and X = press on lever). This finding is similar to blocking in classical conditioning.

3.2.5.3 Reinforcement schedules

a) Four types of partial reinforcement   When an R is always followed by an Sr, one usually speaks of *continuous reinforcement*. In everyday life, however, it is often the case that a certain R is not always followed by an Sr. In such situations, one speaks of *partial reinforcement*. Whenever reinforcement is partial, one must decide when an R is followed by the Sr and when it is not. In doing so, one can follow different schedules. There are, broadly speaking, four different types of (partial) reinforcement schedules (see Michael, 2004, for a more extensive overview): fixed ratio, variable ratio, fixed interval, and variable interval. As can be seen from the names, these four types of schedules emerge when two characteristics are manipulated: a schedule can be fixed or variable, and the administration of the reinforcer can depend on the number of behaviors (a certain ratio between reinforcement and behavior) or on the time interval since the most recent administration of the reinforcer.

In a fixed ratio (FR) schedule, for instance, a reinforcer is delivered every time a certain number of behaviors has been emitted. For example, a fixed ratio 1 to 20 (FR-20) means that a reinforcer (e.g., one food pellet) is delivered every time the organism has performed a certain behavior (e.g., lever pressing) twenty times (see figure 3.4, left). Such fixed ratio schedules are abundant in daily life. Take the example of piecework: workers can be given a certain amount of money every time they finish a certain number of products.

In a variable ratio (VR) schedule, administration of the reinforcer is also dependent on the number of times a behavior is performed, but the number of times a behavior has to be

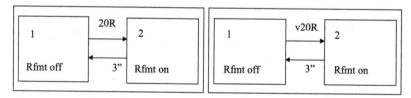

Figure 3.4
A schematic representation of a fixed ratio schedule (left) and a variable ratio schedule (right). In both cases, the transition from a state without a reinforcer (State 1: Rfmt off) to a state with a reinforcer (State 2: Rfmt on) depends on the number of times that a behavior is emitted. With a fixed ratio schedule, this number is constant (e.g., 20R = 20 responses). With a variable ratio schedule, this number is variable (e.g., v20R = on average 20 responses). The transition from State 2 to State 1 happens automatically after a certain time has elapsed (e.g., 3 seconds). Adapted from Michael (2004, p. 86).

performed varies from moment to moment. For example, sometimes a reinforcer is delivered after twenty-two behaviors have been emitted, the next time after seventeen behaviors, then after nineteen behaviors, and so on (see figure 3.4, right). Some gambling machines (e.g., the so-called one-armed bandit) function according to such a schedule. After performing a particular behavior (putting money in the device and pulling a lever) a certain number of times, a reinforcer is delivered (prize money). How many times you have to put money into the device before you win, however, is variable. Nevertheless, the delivery of the reinforcer depends on the number of times the behavior is performed because the device is programmed to provide a winning combination after a variable number of games have been played (which is why gamblers prefer to play on machines that others have played on for a long time without winning).[7]

In a fixed interval (FI) schedule, the first designated behavior that follows a well-defined time interval is reinforced. For example, in a FI-30, the organism receives food the first time it presses the lever after an interval of thirty seconds has elapsed (see figure 3.5). FI schedules are also part and parcel of daily life. Take the example of receiving one's wages or salary. Usually, one gets their salary every month at a fixed time. The pickup of this salary at a counter, for example, can be seen as a behavior that is reinforced according to a FI schedule. After all, this behavior will be reinforced only the first time it is performed after a certain fixed interval. That said, this is not a pure example of an FI schedule, because whether one receives a salary depends also on other behavior (i.e., the quantity and quality of the work that is performed) above and beyond the mere collection of the salary.

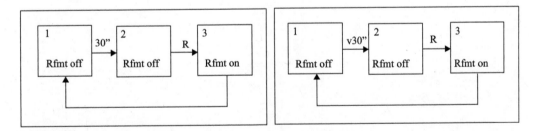

Figure 3.5
A schematic representation of a fixed interval schedule (left) and a variable interval schedule (right). In both cases, the transition is from a state in which the reinforcer is absent and not available (State 1: Rfmt off) to a state in which the reinforcer is absent but available (State 2: Rfmt off). This transition is solely dependent on the course of time. Once in State 2, one will switch to a state with reinforcement (State 3: Rfmt on) as soon as the behavior R is emitted. After a certain period of time in State 3 (e.g., 3 seconds) one will switch back to State 1. The difference between a fixed and a variable interval schedule refers to the time period between State 1 and State 2. With a fixed interval schedule, this time is always the same (e.g., 30 seconds). With a variable interval schedule, this time varies (e.g., 26 seconds, 32 seconds, ... with an average of 30 seconds). Adapted from Michael (2004, p. 86–87).

Finally, in a variable interval (VI) schedule, the reinforcer is presented following the first behavior that is emitted after a variable interval (see figure 3.5). Suppose you try to call someone but the line is busy. Calling them again is a behavior that is reinforced (i.e., you get the person on the line) only after a certain time interval that varies from moment to moment (e.g., sometimes you are immediately successful and sometimes you have to wait half an hour).

b) The influence of reinforcement schedules on the frequency of R   Research shows that there are clear differences in the effects that different schedules have on behavior (Ferster & Skinner, 1957). For example, variable schedules result in much more steady behavior than fixed schedules. We can see this from the cumulative frequency curves in figure 3.6. From such curves, one can deduce how often a behavior (e.g., lever pressing) is emitted over time. Every time a behavior is emitted, the line goes up a little bit. If the line remains flat, it means that no behavior is being emitted at that moment in time. If the line rises slowly, this indicates that the behavior is performed only now and then. If the line rises quickly, this indicates a high frequency of the behavior. From figure 3.6 we can therefore deduce that ratio schedules lead to more frequent behavior than interval schedules do (you can infer this from the fact that the lines for ratio schedules are steeper than for interval schedules). Figure 3.6 also shows that variable schedules lead to more constant behavior than fixed schedules do (you can infer this from the fact

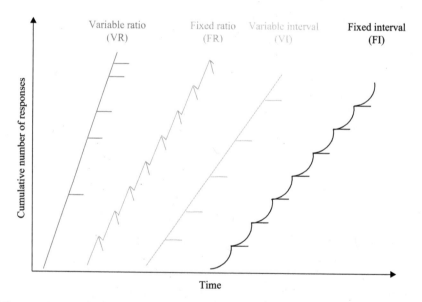

Figure 3.6
Typical cumulative performance curves for variable ratio (VR), fixed ratio (FR), variable interval (VI), and fixed interval (VI) reinforcement schedules.

that the lines for variable schedules are straighter). Cognitive psychologists would immediately wonder which mental processes might produce these kinds of behaviors. Could it be that ratio schedules lead to more motivation to emit a behavior, or that variable schedules lead to more uncertainty about when the reinforcer will be delivered? Although such questions are legitimate, they do not belong at the level of functional psychology. For a functional psychologist, it is sufficient to know that (and how) reinforcement schedules influence behavior. After all, this knowledge can be used to predict when a particular behavior will be emitted more often than another (e.g., that gambling machines that work according to a ratio schedule will be used more often than gambling machines that work according to an interval schedule), and thus also how behavior can be changed (e.g., by adjusting the schedule). Hence, research on reinforcement schedules has many applications, not only in the context of gambling but also in the context of social media use (for an accessible discussion of some of these applications, see https://www.theguardian.com/technology/2019/aug/23/social-media-addiction-gambling).

It is also important to point out that regardless of the schedule that is chosen, partial reinforcement tends to lead to more frequent behavior than continuous reinforcement does. At first this might seem strange because with continuous reinforcement, each behavior is followed by a reinforcer, whereas with partial reinforcement, the behavior is only occasionally followed by a reinforcer. Catania (2013, p. 207) rightly points out that the stronger effect of partial reinforcement can be understood by examining the unit of behavior that determines whether a reinforcer follows. Take the example of an FR-5 (fixed ratio 1 to 5) schedule: a rat has to press a lever five times in order to get one piece of food. Instead of thinking that the behavior "lever pressing" is followed by food in only one of five cases, you could also say that the behavior "pressing the handle five times" is always followed by food. The unit of behavior is thus not "pressing the lever" but "pressing the lever five times." If the behavior "press the lever five times" increases in frequency, the lever will be pressed very often. With variable schedules, the unit of behavior cannot be defined in terms of a fixed number of responses, but in more abstract terms such as "repeatedly pressing." Once again, it becomes clear that a good understanding of operant conditioning is possible only by seeing behavior as not just a certain movement of limbs but a response class that can be aligned on the basis of all sorts of criteria (units). Note that these are analyses that are made by functional researchers who look at the behavior of other organisms. The aim of these functional analyses is not to describe what the organism is thinking (i.e., to uncover the mental causes of behavior) but to arrive at a useful way of describing the behavior and its relation to the environment. Importantly, there is no single correct way of doing so—it is always possible to arrive at different descriptions/analyses of the same behavior. The only criterion for determining the quality of such a description/functional analysis is to see how useful it is—that is, to determine the extent to which it helps the researcher to predict and influence the behavior of interest (see Hayes & Brownstein, 1986).

c) The impact of reinforcement schedules on choice behavior   Reinforcement schedules influence not only the frequency of behavior but also *choice behavior* (i.e., what behavior will be chosen when there are different options available). Choice behavior is very important. In fact, every organism must constantly choose what they will do. At this moment in time, for example, you could write an email, watch TV, or work in the garden. Each of these activities is linked to a certain reinforcement history, and thus the question is, to what extent (based on your reinforcement history) can we predict what your choice here and now will be when there is a choice between different ways of behaving?

Early in learning psychology, a number of experimental procedures were developed in order to answer this question. Historically, it started with the study of nonhuman animals in a T-maze, where the choice given to them was to go either left or right. In a classic article published in 1938, "The Determiners of Behavior at a Choice Point," Tolman argued that all human and nonhuman behavior ultimately constitutes a choice between alternatives, and that a thorough study of the behavior of a rat in a T-maze can be a first step toward a better understanding of choice behavior in other organisms.

Skinner boxes, too, have been used frequently in research on choice behavior. On reflection, it becomes clear that even lever pressing by rats in Skinner boxes constitutes an instance of choice behavior. After all, there is always the choice between pressing the lever (or pecking a key) and "doing something else." However, these behavioral choices in the Skinner box can be made more explicit so that they can be studied in more detail. Most importantly, instead of a single key, two keys can be made available at the same time, each of which is connected to a different reinforcement schedule. Consider the following example. First, we place a pigeon in the Skinner box and make pressing one of the keys (A) result in the delivery of food according to a VI-30 sec schedule. Over time, the pigeon will show a fairly stable and highly frequent rate of behavior. After this happens, we place the second key (B) in the box and make pressing key B result in food according to a VI-10 sec schedule. Over time, the pigeon will lose interest in pressing the first key (A) and instead press (relatively more) on the second key (B). This simple example shows that the performance of a certain behavior is not influenced exclusively by the reinforcement history associated with it, but also by the concurrently present behavioral alternatives that are associated with a different reinforcement schedule. Hence, in this context, one speaks of *concurrent schedules* of reinforcement.

When two behaviors are simultaneously reinforced according to a variable interval schedule, there is a law that describes the relation between (a) the relative frequency with which one of the two alternative behaviors is performed, and (b) the number of reinforcers that each of the alternatives produced. This relation forms the core of what is known as the *matching law*

(Herrnstein, 1970; de Villiers, 1977). In its simplest form, this relation can be represented as follows:

$$RA/RA + RB = r_A/r_A + r_B$$

On the left side of the formula is the relative frequency with which one of the behavioral alternatives (in this case, behavioral alternative A) is emitted. By "relative," we mean the frequency of behavior A in relation to the frequency of both behaviors. If there is no specific preference for A or B, this ratio will be equal to .50. A preference for A or B will lead to a ratio greater than or less than .50, respectively. The right side of the formula expresses the relative reinforcement rate of behavioral alternative A, with rA and rB referring to the number of reinforcers earned by performing behavior A and behavior B, respectively. The matching law points to the fact that there is usually a (fairly) perfect match between both of these ratios.

As with any "law," the matching law is valid only if certain conditions are met. In this case, this law is valid only with variable interval (VI) schedules. With such schedules, it is never certain at what point an interval has elapsed and thus at what point in time a certain behavior is reinforced. That is why it can be useful to continue emitting several behaviors (e.g., sometimes pressing key A but sometimes also key B) because doing so will also lead to the Sr whenever it is the first response after a certain interval. If the two behaviors are reinforced according to a fixed ratio schedule (e.g., FR-10 and FR-25), then the organism will emit only the behavior that is reinforced the most (e.g., FR-10).

The conditional nature of the matching law does not detract from the fact that it is indeed a law. All laws are subject to conditions. Pierce and Cheney (2008, p. 202) illustrate this with the following example. The law of gravity implies that objects with equal mass will fall at an equal rate, but in reality, we see that one kilo of lead falls much more quickly to the ground than one kilo of feathers here on Earth. Thus, predictions derived from of the law of gravity are valid only when we take into account the influence of other elements (such as the resistance of the air). If we drop a kilo of lead and a kilo of feathers into the vacuum of space, then they will indeed fall equally quickly. In everyday life, however, one particular phenomenon (e.g., the speed at which a kilogram of feathers falls) will be a function not only of gravity but also of many other factors. This is particularly true of behavior. Each behavior is probably determined by a huge number of factors, to the extent that you may sometimes get the impression that behavior is itself a random phenomenon that cannot possibly be studied scientifically. But complexity does not exclude that there are laws (of behavior). These laws can be discovered mainly in the laboratory because we can study the influence of one factor or several factors while keeping other factors constant.

The matching law has given rise to a lot of research. This kind of research has also had a big impact on behavioral economics (see Pierce & Cheney, 2008, chap. 9, and Reed, Niileksela, &

Kaplan, 2013, for an overview). The matching law was frequently updated based on this work. For instance, the size of the reinforcer and the time interval of administration (delay) also play a role in some versions of the law. Without going into its mathematical expression (see Schwartz et al., 2002, pp. 224–245), there is a fairly impressive set of findings that has revealed the matching law's heuristic value.

Researchers have gone even further in their attempts to model the complexity of choice behavior. One important experiment is this regard is that of Rachlin and Green (1972), who developed the concurrent-chain procedure, which is often used when studying self-control (see Logue, 1988). Imagine, for instance, that you are given the choice between a small and big reinforcer. You will (rather unsurprisingly) opt for the big reinforcer. Things become more interesting when the delivery of the large reinforcer is delayed and you are asked to choose between either an immediate small reinforcer or a delayed large reinforcer (see figure 3.7, left side). Now, nonhuman animals will often opt for the small immediate reinforcer, with the probability of this choice increasing as the delay for the large reinforcer increases (see Rung & Madden, 2018, for a review). Rachlin and Green (1972) went still one step further by introducing two choices in which the options of the second choice depend on the first choice. In other words, there is a chain of responses (hence the term *concurrent-chain procedure*; see figure 3.7). First, animals have to choose between pecking a left key or a right key. After they peck the left key, they then are given the opportunity to peck another key in order to get a small immediate reinforcer. After they peck the right key, they then have the opportunity to peck a key

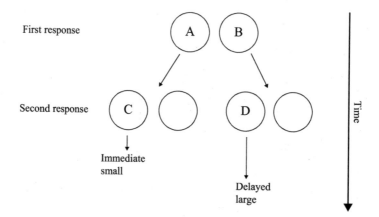

Figure 3.7
Schematic illustration of the concurrent-chain procedure used in Rachlin and Green (1972). If the organism first chooses response A, it is given an opportunity to press a key C for an immediate, small reinforcer. If the organism first chooses response B, it is given an opportunity to press a key D for a delayed, large reinforcer.

that, after a delay, will result in a large reinforcer. Interestingly, on the initial choice, the animals now choose the key that gives them the option to subsequently respond for the delayed large reinforcer (i.e., the right key). In other words, the presence of the initial choice in the concurrent-chain procedure reduces the reinforcing value of the small immediate reinforcer.

This and similar research (see Rung & Madden, 2018, for an overview) has inspired a better understanding of what we mean by self-control and how we can enhance self-control in, for example, hyperactive children (Schweitzer & Sulzer-Azaroff, 1988; see http://www.youtube.com/watch?v=QX_oy9614HQ) or addicts. More specifically, choosing a small immediate reinforcer rather than a large delayed reinforcer is often seen as an instance of impulsive behavior or a failure of self-control. For example, smokers often choose the immediate small reinforcer (smoking a cigarette right now) and thereby reduce the chance of a deferred big reinforcer (longer and healthier life). Studying the conditions under which organisms opt for a small immediate reinforcer over a large delayed reinforcer may provide insights into how to reduce impulsive behavior and increase self-control (see Madden, Price, & Sosa, 2017, for an example of a concrete application in the context of eating behavior).

3.2.5.4 Indirect relations

a) Between R and Sr stimuli   Research on secondary reinforcement has shown that behavior can also be influenced by indirect relations between behavior and stimuli. This research originally took place in the context of Hull's drive theory. As previously mentioned, Hull believed that the reinforcing value of an Sr was determined by the extent to which the stimulus meets a need or drive. Hull distinguished between primary and secondary reinforcers. Primary reinforcers are Sr stimuli that meet a biological or innate need (e.g., food and drink). Secondary reinforcers are (among other things) stimuli that (1) occur together with primary reinforcers, or (2) can be used to obtain other (primary) reinforcers. It has been shown that one can change behavior by relating it to a secondary reinforcer. When this research on secondary reinforcers is disconnected from Hull's theory, we see that it provides evidence for the influence of **indirect relations**: the response never co-occurs directly with the reinforcer but it does co-occur with a neutral stimulus that in turn co-occurs with the reinforcer.

Reinforcement via stimuli that have themselves occurred together with reinforcers is also called *conditioned reinforcement*. To illustrate, imagine that a tone is followed in a contingent manner by food. Afterward, an animal learns to press a lever if this leads to the presentation of the tone. The presentation of the tone thus reinforces lever pressing. Yet, the tone functions as a reinforcer only because it co-occurred with food. The function of one stimulus (e.g., food) can therefore transfer to another stimulus (e.g., tone) as a result of the fact that they co-occur. Note, therefore, that we are dealing here with a special type of classical conditioning—namely, the impact of stimulus presentations on the (reinforcing) function of these stimuli. Conditioned reinforcers play an important role in daily life. Suppose that someone often eats a food with a certain smell. Because of the relation between the smell and the food, the smell becomes a conditioned reinforcer and thus can be used to increase behavior in frequency (e.g., working to gain access to the food that one can smell).[8]

Another type of secondary reinforcer is a stimuli that can be used to obtain other reinforcers. This is known as a *token reinforcer*. A typical example of token reinforcers is money. Often, people will do anything and everything for money. Money is therefore one of the most effective reinforcers. But money in itself does not meet any biological need (e.g., it does not satisfy hunger, thirst, or normally provide heat). Money is effective as a reinforcer because it is linked to obtaining other reinforcers. For example, you can buy food, drinks, or heating with money. Note that token reinforcers can be considered one particular form of conditioned reinforcer. Like other conditioned reinforcers, token reinforcers also co-occur with other (primary) reinforcers. But the relation between token reinforcers and other reinforcers is special. The tokens can be used to obtain other reinforcers. Thus, one has to emit additional behavior (e.g., exchange the tokens or money) so that the primary reinforcers can be obtained. Yet, with other conditioned reinforcers, the relation between the conditioned and primary reinforcers is independent of an additional behavior by the organism.

Both research and daily life show that token reinforcers are a very efficient means of guiding behavior (see Hackenberg, 2009, for an overview of the relevant literature). For instance, in a series of experiments, monkeys were taught that food could be obtained by depositing small plastic discs (like the gambling chips used in casinos) into an apparatus (see Schwartz et al., 2002, pp. 156–160). Afterward, they were taught that they could gain access to these discs or tokens by pressing a lever a certain number of times. They found that the frequency of lever pressing could be influenced to the same extent by tokens as by food. When the trained monkeys were placed together in a cage and tokens were placed in that cage, a battle broke out for possession of the tokens. Some monkeys even started begging for tokens or tried to steal the tokens from other monkeys.

b) Between Sd stimuli and R   So far, we have talked about indirect links only between the R and Sr. Other research has shown that indirect relations between Sds and R can also have an influence on operant conditioning effects. To illustrate, consider a study with rats performed by Colwill and Rescorla (1988).

Phase 1:	Sd1: R1—Sr1
	Sd2: R1—Sr2
Phase 2:	R2—Sr1
	R3—Sr2
Test:	Sd1: R2 or R3?
	Sd2: R2 or R3?

In a first phase, R1 (pressing a button with the nose) was followed by food (Sr1) when a light was turned on (Sd1). The same R1 was followed by sugar water (Sr2) when a tone was presented (Sd2). In the second phase, the rats learned that R2 (pressing a handle) was always followed by food (Sr1) and that R3 (pulling on a chain) was always followed by sugar water (Sr2). Importantly, in this second phase there were no Sds. Finally, in the test phase, the rats had to choose between R2 and R3 (R1 was no longer possible because the button was removed). When they were given the choice during the presentation of the light (Sd1), they opted for R2. However, during the presentation of the tone (Sd2), they chose R3. The Sd thus influenced the choice of R despite the fact that the two were never presented together but were only indirectly linked via a certain Sr. More specifically, Sd1 and R2 were indirectly related to each other because they both occurred with Sr1. The indirect relation between Sd2 and R3 was the result of a common relation with Sr2.

3.2.5.5 Changes in the nature of the relation

a) No relation followed by a relation: R pre-exposure, Sr pre-exposure, and the absence of a contingency Just as presenting a CS or a US alone can weaken the subsequent influence of later CS-US pairings in classical conditioning (see CS pre-exposure and US pre-exposure effects), so too does the occurrence of the R or Sr by itself weaken the later learning of a relation between R and Sr. Most of the research on this topic has focused on the detrimental effect of the absence of an R-Sr relation on later effects of the presence of a R-Sr relation. Originally, this idea was linked to a phenomenon known as *learned helplessness* (Maier & Seligman, 1976; Seligman, 1975). To illustrate, imagine a yoked design where during a first phase, an electric shock is delivered to one group of dogs. These dogs can stop the shock by performing a predetermined escape behavior (e.g., running from one side of the cage to the other). In the other (yoked) condition, other dogs receive exactly the same number of shocks for exactly as long as the dogs in the first group, but they cannot do anything to stop it. In this latter group, the presence of the shock is not contingent on the behavior of the dogs. When during a subsequent phase both groups have to learn an avoidance behavior in another situation, only the first group of dogs succeeds in acquiring that avoidance behavior. Based on results like these, Seligman initially argued that learning a contingency between a R and Sr is undermined if organisms first experience that their behavior has no impact on important events in their environment (Maier & Jackson, 1979). It seems that they learn that they are helpless in controlling their environment. These findings have had a major impact in clinical psychology, where they have led to new insights into depression (Overmier & LoLordo, 1998; Liu, Kleiman, Nestor, & Cheek, 2015) and even new pharmacological treatments for depression (e.g., Vollmayr & Gass, 2013; Yin, Guven, & Dietis, 2016). The phenomenon of learned helplessness has also had a major impact in cognitive (neuro-) psychology (e.g., Maier & Seligman, 2016; Moscarello & Hartley, 2017). It is therefore no exaggeration to state that learned helplessness is one of the more influential findings to have emerged from learning psychology.

Somewhat ironically, in a recent paper, Maier and Seligman (2016) themselves argued that their initial idea was incorrect. Their new explanation implies that repeatedly experiencing aversive events is enough to produce helpless behavior. This impact of repeated aversive events on behavior can be prevented, however, by learning that one has some control over those events. So the new idea is exactly the mirror image of the old one: the two groups (controllable vs. uncontrollable shocks) differ in helplessness behavior not because one group learned that the shocks were uncontrollable, but because the other group learned that the shocks were controllable. It is the learning of control that can counteract the effects of experiencing many shocks. Although this means that learned helplessness effects do not provide evidence for learning the absence of control, it does not negate the many successful applications that resulted from this research. It also illustrates an important lesson for all scientists: the successful application of ideas does not necessarily prove that those ideas are correct.

b) An R-Sr relation followed by the absence of an R-Sr relation   Again, much attention has been paid to the effects of the removal of a contingency. When a behavior (R) (e.g., lever pressing) is followed by a reinforcer (Sr) (e.g., food), this will lead to an increase in the frequency of that behavior (e.g., pressing the lever more often). The term *acquisition* can be used to refer to this change in behavior. If afterward the contingency between R and Sr is removed (e.g., pressing the lever no longer leads to food), the learned change in behavior will disappear. The latter change in behavior is called *extinction* (see figure 3.8). There are some interesting properties of extinction. For instance, immediately after the beginning of the extinction procedure, there is a rise in the frequency of R for a short period of time (see figure 3.8). This "extinction burst" is often accompanied by other side effects such as increased variability in behavior and signs of aggression. After all, breaking the relation between R and Sr typically implies that no Sr is presented anymore, which in itself leads to explorative and aggressive behavior (e.g., even if the food was previously presented separately from the behavior of the animal, stopping the delivery of food will lead to explorative and aggressive behavior). Such side effects of extinction procedures limit the practical applicability of these procedures when changing behavior (Catania, 2013, p. 72). Note, however, that extinction bursts and the increased variability in behavior also have positive effects; more variability offers more possibilities to create new behavior (also see section 3.2.2.2a).

The degree of extinction (i.e., the decrease in the frequency of a previously reinforced R as a result of the extinction procedure) is influenced by the nature of the original relation between the R and the Sr. It is especially important whether R was always followed by the Sr (continuous reinforcement; CRF) or R was only occasionally followed by the Sr (partial reinforcement). When a certain behavior during a first phase is always followed by a reinforcer (CRF) and in a second phase the same behavior is no longer followed by the reinforcer (extinction), then the frequency of the behavior will decrease quite quickly. When a behavior

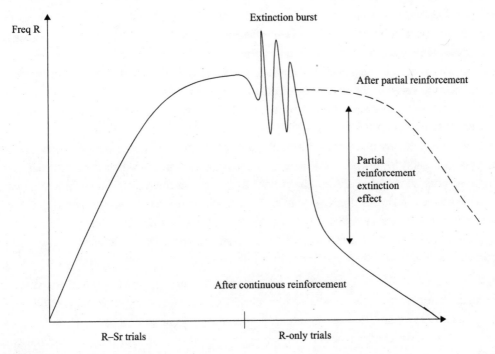

Freq R

Extinction burst

After partial reinforcement

Partial
reinforcement
extinction
effect

After continuous reinforcement

R–Sr trials   R-only trials

Figure 3.8
Acquisition, extinction, extinction burst, and the partial reinforcement extinction effect.

is only partially reinforced during the first phase, it will disappear less quickly during extinction. The fact that extinction procedures are less effective after partial reinforcement than after continuous reinforcement is referred to as the *partial reinforcement extinction effect* (e.g., Harris, Kwok, & Gottlieb, 2019). Thinking about the unit of behavior can help us understand why this behavior occurs. As mentioned earlier (see section 3.2.5.3.b), you can argue that the unit of behavior is different in partial reinforcement (e.g., pressing five times on a lever) than in continuous reinforcement (e.g., once to press a lever). This difference also occurs during extinction if the extinction procedure is defined differently for partial reinforcement (e.g., pressing the handle five times is no longer followed by food) than with continuous reinforcement (e.g., pressing the lever once is no longer followed by food). It thus takes longer before the same number of units of behavior occurs during the extinction procedure (e.g., ten times "five presses without food" versus ten times "press once without food"), and extinction will therefore take longer with partial reinforcement than with continuous reinforcement.

The partial reinforcement extinction effect is also often seen in daily life. Take the example of a child who repeatedly (in a verbal or nonverbal way) asks about his stuffed animal. Most parents initially adhere to this question consistently. However, if the child remains too attached to the toy for too long, or the attachment becomes disruptive for another reason, parents will want to reduce this requesting behavior by no longer reinforcing the request for the toy. Parents who do this consistently apply an extinction procedure. In such cases, it is usually found that the request behavior (i.e., asking for the toy) will decrease quite rapidly in frequency. However, other parents continue to give in to the child's request from time to time, especially if the child does not give up and continues to ask for the toy. In this case, the child is subject to partial reinforcement of the request behavior. Instead of decreasing, the request behavior will actually increase. After all, the unit of behavior has shifted from "asking once" to "ask repeatedly"; the chances of getting the toy are now greater when the child keeps asking even after an initial rejection. The child thus learns that the request behavior is still being reinforced—it is just that the request must be made several times before the toy is delivered. Moreover, it will be very difficult for parents to reduce the frequency of request behavior in this case, even if they never reinforce the request again. The child has learned to keep asking and therefore will have to learn that "constantly requesting" will not lead to the toy.

c) The presence or absence of a regularity depending on the context   In contrast to the study of classical conditioning, the study of operant conditioning paid a great deal of attention to the role of signals that indicate when certain R-Sr relations occur or do not occur. As we noted at the start of this chapter, signals that indicate the presence of R-Sr relations are (descriptive) Sds. It seems obvious that it is at least as important to learn *when* a behavior will have a certain effect as to learn *that* the behavior can have an effect. After all, what follows when a certain behavior is emitted very much depends on the wider context. Operant behavior is therefore adaptive only when it is controlled by stimuli that indicate when the behavior will be followed by certain stimuli. The conditions under which Sds control behavior is investigated in learning psychology in studies on the stimulus control of operant behavior.

As with occasion setters in classical conditioning, a distinction is made between (a) Sds that indicate that a behavior will be followed by an Sr and (b) Sds that indicate that a behavior will not be followed by an Sr (see Michael, 2004, p.77, for the prevailing terminology). Suppose the Sd (e.g., a light) indicates that R (e.g., lever pressing) will be followed by a reinforcer (e.g., food). In that case, the presence of the Sd will lead to an increase in the frequency of R. If R is followed by a reinforcer in the absence of the Sd but not in the presence of the Sd, then the presentation of the Sd will result in a decrease in the frequency of R. Behavior (whether or not R is performed) is therefore under the control of the Sd.

We should briefly point out that, at the level of the procedure, the use of discriminative stimuli is a form of *differential reinforcement*: a procedure whereby a response (R) is followed by a reinforcer under certain conditions (Sr) and not followed by that reinforcer under other conditions (see Catania, 2013, pp. 148–149). The difference between the situations in which the R-Sr relation does and does not hold is indicated in this case by a discriminative stimulus.

In other forms of differential reinforcement, this distinction can be indicated by characteristics of the response itself. For example, pressing a left button is followed by food, whereas pressing a right button is not followed by food. In this case, the location of the button indicates whether button pressing will be followed by food.

Differential reinforcement procedures can result in either discrimination or generalization. Discrimination is said to occur whenever an operant behavior is performed when the R-Sr relation holds, but not when the R-Sr relation does not hold. Stimulus control as an effect (i.e., the impact of Sds on operant behavior) is therefore an instance of discrimination. Generalization, on the other hand, refers to the fact that an R-Sr relation that is valid only under certain conditions (e.g., when the light is on; if the left lever is pressed) also has an influence if these conditions are not met (e.g., if the light is not on; if the right lever is pressed).[9] It is essential for every living organism to achieve a good balance between discrimination and generalization. If discrimination is too pronounced, events in one situation (e.g., the light that was turned on in one specific location at one moment in time) will not affect behavior in very similar situations (e.g., the light is turned on in the same location but at a different moment in time). If generalization is too pronounced, an event in one situation will have an influence on a totally different situation (e.g., another location where there is no light at a different moment in time). Many forms of psychopathology can therefore be understood as an excess of discrimination or generalization. For instance, one could say that people who suffer from posttraumatic stress disorder overgeneralize their traumatic experience to safe situations (e.g., Thome et al., 2017). For these and other reasons, much research has been conducted into both discrimination and generalization (for a brief review, see box 3.3; for more extensive reviews, see Bouton, 2016, chap. 8, and Catania, 2013, chap. 11).

Box 3.3 More on Discrimination and Generalization

The term *discrimination* has a strong negative connotation in day-to-day language. There is, however, nothing wrong with the *ability* to discriminate—that is, to respond differently in the presence of some stimuli than in the presence of other stimuli. In fact, one could argue that all instances of operant behavior involve some kind of discrimination (Catania, 2013). For instance, the mere presence of a lever in a Skinner box can function as an Sd for lever pressing. In most studies on discrimination, however, two clearly distinct (classes of) stimuli are used as Sd. For instance, pigeons might receive food for pecking a key when a green light is on but not when a blue light is on. In such a setup, the pigeon can be said to discriminate when it pecks more often in the presence of the green light than in the presence of the blue light. Often, classes of stimuli are used as Sds rather than individual stimuli. For instance, pigeons can learn to peck a key whenever a photograph is presented with a tree in it, but not when a photograph without a tree is presented.

(continued)

Box 3.3 (continued)

Research has shown that pigeons discriminate on the basis of all kind of stimulus classes, including paintings by famous artists (e.g., pressing one key whenever a painting of Monet is presented and another key whenever a painting of Picasso is presented; Watanabe, Sakamoto, & Wakita, 1995). The fact that they based their behavior on category membership can be inferred from the fact that after training with a subset of items from a category (e.g., ten paintings of Monet and Picasso), they are able to discriminate also on the basis of another subset of items that were never shown before (e.g., a painting of Monet and a painting of Picasso that were never presented during training). These types of studies provide important information about the way nonverbal organisms such as pigeons categorize events in their environment. Discrimination performance can also shed light on many other phenomena such as sensory abilities (e.g., if a pigeon responds differently to two stimuli, it can be said to perceive the difference between the stimuli), time perception (e.g., a pigeon can be trained to respond only when a certain period of time has elapsed), spatial perception (e.g., a pigeon can be trained to respond only to stimuli at certain locations), and memory (i.e., if a pigeon retains over time the ability to respond differently to stimuli, it can be said to memorize the events; see Bouton, 2016, chap. 8, and Catania, 2013, chap. 11, for reviews).

Generalization has also been studied extensively. Because by definition at least two stimuli are involved in generalization (a source stimulus that is established as an Sd during training and a target Sd that is tested to determine whether it functions as an Sd), one can vary the nature of the relation between stimuli in studies on generalization. Most often, the relation between the perceptual properties of stimuli is manipulated. For instance, when a tone of 1000 Hz is established as an Sd for key pecking in pigeons, one can test whether the pigeons also peck for test stimuli of 700 Hz, 800 Hz, 900 Hz, 1100 Hz, 1200 Hz, and 1300 Hz. Typically, a generalization gradient is observed such that the test stimuli that are perceptually most similar to the training stimulus (i.e., 900 Hz and 1100 Hz) result in more responding than test stimuli that are less similar to the training stimulus (i.e., 700 Hz and 1300 Hz). Generalization can be tested not only for training stimuli that signal the availability of reinforcers (feature positive Sds; e.g., a tone of 1000 Hz that signals that pressing a lever will result in food) but also for training stimuli that signal the unavailability of reinforcers (feature negative Sds; e.g., a tone of 500 Hz that signals that pressing a lever will not result in food). In studies that involve discrimination training, both types of training stimuli are used, thus allowing one to examine simultaneously the generalization effects of both training stimuli (e.g., by presenting tones of 300, 400, 600, 700, 800, 900, 1100, and 1200 Hz). These types of studies have revealed an interesting phenomenon called *peak shift* that entails that the generalization gradient for feature positive Sds shifts as the result of including a feature negative Sd during training (Purtle, 1973). For instance, after training with a feature positive tone of 1000 Hz and a feature negative tone of 500 Hz, a generalization stimulus of 1100 Hz will lead to stronger responding than a generalization tone of 900 Hz. In contrast, when training involves a feature positive tone of 1000 Hz and a feature negative tone of 1500 Hz, a generalization stimulus of 900 Hz will lead to more responding than a generalization stimulus of 1100 Hz. In some cases, responding to a generalization stimulus (e.g., a tone of 900 Hz) can even be stronger than responding to the original training stimulus (e.g., a tone of 1000 Hz).

Returning to the main subject of this section, much research has been carried out on the stimulus control of operant behavior (see Catania, 2013, and Pierce & Cheney, 2018, for a comprehensive overview). In essence, this research looked at the moderators of stimulus control (the nature of the Sd, the R, or the R-Sr relation; the nature of the organism; the broader context; [changes in] the Sd:R-Sr relation). We will not review all of this research but will only describe different types of stimulus control that differ with regard to the specific aspects of stimuli in the environment that function as the Sd (i.e., what controls the operant behavior).

A first type has already been discussed extensively: control by a single stimulus. This leads to *nonrelational responding*. For instance, imagine that pressing a lever (R) is followed by food (Sr) when a light is lit (Sd). By exposing the organism to this Sd: R-Sr contingency, the light will give rise to the response "lever pressing." One stimulus therefore controls the behavior resulting from the prior experience of the Sd: R-Sr contingency.

A second type of stimulus control occurs in *nonarbitrarily applicable relational responding* (NAARR). This behavior is determined by a relation between two stimuli. To see this more clearly, consider the example in figure 3.9.

In this matching-to-sample task, participants press a left or right button in order to receive a reinforcer. On each trial, three stimuli are presented: a sample stimulus at the top middle of the screen and two comparison stimuli at the bottom, one on the left and one on the right. Which stimuli are presented during the training phase differs from trial to trial (see numbers 1 and 2 in figure 3.9). Pressing the left button is followed by a reinforcer if the left comparison stimulus is identical to the sample stimulus (as in Trial 1). Pressing the right button is reinforced when

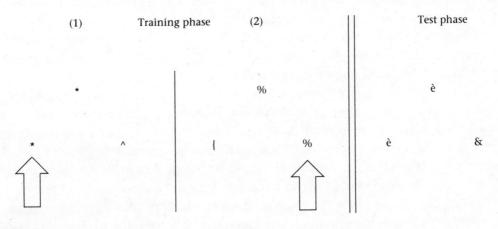

Figure 3.9
Trials from a matching-to-sample task. This experimental setup is often used in research on non-arbitrarily applicable relational responding.

the right comparison stimulus is identical to the sample stimulus (as in Trial 2). The arrow at the bottom of figure 3.9 indicates which response is reinforced. As a result of this training procedure, participants will increasingly press the reinforced responses (left for 1 and right for 2). In principle, it is possible that the behavior is under the control of the sample stimulus alone. If the sample stimulus is *, then they should press left, whereas if the sample stimulus is %, they should press right. If so, then this would be an example of nonrelational responding. During the test phase, however, participants are exposed to stimuli that were not presented during the earlier learning phase (see figure 3.9). Based on the sample stimulus è, they cannot decide whether to press left or right because it is the first time they see that stimulus è. However, both humans and nonhumans select the left more often than the right response during the test phase. From this, we can deduce that the behavior is under the control not of the sample stimulus alone but of the *relation* between the sample and the comparison stimuli: one chooses the response on the same side as the comparison stimulus that is identical to the sample stimulus. This relation predicts the correct response during the training phase and can thus be used to select a response during the test phase. This is an example of *relational responding* because operant behavior (responding left or right) is controlled by a relation between stimuli. The criterion that is used to delineate the response class (the class of behaviors that are reinforced) is thus defined on the basis of a relational characteristic—namely, the relation between the upper and lower stimuli. This example concerns *nonarbitrarily applicable relational responding* because it is based on a nonarbitrary relation between (in this case, physical) characteristics of two stimuli (i.e., the two stimuli look exactly the same). The relation between the physical characteristics of stimuli is nonarbitrary (not coincidental) in the sense that the physical characteristics are specific to each individual stimulus. Research shows that both humans and other animals are able to adjust their behavior to nonarbitrary relations between stimuli (e.g., respond to one stimulus as being larger, smaller, different from, above something, under something, earlier, later than another).

A third form of stimulus control is *arbitrarily applicable relational responding* (AARR). Again, behavior is under the control of the relation between stimuli, not one stimulus (in other words, it is a type of relational response). However, this time, the relation is arbitrary because it is not dependent on the inherent physical characteristics of the stimuli involved. In essence, it means that people "act as if" stimuli are related in a certain way. A first indication for the existence of AARR was found when studying a phenomenon known as *stimulus equivalence* (e.g., Sidman, 2009). In studies on stimulus equivalence, the stimuli presented are randomly selected and therefore not systematically similar to each other in terms of physical characteristics. An example can be seen in figure 3.10.[10]

During the training phase, participants learn to press the left button under the comparison stimulus ù when they see the sample *. They also learn to press the right button under

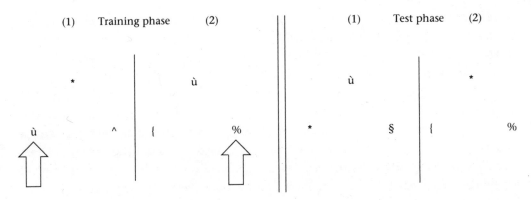

Figure 3.10
Matching-to-sample design used to study stimulus equivalence.

the comparison stimulus % when they see the sample ù. Then they get a test phase where they have to choose between the left or right button when they see the sample ù or the sample *. If the behavior were under control of the sample stimulus itself (i.e., if it were an instance of nonrelational responding), then they would choose right for ù and left for *, because during the training phase, pressing left in the presence of * and right in the presence of ù was followed by reinforcement. Interestingly, in humans but not nonhumans (see below), we typically find that in the test phase, they choose left for ù and right for *. In other words, participants behave as if they think that * "is the same as" ù and that ù "is the same as" %. If you respond based on the relation "is the same as," then you choose ù if * is the sample and also choose * if ù is the sample. The relation "is the same as" is *symmetrical* (if A is the same as B, then B is the same as A; i.e., the opposite is also true). The relation "is the same as" is also *transitive* (if A is the same as B, and B is the same as C, A also is the same as C). Therefore, the response under % is chosen if * is the sample, because * and ù are considered to be *equivalent* to one another. In this kind of study, people do not choose the response on the basis of the sample stimulus alone. Instead, they choose the response under the comparison stimulus that "is the same as" the sample stimulus. They thus seem to respond to a presumed relation between two stimuli. This phenomenon shows once again how broad and abstract response classes and operant classes can be: even a unit like "act as if A, B, and C are equivalent" can be used to align these classes, just as "do the same as that other person" or "press the lever" serve as units of behavior. Just as the unit "press numerical code 6823" can be seen as a certain pattern of behaviors extending across time, so too can the unit "act as if A, B, and C are equivalent" be seen as a pattern of behaviors that extend across time (if A choose B, if B choose A, if A choose C, etc.). The only unique feature of a unit such as "act as if A, B, and

C are equivalent" is that it refers to the relation between stimuli, or more specifically, to a relation that is not grounded in physical characteristics.

The question, of course, is how one learns to "act as if" stimuli are related to each other. If the relation between stimuli is not grounded in their physical characteristics, then how do people decide that * and % are related to each other? Perhaps making certain choices during the training phase is already enough to act as if those stimuli are related to each other. For example, the fact that the response under ù is reinforced in the presence of sample * might already be enough to allow you to "act as if" ù is related to the sample *. If this is the case, one can say that the act of reinforcing a choice functions as a contextual cue that specifies the nature of the relation between stimuli (i.e., reinforcement functions as a *relational contextual cue*).

But sometimes there are more direct cues for AARR. Suppose I tell you that ù is related to * and that % is related to ù. Perhaps you will then during the test phase immediately choose * when you see ù as a sample and choose % when you see * as a sample, even if you have not been exposed to the training phase of figure 3.10. The verbal expression "is related to" is a sufficient indication for you to start behaving as if certain stimuli indeed are related. This example also allows us to make clear that one can act as if stimuli are related in all kinds of ways. Suppose, for example, that I tell you that * is more than ù and that ù is more than %. Thereafter, I ask if you want * or % number of coins. You may choose "* number of coins." If you do this, your behavior depends on an arbitrarily applicable relation between * and % (i.e., that * is more than %; see Törneke, 2010).

So far, research suggests that only verbally able humans are able to act as if stimuli are related in a certain way (i.e., to show AARR). The phenomenon of stimulus equivalence, for example, has still not been firmly established in nonhuman animals, despite intensive attempts to do so (see Hughes & Barnes-Holmes, 2014, for a discussion). This supports the assumption made by several functional learning psychologists that language is a complex instance of AARR. The following example from Törneke (2010, p. 65) might help clarify this. Imagine that I reinforce both a parrot and a child to say "Carla" each time a certain girl enters the room. With sufficient training, both the parrot and the child will learn to do so. However, we can show that what appears to be the exact same behavior (at least on the surface) is actually due to different forms of stimulus control in the parrot and the child. For example, when I suddenly say "Carla" aloud, chances are that the child will look toward the entrance to the room as if they were expecting the girl to enter the room. The parrot, on the other hand, will not react at all. So the child attaches "meaning" to the word. The child has learned that the sound "Carla" is related to the actual girl, so if someone says "Carla," chances are that the girl is somewhere close by. This is the core of language: you attach meaning to sounds and words by relating them to other things, even though the characteristics of those sounds and words often have nothing in common with the characteristics of the things they refer to (i.e., they are arbitrarily related). The parrot, on the other hand, does not learn the meaning of the sound "Carla"; it learns only that it has to say "Carla" when the girl enters. The behavior of the parrot is thus an example of nonrelational responding, whereas the behavior of the child is an example of arbitrarily applicable relational responding, because the latter depends on the arbitrary relation between the actual girl and the sound "Carla."

More generally, some functional psychologists view AARR as the essence of "meaning giving." This idea lies at the core of relational frame theory (RFT), which in turn inspired a new approach in clinical psychology called acceptance and commitment therapy (ACT) that views psychopathology as primarily a problem of meaning giving. (For more on ACT and RFT, see Törneke, 2010; Hughes and Barnes-Holmes, 2016; and Zettle, Barnes-Holmes, Hayes, and Biglan, 2016.) Finally, we will return to the phenomena of NAARR and AARR in chapter 4 when we discuss complex forms of learning.

Box 3.4 Is Punishment Desirable?

The functional knowledge we have so far discussed in this chapter was focused mainly on reinforcement. However, the majority of this knowledge can also be applied to punishment. Knowledge about the moderators of punishment is essential to correctly assess the importance of punishment. After all, there are often doubts about the effectiveness and desirability of punishment as a procedure for changing behavior. This is especially true for procedures in which behavior is coupled with the administration of aversive stimuli (such as parents who beat their children; see Gershoff et al., 2018, for a recent review). It is interesting to note that the negative view of punishment currently prevalent in our society is based to some extent on the vision of early learning psychologists. Early in the twentieth century, Thorndike (1932) argued that punishment is not an effective method for achieving meaningful and long-lasting changes in behavior. Skinner (1953) and more recently Sidman (2001) also strongly advocated for the reduced use of punishment in society. Earlier, we noted that administering a negative stimulus (e.g., reprimands) often leads to a temporary change in behavior but that these changes are not necessarily instances of punishment: often, a change in behavior during a punishment procedure will be due not to the punishment of the behavior (the R-Sr relation) but merely to the administration of the negative stimulus (the Sr itself). Moreover, because the stimulus is often administered by a certain person (e.g., the parent), punishment also installs a relation between that person and negative stimuli, which in itself can lead to changes in the behavior toward that person.

Although there are risks associated with the use of punishment procedures, it is clear that punishment is a fact of life. Azrin and Holz (1966, p. 438) rightly pointed out, "One type of punishment, however, seems impossible to eliminate, and that is the punishing contingency that is arranged by the physical world." We experience pain when we bang our heads against a wall, no matter how much we reject the use of punishment procedures. It is therefore important to understand punishment well. We also need to conduct in a scientific way a debate on the desirability of punishment.

(continued)

Box 3.4 (continued)

We therefore agree with Domjan (2000, p.136) when he states that learning psychology can make an important contribution to the societal debate on punishment. After all, learning psychologists can determine empirically whether and under which conditions punishment has a (long-term) influence on behavior. And there are indeed conditions under which punishment is very effective. Following Domjan (2000), we discuss these conditions in the context of an example where punishment does work and an example where it does not work. It is not difficult to find examples in daily life that show that punishment is not always effective. Take punishment of speeding offenses. Through laws, fast driving is linked to negative consequences (e.g., paying a fine, losing the driving license, serving a prison sentence). Yet, such laws (which can be regarded from a psychological point of view as punishment procedures) are not very effective. On the other hand, there are also situations where punishment can be very effective. Take the example of a child who puts his fingers into an electrical outlet and receives a (nonfatal) shock. It is very likely that after this one incident, the child will never put his fingers in an electrical outlet again. Punishment is very effective here: a single punishment suffices to completely eliminate a behavior. Why is punishment so effective here while it seems to be making little difference in speeding offenses? Based on our functional knowledge about operant conditioning, we can see several reasons (see Domjan, 2000, for more details):

– Contiguity

The effectiveness of the punishment will increase as contiguity (proximity in time and space) between the R and Sr increases. When punishing a speeding offense, there is usually a lot of time between the offense and the punishment (often several weeks or even months). The child who puts his fingers in the socket, however, immediately gets a shock.

– Contingency

As with any other operant learning procedure, the effectiveness of punishment will increase as the contingency between R and Sr increases. The contingency between making a speeding violation and getting a fine is quite low (i.e., there is a very low chance of being caught). Yet the contingency between putting your fingers in a socket and receiving a shock is very high.

– Changes in the intensity of the Sr

Earlier, we discussed the research by Azrin and Holz (1966) that showed that a negative Sr with a certain intensity has less effect if less intense Sr stimuli were used previously (see section 3.2.1.2). This is similar to what often happens in the punishment of speeding offenses. The first time one is caught, the fine is rather small; the more often one gets caught, the higher the fine. By the time a truly hefty fine is given, (some) people have already gotten used to getting fines, and the effect of a heavy fine will be less than if the heavy fine was already applied at the first violation. A child who puts his finger into the socket, however, is immediately confronted with a strong aversive stimulus. This is one of the reasons why punishment is so effective in this case. Both educators and legislators often work with punishments that are initially light for humanitarian and moral reasons. Although learning psychology cannot comment on the value or meaningfulness of these

Box 3.4 (continued)

nonscientific reasons (Domjan, 2000), research does show that the use of initially light punishments can actually be counterproductive. It can lead to situations where one eventually has to apply far more severe punishments (e.g., prison sentences) than if they had applied harsher punishments from the beginning (e.g., high fines).

– Stimulus control: The influence of Sds

In all forms of operant learning, there can be stimuli that indicate when a response will lead to a certain result (i.e., a Sd; see section 3.2.5.5). Sds can also have a significant impact on the effectiveness of punishment. Suppose a driver knows in advance where speed controls are being held (sometimes such information is indeed made public). Chances are that the driver will adjust his speed at the places where speed checks are held, but not at other places. The effect of the punishment procedure (i.e., the law that states that excessive speed will be fined) will therefore not (or will to a lesser extent) generalize to situations where it is known that speed will not be checked and therefore the law will not be enforced. Let's take another example: suppose the parents of a child punish that child for running through the living room but the grandparents of the child do not punish this behavior. The child may not run through the room if the parents are there but might if only the grandparents are present. In this case, the parents are the Sd for punishment of the running behavior.

– Sd: R-Sr relations in the broader context: Choice behavior based on a cost-benefit analysis

From a learning perspective, every operant behavior is established and maintained because it leads to certain outcomes. This is also the case for behavior that one wants to punish. Let's return to the example of excessive speeding once again. The behavior "fast driving" is performed because it results in various positive outcomes. For instance, it ensures that you reach your destination more quickly. Others get a "kick" from fast driving. When one wants to punish a behavior, one cannot separate this entirely from the reinforcers that sustain the behavior. If you want to punish a behavior by linking it to an aversive outcome (i.e., by creating a new R-Sr relation), you have to realize that this aversive outcome will have an effect only to the extent to which it "outweighs" the positive outcomes that are also connected to the behavior (other R-Sr relations with the same R). The effectiveness of such a punishment procedure will therefore depend on how the individual weighs the costs and benefits of the punished behavior.

   Different alternatives to punishment make use of the fact that every behavior takes place in a broader context that includes a whole network of Sd: R-Sr relations. Earlier, we discussed differential reinforcement of other behavior (DRO; see section 3.2.4.1). Instead of linking new (negative) outcomes to undesirable behavior (punishment), new (positive) outcomes can be linked to desired behavior. Because every behavior is a choice (you can engage in only one or a limited number of behaviors at the same time), an increase in the frequency of another behavior will lead to a decrease in the frequency of the undesired behavior. DRO can be extra efficient if the other, more desirable behavior leads to the same outcome as the undesirable behavior. For instance, suppose that you have children and they are arguing in the backseat of the car during a long drive. One

(continued)

Box 3.4 (continued)

possible reason for this is that quarreling takes away the boredom of the car ride. You can punish this behavior, but this does not make the boredom disappear, and chances are that the children will start to argue again later on. A better alternative is to combine punishment with the possibility to adopt a different behavior that can take away the boredom (e.g., give the children an iPad to keep them busy).

Sometimes administering a negative stimulus increases the frequency of a behavior instead of decreasing it. Once again, this can be understood from a learning perspective. For example, it is possible that the behavior has benefits as well as costs. Suppose a child never gets attention from their parents unless they are punished for disturbing behavior. In such a situation the disturbing behavior can increase in frequency because it is followed not only by a negative result (e.g., receiving a verbal reprimand) but also by a positive result (e.g., parental attention). Again, the behavior will depend on a consideration of costs and benefits. From this insight, effective therapies have been developed for self-injury (see Schwartz et al., 2002, pp. 195–197). Note that often, what is important is not the real costs and benefits but the perceived costs and benefits (i.e., what one thinks the costs and benefits are). Perhaps the most effective way to change behavior is to make the costs visible and try to eliminate the benefits as much as possible. This brings us to the domain of theories about the mental processes that mediate operant conditioning, a topic we discuss in the second part of this chapter.

3.3   Mental Process Theories

3.3.1   Associative Models

All associative models of operant conditioning are based on the assumption that the effect of relations between behavior and stimuli is mediated by associations between representations in memory. We first discuss models that assume that S-R associations are responsible for learning. We then review the evidence arguing against such a vision. Thereafter, we briefly outline associative models in which R-Sr and Sd-Sr associations are central.

3.3.1.1   S-R models

a) The core of S-R models   According to a typical S-R model (e.g., Thorndike, 1911; Hull, 1943), learning boils down to the acquisition of a kind of internal structure that consists of an association between the sensory aspects of the stimulus and the motor aspects of the response.

Think It Through 3.2: Extrapolate Mental Process Theories of Classical Conditioning

In the previous chapter we discussed mental process theories of classical conditioning. Before you read on, first try to see if these theories can also be applied to operant conditioning.

In more modern terms, you can state that it is about an association between representations of stimuli and responses. Again, take the example of the rat pressing the handle when a light is on and gaining access to food as a result. According to the S-R vision of Thorndike, access to the food (Sr) will ensure that an association is formed between the light (Sd) and pressing the lever (R). As a result of that association, the presentation of the light will automatically result in the lever being pressed. The food (Sr) is thus something via which one "learns" (in the sense of forming associations), not something about which one learns.[11]

b) The two-factor model of Mowrer   One of the most influential S-R models was formulated by Mowrer in the context of avoidance learning. It was so influential because it offered an answer to an important problem for the S-R model of Thorndike (1911): if the presence of the Sr is a necessary condition to learn, then how can you explain avoidance? After all, avoidance behavior results in the absence of a Sr. How can S-R models explain that the absence of a stimulus can also lead to operant conditioning? Let us take a concrete example: the behavior of rats in a shuttle box. A shuttle box is a cage that is divided into two rooms separated by a wall with a passage at the bottom (see figure 3.11). The animal is placed in one of the two chambers. After a while, a light is turned on and then (e.g., after ten seconds) an electric

Shock

No shock

Figure 3.11
Basic model of a shuttle box.

shock follows. This shock persists until the animal passes through the opening to the other room. After a while, the light is turned on again and followed by an electric shock that animal can escape by going back to the first room. And so the procedure continues. Over time, the escape behavior changes into avoidance behavior: when the light turns on, the animal passes to the other room before the shock is delivered.

Learning an escape response (R is followed by the termination of a negative Sr) poses few problems for a S-R theory: stopping a negative stimulus is a positive outcome that can lead to the strengthening of the association between the light (S) and moving to the other room (R). As soon as the escape behavior changes into avoidance behavior, however, there is no longer a physical stimulus present that serves to reinforce behavior. Hence, the S-R association between the light and behavior should weaken and the avoidance behavior should decrease in frequency. When the avoidance behavior is no longer emitted, the shock is re-administered and the escape-avoidance cycle can start again. According to an S-R theory, one would therefore expect that avoidance behavior is not stable insofar as it will revert to escape behavior. Yet, we see that avoidance behavior is often very stable, which contradicts a core prediction of an S-R theory.

Mowrer (1947, 1960) formulated the two-factor theory as a solution to this problem. According to Mowrer, there are two S-R relations that are learned (hence, two-factor theory). First of all, a Pavlovian S-R association is formed based on the contiguity between the Sd and the Sr. As a result, the Sd will elicit reactions that were initially elicited only by the Sr (see S-R statement of classical conditioning). One of those reactions was thought to be fear. In addition, an operant S-R association is formed as a result of the fact that emitting R in the context of the Sd leads to positive results. In the escape phase, the most important positive result of R is stopping the Sr. In the avoidance phase, this positive result is no longer present, but as a result of the Pavlovian S-R relation there is still another positive result. After all, emitting R in the context of the Sd leads to the removal of the Sd and thus to the cessation of the conditioned fear that is elicited by the Sd. Let us return once more to the example of a rat placed in a shuttle box (see figure 3.11). Once the rat emits an avoidance behavior, this behavior will no longer be followed by the termination of the shock but will still be followed by the disappearance of the fear-eliciting light. Crucially, the disappearance of that light is also a positive result that can maintain avoidance behavior even when no more shocks are delivered.

That said, the unique aspect of the two-factor model (i.e., the assumption that escape from conditioned fear serves to reinforce avoidance behavior) is not without its own problems. First, the fear that is elicited by the Sd should also be extinguished over time. This also removes the second source of reinforcement of R, so R should eventually also be extinguished. The assumption of a second source of reinforcement therefore only postpones the problem and does not provide a fundamental solution for the inability of S-R theories of operant conditioning to explain the stable nature of avoidance behavior. Second, the two-factor model assumes an S-R theory of classical conditioning. It therefore falls prey to all criticisms that apply to S-R theories of classical conditioning (see chapter 2). For example, the idea that fear is a part of the UR that later can be elicited also by the CS is highly problematic. Fear is not a condition that follows the administration of an aversive stimulus (it is therefore not part of the UR) but rather the anticipation of the aversive stimulus. An aversive stimulus causes pain, which is different from fear. Fear arises only when you expect pain.

c) General evaluation of S-R models   S-R models fail, not only as an explanation of avoidance learning, but also as an explanation of operant conditioning in general. When we look at the functional knowledge of operant conditioning as we summarized earlier, we notice that different findings directly refute the predictions of S-R models. For example, Colwill and Rescorla (1985) showed that nonhuman animals will no longer emit a behavior (e.g., press a lever) that leads to a positive stimulus (e.g., food) after the positive stimulus has become negative (e.g., because the food was accompanied by nausea). This shows that operant conditioning (the change in behavior as a result of presenting stimuli together) is based on knowledge about the Sr. According to S-R models, however, knowledge about the Sr does not play any role in operant conditioning. After all, operant conditioning involves learning not *about* the Sr but *because of* the Sr (i.e., the Sr provides the cement with which the S-R association is built). Once the presentation of the Sr has led to the strengthening of the S-R relation, the role of the Sr is finished and changes in the Sr can no longer have any impact on conditioned behavior. The findings of Colwill and Rescorla show that this argument is incorrect.

A study by MacFarlane (1930, in Bouton, 2016) also offers a nice illustration of the fact that organisms acquire knowledge about the Sr and that operant conditioning thus involves more than the formation of new S-R associations. MacFarlane placed a rat in a bath of water, where it learned to swim to a certain feeding spot. After it learned to quickly swim to the feeding spot, MacFarlane emptied the bath. When the rat was placed in the empty bath, the rat walked to the feeding location. So the rat did not learn a specific motor behavior (swimming to a location) but did learn the location where it could get food. Note, however, that this analysis assumes a very limited view of behavior as a certain motor activity. When we view behavior as a class of responses aligned with a particular unit (Catania, 2013), it becomes clear that we can also understand MacFarlane's findings at the functional level as illustrating the formation of an operant class of behavior (namely, the class of behaviors that brings the animal closer to the location of the reinforcer). However, at the level of mental processes, this behavior can be learned only if the animal acquires knowledge about the location of the reinforcer.

Nevertheless, S-R models cannot be completely rejected. After all, research shows that under certain conditions, changes in the Sr have no influence on conditioned behavior. Behavior that is not influenced by changes in outcomes is sometimes called a *habit*. It is often assumed that habits are crucial in everyday life (e.g., Wood & Rünger, 2016). However, it is very difficult to study habits because determining whether something is a habit is based on not finding an impact of changes in an Sr. What is often forgotten is that such null findings do not always point to the existence of a habit (De Houwer, Tanaka, Moors, & Tibboel, 2018). For example, it is possible that the manipulation of the Sr has no effect because this manipulation was too weak or because the behavior is controlled not by the Sr being manipulated but rather by a different outcome.

3.3.1.2 R-Sr and Sd-Sr models   According to R-Sr models, operant conditioning is mediated by the strength of the association between the representation of behavior and the representation of the outcome of that behavior. If R is associated with a positive Sr, then the frequency of the behavior will increase. If there is an association between R and a negative Sr, the frequency of the behavior will decrease. As noted previously, however, it is not entirely clear how one can establish that an Sr is positive/appetitive or negative/aversive. It is also not entirely clear how R-Sr associations can affect behavior. One possibility is that activation of the representation of a positive Sr can lead to activation of the representation of the R. The latter can increase the chances that R will be performed. The activation of a representation of a negative Sr would then lead to the inhibition of the representation of R (and thus a reduction in the frequency of R).

However, there are few specific models about the mental processes that are assumed to be responsible for the formation and activation of R-Sr associations. Instead, cognitive psychologists focused their attention mainly on developing mental process theories of classical conditioning. They had two reasons for that. First, it is much easier to study classical rather than operant conditioning because the researcher has much more control over the situation in classical conditioning procedures (see also box 2.2). A second reason is that the conviction quickly arose that the formation of R-Sr associations is based on the same mental processes as the formation of S-S associations. From our overview of the available functional knowledge about classical and operant conditioning, we have seen that both forms of learning do indeed seem to occur under the same conditions. This may indicate that the underlying mental processes are similar as well. Especially the fact that both forms of learning are dependent on (conditional) contingency can be seen as an argument for the assumption that R-Sr and S-S associations are formed by the same processes. If the processes in operant and classical conditioning are the same, then one can better study these processes by studying classical conditioning because one has more control over the presented relations (but see Bouton, 2016, p. 451, for arguments why there still might be differences between the mental processes underlying classical and operant conditioning).

If one assumes that operant conditioning is indeed based on R-Sr associations that are formed in the same way as S-S associations (e.g., according to the processes described by Rescorla & Wagner, 1972), then R-Sr models can account for some important functional properties of operant conditioning. For example, a Rescorla-Wagner–based R-Sr model is compatible with the fact that operant conditioning is determined not by mere contiguity but by (conditional) contingencies. The moderating effects of Sr devaluation on operant conditioning (Colwill & Rescorla, 1985) also support R-Sr models because they show that operant conditioning effects depend on knowledge about the Sr, as postulated by R-Sr models.

However, we should point out that R-Sr models are insufficient when it comes to explaining all the functional knowledge that has been accumulated on operant conditioning because, among other things, they say nothing about the important role that Sds play in operant conditioning. Nevertheless, the influence of Sds can be taken into account by also including representations of the Sds into R-Sr models. A first solution is to assume that the influence of R-Sr associations on behavior is moderated by Sd representations (see also Bouton, 2016, pp. 454–456). Such a model is similar to the associative model that Bouton (1993) forwarded for classical conditioning (also see Rescorla, 1991). For instance, suppose that lever pressing is followed by food when a light is on but not when the light is off. This can lead to the following associative structure in the memory. Schematically, this is as depicted in figure 3.12.

There is an excitatory association between R and Sr (the full line) so that activation of the Sr can lead to activation of R. This association is active only when the Sd is present. As a result, R will be emitted only if the Sd is present and not when it is absent.

A similar model can be created for situations in which the Sd indicates that the R-Sr relation does not hold. Suppose that pressing a lever is followed by food except when a light is on. An associative structure can be created that is equivalent to that which, according to Bouton, is responsible for the extinction of classical conditioning. This is shown schematically in figure 3.13.

There is an excitatory association between Sr and R (the full line) that is always active. However, the effect of this excitatory association is counteracted by an inhibitory association (the dashed line) that is active only when the Sd is present. Activation of the Sr can therefore lead to the performance of the R when the Sd is absent (because then the inhibitory association is not active) but not when the Sd is present (because then the inhibitory association is active).

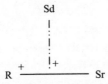

Figure 3.12
A schematic presentation of an associative model in which activation of the Sd representation activates the (excitatory) R-Sr association.

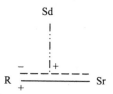

Figure 3.13
A schematic presentation of an associative model in which activation of the Sd representation activates the inhibitory R-Sr association.

A second way an Sd can exert influence on R-Sr models is through an association between the Sd and Sr. Such an association can influence operant behavior in different ways. First, the presentation of the Sd can (via the Sd-Sr association) lead to the activation of the Sr representation. This activation in turn leads to activation of the representation of R. On the basis of these additional assumptions, R-Sr models can offer an explanation for the findings of Colwill and Rescorla (1988). They showed that an Sd can influence the selection of an R even when the Sd and R are only indirectly related to each other. For example, when the presence of a tone is an Sd indicating that food can be obtained by pressing a button, and afterward it is learned that (in the absence of the tone) food can also be obtained by pressing a lever, then the subsequent presentation of the tone will increase the chance that animals will press the lever. One can explain these findings in terms of associative processes if one assumes that Sd-Sr associations are formed during operant conditioning and that the Sd, via the activation of the Sr representation, can also activate the representations of behaviors related to that Sr. Thinking can therefore lead to action: because of a certain stimulus in the environment (e.g., the smell of a cake when you pass a baker), you think of another stimulus (e.g., the cake), which leads to a behavior that in turn results in that stimulus (e.g., you go to the bakery and buy the cake). This idea is in line with the so-called ideomotor theory found in cognitive research on planned actions (e.g., Greenwald, 1970; Hommel, Müsseler, Aschersleben, & Prinz, 2001; Lotze, 1852). This is shown schematically in figure 3.14.

Dickinson (2012) described another way Sds can be involved in R-Sr models—namely, via S-R learning. His model can therefore be seen as a combination of an S-R model and an R-Sr model. In a first step, the combination of an Sd and an R would result in the formation of S-R associations. For example, when rats get food for pressing a lever, the sight of the lever can be thought of as an Sd that often goes together with pressing the lever (R). As a result of these pairings, an S-R association is formed between the representation of the lever and the representation of pressing the lever. Once the S-R association is strong enough, the mere sight of the lever can result in a tendency to press the lever. Once R-Sr associations have also been formed (as the result of the fact that lever pressing is followed by food), activation of the R

Figure 3.14
A schematic presentation of an associative model in which activation of the Sd activates the representation of the Sr, which in turn activates the representation of the response.

Figure 3.15
A schematic presentation of the associative model of Dickinson (2012) in which activation of the Sd representation activates the representation of the response (R), which—if the R-Sr association is strong enough—can lead to the activation of the representation of the reinforcer (Sr), which in turn can strengthen the activation of the response representation (R).

representation can in turn lead to activation of the Sr representation. For example, seeing the lever is reminiscent of pressing the lever, which in turn is reminiscent of the food that was presented in the past after pressing the lever. Once the idea of food has arisen, the organism will examine how valuable the food is for it at that moment in time. If it is valuable, this will increase the likelihood that the lever will be pressed. These ideas are depicted in figure 3.15.

The Dickinson (2012) model offers an elegant explanation for a wide range of functional knowledge related to operant conditioning. For example, if the Sd-R association is very strong, a behavior can be elicited purely on the basis of the presence of an Sd, even if that behavior no longer leads to a valuable Sr. In this way, the model explains habitual behavior. However, in situations where the Sd-R association is not strong enough to lead to behavior, it can lead to a behavioral trend (activation of the representation of R) that can be amplified when it is linked to an Sr that is valuable to the organism. In those situations, behavior will occur only if the Sr is valuable for the organism at that time. The model can therefore also explain the effects of Sr devaluation. Despite the fact that Dickinson's (2012) model is rather vague about certain crucial aspects, such as the way Sd-R and R-Sr associations are formed, it is a commendable attempt to capture important aspects of operant conditioning in terms of associative principles.

Box 3.5 Is Avoidance Learning a Form of Classical Conditioning?

Research has shown that some behaviors (e.g., running from one room to another) will increase in frequency more quickly than other behaviors (e.g., pressing a lever) if they lead to the avoidance of a negative stimulus. Bolles (1972) explained this by assuming that certain Sds become a signal for the arrival of a negative stimulus. For example, the room in which a shock is delivered will become a threatening Sd indicating that a negative stimulus can occur. According to Bolles, the

(continued)

Box 3.5 (continued)

Sd acquires that signal value because of the formation of an Sd-Sr association, where we see the negative stimulus (the shock) as the Sr. Bolles further assumes that each organism exhibits a whole range of responses as soon as it is threatened or in danger. Bolles called this the *species-specific defensive reactions* (SSDRs). As the name suggests, such reactions may vary from species to species. The most common reactions are running away, sitting still (freezing), or aggression (i.e., fight or flight). These reaction patterns can show a certain hierarchy in each species, meaning that an animal will try out the first response (e.g., running away) before it will try the second response (e.g., freezing), and so on. Which response is at the top of the hierarchy (i.e., which will be emitted first) can depend on the context in which the organism is threatened (Fanselow, 1989). Bolles believed that in most cases, avoidance learning can be explained as an SSDR that occurs as soon as a situation or a discrete stimulus becomes a signal for the US. In situations where the spontaneously occurring SSDR (e.g., running away as the result of being threatened) corresponds to what must be learned as avoidance behavior (e.g., running away stops or prevents the shock), the entire learning process is reduced to classical conditioning; that is, a neutral stimulus or situation (CS; e.g., being in a certain room) becomes a signal for an aversive US (e.g., an painful electric shock). As a result of these pairings (sometimes even a single CS-US presentation suffices), presentation of the CS will lead to the defensive response (running away) even before the shock is presented. Bolles's account therefore implies that avoidance behavior can arise without the need for reinforcement. In situations where the spontaneously occurring SSDR (e.g., running away) does not comply with what was provided as avoidance behavior (e.g., when the rat needs to press a lever to stop or prevent the shock), there is obviously a punishment of this spontaneous SSDR (because running away does not stop or prevent the negative stimulus). The animal is then obliged to try another SSDR until it finally succeeds in avoiding the negative stimulus. In situations that require an avoidance behavior that does not belong to the SSDR repertoire (e.g., pressing a lever), avoidance behavior will never be learned (unless, in exceptional cases, by chance). Bolles's theory can thus be reduced to an explanation of avoidance learning in terms of classical conditioning (the effect of relations between stimuli), which, in his view, is based on the formation of S-S associations. R-Sr associations therefore play no role in the Bolles model. The Sd-Sr association leads to a CR (threat) that functions as a US that provokes URs. Schematically, this is as depicted in figure 3.16.

$$Sd \longrightarrow Sr \longrightarrow CR \longrightarrow SSDR$$

Figure 3.16
A schematic presentation of the associative model of Bolles (1972) in which activation of the Sd representation activates the representation of shock (Sr), which is assumed to lead to an expectancy of the shock. Because the shock is expected, fear is evoked (CR), which leads to a defensive response (SSDR).

Bolles's explanation of avoidance behavior also shows that it is often difficult to determine whether (avoidance) behavior can be seen as an example of classical or operant conditioning. In almost all procedures of operant conditioning, stimuli also co-occur (e.g., Sd and Sr), making it

Box 3.5 (continued)

possible (in principle) that observed changes in behavior are due to stimulus-stimulus relations. It is therefore always necessary to carefully consider whether the change in behavior is due to S-S or S-R relations; simply looking at the procedures does not suffice. To call something operant or classical conditioning is always a hypothesis about the environmental causes of behavior and needs to be backed up with arguments and evidence.

Think It Through 3.3: Fear Extinction and Avoidance

According to Bolles, the Sd functions as a signal for the presence of the aversive Sr (e.g., shock) and will therefore evoke fear. However, once the animal successfully avoids the Sr, the Sd will no longer be followed by the US, and hence, it should stop eliciting fear (i.e., extinction). Nevertheless, research shows that the Sd still elicits fear when, after long periods of successful avoidance, it is presented in a situation in which the avoidance behavior can no longer be emitted. How could we explain this if we assume that the formation of Sd-Sr associations occurs in line with the Rescorla-Wagner model?

3.3.2 Propositional Models

3.3.2.1 The core of propositional models Propositional models, like associative models, are largely derived from research on classical conditioning. However, they can also be applied to operant conditioning. The idea is that people and other animals try to figure out the conditions under which their behavior has an influence on the environment. They formulate hypotheses that they evaluate on the basis of all available evidence. Behavior is then assumed to be based on the propositions that they take into account. For instance, based on the available propositional knowledge that they have, they might deduce which behavior has the most favorable consequences. This behavior is then emitted.

The Lovibond model (2006; see De Houwer, Crombez, & Baeyens, 2005, for a related model, and Declercq & De Houwer, 2009, for an adaptation of the Lovibond model) on avoidance learning is one of the only propositional models that explicitly focuses on explaining operant conditioning. To illustrate, suppose a rat gets a shock in room A unless it goes to another room B. According to Lovibond, the rat will learn two propositions: (1) "In room A (Sd) I get a shock (Sr)"; (2) "I can avoid the shock (Sr) by walking to another room (R)." The animal thus acquires a proposition about the relations between stimuli and a proposition about the relation between behavior and stimuli. It uses these propositions to decide which behavior is best. When it is in room A, it will walk to room B because it knows that this will lead to a better outcome: if it stays in room A, a shock will follow. If it goes to room B, no shock will follow.

3.3.2.2 General evaluation of propositional models According to propositional models, organisms can form propositions about the consequences of their behavior. Operant conditioning is therefore the result of causal learning (see also Dickinson, 1980). There are findings that directly support this assumption. Consider the Watson study (1967, 1971) involving babies. In this study babies were placed lying in a cradle with their heads on a pillow. In the contingency condition, a rotational movement of the baby's head was immediately followed by the movement of an object above the cradle. In the noncontingent condition, this object was moved just as often but independent of what the baby did. Whereas the rotational movement of the head rose in frequency in the first group, this was not the case in the second group. But there is more: in the first group, the babies seemed to find the movement of the object more and more pleasant, while in the second group they initially responded with a smile to the movement, but this smile quickly disappeared. Babies therefore seem to make a clear distinction between environmental changes that they cause themselves and those that arise independently of their behavior.

One of the important advantages of propositional models is that propositions can specify not only that there is a relation between two stimuli or between a behavior and a stimulus, but also how the two elements are related. For an organism it is important to know the nature of relations in the environment (see Lagnado et al., 2007, for an excellent discussion of this point). The fact that propositions may contain information about the nature of the relation between two stimuli also fits well with the phenomenon of AARR (see section 3.2.5.5.c). After all, humans are able to relate stimuli to each other in many different ways (e.g., [*] is related to [ù]; [*] is more than [ù]). Standard associative models cannot explain that people are capable of this because they can only represent that two stimuli are linked to each other but not how the two stimuli are related (see De Houwer, Hughes, & Barnes-Holmes, 2016, for a more detailed discussion of the implications of AARR for propositional theories as they apply to human and nonhuman animals).

Sometimes it is argued that propositional models can only offer an explanation for rational behavior (e.g., McLaren et al., 2014). There are, however, several reasons why organisms can opt for a behavior that is not the most optimal behavior from an objective point of view.

– Incorrect propositions If one starts from false premises (i.e., false propositions about relations in the environment), then one will also arrive at erroneous conclusions (normative maladaptive behavior). Forming erroneous propositions about relations in the environment can be due to many different factors such as nonrepresentative experiences (e.g., bad luck that one experiences only negative and no positive outcomes of a behavior) or receiving incorrect information from others.

– Incorrect conclusions People (and perhaps other animals; see De Houwer, Hughes, & Barnes-Holmes, 2016) can reason. But they also make mistakes in their reasoning. Such errors can lead to irrational behavior.

– *Automatic effects of old propositions*   Once a certain proposition has been formed, it can be stored in and retrieved from memory automatically. For instance, someone who learns to count will have to think hard about whether the proposition "$3 + 5 = 8$" is true. After a while, however, people automatically remember that this proposition is true without having to rethink the reasons for this. So if you have reached a certain conclusion very often, that conclusion can automatically influence your behavior, even in situations where that conclusion may no longer be correct (De Houwer, 2014, 2018c).

We can therefore conclude that propositional models are capable of explaining many aspects of operant conditioning. Yet these models remain rather vague and have had little impact on operant conditioning research. The real heuristic and predictive value of these models therefore remains unclear.

Box 3.6 Is Reinforcement Desirable?

Some psychologists argue that people should primarily do the things that they are "intrinsically" motivated to do (i.e., because they get satisfaction from doing those things). They argue that reinforcing a behavior could have a negative effect because it can undermine the organism's intrinsic motivation. Take the example of children who are intrinsically motivated to draw. If one then starts to give the child money every time he or she sketches, so the argument goes, the child will eventually draw not because he or she likes to draw but because he or she receives money for drawing. In other words, rather than being **intrinsically motivated**, the behavior becomes **extrinsically motivated**. It has been argued that providing rewards such as money is harmful in the long run because it undermines intrinsic motivation. Imagine that, after a long period of receiving money for each picture drawn, the child no longer receives money. This removes the extrinsic motivation for drawing. But the intrinsic motivation for drawing will have disappeared too—the child will have lost the passion for drawing. Hence, the child will stop drawing all together. A similar argument can also be applied to studying. If you consistently reinforce studying in children, the intrinsic motivation for studying will decrease and the child will start studying less in the long term.

In the 1970s, various experiments were carried out to determine whether reinforcement can indeed have such negative effects. For instance, Deci (1971) conducted a study in which, in a first phase, children were given "intrinsically motivating" tasks (e.g., making puzzles). In a second phase, the children of the experimental group were given a reinforcer each time they solved a puzzle. Children from the control group received no reinforcer. In a third phase, the children were given the opportunity to solve puzzles, but now nobody was reinforced for solving puzzles. The results showed that during the third phase, children from the experimental group solved fewer puzzles than children from the control group. In the experimental group even fewer puzzles were solved during the third phase than during the first phase. This suggests that the intrinsic motivation for solving puzzles had been reduced by the second phase reinforcement schedule.

(continued)

Box 3.6 (continued)

Such findings had a dramatic impact on practice, perhaps also because they fit well in the post-1960s antiauthoritarian zeitgeist. They led to slogans such as "a reward a day makes work out of play" (Zimbardo, 1992) and textbooks were explicitly discouraged from using reinforcement in educational settings. However, these conclusions can be questioned for various reasons. For example, the effect of the original work has failed to replicate (e.g., Eisenberg & Cameron, 1996) and alternative explanations are equally possible (e.g., a decrease in the frequency of puzzle solving behavior could have also been due to fatigue).

But perhaps more importantly, the contrast between reinforcement and intrinsic motivation is based on a misunderstanding. Doubts about the desirability of reinforcement are based on the observation that "rewarding" a behavior sometimes seems to lead to a decrease in the frequency of behavior. However, this conclusion is based on the erroneous assumption that reinforcement is the same as rewarding and that a **reinforcer** is the same as a **reward**. This error is the result of not distinguishing the functional and cognitive levels of explanation. A reinforcer is a purely functional concept; it refers to the function of a stimulus: a reinforcer is a stimulus that leads to an increase in the frequency of behavior when this behavior is linked to that stimulus. Therefore, by definition, reinforcement leads to an increase in the frequency of behavior. If the behavior should decrease in frequency when it is linked to a stimulus, then that stimulus is not a reinforcer but a punisher. The question of whether reinforcement (i.e., linking a behavior to a reinforcer) can lead to a decrease in the frequency of behavior is therefore a pointless question whenever you talk about reinforcers instead of rewards.

The term *reward*, on the other hand, is not a functional term but belongs to the mental level of explanation. Whether something is called a reward does not depend on the function of that stimulus but on the structure or nature of that stimulus. For example, one could say that food is a reward because it has a certain energy value or that money is a reward because it elicits a positive feeling. It is indeed possible that rewards such as food sometimes do not function as reinforcers (e.g., when people have eaten a lot). At best, studies on intrinsic motivation point to the possibility that rewards such as giving money sometimes have negative consequences. But of course, this says nothing about reinforcement in general. The fact that some rewards sometimes do not function as reinforcers does not mean that stimuli can never function as reinforcers. There can be no doubt that reinforcement as an effect is a real fact.

For cognitively oriented learning psychologists, it is interesting to know that stimuli referred to as rewards sometimes do not function as a reinforcers. Indeed, it contradicts simple S-R process theories of operant conditioning (e.g., Thorndike, 1911, see section 3.3.1). Money and food seem to be positive stimuli and should therefore, according to Thorndike, strengthen S-R associations. Hence, one would expect that linking a behavior to money or food should always lead to an increase in the frequency of the behavior. However, the functional knowledge that money and food can sometimes function as punishment can be reconciled with self-determination theory (Deci & Ryan, 2000): linking stimuli such as money and food to behavior can, under certain conditions, be the intrinsic motivation for decreased behavior. The mental concept of "intrinsic motivation" thus helps to explain functional knowledge about reinforcement. So there is no

Box 3.6 (continued)

contradiction between reinforcement and intrinsic motivation. The first is an effect and thus situated at the functional level of explanation while the second is a mental concept that is situated at the mental level of explanation. Mental process theories such as self-determination theory can even help to discover new functional knowledge about reinforcement. The entire debate about the desirability of reinforcement is therefore the result of confusing the functional and cognitive approaches within psychology.

The fact that cognitive psychologists often do not distinguish between the term "reinforcer" and "reward" probably has to do with the fact that they see a purely functional definition of "reinforcement" as circular: if you say that reinforcement (increase in frequency R as a result of the R-Sr relation) occurs because the Sr is a reinforcer, then this is purely circular because the Sr can only be called a reinforcer because reinforcement occurs. However, the term "reinforcer" is not intended to explain reinforcement but to describe the function of the Sr. In order to explain reinforcement as an effect, we do indeed need mental concepts such as rewards and associations. But that does not mean that the term "reinforcer" is meaningless. When we say that a stimulus functions as a reinforcer, this implies the hypothesis that an increase in the frequency of behavior is due to the relation between the behavior and the specific stimulus. In this way, the term reinforcer does provide an explanation for the increase in behavior: the increase is due to that specific R-Sr relation and not to other R-Sr relations. This functional knowledge is sufficient to influence the behavior (e.g., the removal of the R-Sr relation should reduce the frequency of the behavior). The naming of a stimulus as a reinforcer does not say *why* the stimulus has that function, but it does say *that* it has that function, which is also an important thing to know.

4 Complex Forms of Learning: Joint Effects of Multiple Regularities

After reading this chapter, you should be able to:

- Give different examples of learning in which multiple regularities jointly influence behavior.
- Distinguish between different types of complex learning.
- Indicate how "Learning 2.0" differs from the traditional approach to learning as outlined in chapters 1 to 3.

Introductory Task

Try to find in chapters 1 to 3 four examples of learning effects wherein multiple regularities jointly determine a change in behavior.

4.1 Some Basic Terms and an Overview

Throughout this book we have defined learning as the impact of regularities in the environment on behavior. In most cases we have focused on **simple learning**—that is, changes in behavior that are due to a single regularity. However, we also highlighted some examples of **complex learning**, which we defined as changes in behavior that are due to multiple regularities in the environment (see section 0.2.2). In this chapter, we revisit a number of these phenomena in order to (a) identify how they might be related to one another and (b) link them to a number of insights that are currently emerging from the learning literature. We will focus on two types of complex learning that we introduced in the introductory chapter: *moderated learning* and *effects of metaregularities*. Whereas moderated learning refers to the joint impact of **standard regularities** (i.e., regularities with individual stimuli or responses as elements), effects of metaregularities are changes in behavior that are due to **metaregularities** (i.e., regularities in the presence of regularities).

Figure 4.1
Moving from simple to complex learning.

After discussing these two types of complex learning, we consider the provocative idea that in verbal humans, even seemingly simple types of learning such as classical conditioning might qualify as instances of complex learning. If correct, this idea has far-reaching implications for our understanding of human learning and the future of research on learning. The chapter closes with a brief discussion of which mental processes might mediate complex forms of learning.

4.2 Functional Knowledge

4.2.1 Two Types of Complex Learning

4.2.1.1 Moderated learning As noted in the introductory chapter, moderated learning refers to changes in behavior that arise because of the joint impact of multiple standard regularities. Throughout this book ,we have seen many examples of moderated learning. Take, for example, sensory preconditioning in which a light is paired with a tone (Regularity 1) and the tone is subsequently paired with an electric shock (Regularity 2). Once both regularities have been experienced, the light elicits a fear response even though it was never directly paired with the shock. Both regularities are standard regularities because they have only individual stimuli as elements. Neither regularity alone would produce this change in behavior. Hence, sensory preconditioning qualifies as an instance of moderated learning.

If you flip back through the pages of this book, you will see that we have discussed many other phenomena in which behavior changes as the result of multiple standard regularities (e.g., higher-order conditioning, conditioned reinforcement, effects of indirect links between Sd and R, differential outcomes effect). The ones mentioned in chapters 1 to 3 are certainly not the only known instances of moderated learning; many others exist. Take, for example, a phenomenon called *Pavlovian-to-instrumental transfer* (PIT) (see Cartoni, Balleine, & Baldassarre, 2016, for an overview), which refers to changes in behavior that result from the interplay between a regularity in the presence of two stimuli and a regularity in the presence of stimuli and behavior. Imagine that you set up an experiment where first a light is paired with food (Regularity 1) and then the organism learns that pressing a left button will lead to the delivery of food (Regularity 2). Both regularities together ensure that subsequent presentations of the light increase the chances that the organism will press the left button.

It should be clear that the aforementioned phenomena are not new and have already been documented by others. What is new, however, is the proposal to bring all of these phenomena together under the umbrella of "moderated learning" (see De Houwer et al., 2013, for a related but slightly different proposal; see introduction, note 6). This idea has heuristic value in that it highlights that each of these phenomena results from the interplay between separate standard regularities. It also sets the stage for a systematic analysis of the similarities and differences between different instances of moderated learning.

When analyzing instances of moderated learning in this way, it quickly becomes apparent that regularities that interact to produce a certain effect often have one or more elements in common. To illustrate, let's return to the example of sensory preconditioning (e.g., fear responses elicited by a light after light-tone and tone-shock pairings). The two regularities that are involved in this effect share a common element: the tone. Drawing on this idea, Hughes et al. (2016) recently introduced the concept of *intersecting regularities*. Instead of considering each regularity separately, one can see the combination of regularities as a whole (i.e., as a compound) that is more than the sum of its parts (just as one can see two stimuli together as a compound stimulus that is more than the sum of its parts; see section 2.2.5.2.c). Put simply, multiple standard regularities form one intersecting regularity when they share one or more elements with each other. Thus, in sensory preconditioning procedures, one can speak of two stimulus-stimulus relations that together form an intersecting regularity because of a common stimulus element (e.g., the tone). In Pavlovian-to-instrumental transfer, the intersecting regularity is formed by a stimulus-stimulus relation (e.g., light-food) and a behavior-stimulus relation (e.g., pressing the left button → food) that share one element (e.g., the food). Such intersecting regularities can thus be regarded as a fourth type of regularity (in addition to regularities in the occurrence of one stimulus, regularities in the occurrence of two stimuli, and regularities in the occurrence of behavior and stimuli in the environment). It then follows that the effects of such intersecting regularities can be regarded as a fourth type of learning effect (along with effects due to noncontingent stimulus presentations, classical conditioning, and operant conditioning).

The proposal by Hughes et al. (2016) not only has a heuristic value (i.e., it provides a new way of looking at well-known effects) but also has predictive value (i.e., it generates new ideas). For instance, it points to the possibility that all kinds of intersecting regularities can influence behavior, including those that have not yet been examined. Hughes et al. tested this idea in the context of evaluative learning (i.e., the impact of regularities in the environment on evaluative responses). In one of their studies they created four operant contingencies (i.e., regularities in the presence of behavior and stimuli), shown in figure 4.2.

On the one hand, when participants saw a positive image (e.g., a tasty-looking piece of cake) they had to press a computer key (R1), then they were shown a first neutral Chinese letter (neutral ideograph O1). On seeing a novel brand product name (e.g., Ailbe), they had to press a second key (R2), then they again saw the first neutral Chinese letter (O1). These two regularities form an intersecting regularity because they both share a common element (the neutral Chinese letter O1). On the other hand, after seeing a negative image (e.g., a rotten piece of meat), pressing a third computer key (R3) caused a second neutral Chinese letter to appear (O2). The same letter also appeared when participants pressed a fourth key (R4) after seeing a second unknown brand product name (e.g., Sile). Thus, the third and fourth regularity also form an intersecting regularity because they share a common element (i.e., the second neutral Chinese letter O2). Each regularity was repeatedly presented in random order in successive blocks of trials. The authors found that participants came to prefer the

Stimulus		Response	Outcome
Positive image (S1)	→	*Response 1* (R1) →	Neutral ideograph (O1)
Neutral brand (S2)	→	*Response 2* (R2) →	Neutral ideograph (O1)
Negative image (S3)	→	*Response 3* (R3) →	Neutral ideograph (O2)
Neutral brand (S4)	→	*Response 4* (R4) →	Neutral ideograph (O2)

Figure 4.2
A schematic overview of the learning phase of Hughes et al. (2016, Experiment 2). The neutral ideographs are Chinese letters (retrieved from Hughes et al., 2016, figure 3).

first over the second brand product. It therefore seems that the valence of the image (positive or negative) of one regularity transfers to the brand product that is part of another regularity because both regularities involve the same Chinese letter.[1] Research on the effects of intersecting regularities, still in its infancy, constitutes an exciting new direction for exploration. For instance, future work needs to examine whether intersecting regularities lead to changes in other types of behavior (e.g., the ability for stimuli to elicit fear or disgust) and to identify the moderators of this class of effects (e.g., whether effects of intersecting regularities can be undone by presenting stimuli on their own).

4.2.1.2 Effects of metaregularities: On the functions of relations and regularities As mentioned above, behavior can change also as the result of metaregularities—that is, regularities in which at least one element is itself a regularity. Examining the effects of metaregularities is particularly important because it can shed light on the functions of stimulus relations and the functions of regularities. Both issues are discussed in this section.

a) The functions of relations: Relational learning As noted in the introductory chapter, a regularity refers to any state in the environment that entails more than one event at one point in time. Hence, when there is a regularity in the environment, by definition there are multiple events, which make it possible for researchers to identify relations between those events. Take, for instance, a situation in which two images (e.g., a picture of a lemon and a picture of a banana) are presented together on a computer screen. This regularity allows one to identify multiple relations between those images such as relations in terms of shape or color (e.g., the fact that the lemon and the banana have a different shape, as well as the fact that both are yellow). We thus conceive of a relation as something in the environment, just as individual stimuli or regularities can be conceived of as situated in the environment. It offers an additional tool for constructing descriptions of the environment and for analyzing how behavior is a function of that environment. It is a highly valuable tool because it allows for complex and flexible descriptions of the environment that involve multiple events using a large variety of types of relations (e.g., same, opposite, bigger, smaller, part of, etc.). If we allow for relations in our functional analyses, then the scope and power of

---

Think It Through 4.1: Create Your Own Intersecting Regularities Procedure

The study by Hughes et al. (2016, Experiment 2) with the Chinese letters (figure 4.2) is just one of many possible procedures with intersecting regularities that can be created with operant contingencies. Create your own procedure by designing two operant contingencies that don't share their outcome but do share their antecedents and/or responses.

our analyses greatly expands, especially given that behavior often seems to be a function of relations rather than individual events (for many such examples, see Hughes & Barnes-Holmes, 2016).

At this point it might be useful to draw the distinction between relational behavior (which is referred to as "relational responding" or "relating") and relational learning. Relational behavior refers to any behavior that is a function of relations in the environment. For instance, picking a large rather than a small piece of food qualifies as a relational behavior if this choice was based on the difference in size between the two pieces of food (rather than the absolute size of one of the two pieces of food). **Relational learning**, on the other hand, refers to the effect of *regularities* in the environment on behavior, like any other type of learning. What distinguishes relational learning from other types of learning is that behavior changes as the result of regularities in which relations function as stimuli.

What does it mean to say that relations function as stimuli? In the previous chapters, we saw that a stimulus such as a tone or light can have many different functions in learning: it can function as an Sd, Sr, CS, US, occasion setter, establishing operation, and so on. In principle, relations can function as stimuli in that they can have the same stimulus functions. This idea makes sense if one considers the fact that stimuli are typically classes of events that are defined in terms of a unit—that is, in terms of a feature that all the events in a stimulus class share and that differentiates events within the class from those outside of the class (see section 3.1.1.1). For instance, the class of red stimuli encompasses all stimuli that have a red color. If we take this idea (i.e., that the unit is defined in terms of the feature that all events in the class share) and push it one step further, then we see that the unit that defines a stimulus class can also refer to *the relation between events*. In these cases, one can examine whether relations can acquire specific stimulus functions.

These are all quite abstract ideas, so let's stop and consider a concrete example. Think back to chapter 3, where we introduced a paradigm known as the matching-to-sample task. In that task, a sample stimulus is presented at the top of the screen and two comparison stimuli are presented at the bottom of the screen. Participants need to select the comparison stimulus at the bottom that is identical to the sample stimulus at the top (see figure 3.9). In this case, all events in which the sample stimulus is identical to the left comparison stimulus are part of the stimulus class that signals that a left response is correct. Hence, the unit that defines this stimulus class is the *relation* between sample and comparison stimuli. Now think back to the relational matching-to-sample task discussed in the introductory chapter (see figure 0.3). In that task, one pair of sample stimuli are presented at the top of the screen (e.g., 1–1) and two pairs of comparison stimuli are presented at the bottom of the screen (e.g., 3–3 and 3–2). During the task, a correct behavior depends on the relation between relations (e.g., choosing the stimulus pair 3–3 is reinforced whenever one sees the sample pair 1–1 because both pairs consist of identical stimuli; see figure 0.3). In this case, all events in which the relation between the elements of the sample pair (e.g., 1–1) is identical to the relation between the elements of the left comparison pair (e.g., 3–3) are part of the stimulus class that signals that a left response is correct. Thus, in this case, the unit that defines the stimulus class refers to the *relation between relations*.

Just as standard regularities allow one to study changes in the function of the individual stimuli that are elements in that regularity, so too do metaregularities allow for the study of changes in the function of the relations that are elements of the metaregularity. Metaregularities offer an ideal tool to study relational learning because they have at least one regularity as an element, which makes it possible to identify relations between the stimuli or responses involved in that regularity, and thus to examine changes in the functions of those relations. Consider a matching-to-sample task in which participants succeed in systematically selecting the comparison stimulus that is identical to the sample stimulus (i.e., show evidence of NAARR; see section 3.2.5.5.c). In this case, the identity relation between the sample and comparison stimulus can be said to have acquired the function of an Sd: it determines the responses of the organism on the basis of the fact that it signals which response will be reinforced. In a relational matching-to-sample task, on the other hand, it is not a single relation between stimuli that functions as an Sd, but a relation between relations. Just as researchers have looked at the conditions under which individual stimuli acquire the function of an Sd, learning researchers can also study the conditions under which relations become Sds. The same applies for all other stimulus functions.

One can distinguish different types of relational learning depending on the nature of the regularity that is involved. For instance, one can distinguish effects of (1) regularities in the presence of a single relation; (2) regularities in the presence of two relations (see Think It Through 4.2 for a concrete example); (3) regularities in the presence of a relation and a behavior; and (4) intersections between multiple metaregularities that each have one or more relations as elements. As you undoubtedly noticed, these types of relational learning are conceptually similar to the types of (nonrelational) learning that we distinguished earlier on in this book. The only difference is that one or more of the elements in these regularities are relations rather than (nonrelational classes of) individual events.

The distinction between these types of relational learning provides a heuristic framework for research on relational learning, which not only allows one to systematize known instances of relational learning (i.e., the framework has heuristic value) but also generates new ideas about relational learning (i.e., the framework has predictive value). Its heuristic power can be illustrated in the context of matching-to-sample and relational matching-to-sample tasks. Successful performance on both tasks can be seen as instances of operant relational learning: in both cases, the metaregularity is operant in that a response (selecting a comparison) is reinforced (feedback that a response was correct) in the presence of a relational Sd. The two cases differ, however, with regard to the nature of the relation that functions as an Sd. Whereas in matching-to-sample, a relation between individual stimuli functions as the Sd, in relational matching-to-sample, a relation between relations functions as the Sd. Hence, our definition of (different types of) relational learning allows one to highlight similarities and differences between different learning phenomena.

The framework also has predictive value. Until now, research on relational learning has focused mainly on situations where relations have the function of an Sd (see section 3.2.5.5.c). However, relations could also have other functions. For example, it would be interesting to investigate whether relations can function as a CS (as would be the case when a pair of identical stimuli elicits fear because a shock previously followed the presentation of two identical stimuli but not the presentation of two different stimuli), as a US (as would be the case when two stimuli are perceived as more similar because they were previously presented together with a pair of identical stimuli), as an occasion setter (as would be case when the fear elicited by a light depends on the presence of identical stimuli because the presence of identical stimuli previously signaled the light-shock contingency), as an Sr (as would be the case when the presentation of identical stimuli reinforces a response because identical stimuli were previously paired with food), and an establishing operation (as would be the case when the presence of identical stimuli increases the extent to which food reinforces a response because identical stimuli were previously paired with food). For each of these functions, one can examine what variables moderate relational learning. Only a tiny fraction of these possibilities has already been explored.

So far, we have focused on functions that are studied in nonrelational types of learning (e.g., CS and US in classical conditioning; Sd and enabling condition in operant conditioning).

Think It Through 4.2: Learning via Analogy

In a yet unpublished study conducted at our lab in collaboration with Ian Hussey (see https://osf.io/36f99/), two pairs of stimuli were presented simultaneously on a computer screen: one pair on the left side of the screen and a second pair on the right side of the screen. The first pair consisted of a positive word (e.g., FLOWERS) and a neutral unknown word (e.g., VEKTE). For one group of participants, the second pair of stimuli consisted of two identical words (e.g., FULL and FULL). For another group of participants, the second pair of stimuli consisted of two antonyms (e.g., EMPTY and FULL). Results showed that the neutral word of the first pair was subsequently rated more positively by the first group than by the second group. Try to analyze this study from the perspective of relational learning. What is the metaregularity that produces the change in liking? What type of relational learning could this be?

However, there is one function that is unique to relational learning—namely, the function of a **relational contextual cue** (Hayes, Barnes-Holmes, & Roche, 2001). As noted at the outset of this section, whenever there is more than one event, it is possible to identify multiple relations that each refer to a different property of those events. A relational contextual cue signals which of those relations is relevant in the current context and can thus determine which of those relations has a particular function. To illustrate, let us return to performance in matching-to-sample tasks. Suppose that on each trial of a matching-to-sample task, you see three stimuli: one at the top (the sample stimulus) and two at the bottom of the screen (the two comparison stimuli). These stimuli vary in terms of their identity (* versus ^) and their color (blue or green; see figure 4.3). In this example there are two stimulus relations that can function as an Sd: the physical identity relation (e.g., selecting the comparison stimulus with the same identity as the sample stimulus, regardless of their color) and the color relation (e.g., selecting the comparison stimulus with the same color as the sample stimulus, regardless of identity). In such situations, contextual cues (e.g., the circle and square in figure 4.3) can be used to indicate which stimulus relation signals the correct relational response (e.g., in the presence of a circle, select the comparison stimulus with the same shape as the sample stimulus; in the presence of a square, select the comparison stimulus with the same color as the sample stimulus). Those cues can be said to function as a relational contextual cue when performance depends on the presence of those cues (e.g., participants select the comparison

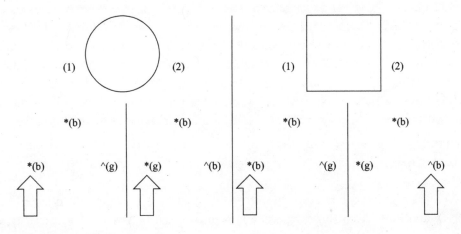

Figure 4.3
A relational contextual cue (circle or square) indicates which relation participants should respond to—either the match between the shape (circle) or the color (square) of the stimuli. The arrow indicates the correct choice on a given trial. The letter between parentheses indicates the color (blue or green) of the stimulus.

with the same identity as the sample in the presence of the circle, and the comparison with the same color as the sample in the presence of the square).[2]

Just as individual stimuli (such as circles and squares) can function as a relational contextual cue, so too can stimulus relations. For instance, on each trial, one could present two images at the top of the screen, the content of which changes from trial to trial. If the content of the images is identical (e.g., two pictures of a lion or two pictures of a chair), then participants need to select the comparison stimulus with the same shape as the sample stimulus; if the content of the images is different (e.g., a picture of a lion and a picture of a chair; a picture of a house and a picture of a flower), then participants need to select the comparison stimulus with the same color as the sample stimulus. If the relation between the content of the images influences responding in line with these contingencies, it can be said to function as a relational contextual cue. Considering relations as relational contextual cues opens up some interesting new possibilities for learning research. For instance, it is likely that the speed with which a relation can acquire the function of a relational contextual cue will depend on the similarity between the different relations. Imagine a situation in which two geometric shapes are presented in blue or green at the top of a screen. In one condition, a match in the identity of the shapes (e.g., a blue circle and a green circle) signals that a match in the identity of the sample and comparison stimulus is relevant for selecting the correct response. A match in the color of the shapes (e.g., a blue circle and a blue square) signals that a match in the color of the sample and comparison stimulus is relevant. In a second condition, however, a match in the identity of the shapes signals that color match is relevant, whereas a match in the color of the shapes signals that identity match is relevant for selecting the comparison stimulus. In all likelihood, fewer trials are needed to establish the relation between the shapes as a relational contextual cue in the first condition than in the second condition. Surprisingly little is known about when and how events (including relations) acquire the function of relational contextual cues. Because these cues are crucial for relational learning, it would be good to devote more attention to this issue in future research.

b) The functions of regularities: Regularities as relational contextual cues   Just as individual stimuli can have different functions, so too can regularities have different functions. In terms of stimulus classes, one could say that the unit that defines the stimulus class can refer to the relation between the spatiotemporal properties of events—that is, the way in which events occur in space and time. From this perspective, a regularity can be viewed as a special type of relation—namely, a relation in terms of the time and place at which different events occur. For instance, consider a situation in which lever pressing is followed by food whenever two stimuli are presented on the screen, but not when only one stimulus is presented or no stimulus is presented. All events in which two stimuli appear together on the screen are part of the stimulus class that signals that lever pressing will be followed by food, irrespective of the other properties of those stimuli (e.g., their identity or color). In this situation, the presence of two stimuli is a regularity that is itself one element in a larger operant metaregularity that also involves lever pressing and food. As a result of this metaregularity, the mere presence of two stimuli (i.e., presenting two stimuli together in space and time on a screen) could take on the function of an Sd that influences the rate of lever pressing. Likewise, regularities could in principle serve the function of a CS, occasion setter, establishing operation, and so on. Changes in each of these functions can be studied using metaregularities that relate regularities to other events (e.g., stimuli, responses, relations, other regularities).

As we mentioned in our discussion of AARR (see section 3.2.5.5.c), there are reasons to believe that regularities can function as relational contextual cues. More specifically, we argued that the mere act of reinforcing a certain response in a matching-to-sample task could signal that the sample and the to-be-selected comparison stimulus are equivalent. For instance, reinforcing participants to select the comparison stimulus ù in the presence of the sample stimulus * during a learning phase could function as a relational contextual cue for acting as if ù and * are equivalent during a subsequent test phase (see figure 3.10). This would explain why participants select * on test trials where ù is presented as the sample stimulus and * is presented as one of the comparison stimuli: it is one way of "acting as if" ù and * are equivalent.

Note that in these studies on AARR, regularities do not acquire the function of relational contextual cue during the course of the experiment. Instead, this function has probably been acquired before the start of the experiment. Unfortunately, little is known about the learning history via which regularities can acquire their function as relational contextual cues. There are some studies suggesting that this function is context dependent. For instance, under certain conditions, reinforcement can function as a contextual cue for opposition—that is, for acting as if stimuli are opposite to each other (see Hayes et al., 2001, Hughes & Barnes-Holmes, 2016, and Perez, de Almeida, & de Rose, 2015; Perez et al., 2017 for more details). More generally, there is little to no research on the functions of regularities or how those functions are acquired. This lack of knowledge stands in sharp contrast to the central role of regularities in learning research. As we will discuss in the next section, research on the functions of regularities could indeed shed a completely new light on learning in general.

4.2.2 Learning 2.0

One of the cornerstones of this book is the idea that learning can be defined as changes in behavior that are due to regularities in the environment. But what does "due to" mean? What exactly is the role of regularities in changing behavior? In this section, we examine the intriguing idea that regularities influence behavior because they function as a relational contextual cue for AARR (see Hayes et al., 2001, and De Houwer & Hughes, 2017, for more details). In the previous section, we proposed that regularities can have this function in matching-to-sample tasks where participants need to respond on the basis of the relation between stimuli (see figure 3.10). But maybe regularities can function as relational contextual cues in many other situations, too?

To illustrate this idea, let us consider evaluative conditioning. Assume that a first novel nonword is repeatedly paired with a positive word (e.g., AMBIK–LOVE), whereas a second novel nonword repeatedly co-occurs with a negative word (e.g., SAFROM–CANCER). After being exposed to this procedure, participants typically respond more positively to the first nonword than to the second one (e.g., Hughes, Ye, & De Houwer, 2019). We have recently argued that this evaluative conditioning effect occurs because the pairing of stimuli functions as a relational contextual cue signaling that the paired stimuli are equivalent (De Houwer & Hughes, 2016; Hughes, De Houwer, & Barnes-Holmes, 2016). For instance, after seeing AMBIK together with LOVE, participants start acting as if AMBIK has the same meaning as LOVE, which includes responding in positive ways to AMBIK. Note that this functional analysis implies that the evaluative conditioning effect is an instance of AARR. In other words, the change in liking of the CS is seen not as a change in a nonrelational (evaluative) response (e.g., AMBIK now evokes positive rather than neutral responses) but as the emergence of or a change in relational responding (e.g., responding to AMBIK as if it is equivalent to LOVE). The evaluative conditioning effect remains an evaluative conditioning effect (i.e., a change in liking due to stimulus pairings), but the ideas about the function of the pairings (i.e., a relational contextual cue rather than a mere functional cause) and the nature of the change in behavior (i.e., a change in relational responding vs. nonrelational responding) are different (see De Houwer & Hughes, 2016, 2017, for more details).

A similar argument can be constructed for other forms of learning (in verbal humans). For instance, in the context of effects of noncontingent stimulus presentations, perhaps the mere repetition of a novel stimulus sometimes has the function of a relational contextual cue, or more specifically, a cue indicating that the frequently presented stimulus is equivalent to other frequently presented stimuli. If we assume that positive stimuli occur more often than negative stimuli (see Unkelbach, Fiedler, Bayer, Stegmüller, & Danner, 2008), then we can understand why the repeated presentation of a stimulus leads to a more positive evaluation of that stimulus (see the mere exposure effect, section 1.1.2). In other words, (1) the fact that a novel stimulus frequently occurs is a cue indicating that this stimulus is similar to other frequently occurring stimuli; and (2) frequent stimuli are often positive; so (3) responding to the stimulus as if it is similar to other frequent stimuli includes responding to the stimulus in positive ways.

The idea that regularities influence behavior because they function as a relational contextual cue for AARR could have immense implications for the psychology of learning. Because of this reason, we proposed the concept of Learning 2.0 to describe this new perspective (De Houwer & Hughes, 2017). First, it sheds new light on how learning via instructions and observation are related to other modes of learning. It is likely that learning via instructions and observation (see section 2.2.1.1) are examples of AARR. For instance, participants might be told that a tone will be followed by an electric shock. As a result, the tone will elicit fear even if the tone and shock are never paired (e.g., Cook & Harris, 1937). It is unlikely that the message "tone is followed by shock" has this effect simply because the words *tone* and *shock* occur together in space and time (see De Houwer & Hughes, 2016, for a discussion). Instead, this type of instruction probably has an impact because it functions as a relational contextual cue (e.g., it makes people respond as if the tone is a predictor of the shock). Likewise, when you observe that someone else responds fearfully to an object that you do not know, this event might function as a relational contextual cue for acting as if the object is similar to other fearful objects. Hence, also observational learning could be an instance of AARR. From this perspective, one could argue that all types of learning in verbal human beings are instances of AARR but that different types of learning differ with regard to the nature of the relational contextual cue that controls AARR (De Houwer & Hughes, 2017). Whereas in most types of learning, spatiotemporal regularities (e.g., the pairing of stimuli) function as a relational contextual cue, words serve this function in learning via instructions and observed events serve this function in learning via observation.

A second implication of the "Learning 2.0" perspective is that the effects of a regularity should be context dependent because its function as a relational contextual cue is context dependent. When discussing the idea that reinforcement can function as a relational contextual cue (section 4.2.1.2.b), we already mentioned that this function can itself be context dependent (i.e., reinforcement can function sometimes as a cue for equivalence and sometimes as a cue for opposition). Recent studies suggest that the same is true for stimulus pairings. For instance, Hughes et al. (2019) not only paired nonwords with positive or negative words (e.g., AMBIK–LOVE; SAFROM–CANCER) but also presented context trials on which either a pair of identical words (e.g., UP–UP) or a pair of opposite words (e.g., UP–DOWN) was presented. They observed that the evaluative conditioning effect (i.e., a preference for AMBIK over SAFROM) was reduced or even eliminated when the context trials displayed opposite words. One interpretation of this finding is that the context trials changed the relational cue function of the stimulus pairings (see Think It Through 4.2 for another interpretation). Whereas pairings typically function as a cue for the equivalence of the paired stimuli, this function can be counteracted by presenting context trials in which words with opposite meanings are paired. Although these results are preliminary, they illustrate the generative power of the idea that seemingly simple forms of learning such as evaluative conditioning in humans might actually be instances of AARR. Without this idea, we probably would not have examined the impact of context trials on evaluative conditioning.

Third, the "Learning 2.0" perspective implies that there might be fundamental differences between learning in humans and learning in nonhuman animals. As noted earlier (section 3.2.5.5.c), there are reasons to suspect that AARR can be found only in humans who are verbally able because of a long learning history dealing with relational events (e.g., see Hayes et al., 2001, for details on what that learning history might entail). If seemingly simple forms of learning in humans can be instances of AARR, then there might be fundamental differences in simple forms of learning between humans with a learning history that supports AARR (for whom regularities could function as relational contextual cues for AARR) versus other animals or humans who did not experience the learning history that gives rise to AARR (for whom regularities would not function as relational contextual cues for AARR). Until now, most learning researchers assumed that human and nonhuman animals learn in more or less similar ways (but see Hayes et al., 2001). This was one of the main reasons why so much learning research has been conducted with nonhuman organisms such as rats and pigeons. But from the perspective of Learning 2.0, this fundamental assumption needs to be questioned. When looking at the moderators of learning, it is undeniable that there are many parallels between learning in human and nonhuman animals. But these similarities might hide fundamental differences (see also the idea of convergent evolution, discussed in section 2.2.3). Learning 2.0 offers us ideas about possible differences in moderators of learning (e.g., the impact of relational contextual cues for AARR and the role of learning history), ideas that have already inspired and will continue to inspire future research. The fact that conditioning in humans often depends on conscious rules (rule-governed behavior) instead of contingencies (contingency-shaped behavior; Skinner, 1966, 1969; see section 3.2.2.2.c) is an indication that there are important differences between learning in humans versus nonhumans. Although many questions remain with regard to how exactly learning in (verbally able) humans and nonhumans might differ (see De Houwer et al., 2016, Hayes et al., 2001, Hughes & Barnes-Holmes, 2014, for a discussion), it would be wise to critically reexamine the long-standing assumption that the principles and mechanisms of learning are the same in humans and other animals.

Finally, the idea of Learning 2.0 highlights the importance of studying relational contextual cues. How do individual stimuli and regularities come to acquire these functions? For example, is it possible that a stimulus can become a relational contextual cue via the joint presentation of that stimulus and another stimulus that already functions as a relational contextual cue (e.g., Perez et al., 2015, 2017)? How can relational functions be changed once they have been learned? For example, is it possible to extinguish this function by repeated stimulus presentations? How do different relational contextual cues interact? Does it matter whether the relational contextual cue is an individual stimulus, a class of stimuli, a relation, or a regularity? Or does the type of regularity matter (see De Houwer & Hughes, 2017, for a discussion)? We still know very little about the answers to these questions (but see Hughes & Barnes-Holmes, 2016). A new era of psychological research on learning is thus emerging.

Box 4.1 The Shared Features Principle and Related Features Principle

We recently proposed the shared features principle, which states that whenever two stimuli share one feature, people act as if they also share other features (Hughes, De Houwer, Mattavelli, & Hussey, in press). Put differently, the sharing of features can function as a relational contextual cue for equivalence.[3] There are many examples of the shared features principle in the psychological literature. For instance, people will act as if members of the same group are more similar to each other than to members of other groups (e.g., Otten, 2016). In this case, the shared feature is group membership. Likewise, the success of counterfeit brands suggests that unknown brands that share features with well-known brands (e.g., their brand names are written in similar fonts or the products are packaged in a similar way) tend to be treated in similar ways as the well-known brands that they resemble (e.g., as valuable and thus worthy of purchase). Whereas these individual phenomena are typically studied in isolation, the shared features principle highlights the communality between these phenomena. Moreover, it implies that there might be many other, as yet undiscovered instances of the shared features principle.

What is particularly interesting for research on learning is that environmental regularities can be thought of as involving events that share spatiotemporal features. For instance, when two stimuli are presented together in space and time, they share the time and location in which they occur. Hence, based on the shared features principle, one can predict that people will often respond as if the paired stimuli are also similar in other ways. Consider an evaluative conditioning study in which the nonword AMBIK is repeatedly presented together with the positive word LOVE. As a result of these pairings, AMBIK and LOVE have spatiotemporal properties in common. Hence, the shared features principle predicts that people will respond as if AMBIK and LOVE also have the same valence; that is, they will respond to AMBIK in a positive way. Evaluative conditioning might thus be one instance of the shared features principle. Hughes, De Houwer, Mattavelli, & Hussey (in press) reasoned that if this idea is correct, changes in liking will also occur for stimuli that have other features in common. In a series of studies, they indeed found evidence for changes in liking that were based on the fact that two stimuli were presented in the same color or the same font.

At our lab, we are currently exploring whether the shared features principle itself is just one instance of an even broader principle that we refer to as the "related features principle." Events not only can share features but also can be related in other ways. For instance, stimuli can be located at opposite locations (left vs. right), differ in size (small vs. large), be related in a hierarchical manner (A is a member of B), and so on (see Hayes et al., 2001). The related features principle states that if events are related in a particular way with regard to one feature, participants often act as if those events are related in the same way with regard to other features. Hence, if two stimuli share a feature (e.g., group membership, their presence in space and time, color), people will act as if they also share other features (e.g., intelligence, whether they are good or bad). However, if two stimuli are opposite with regard to one feature, people will respond as if they are opposite with regard to other features, too. In an initial, yet unpublished test of this idea that was conducted in collaboration with Ian Hussey (see https://osf.io/8zqs6/), participants were asked to discriminate between presentations of a nonword and presentations of existing words by pressing a left key for

(continued)

Box 4.1 (continued)

one type of stimulus and a right key for the other (e.g., press left for nonwords and right for existing words). As such, nonwords and existing words were opposite in terms of the response to which they were assigned (left or right). For some participants, all existing words had a positive valence, whereas for other participants, all existing words had a negative valence. In line with predictions, participants who distinguished the nonwords from positive words liked the nonwords less than participants who distinguished the nonwords from negative words. Hence, stimuli that are opposite in one respect (i.e., the location of the response to which they are assigned) are responded to as if they are also opposite in another respect (i.e., whether they are good or bad). Future studies are needed to confirm these initial findings, to extrapolate them to other types of stimuli and relations, and to identify the boundary conditions and moderators of related features effects.

Another way of extending research on the shared (and related) features principle is to apply these principles to (meta-) regularities that share elements. Just as people might act as if stimuli that share features are also similar in other ways, they might act as if regularities that share elements also have other things in common. This idea is compatible with some of the effects of intersecting regularities that we have observed in our lab. Consider the evaluative learning study of Hughes, De Houwer, & Perugini (2016) that involved four regularities consisting of positive or negative images, novel brands, responses on a keyboard, and Chinese letters (see section 4.2.1.1). When two regularities shared a Chinese letter as the outcome stimulus, people acted as if the neutral brand of second regularity and the images of the first regularity had a similar valence. Hence, they acted as if the regularities were similar in other ways too (i.e., with regard to the valence of the first stimulus in each regularity). In sum, many instances of learning could be seen as instances of the shared or related features principle, which provides a bridge between learning research and other instances of these principles such as minimal group membership effects.

4.3 Mental Process Theories

Although much research has been carried out on individual instances of complex learning (e.g., sensory preconditioning, Pavlovian-to-instrumental transfer), this research has been fragmented, and few attempts have been made to relate the different forms of complex learning. Given the dominance of associative models in learning research, mental process accounts of individual instances of complex learning have typically been formulated in terms of association formation in memory. In section 2.3.1.2, we saw how sensory preconditioning has been explained from the perspective of associative S-S models (see figure 2.16; see Wagner, 1981, for an account of interactions between repeated stimulus presentations and stimulus pairings). The basic idea is that each stimulus-stimulus relation results in an association in memory, which results in the formation of a chain of associations that allows activation to spread from one stimulus representation to the other. Although this "chain of associations" idea might explain some forms of complex learning, it seems difficult to reconcile with others. For example, consider the example of learning via intersecting regularities, discussed in section 4.2.1.1. In order to explain these effects, one has to assume that activation can spread across an association in both directions. For instance, to explain the effect observed by Hughes et al. (2016; see section 4.2.1.1), it is necessary not only that the presentation of Product 1 leads to the forward activation of the representation of the first neutral Chinese letter, but also that this in turn leads to the backward activation of the representation of the positive image. That second step presupposes a reverse spreading of activation: from the representation of a result (the first Chinese letter) to the representation of a stimulus that always precedes that outcome (the positive image). From research on animals, however, there is very little evidence for such a reverse spreading of activation (see Ward-Robinson & Hall, 1996, but see also Prével et al., 2016). In chapter 3, we also discussed the fact that associative models have difficulties with the phenomenon of relational responding (NAARR and AARR). Because simple associations do not provide information about the precise way in which stimuli are related (e.g., similar, opposite, larger or smaller than), they also cannot explain the fact that behavior can depend on the way in which stimuli are related. This leads us to conclude that associative models are limited in their ability to explain complex forms of learning. On the other hand, it needs to be acknowledged that, as a class, associative models can account for a wide range of seemingly complex types of behavior (see Haselgrove, 2016, for an excellent discussion of the power of associative models).

Complex learning seems more in line with the assumptions of propositional models. One of the great advantages of propositions is that they can be combined via inferential reasoning to arrive at entirely novel propositions: new knowledge can be derived or "inferred" from existing knowledge. When different regularities occur in the environment, each regularity can lead to a separate proposition. Complex learning can then be the result of the fact that these propositions give rise to novel propositions that in turn influence behavior. Let's return to the example of sensory preconditioning once more. If you know that a light is followed by a tone, and the tone is followed by a shock, then (given certain assumptions) you can infer that the light will be followed by the shock. Both stimulus-stimulus relations thus lead to a proposition, and when combined, these propositions lead to a conclusion that has an impact on behavior. As we noted earlier (see section 3.3.2.2), it is not necessarily the case that every inference one makes is logical. But if inferences form the basis of complex forms of learning, one should be able to influence such effects by influencing the inferences (e.g., by providing information that influences the probability of a certain inference). If, for example, sensory preconditioning is based on an inference about the sequence of events, you could negate this effect by making people doubt that the tone is always followed by the shock. For example, if participants are confronted with trials in which the tone is preceded by a stimulus (e.g., a square or the sound of a bell) but not followed by the shock, they might decide that the tone is followed by the shock only when the tone is presented by itself. This may lead them to infer that the light will not be followed by the shock. To the best of our knowledge, such predictions have not yet been tested.

Finally, we repeat our conclusion that propositional models fit nicely with the phenomenon of NAARR and AARR (see also section 3.3.2.2). The fact that behavior can depend on the precise relation between stimuli seems explicable only if one presumes that organisms have propositional knowledge about the nature of relations (De Houwer, Hughes, & Barnes-Holmes, 2016). In this chapter, we have also argued that even apparently simple forms of learning such as classical and operant conditioning can qualify as instances of AARR for certain organisms with certain learning histories. This idea fits nicely with our earlier conclusion that propositional models offer a good explanation for classic and operant conditioning (see sections 2.3.2 and 3.3.2). After all, if classical and operant conditioning (at least in humans) is a form of AARR, and if AARR can be explained only on the basis of propositional models, then it is also logical that classical and operant conditioning (in humans) is mediated by the formation of propositions. We are therefore convinced that propositional models of learning will provide a lasting inspiration in studying both seemingly simple forms of learning and more complex forms of learning. Nevertheless, propositional models of complex learning also face challenges. Consider the fact that NAARR can be observed in both human and nonhuman animals, whereas AARR has been observed only in humans. If both NAARR and AARR rely on propositions, then why does this difference between human and nonhuman animals arise? One might argue that human and nonhuman animals have different types of propositions, but so far, little has been said about what those differences might be (see De Houwer, Hughes, & Barnes-Holmes, 2016, for a discussion of this issue).

5 Applied Learning Psychology: Using the Principles of Learning to Improve the Well-Being of Individuals, Groups, and Societies

After reading this chapter, you should be able to:

- Specify three domains where the principles of learning have already been used to improve human well-being.
- Identify the core features of a functional analysis and clarify how one can test to see whether an intervention successfully changed behavior.
- Apply the principles of learning to an individual- or group-level problem in your own life or in an area that you care about.

Introductory Task

Can you think of three ways in which the principles of learning developed in the laboratory could be used to promote well-being in daily life (at either the individual or group level)?

5.1 Introduction: From Experimentation to Application

Chapters 1 to 4 tell the story of how learning psychologists identified a small but powerful set of regularities, as well as the factors that moderate their impact on behavior. These regularities are quite remarkable: when properly understood and arranged, they allow us to predict and influence the behavior of many (if not most) organisms on our planet. Think about that for a moment. Nearly every organism on planet Earth has been prepared via evolution to adapt to the world in specific ways. By understanding how they learn, we can better explain their past actions and predict (as well as influence) their future behavior. The chapters in this book have highlighted how different types of regularities constitute important pathways via which organisms are shaped by and in turn, shape their environment.

Figure 5.1
In the pursuit of well-being.

At this point, you might assume that what we discussed in chapters 1 to 4 is applicable to only our nonhuman counterparts and insufficient to fully grapple with the complexities of our own species. Surely, humans are endowed with unique abilities (e.g., language, imagination, creativity, and free will) that distinguish them from other species in the animal kingdom, which thus makes their thoughts, feelings, and actions difficult to predict, never mind influence. Flipping back through the pages of this book might also reinforce such an idea, given that we have generally relied on simple organisms (e.g., rats and pigeons) interacting with simple procedures (e.g., mazes and Skinner boxes) to explain behavioral effects, principles, and their moderators. But if you arrive at such an assumption (e.g., "the psychology of learning is only relevant to rats and pigeons") then you are making a big mistake, and missing out on the true power, scope, and potential of what the psychology of learning actually has to offer. In other words, if you take only one message from this book, it should be this: what shapes the behavior of simple organisms such as plants, fish, rats, and pigeons also influences the behavior of more complex ones such as dolphins, octopi, bonobos, and yes, even humans.

The concepts we covered in this book (e.g., classical and operant conditioning) are being used each and every day to improve human well-being. They form the core of treatment programs that are dramatically improving the lives of millions of children and adults living with developmental and intellectual disabilities (see Virués-Ortega, 2010). They are shaping people into better parents, teachers, colleagues, and friends (see Biglan, 2015). They are being used to radically cut drug and alcohol use in people struggling with addictions (see, e.g., Prendergast, Podus, Finney, Greenwell, & Roll, 2006). Concepts and procedures derived from the psychology of learning are the beating heart of many clinical therapies used to treat phobias, panic and anxiety disorders, and chronic pain–related issues, as well as psychosis, depression, and substance abuse (see Messer & Gurman, 2011). Those same ideas are deployed to train disobedient pets and improve the welfare of zoo animals and livestock (e.g., Friedman, Edling, & Cheney, 2006; Maple & Segura, 2015; see http://www.Behaviorworks.org and http://www.Behave.net), address health behaviors (e.g., Friman & Piazza, 2011), help athletes improve their performances and pathological gamblers beat their addictions (Daar & Dixon, 2015; Luiselli & Reed, 2015), promote recycling and reduce pollution (Lehman & Geller, 2004), and much, much more (see Roane, Ringdahl, & Falcomata, 2015; Schneider, 2012). The takeaway message is that the procedures, effects, and principles we discussed in chapters 1 to 4 drive human behavior and can help us save lives and improve well-being.

Yet, the true potential of learning psychology extends even beyond the level of an individual organism: regularities and their moderators govern the behavior of groups just as they do individuals, and they are helping us improve the functioning of families and schools (see Biglan, 2015). They are contributing to our understanding of the financial behavior of people and markets (behavioral economics; Foxall, 2016; Reed et al., 2013) and helping us optimize the functioning and well-being of companies and their employees (Ludwig, 2015). Perhaps most importantly, given the global challenges we all face, the principles of learning have the potential to help us predict and influence the behavior of the large-scale groups in which we are embedded (e.g., cultures, societies, and systems).

Therefore, in chapter 5, we move away from experimentation and toward application. We first provide a short recap of what we learned in chapters 1 to 4 to showcase how work in the laboratory can help us influence behavior in the real world. Thereafter, we discuss how the principles of learning are currently being used to devise interventions that improve the lives of individuals and shape the well-being of groups. As we shall see, applied functional learning psychologists have had much success with behavioral change at the individual and small group levels, and to a lesser extent, with changing the behavior of larger systems such as corporations, societies, or species. Although the ideas outlined in this book are highly relevant to the societal and environmental problems we all face, few learning researchers have ventured into these waters (for notable exceptions see Biglan, 2015; Zettle et al., 2016). We will try to follow them in this endeavor. We then conclude the chapter with a short introduction to a new functional-cognitive approach to behavior change known as *psychological engineering*. This approach argues that understanding the environmental moderators and mental mediators of learning can better equip people with the knowledge necessary to improve their own well-being and the world around them.

One last point before we begin. It is important to note that we cannot (nor do we intend to) provide a complete overview of every area in which concepts from the psychology of learning are currently being applied or could be applied. Doing so would require too much time, and the examples are simply too diverse. Instead, our aim is to provide a brief overview of the current directions in this work and convey its potential for improving well-being on both small and large scales. When reading this chapter, try to keep in mind what you have learned in chapters 1 to 4. If you can recognize what the principles of learning are, then you are better able to identify when they are being used (intentionally or unintentionally) to shape your own behavior as well as that of the people and society around you. Indeed, as you will see, just as nuclear energy can be used for prosocial (e.g., cheap, clean energy) and selfish reasons (e.g., nuclear weapons), so too can the principles of learning be used for good and ill.[1]

5.2   On the Relationship between Learning and Application

Throughout this book we have defined learning as an *effect* (i.e., as a change in behavior due to regularities in the environment). *Regularities* refers simply to patterns or systematic occurrences that take place across time and/or space. As we have seen, there are three important types of regularities: regularities in the presence of (a) a single stimulus, (b) multiple stimuli, or (c) stimuli and responses. Each of these different ways of arranging the environment leads to a *behavioral effect*. Moreover, different regularities can also jointly influence behavior (i.e., complex learning). All these learning effects can be moderated by (at least) five different factors: the nature of the stimuli and behaviors that constitute the regularity, the behavior used to test the impact of the regularity, characteristics of the organism, the context in which the organism is embedded, and the nature of the regularity itself. When formulated in an abstract manner (i.e., without referring to specific stimuli or responses), these effects

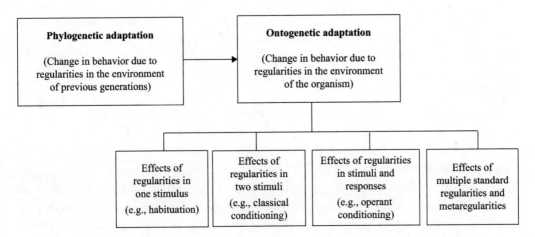

Figure 5.2
Schematic overview of the relationship between different types of learning.

and their moderators form the basis of several general concepts known as *principles*. We have encountered examples of several principles throughout this book: sensitization, habituation, classical conditioning, operant conditioning, generalization, and discrimination.

From a psychology of learning perspective, changing our own behavior and that of others requires that we first identify existing regularities in the environment or create novel ones. Given that regularities consistently influence behavior in the laboratory, it is very likely that they also guide human and nonhuman behavior in the everyday world. Before we examine how they do so, we need to consider several points.

First, applied learning psychologists can, in principle, use regularities to change any type of behavior, from responses observed *within* the individual (e.g., genetic, neural, hormonal) or emitted by the "whole" individual (e.g., what a person thinks, feels, or does) to responses emitted by entire groups of individuals (e.g., couples, families, corporations, communities, and societies). That is, we can operate on behavior at the biological, individual, and group levels. Second, effective interventions require that we consider not only regularities but also the moderators of learning. In certain cases, our analysis might incorporate *phylogenetic adaptation* (i.e., the impact of regularities on the behavior of previous generations, which lead to behaviors such as "fixed action patterns" or "instincts"), *ontogenetic adaptation* (i.e., regularities that impact the organism's behavior within its lifetime), and/or the interaction between the two (e.g., Jablonka & Lamb, 2005; Wilson, Hayes, Biglan, & Embry, 2014). Third, the types of interventions and analyses we outline later in this chapter are usually situated at the functional level (i.e., focused on the relationship between environment and behavior). We focus on these because most interventions stemming from learning psychology (at least as far as we can see) have emerged from the functional wing of the discipline. We certainly do not exclude the idea that applied cognitive learning psychology can contribute much to our understanding of behavioral change; we simply cannot find many examples of such contributions. We will return to this issue later in the chapter.[2]

5.3   The Functional Approach to Behavior Change

5.3.1   Applied Behavior Analysis

Chapters 1 to 4 were concerned with the *experimental analysis* of behavior that typically takes place in the lab. In this way, researchers try to understand behavior in general. In contrast, applied learning psychologists seek to develop interventions or technologies that can change specific types of real-world behavior. They do so in one of two ways: by focusing on those environmental regularities and moderators that lead to real-world behavioral change (**applied functional learning psychologists**) or on the mental processes that mediate between those regularities and behavior (**applied cognitive learning psychologists**).

Many applied functional learning psychologists have banded together and formed a field known as *applied behavior analysis* (ABA) (for book-length treatments, see Fisher, Piazza, & Roane, 2011; Roane et al., 2015). This group is interested in the scientific study of behavior change that relies on the principles of learning to evoke or elicit targeted behavioral change (Furman & Lepper, 2018). ABA differs in several ways from other applied disciplines. First, and unlike applied cognitive learning psychologists, applied behavior analysts view issues such as marital problems, aggressive children or animals, excessive consumption and pollution, academic problems, and phobias as problematic *behavior* (rather than mental processes). The interventions they devise are designed to target the environmental events that give rise to and sustain these behaviors. Applied functional learning psychologists are interested in the direct observation, measurement, quantification, prediction, and influence of behavior (*dependent variable*) and set out to achieve this by manipulating environmental regularities and their moderators (*independent variable*).

Second, this approach is built on the belief that the principles of learning can help us understand where adaptive and maladaptive behaviors come from and influence their probability of occurring in the future. To illustrate, imagine there is a busy kindergarten where three staff members are responsible for thirty children. The staff are busy every day and, unless called for, will not interact with well-behaved children outside of their regularly scheduled feeding and play times. This results in some children being deprived of attention or social interaction (this deprivation may function as an *establishing operation*). Now imagine that one of the children accidentally hurts her leg (R) and a staff member rushes in to help (Sr). It is possible that problematic (e.g., self-injurious or crying) behaviors increase in frequency because

Figure 5.3
The principles of learning can help us understand the origins, and influence the probability of, adaptive and maladaptive behavior in everyday settings (e.g., kindergarten).

they lead to an increase in attention (i.e., reinforcement). According to ABA, the same principles of learning that give rise to problematic behavior can be used to replace it with more adaptive behaviors. For instance, one could decrease the frequency of maladaptive behavior by removing reinforcers (such as attention in the above example) or introducing punishers (verbal reprimands), and then use shaping and differential reinforcement of other behavior (DRO; see section 3.2.4.1) to strengthen responses that are incompatible with self-injury and attention seeking (e.g., by reinforcing play or academic activities through access to approval or attention from caregivers). When implementing this strategy, the staff could bring the new behavior under stimulus control by using discriminative stimuli to alert the child to those contexts in which reinforcers follow desired behavior. The point here is that the principles of learning can give rise to problematic behaviors just as they can give rise to adaptive ones, and that by understanding these principles, we can intervene on the behaviors of interest.

Third, ABA leads to interventions that do not focus on changing the mental mechanisms that mediate between environment and behavior. Instead, they focus on manipulations of the environment in order to influence behavior. Prior to such interventions, the analyst first engages in a *functional analysis* of the behavior they want to target for change. A functional analysis involves identifying what events proceed (antecedents) and follow (consequences) the behavior in which they are interested. A functional analysis tells us what controls that behavior and what contingencies are reinforcing it. This equips the analyst with baseline data about the target behavior before they try to intervene, and enables them to define that behavior *functionally* (i.e., in terms of what it is a function of) and not just *topographically* (i.e., in terms of the structure or form that the behavior takes). Without this baseline data, it is difficult to determine how well (or poorly) an individual will respond to the subsequent intervention.

Once the functional analysis is carried out, the applied behavior analyst then specifies what they want to achieve with the intervention and what it will consist of (i.e., they create a **behavioral contract**). When constructing behavioral contracts, the aim is to ensure that (a) the targeted behavior can be observed and measured, (b) descriptions of that behavior can be read and understood by others, and (c) the behavior can be distinguished from other types of behavior. Once this is done, the behavior needs to be recorded, and there are several ways of doing so (e.g., record every instance of behavior [event recording], record specific periods of time during which behavior occurs [interval recording], or record behavior over a long time scale [time sampling]). Thereafter, the applied behavior analyst manipulates the contingencies controlling the target behavior to alter its occurrence (i.e., they engage in *direct contingency management*). When doing so, they mostly focus on those contingencies that influence the individual and their immediate social environment. Treatment is usually carried out in schools, hospitals, homes, and prisons, while those who typically signal (control) the reinforcers maintaining the targeted behavior (e.g. parents, teachers, friends, coworkers, bosses, and romantic partners) are involved in the intervention and instructed on how to influence the client's behavior.[3]

5.3.2   Testing the Effectiveness of ABA Interventions

Once the analyst has intervened on the environment to change targeted behavior, they then need to identify if their intervention actually worked. Whereas applied cognitive learning psychologists often employ group-comparison designs and use inferential statistics to identify differences between groups, applied functional learning psychologists often use *single-subject designs* (see Tate et al., 2016). In single-subject designs, the behavior of individual subjects prior to treatment (or in the control condition) is compared to the behavior of those same subjects in the intervention condition.

Two common ways of measuring whether an intervention works are A-B-A-B and multiple baseline designs. Both are instances of single-subject designs. *A-B-A-B designs* are a powerful tool for demonstrating causal relations between antecedents (Sd), behavior (R), and consequences (Sr). Here the investigator alternates between a baseline (A phase) in which the intervention is not applied and a testing context (the B phase) where the intervention is applied. To illustrate, imagine that your household pet (dog) has developed a nasty habit of biting the postman, and you are attempting to train it to be less aggressive. During the A-phase, you would repeatedly measure behavior to establish a baseline prior to the intervention (e.g., observe that the dog bites the postman four times a week). In the B-phase the relation between environment and behavior is manipulated and subsequent behavior repeatedly measured (e.g., you reinforce the dog with praise [Sr] for not biting the postman [R] in your presence [Sd]). If there is a change in the behavior you are targeting (e.g., the dog no longer bites the postman), and the intervention was causally responsible for this change, then reintroducing the A-phase should cause behavior to return to baseline (i.e., reinforcement is removed and the dog returns to biting the postman when you are not around). Reintroducing the B-phase should cause the behavior to change back to what was originally observed in the first B-phase.

Although useful, A-B-A-B designs are sometimes problematic; for example, in the above example, we could not use an A-B-A-B design because it is not ethical to expose people to potential harm—one cannot sit idly by and watch one's dog attack the postman. Therefore, alternatives (such as multiple baseline designs) are available. *Multiple baseline designs* involve (a) targeting two or more behaviors, settings, or individuals, and (b) collecting baseline data at the same time. There are three different types: multiple baselines across settings (e.g., reinforcement is applied in one situation but not another), across subjects (e.g., reinforcement is

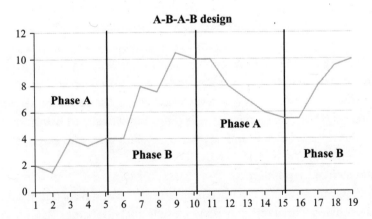

Figure 5.4

Fictitious results in an ABAB design, showing an increase in responding when Phase B starts, a decrease when Phase A is reinstated, and an increase in responding when Phase B is implemented for the second time.

applied to different participants who exhibit the same target behavior), and across behaviors (e.g., a reinforcement procedure is progressively applied across different behaviors). Note that other designs are also used to measure the effectiveness of interventions in this area (e.g., changing-criterion and multiple-treatment designs; see Fisher et al., 2011; Kazdin, 2011).

5.3.3   Training for Generalization

Once the target behavior has been identified and modified, one has to ensure that the changes are not restricted to a single instance of behavior emitted in a single context or time. In other words, the new behavior must last and occur in many different situations. For instance, imagine that a child has been acting aggressively at school, hitting and biting his peers, and that following treatment, he no longer does so. If the child's aggressive and disruptive behaviors are successfully eliminated in a clinic but return at school or at home, then the behavior change has not *generalized* (see section 3.2.5.5). Thus, the behavioral intervention is beneficial only if it decreases problematic behavior across different settings when different individuals implement it. The behavior analyst will train for generalization in three ways: **stimulus generalization** (e.g., ensure that a variety of stimuli and contexts occasion the child's behavior), **response generalization** (e.g., ensure that the child's behavior spreads to other related responses), and **behavioral maintenance** (e.g., ensure that behavior change persists when the contingencies that constitute the intervention are removed). In short, the most effective way to ensure that the generalization occurs is to directly train it during the intervention phase.

5.4   Applied Learning Psychology: Shaping the Behavior of Individuals

So far, we have seen that applied functional learning psychologists design interventions that manipulate environment-behavior relationships in order to change behavior. This typically involves (1) carrying out a functional analysis to identify what aspects of the environment give rise to and sustain behavior, (2) manipulating those contingencies, and (3) generalizing the new behavior across stimuli, responses, and contexts. The following sections highlight how this strategy has been implemented to improve individual well-being and alleviate suffering in domains such as autism, clinical psychology, and substance abuse.

5.4.1   Developmental Disabilities

One major success of ABA is that it has led to interventions that have significantly improved the lives of those living with developmental or intellectual disabilities. Before applied behavior analysts started using operant techniques to help these children and adults acquire key skills (e.g., self-care, social, and communication repertoires), many people with disabilities lived short and unfulfilled lives, isolated in institutions. Consider autism spectrum disorders

(ASDs), which include autism, Asperger's syndrome, and childhood disintegrative disorder. Individuals with ASD are commonly characterized by three core complaints: (a) impaired communication such as repetitive speech patterns and delayed or impaired linguistic development, (b) deficits in social interactions such as poor eye contact, social relations, or emotional reciprocity, and (c) abnormal behavioral patterns, including restricted, repetitive, or stereotypical interests (e.g., eating only certain foods) and activities (e.g., rocking back and forth; American Psychiatric Association, 2013). Individuals with ASD often suffer from a host of related issues, such as sleeping and feeding disorders; delays in toilet training; self-injurious, aggressive, and disruptive behavior; genetic and medical conditions; and cognitive impairments (Frith & Happé, 2005; Fisher & Zangrillo, 2015). These deficits can vary from severe (e.g., an inability to communicate even basic needs) to mild (e.g., intact communication abilities with social skill deficits and repetitive interests). Without treatment, the long-term prognosis is disheartening, with many individuals requiring extended care and supervision. Thankfully, many of these behavioral problems and deficits can be addressed using interventions derived from the learning psychology literature.

For instance, *early and intensive behavioral interventions (EIBI)* are ABA procedures for remediating many of the behavioral deficits and issues associated with ASD. EIBIs are currently among the most scientifically established and evidenced-based approaches available, and they often outperform nonspecific or eclectic treatments in this area (Foxx, 2008; Peters-Scheffer, Didden, Korzilius, & Sturmey, 2011; Reichow & Wolery, 2009; but see Warren et al., 2011). People speak of EIBIs whenever a "package" of these procedures is created and systematically applied to tackle developmental or intellectual deficits. EIBIs typically consists of a comprehensive, hierarchically arranged curriculum implemented across several years, which is designed to improve the child's overall functioning (e.g., increase social behavior, develop speaking and communication skills, eliminate self-stimulation and aggressive behavior). The child is provided with numerous learning opportunities that shape the desired behavior in a progressive, developmental sequence, starting with basic behaviors and then moving on to more complex skills and repertoires. Although there are several different types of EIBIs, they typically begin treatment from an early age (three to four years), are intensive (twenty to forty hours per week), provide individualized and comprehensive treatment, and train parents and caregivers to serve as co-therapists. EIBIs target a variety of issues, such as challenging behaviors, stereotypes, rituals, and life skills. Addressing such issues usually involves steps similar to those outlined in the previous section (functional analysis of the target behavior, construction of a behavioral contract, implementation of the intervention, and training for generalization and persistence), which are often used in conjunction with one another.

One of the most important targets is the language deficits at the core of ASD, given that the capacity to communicate one's thoughts and feelings drastically improves the social community's ability to meet the individual's needs (see Barnes-Holmes, Kavanagh, & Murphy, 2016; Matson et al., 2012). There are several different EIBIs designed to tackle problems with communication. For instance, *natural environment training* is typically conducted in natural settings (e.g., the home) with an emphasis on training caregivers to promote learning opportunities during playtime (see Weiss, 2001). This intervention uses naturally occurring establishing operations to teach functional language skills. For instance, a parent may use the hunger their child naturally experiences throughout the day (establishing operation) as an opportunity to reinforce a particular language skill (e.g., having the child say a phrase such as "I'm hungry" or answer a question such as "Are you hungry?") through access to food (whose reinforcing value is relatively high in this context). Generalization is built into the training (e.g., use of different stimuli, settings, and therapists, and intermittent contingencies) so that the desired verbal responses are more likely to occur in different settings. The *applied verbal approach* is based on Skinner's (1957) theory of verbal behavior, where the aim is to get the individual to respond not just to what a word sounds or looks like, but also to the antecedents (e.g., parent points to a blue truck in a book) and consequences ("That's correct ... it is blue") that give rise to and sustain verbal responding (e.g., a child saying "blue"; for more, see Rehfeldt & Barnes-Holmes, 2009). Finally, the Promoting the Emergence of Advanced Knowledge (PEAK) Training System has also sought to address language and cognitive deficits in children with autism (see McKeel, Dixon, Daar, Rowsey, & Szekely, 2015). Unlike the other EIBIs mentioned above, PEAK incorporates recent developments in relational learning (i.e., AARR) and aims to address deficits in relational (verbal) skills (see section 3.2.5.5), among other things. Early evidence on this is promising (McKeel et al., 2015; see also Rehfeldt & Barnes-Holmes, 2009; Ming, Moran, & Stewart, 2014).

In sum, although seemingly time-consuming and resource-intensive, EIBIs are far more cost-effective than providing a lifetime of supervision or institutionalization. More importantly, they transform the lives of those with ASD and rescue many from an otherwise isolated and impoverished existence. EIBIs are equipping children and adults with daily living skills, improving intellectual functioning, language development, and communication skills, and allowing many to live in ways that would be unimaginable without the help of such interventions.

5.4.2 Maladaptive (Clinical) Behaviors and Their Treatment

The principles of learning discovered in the lab have guided our understanding of how, when, and why many clinical problems develop, and helped us craft effective treatments to alleviate those problems. During the twentieth century these principles played a key role in many psychotherapies, from behavior therapy and cognitive behavior therapy to recent approaches such as dialectical behavior therapy (DBT; Linehan, 1993), functional analytic

Figure 5.5
The principles of learning have historically played, and continue to play, a guiding role in many different therapeutic approaches, and they are central to the treatment of many different clinical phenomena.

psychotherapy (FAP; Kohlenberg & Tsai, 1991), behavioral activation (BA; Jacobson, Martell,
& Dimidjian, 2001), and acceptance and commitment therapy (ACT; Hayes, Strosahl, & Wilson, 1999). (For more on this, see Barlow, 2016; Hayes, 2016.)

– Traditional behavior therapy Learning principles first guided clinical practice with the
emergence of behavior therapy, which was based on the idea that the source and solution
to many clinical issues is located in the relationship between environment and behavior.
From the beginning, behavior therapy placed heavy emphasis on classical and (later) operant
conditioning in order to explain and treat a variety of problems such as phobias, depression,
and obsessive-compulsive, panic, and anxiety disorders (see Antony & Roemer, 2011; Spiegler & Guevremont, 2010). The core aim of this approach is to directly change those environmental factors that predispose, trigger, strengthen, or maintain maladaptive behaviors

(i.e., to engage in a functional analysis of the problem behavior—often through single-case designs—and then operate on the contingencies maintaining that behavior).

To illustrate, imagine that a person enters the clinic with a debilitating phobia of flying and tells the clinician that this phobia first emerged when they experienced extreme turbulence on a flight. The clinician would initially engage in a functional analysis to determine which properties of the antecedent and consequential stimuli, responses, organism, and context need to be modified in order to decrease the problem (target) behavior and increase the probability of alternative behaviors. This analysis might lead them to conclude that the fear of flying represents a conditioned fear response stemming from an environmental event (e.g., turbulence during a flight) in which flying was paired with an aversive experience (just as the pairing of a light and shock in the lab can lead to fear responding). Avoiding flying is likely reinforced because it serves to decrease contact with that fear response (just as avoidance responses in the lab reduce contact with aversive stimuli). This functional analysis would be the first step toward building an individualized treatment plan that involves operating on the fear and avoidance behavior by altering the relevant contingencies. The effectiveness of this intervention would be gauged by comparing pretreatment measures of the target behavior at baseline to the rate of problem behaviors during and after treatment.

Behavior therapy yielded a variety of procedures for treating clinical issues. Two that gained popularity early on were systematic desensitization and exposure techniques (see Spiegler & Guevremont, 2010). For fear of flying, systematic desensitization involves creating a hierarchy of situations ranging from mildly distressing (e.g., imagine seeing an airplane while standing at the airport) to highly distressing (e.g., imagine sitting in a turbulent plane) in order to decrease fear by pairing the presence of the feared stimulus with relaxation. The therapist would train the patient to relax using a progressive relaxation exercise, asking them to visualize increasingly feared events while implementing the relaxation technique. More recently, exposure techniques have largely replaced desensitization. Rather than having the patient imagine the airplane, these techniques gradually exposed them to the feared event (air travel) itself, with the aim of decreasing fear responding (for more, see Tryon, 2005).

– Cognitive (behavior) therapy As the twentieth century progressed, researchers and clinicians increasingly came to realize that the internal content of the individual (e.g., their thoughts, and feelings, desires, motivations, goals, and "talk") needed to be incorporated into treatment, given that these factors seemed to exert a powerful influence over past and present behavior. The growing interest in the mental level of analysis in the academy started to influence developments in the clinic and gave rise to "early" cognitive therapy (e.g., Beck, Rush, Shaw, & Emery, 1979; Mahoney, 1974; Meichenbaum, 1977). This approach arguably pushed the environment off center stage and focused attention instead on the mental level, specifically on "cognitive errors" (such as irrational thoughts, pathological cognitive schemas, or faulty information-processing styles) that were assumed to mediate between environment and behavior. The idea was that these cognitive errors were the source of maladaptive behavior (such as fears of flying) and its solution could be found in their detection, correction, or elimination, which typically involved installing novel mental content (e.g., schema-based therapy; Beck et al., 1979). Thus, research and methodological developments centered on ways to restructure and reappraise core beliefs. Eventually, elements of behavioral and cognitive therapy were combined to form a family of techniques and approaches known as cognitive behavioral therapies (CBT; for reviews, see Butler, Chapman, Forman, & Beck, 2006; O'Donohue & Fisher, 2008). These therapies combined the two approaches and targeted both problematic behaviors and maladaptive cognitions (see De Houwer, Barnes-Holmes, & Barnes-Holmes, 2016, for a functional-cognitive analysis of the relation between behavior therapy, cognitive behavioral therapies, and more recent therapies).

– Recent developments   Although an increased focus on cognition, emotion, and language in the therapeutic context was certainly a step forward, a number of anomalies started to emerge (see Longmore & Worrell, 2007; Young, Klosko, & Weishaar, 2003). These issues contributed to a renewed interest in the environmental (contextual) factors that serve to shape overt as well as covert behaviors (e.g., thoughts and feelings). Increasing attention was paid to the idea of "contacting the present moment," and treatment was redirected away from changing cognitive errors and toward the psychological context in which cognition occurs. Emerging therapeutic approaches such as dialectical behavior therapy, functional analytic psychotherapy, integrative behavioral couples therapy, and acceptance and commitment therapy shared two core ideas: (a) an emphasis on behavioral principles and environment is crucial if we are to understand and operate on clinical behaviors, and (b) unlike traditional behavioral therapies, language and cognition also govern human behavior and therefore should be incorporated into one's functional analysis (see behavioral activation, which mainly focus on the first rather than the second assumption). These treatments tend to reinforce broad, flexible, and effective behavioral repertoires, through the use of the principles of learning. Most therapies (e.g., ACT) do not emphasize the need to restructure or reappraise one's thoughts or feelings; instead, they focus on what "functions" those thoughts and feelings have for the individual, and how the environment gives rise to and sustains those functions. These modern cognitive behavioral therapies have also incorporated a variety of procedures that were developed in and outside of the learning literature (e.g., exposure-based strategies, behavioral activation, modeling, acceptance-based strategies, and emotion regulation).

– Conclusion   Many traditional and modern therapies rely on an idea that stems from the psychology of learning: maladaptive "clinical" behaviors are the result of people's ongoing interactions with the environment, and they can be modified by manipulating the nature of those interactions. These therapies, and the principles of learning and procedures they typically rely on, work: they help people suffering from a wide range of issues, from depression, ADHD, and OCD to panic and anxiety disorders, fears, and phobias (see Dobson & Dobson, 2017; Messer & Gurman, 2011; Spiegler & Guevremont, 2010). Interestingly, some of the most effective treatment procedures in clinical therapies are those that emerged from the learning psychology literature, highlighting the applied value of this area (e.g., exposure-based approaches, behavioral family therapies, skills training, and other strategies for changing behavior; see Antony & Roemer, 2011; Nathan & Gorman, 2007).

5.4.3 Substance Abuse

Substance abuse is a pervasive and costly issue facing many societies around the world. The principles of learning are having a direct impact here as well: evidence indicates that drug addiction can be viewed as an operant behavior and drug use as a particular type of operant (i.e., a *choice* between drug use and abstinence; see section 3.2.5.3 for more on choice behavior). From this perspective, there is a dynamic competition between the reinforcing (or punishing) consequences for drug use versus abstinence. The relative reinforcing (or punishing) value of drug and nondrug stimuli exerts powerful control over a person's choices. If one conceptualizes drug use as an operant, then it follows that drug abuse can be treated through what we know about operant conditioning (for more on this, see Higgins, Silverman, & Heil, 2008; Silverman, Kaminski, Higgins, & Brady, 2011; Stitzer & Petry, 2006).

For instance, we now know that humans and nonhumans will self-administer (R) drugs (Sd) such as cocaine, opiates, alcohol, benzodiazepines, nicotine, and marijuana, and that the physiological consequences of doing do (Sr) can exert overwhelming control over their behavior, regardless of the costs. Indeed, studies show that in situations where there is unlimited access to drugs, nonhuman animals will persistently self-administer them over and over again, even to the point of death (e.g., Johanson, Balster, & Bonese, 1976). Many environmental factors can transform drugs into reinforcers and moderate drug use. For instance, the extent to which people self-administer drugs depends on schedules reinforcement, the extent to which alternative incompatible responses are reinforced (DRO), the magnitude of the reinforcer, and the temporal gap between response and reinforcer (for a review, see Silverman et al., 2011). Given that human drug users operate in environments rich with drug and nondrug reinforcers, concurrent-chain schedule procedures are often used to model a multi-response, multistimulus world in the laboratory (see section 3.2.5.3). This work reveals that decreases in drug use due to the presence of nondrug reinforcers varies depending on factors such as the relative reinforcing value of drugs to nondrugs, schedule requirements, length of access to drug, and whether access to the nondrug stimulus is mutually exclusive to drug use itself (e.g., Perry & Carroll, 2008).

Figure 5.6
The principles of learning can help us better understand and treat a range of substance abuse problems.

This laboratory work has led to the development of *contingency management treatments* for drug addiction, with the most effective being abstinence reinforcement interventions.[4] **Abstinence reinforcement interventions** introduce operant contingencies that reinforce an alternative behavior (drug abstinence) that is incompatible with drug use. For instance, an abstinence reinforcement intervention designed to treat cocaine addiction might require participants to provide biological samples (R) (e.g., urine) that are tested for the presence of the target drug. Biological samples allow for an objective assessment of drug use, especially given that verbal reports of drug use are often unreliable and fabricated to gain access to reinforcers. Reinforcement is effected when the test confirms the absence of the drug in the individual's system; it typically takes the form of tokens/vouchers (conditioned reinforcers) that can be exchanged for money at a later time. If the drug is present in the system, reinforcers are withheld or punishers introduced (e.g., reset of the reinforcer value to a lower level).

Some of these programs (*deposit contracting procedures*) require that people deposit a certain sum of money (secondary reinforcer) prior to the program, and this amount can be earned back over time by demonstrating reductions in drug intake (e.g., smoking). This up-front commitment of resources serves as a "contract" between the person trying to quit and the clinician or researcher, and unlike in other procedures, the person's own funds are used to reinforce abstinence. Other treatments (*voucher-based procedures*) deliver vouchers (Sr) that can be exchanged for goods or services contingent on drug abstinence (R). *Intermittent prizes* (variable reinforcement schedules) are often used in situations where it is not possible to continuously reinforce abstinence or measure abstinence via biochemical measures, for practical or economic reasons. Contingent on their drug abstinence (R), participants draw from a bowl slips of paper (Sr) that refer to reinforcers, which can vary in their reinforcing value (from no prize to a large prize).

In sum, abstinence reinforcement interventions represent yet another application of concepts (operant) that emerged from the psychology of learning. These interventions have proven highly effective in promoting abstinence from a range of drugs in many different types of people, contexts, consequences, and contingencies, especially when combined with other strategies (see Stitzer & Petry, 2006).[5]

5.5 Applied Learning Psychology: From Individuals to Groups

So far, we have seen how the principles of learning can be used to improve the lives of individuals living with developmental or intellectual disabilities, suffering from mental health problems, or struggling with substance abuse. Yet, if we take a step back, we see that individuals (e.g., children and parents) are nested within small groups (families) that are in turn nested within larger groups (e.g., communities), which in turn are nested within even larger groups (e.g., political and economic structures such as societies and ideological systems). Individuals and groups are constantly learning and reacting to and shaping the world around them, sometimes for better (e.g., development of social welfare systems) and sometimes for worse (e.g., unchecked materialism and runaway capitalism). If not just individuals but also groups of individuals (e.g., societies) behave, and if behavior is shaped by its consequences, then it should be possible to intervene in the environment in order to promote health and happiness at the group level. Exerting change over complex systems is certainly an ambitious and difficult goal. One way this could be achieved is by using the principles of learning to craft interventions, which lead to what Biglan (2015) calls "nurturing environments." The idea here is that many problem behaviors (and associated issues) stem from our failure to ensure that people live in environments that "nurture" their own and others' well-being. Therefore, if we are to shape a better society, we need to shape nurturing environments at every level of it, from couples and families to communities and schools, businesses, and governments. According to Biglan (2015), we can create nurturing environments by promoting and reinforcing prosocial behavior, minimizing social and biologically toxic conditions, monitoring and setting limits on influences and opportunities to engage in problem behavior, and promoting the pursuit of prosocial values. Next, we highlight how the principles of learning are already being used to create nurturing environments in family and school contexts.

But before we do, two points are worth mentioning. First, the interventions we will encounter fall into one of two categories: those that were actively designed to use the principles of learning in order to change behavior, and those that do not explicitly use learning principles but are nevertheless effective because they manipulate contingencies and arrange consequences in some way. Second, we will encounter three types of interventions: highly specific *practices*, general *programs*, and even more general *policies* (see box 5.1). As we shall see, the repeated (and widespread) use of certain practices to prevent or reduce problematic behaviors and improve well-being (either independently or as part of a larger program) can be viewed as a sort of "behavioral vaccine." Just as medical vaccines protect people from the risk of future infections, behavioral vaccines "immunize" the person against "contagions" present in toxic environments (e.g., coercive patterns of control) that would otherwise increase the risk of unwanted downstream outcomes (e.g., aggressive children, parents, and partners). And just as a medical vaccine is a simple action that yields large results, so too is a behavioral vaccine: it is a simple, scientifically proven routine or practice that, when put into widespread daily use, can have large-scale benefits (for more on behavioral vaccines, see Embry, 2002).

5.5.1 Nurturing Families

The family environment is a context in which most people are embedded, and it that can exert either an adaptive or maladaptive influence on children from the earliest ages. What happens in families moment-to-moment, day-by-day, has a profound influence on how children (individuals) will develop. For example, growing evidence suggests that during pregnancy, stressful maternal experiences including social threats and nutritional shortages lead to epigenetic processes that can "wire" offspring to become hypervigilant to threat and quick to become aggressive (Gatzke-Kopp, 2011; Kaiser & Sachser, 2005). Other properties of the family environment (e.g., underage pregnancy, parental mental health issues, lack of social support and education, and poverty) can negatively influence the child's early development as well (see Biglan, 2015).

Minimizing toxic environments is important for both parents and children during their early years. In toxic environments, parents are harsh and inconsistent in how they deal with unwanted behavior, increasing the chances that they and their children develop a growing repertoire of angry, cruel, and even dangerous ways of interacting (i.e., develop coercive patterns of behavior). Coercion is defined as the control of behavior through (a) punishment or the threat of punishment, or (b) negative reinforcement that involves the removal of the punisher (see Sidman, 2001).

Box 5.1 Practices, Programs, and Policies

There are three main routes to delivering interventions for behavior change: practices, programs, and policies. *Practices* refers to simple procedures that are designed to immediately influence the behavior of individuals or groups, usually in a specific context. Consider one common example: the "time-out". The time-out is a simple practice wherein a certain behavior (e.g., hitting a sibling) is consequated with the removal of an appetitive stimulus (e.g., access to the television), and as a result, the targeted behavior typically decreases in frequency. *Programs* are collections of practices that establish contingencies with the aim of shaping the behavior of individuals and groups. We will encounter several programs in the following section. Finally, *policies* refers to laws and regulations (contingencies) that specify relations between behavior and environment; they typically apply at the population level (Wagenaar & Burris, 2013). Examples include "fat taxes" that attempt to punish soft-drink or fast-food consumption, carbon taxes designed to minimize pollution, and prohibitions on advertising certain products to certain populations (e.g., cigarette advertisements during children's TV programs). Practices, programs, and policies differ in their scope. Policies are often the most efficient way of impacting behavior at the population level. For instance, raising the price of alcohol has helped reduce alcohol consumption in youth, alcohol-related car crashes, and the development of alcoholism (see Biglan et al., 2004), all without the need to implement specific practices or programs (for more on behaviorally inspired programs and practices, see Embry & Biglan, 2008, and for policies that are improving public health, see Wagenaar & Burris, 2013). That said, certain problems do not require lengthy, complex, or costly interventions, such that practices are sometimes more effective than programs or policies in certain contexts. These three strategies are also interconnected: practices and programs often serve as the basis for policies, which then implement them (for more see Biglan, 2015).

A good example of this can be found in a seminal study by Patterson (1982), who observed interactions between aggressive children, their parents, and siblings in their homes. Patterson studied the consequences that each person provided to other family members' behavior and the effects of those consequences. They found that families with aggressive children experienced more conflict and handled conflict differently than other families. To illustrate, imagine that one sibling criticizes another, who responds in kind. Because neither finds such behavior appetitive, they get angry, shout, or hit (R), and this ends (negatively reinforces) the entire interaction (Sr). Likewise, in a coercive parent-child exchange, the parent asks the child to engage in some activity (R) (e.g., do chores or homework), causing the child to respond aversively (Sr) (e.g., scream, hit, or flee) in an attempt to avoid that behavior. If the child is "successful" and the parent backs down, then two things occur: (a) the avoidance of the unwanted behavior reinforces the child's aversive responding, and (b) the termination of the child's aversive behavior reinforces the mother's backing down. Finally, spouses often

Figure 5.7
The principles of learning can help us better understand the origins of maladaptive patterns within groups such as families (e.g., coercion). They also highlight ways that we can address such behaviors and promote more healthy and nurturing families.

respond to each other's verbal criticisms and complaints (Sd) with their own nasty reactions (R). A cycle of negative reinforcement occurs when one occasionally responds with angry behavior and this temporarily terminates their partner's unpleasant behavior (Sr).

Therefore, just like rats that press a lever to stop an electric shock, family members act in ways that reduce their contact with aversive stimuli, and verbal and physical attacks are often some of the most powerful consequences available to them. And like rats that continue pressing a lever to avoid a shock, family members keep providing aversive consequences to minimize unwanted outcomes. Although effective in the short term, these coercive patterns can be devastating in the long run. For instance, cycles of coercion learned within the family equip aggressive children (by the age of five) with a repertoire of aggressive behavior and a deficit of prosocial skills such as cooperation and impulse control. At school, aggressive children fail to cooperate with teachers (R) and do not learn as much as their nonaggressive peers (Sr). They annoy those peers (R), who in turn actively avoid them (Sr). When they reach high school, they are falling behind academically and have fewer friends. The conflict created at home means that their parents have also given up trying to monitor their adolescent behavior or set limits on their activities, so they are free to interact with their aggressive peers (Dishion & Dodge, 2005). These deviant peer groups become training grounds for the development of multiple problem behaviors (Capaldi, Pears, & Kerr, 2012; Patterson, DeBaryshe, & Ramsey, 1989). As adults, they are more likely to engage in conflict with their partners, get divorced, and raise children with similar problems, thus perpetuating the coercive cycle (Biglan et al. 2004).

In order to change the coercive behavior of children, parents, and partners, we first have to change the family environment they are embedded in (i.e., contingencies within families). We can do so by establishing contingencies that reinforce prosocial interactions and disrupt cycles of coercion between parents and children, thus "immunizing" both from, and serving as an antidote to, the aforementioned problems. For instance, we can train parents in how to change disruptive child behavior (i.e., administer behavioral parent training). Behavioral parent training, which grew out of the application of contingency analysis to family interactions, typically involves arranging immediate contingencies for the parent and child that are designed to influence the child's behavior for the better (see Maughan, Christiansen, Jenson, Olympia, & Clark, 2005). These programs teach parents to avoid coercive practices (e.g., explosive anger, criticism, pleading, or physical deterrents) that punish unwanted child behavior. Instead, they are taught to reinforce desired behaviors, using time-outs and explanations rather than spanking. And it seems to work: evidence suggests that behavioral parent training significantly reduces coercive processes in families, increases positively reinforcing interactions, and reduces children's aggressive social behavior (Forgatch & Patterson, 2010). This approach has led to the development of new methods for reducing child disruptive behavior, which are used in different settings (Forehand, Jones, & Parent, 2013; Michelson, Davenport, Dretzke, Barlow, & Day, 2013). Finally, there are a number of new parenting interventions that focus not only on direct contingency management —but also on the verbal behavior ("thoughts, feelings, and talk") at the core of many family interactions. These interventions have investigated coercive family interactions through the lens of learning theories such as relational frame theory and therapies such as ACT (see section 3.2.5.5). Early evidence suggests that this approach might contribute above and beyond the impact of traditional parenting interventions alone (see Jones, Whittingham, Coyne, & Lightcap, 2016).

5.5.2 Nurturing Schools

Creating nurturing environments that govern the behavior of schools and their members (students and teachers) requires that we create conditions similar to what we did in the family. First, we need to minimize the impact of coercion. For instance, teachers often pay more attention to problem students than to their well-behaved counterparts because (a) problem students interrupt the lesson, and (b) doing so is reinforcing (i.e., if the problem student complies with the teacher's command, the termination of the problem behavior increases the likelihood that the teacher will deliver punitive action in the future). But the teacher's attention can also reinforce the student's problematic behavior, which can lead to a vicious cycle of coercion like that in the family setting described earlier (i.e., doing something aversive to someone who is annoying you often makes them stop, reinforces your behavior, and sets up a punitive pattern of behavior). When this happens, teachers and students both fall under the control of the aversive consequences of their actions.

Skilled teachers avoid this "coercive trap" and learn to use positive reinforcement to increase desired behaviors and reduce problematic ones (e.g., by praising cooperative and on-task behavior and ignoring disruptions). The principles of learning have been used to design practices that help teachers establish prosocial behavior in their students. One well-known example is the Good Behavior Game (GBG; Barrish, Saunders, & Wolf, 1969; Embry, 2002). In this game, the teacher specifies the contingencies that will be reinforced in the classroom (i.e., what will make the classroom a good place to learn, more enjoyable, and pleasant). They then specify the behaviors that are incompatible with those outcomes (i.e., the behaviors that will be put into extinction) and the consequences for acting in these ways (i.e., punishers or "fouls"). Examples of both are presented so that students can learn what will evoke reinforcement or punishment. The teacher also implements the game at certain times but not others (i.e., they use interval-based schedules). Children are divided into groups (so that group-level contingencies can operate on and shape the behavior of the individual), and the groups with the fewest "fouls" gain access to some reinforcer. A scoreboard is presented, allowing each group to keep track of their own and other groups' performances (for more, see Embry, 2002). Remarkably, in more than fifty studies in all sorts of classroom settings, this relatively simple game motivates children to work cooperatively and reduces disruptive behavior as well as teacher distress (see Leflot, van Lier, Onghena, & Colpin, 2013). Interestingly, those exposed to the GBG were less likely to be arrested or to become smokers later in adolescence, and less likely to be addicted to drugs, to be suicidal, or to have committed crimes in adulthood (Kellam, Mayer, Rebok, & Hawkins, 1998; Kellam et al., 2008). In short, this simple behavioral practice (GBG) saves lives.

The principles of learning can help us not only to optimize the learning environment but also to accelerate the speed and quality of the learning that takes place. A good education trains students to combine and apply various simple skills in order to solve more complex problems, to maintain those skills over time, and to generalize them to other situations and problems. Many pedagogical methods have drawn on the principles of learning to help meet these outcomes. One example is *direct instruction* (see Binder & Watkins, 2013; Stockard, Wood, Coughlin, & Rasplica Khoury, 2018). Direct instruction is a contingency-shaping method. A functional analysis is initially carried out to determine the student's current abilities in a content area, and then used to allocate them to a given group. A mastery approach is then adopted, such that instruction begins with the necessary prerequisite skills and progresses only when students can demonstrate mastery over a particular skill. To illustrate, imagine a teacher who is attempting to teach young children how to read. Typically, the teacher models the required response (e.g., "This letter is *S*") and asks students to emit that same response ("Say *S*"). Students are given extensive practice in responding throughout the lesson, and all responses are followed by immediate feedback (reinforcing either a correct response or, in the case of error, a correction that models the right response). Direct instruction programs require mastery for all activities and all content. If students are not at mastery, the teacher provides modeling, feedback, and additional practice until it is achieved. Students tend to quickly come in contact with a powerful reinforcer—being competent. Frequent measurement of behavior tied to certain educational objectives guides future decisions about what instructional methods to use. Direct instruction is associated with increased scholastic skills, cognitive skills, and affective outcomes, and often outperforms alternative instruction methods (see Moran & Marlott, 2004; Stockard et al., 2018).

Finally, the principles of learning are helping us design procedures that not only improve behavior and learning in the classroom but also shape better behavior at the level of the school. One such intervention, Positive Behavioral Intervention and Support (Muscott, Mann, & LeBrun, 2008), involves consistently reinforcing desired behavior while implementing contingencies to curtail problem behavior. The program typically begins with a functional assessment that targets behavior at three different levels (individual, classroom, and school). At each level, behavioral expectations (i.e., contingencies) are articulated, reinforcers are provided to students who meet those expectations, and a strategy is specified for managing problem behavior when it arises (Bradshaw, Mitchell, & Leaf, 2010). This intervention is linked to fewer suspensions, better academic performance, reduced harassment and bullying, and increased prosocial behavior (Bradshaw et al., 2010; Horner et al., 2009; Sugai, Horner, & Algozzine, 2011). Thus, to conclude, the concepts derived from the psychology of learning have been used to build technologies that lead to superior educational outcomes and functioning in schools.

5.6   Future Directions for Application

As we outlined in the introduction, we have highlighted only some of the areas where the principles of learning are currently making a difference in (for more see Fisher et al., 2011; Foxall, 2016; Roane et al., 2015; Schneider, 2012; Zettle et al., 2016). There are other areas where applied functional learning psychology has only begun to make an impact, from behavioral economics (Foxall, 2016) and sports psychology (Luiselli & Reed, 2015) to educational practices (Moran & Malott, 2004) and product design (Wendel, 2014). And there are still other areas that have not benefited from the systematic input of applied functional learning psychology but certainly could, from behavioral medicine (Greenwald, Roose, & Williams, 2015) and political science to areas within psychological science (e.g., personality; Perugini, Costantini, Hughes, & De Houwer, 2016) and beyond. Next, we highlight one vital issue where the principles of learning could be used to help change human behavior for the better: the climate emergency.

Converging evidence indicates that the earth is warming, that this warming is due to human activity, and that potentially catastrophic changes are just over the horizon (IPCC, 2007). Those living in coastal cities and low-lying countries are already dealing with rising seas, whereas many others are faced with persistent droughts and water shortages. Worldwide agriculture and food supply networks are also being pushed to their limits by droughts, flooding, and growing populations. Rising sea levels bring salt water into rivers, destroying drinking wells and fertile farmlands. Extreme weather patterns are occurring more frequently and giving rise to "climate migrants" fleeing increasingly inhospitable regions. Militaries see climate change as a "threat multiplier" and are preparing for action (e.g., how to control for armed conflict, maintain security, and provide humanitarian aid to victims of climate-related disasters). These changes are happening here and now, accelerating (Hansen & Sato, 2011), and affecting millions around the world (IPCC, 2007; also see Alavosius, Newsome, Houmanfar, & Biglan, 2016; Emmott, 2013; Thompson, 2010).

One of the main drivers of climate change is human behavior. We fuel our societies and run our cars, homes, airplanes, and cities by burning fossil fuels. Our agricultural practices release millions of tons of greenhouse gases into the atmosphere, while we continue to cut down huge swathes of forests and destroy green lands for ourselves and livestock. At this point, it is too late to stop climate change—it is already happening—but as Thompson (2010) points out, there are three remaining options available to us: mitigate, adapt, or suffer. *Mitigation* involves reducing the pace and magnitude of these changes by altering the underlying causes (i.e., our behavior). From a learning psychology perspective, it is the contingencies that shape the daily behavior of individuals, businesses, governments, and societies that will determine whether we collectively step up to the challenges presented by climate change, or face the repercussions of not doing so. Some of the behaviors we need to address are relatively straightforward (e.g., adopt energy-conservation practices, improve the rate and efficiency of recycling, and reduce our reliance on fossil fuels). We also need coordinated action (policies) at the national and international levels that help us transition our energy and transportation industries toward renewable alternatives; smart urban design that cools overheated cityscapes; worldwide carbon taxes that reinforce environmentally sustainable industry;

Figure 5.8
The climate emergency is reshaping the world as we know it. The principles of learning can help us better understand the contingencies that give rise to and maintain the human activity at the heart of this crisis. They can also help us design interventions to mitigate the crisis, better adapt to it, or lessen our suffering from it.

raises in minimum mileage standards on cars; artificial and natural carbon sink systems that capture and contain greenhouse gases, and much more.

If we cannot mitigate, then our second option becomes *adaptation* (i.e., adapting to habitats created by climate change and reducing the adverse impact of its consequences). If this happens, then we will have to invest even more in infrastructure projects such as constructing sea barriers, relocating coastal towns and cities inland, changing agricultural practices to counteract shifting weather patterns, and strengthening human and animal immunity to climate-related diseases. If we fail here, then our third option, *suffering*, means enduring those consequences that cannot be prevented via mitigation or adaptation. Although everyone will be affected by global warming, those with the fewest resources are already suffering the most, and that will continue. And it will not only be humans that suffer: the Anthropocene (the current geological epoch defined by mankind's impact on the planet) has witnessed a sixth great extinction event that is currently wiping many species from the face of the earth (Kolbert, 2014).

Unfortunately, there is no magic bullet that will solve these problems. But the psychology of learning can help. The concepts covered in this book represent tools that we can use to alter human behavior and by implication, climate change itself. For instance, behavioral principles such as classical and operant conditioning have already been used to design interventions that influence domestic and industrial energy consumption, litter control, recycling, transportation decisions, and consumer behavior (see Lehman & Geller, 2004; for related work, see Thaler & Sunstein, 2008). They can continue to help us do so. The matching law can also help us gain better insight into the relationship between our choices (e.g., a meat-eating vs. vegetarian lifestyle) and the relative reinforcing value of those options. This law helps us appreciate that although certain behaviors may seem "irrational" (e.g., eating meat is associated with cancer and is destroying the environment), they are actually lawful, and our choices are sensitive to certain types of consequences and insensitive to others (for more on this, see Foxall, 2016).

Evidence from the operant learning literature also tells us that the strength of reinforcers decreases as their temporal distance from behavior increases (e.g., Fantino, Preston, & Dunn, 1993; Skinner, 1938). Simply put, humans choose immediate reinforcers over larger but delayed ones. We engage in immediately satisfying actions (e.g., eat meat, drive cars, consume plastic goods) at the expense of their delayed aversive consequences (environmental destruction). This research help us address these issues, too (see section 3.2.5.3). Recent developments in the domain of relational learning also inform us about how verbal and cognitive processes drive environmentally destructive behavior, suggesting that our interventions need to incorporate more than just direct contingency manipulations (e.g., educational initiatives, marketing, entertainment, and advocacy campaigns; see Alavosius et al., 2016). Therefore, at the individual level, we must change the immediate consequences of behavior directly or indirectly related to environmentally destructive behaviors. Employing economic consequences (e.g., increasing the cost of fossil and lowering the cost of renewable fuels, raising or reducing taxes on high- or low-emission vehicles) as well as interpersonal reinforcers and punishers (e.g., approval from one's social circle) are one place to start. We need to find ways of making people understand and care about the long-term consequences of their consumption. These strategies will need to take into account avoidance behavior (elicited by aversive consequences associated with failures to act) and utilize positive and personal long-term consequences when doing so (e.g., benefits or consequences for them, their children, and their community in adopting pro-environmental behaviors).

Yet, even this will not be enough. One major shortcoming of the learning literature (especially when it comes to climate change) is its focus on the individual level and lack of work on the larger systems (contexts) in which the individual is embedded. Therefore, we also need to analyze and influence how large-scale organizations and systems operate. Although a functional analysis of organizational practices has begun, more is clearly needed (see Biglan & Embry, 2013; Houmanfar, Rodrigues, & Ward, 2010; Luke & Alavosius, 2012; Malott & Glenn, 2006). Indeed, the level of behavioral change required to combat global warming means that virtually every organization will have to alter its behavior in some way. This is not going to be easy: the contingencies governing certain for-profit corporations and countries mean that a reduction in fossil fuel use (R) might translate into a loss in revenue or taxes (Sr), an aversive consequence that is likely to elicit corresponding escape or avoidance behavior. Other companies create technologies that rely directly on fossil fuels (e.g., cars and trucks consume petrol and diesel), or utilize energy derived from nonrenewable sources in their manufacturing and transportation processes. Still others create greenhouse gases as a by-product of their actions (e.g., methane produced by livestock in the farming industry). Recall that individual behavior is controlled more by its short-term than its long-term consequences. The same may be true for organizations: some companies dump their waste products in rivers and seas or release greenhouse gases into the atmosphere during transportation and manufacture because of the short-term gain (e.g., profits). Yet, doing so reduces air quality and raises global temperatures—these are long-term effects that are in no one's best interest but do not seem to control individual or group-level behavior.

As Houmanfar et al. (2010) points out, the interlocking behavior of organizational members (R) leads to products or services that are purchased (or not) by consumers (Sr). The consumption of these products reinforces their production as well as the practices that lead to their creation. In other words, for-profit organizations will maintain or increase those practices that benefit their profits, whether they be marketing strategies, public relations, or lobbying efforts. These companies will also work to escape or avoid any practice, program, or policy that threatens to remove reinforcers (profits). For instance, corporations exert a powerful influence on policy development (Sr) through lobbying efforts (R), as do nonprofit organizations and advocacy groups that lobby (sometimes on the behalf of industry players) to prevent policies that would lead to a reduction in fossil fuel use. This means that the network of contingencies linking organizations to one another (and governments) is an important additional source of behavioral control that we must consider—the contingencies governing "governance.".

While tackling the contingencies driving these organizations, we need to simultaneously reinforce organizations that gain from a reduction in fossil fuels because they either sell alternative products (e.g., solar panels, vegetarian foods, electric vehicles) or adopt practices that reduce the company's costs and improve its profits via renewable energy. We also need to introduce contingencies that shape up pro-environmental behaviors in companies that would neither benefit from nor be harmed by policies that reduce fossil fuel use. One such example is "cap and trade" policies. These policies specify the limit or "cap" (Sd) on the amount of pollution a company can release (R) and reinforce reductions in pollution levels by allowing the company to sell or "trade" (Sr) what they have not used in their limit. At the same time, better funding and education for nonprofit organizations and advocacy groups working to reduce greenhouse gas emissions is needed (for more see Biglan, 2009). For instance, churches, universities, foundations, and civic organizations could influence the behavior of their members (as well as that of the individuals and organizations which which those members are connected) to support efforts to reduce greenhouse emissions and adopt sustainable practices.

Finally, we need to consider the behavior of governments at the city, state, and federal levels. These groups also act in ways that involve the emission of greenhouse gases (e.g., use of private jets vs. public transport). Perhaps more importantly, they can adopt and enforce policies for individuals and other organizations that influence emissions and sustainable patterns of behavior. They can arrange contingencies (e.g., taxes, emission standards, education programs) and consequences (e.g., tax reductions, sanctions) that increase the pro-environmental behavior of individuals and organizations (Luke & Alavosius, 2012). Clarifying the contingencies linking (a) profit and nonprofit organizations, (b) those organizations to governments, and (c) the values of their respective members may reveal avenues for promoting efforts to affect environmental issues.

So what can we conclude? In 1987 B. F. Skinner asked a relatively simple question: why are we not acting to save the world? He believed that the answer lay in the fact that our species did not possess the verbal behavior necessary to analyze the problems we face or to change the environment in ways that would promote cultural (and possibly species) survival. What was missing, he argued, was the language of an experimental analysis of behavior— specifically, the practice of analyzing those contingencies that maintain individual, group, and societal actions, and a language that would allow us to predict and influence those contingencies for the better.

What we have covered in the foregoing section is far from comprehensive; it does not tackle all the contingencies or factors relevant to climate change or those threatening our species (e.g., environmental destruction, species extinction, growing population levels). But it is a first step. The science of individual behavior is relatively clear about those contingencies that could influence people to reduce their greenhouse gas emissions and lead more sustainable lives. Yet, in the absence of strategies that "scale" interventions up to the group, organizational, and population level, this research is unlikely to impact on the problem. Little empirical and only emerging theoretical work indicates how we can affect the behavior of populations by manipulating the complex network of contingencies that control behavior at these levels. We realize that the problems we face are great and that the solutions are not going to be simple or easy. But we do have the conceptual tools (functional analyses and behavioral principles) necessary to start making a meaningful difference.

5.7   Applied Cognitive Learning Psychology

So far, we have focused on those areas where applied *functional* learning psychologists have, or could, influence behavior. But what about applied *cognitive* learning psychologists? Although some cognitive learning psychologists would claim that they are interested primarily in understanding the mental mechanisms underlying learning for its own sake, others hope that studying those mental mechanisms will eventually also lead to applications that can help solve real-world problems such as psychological suffering.

Despite our best efforts, however, we could not find many real-world interventions that directly stem from cognitive theories of learning such as the Rescorla-Wagner model, SOP, or Bouton's, Pearce's, or Mackintosh's model.[6] One notable exception is the idea of context-dependent inhibitory associations, which has played a role in clinical research and practice (e.g., Craske et al., 2014; see box 2.6). Relatedly, clinical researchers have been inspired by the idea that (inhibitory) learning during extinction is a function of expectation discrepancy, as is posited by the Rescorla-Wagner model (see section 2.3.1.2.c). As result, they have examined whether exposure therapy might be enhanced by *increasing* the fear that patients initially experience during exposure (and thus the discrepancy between the expectancy that something bad will occur and the fact that nothing bad occurs during therapy; see Craske et al., 2014).

We also see few indirect contributions of cognitive learning theories toward solving real-world problems. Whereas contributions such as those mentioned in the previous paragraph result directly from the ideas incorporated in cognitive learning theories (e.g., maximizing expectation discrepancy), indirect contributions result from new empirical phenomena discovered as the result of predictions made by those theories. Many of the learning phenomena that inspired applications were described long before cognitive learning theories were developed. For instance, CS pre-exposure effects led to interventions for reducing children's fear of dentists that involved exposing the children to dentists and dental equipment before the first dental treatment took place (Surwit, 1972). Although these phenomena and their applications can be interpreted on a post hoc basis from the perspective of cognitive learning theories (e.g., as preventing the development of associations in memory), it would be incorrect to see these applications as examples of the successful application of cognitive learning theories themselves. When applications such as these are removed from the list of applied cognitive learning psychology's contributions, there seems to be little left on that list.

We see two possible reasons for these conclusions. The first is that we have simply missed those interventions that are inspired by cognitive learning theories. If so, then we hope readers can point these out to us. The second possibility is more troubling. If it turns out that there are indeed few interventions that were inspired by cognitive learning theories, then it may be that these theories are exceptionally good at generating questions about the mental mechanisms underpinning learning effects but relatively poor at inspiring solutions for real-world problems. One could of course argue that it is not the role nor responsibility of cognitive learning theories or researchers to address societally relevant issues. Indeed, for cognitive learning researchers, there is value as such in shedding light on the mental mechanisms that mediate learning. But for cognitive learning researchers who examine mental processes in the hope that it will lead to applications, our conclusion is highly disturbing. Perhaps they can continue to believe that, eventually, cognitive learning theories will lead to applications. Nevertheless, after forty years of basic research, these rationalizations increasingly seem like "promissory notes" that push responsibility for change onto others, or down the road. When applied cognitive learning psychologists adopt an immediate, proximal goal to uncover mental mechanisms in service of their ultimate, distal goal of solving practical problems, they must check on a regular basis whether there are reasons to continue to believe that the proximal goal actually serves the distal goal. If such reality checks provide little indication for this assumption, we believe that they should be willing to move on and look for other ways to achieve their distal goal (for more on these and related issues, see De Houwer et al., 2017). Moving forward, we hope that applied cognitive learning psychology can rise to the challenge of promoting well-being at the individual, group, and societal levels. As we discuss in the next section, we believe that by adopting a functional-cognitive perspective, this tradition may be better able to do so.

5.8   Psychological Engineering: A Functional-Cognitive Way Forward

Until now, applied functional and cognitive learning psychologists have rarely interacted, due to differences in their respective goals and ways of conducting analyses. With regard to trying to solve real-world problems, this means that developments in one wing of the learning tradition have rarely fed into and driven progress in the other. It is disconcerting that in an era when interdisciplinary research has become commonplace, there is still so little interaction between (applied) functional and cognitive researchers (De Houwer et al., 2017). We firmly believe that the application of learning psychology, like learning psychology itself, would benefit from closer interactions between functionally and cognitively inspired researchers. As this chapter shows, applied functional learning psychologists are interested in a vast range of applied issues, including intellectual and developmental disabilities, drug use, healthy individuals, families, schools, and much more. Although so far, cognitive learning theories seem to have provided little input to this work, directly relating those theories to applied issues (rather than predominantly to phenomena studied in the lab) could increase the applied value of cognitive learning psychology. Also, cognitive theories of phenomena other than learning (e.g., memory) could feed into the applied work that functional researchers are currently engaged in. Such closer interactions between functional and cognitive researchers at the applied level is bound to also feed back into the development of cognitive theories, creating a win-win situation.

Throughout this book, we have highlighted the conditions that need to be met if functional and cognitive psychologists are to successfully interact: as much as possible, all researchers (functional and cognitive) must describe the behavioral phenomena they are studying in abstract functional terms (e.g., reinforcement, stimulus control, etc.). Doing so fosters rather than hampers cognitive theorizing because it separates the to-be-explained phenomena from explanatory mental processes (see the introduction). At the same time, it encourages cognitive researchers to speak the same language as their functional colleagues, which provides the basis for more fruitful collaborations. Exactly the same can be done in applied research. Describing real-world problems in abstract functional terms provides a common language and new opportunities for cognitive theorizing. In a recent paper, we referred to this functional-cognitive framework for applied psychology as psychological engineering and noted that

> within such a discipline, applied psychologists of all types (both functional and cognitive) can contribute to a joint body of knowledge that can be consulted by all current and future applied psychologists. At the same time, applied research interests can remain diverse, both in terms of topics studied and approaches adopted. Just as different types of engineers explore a diverse set of phenomena (e.g., bridges, oil rigs, buildings) from a common core (principles of physics), so too can different applied researchers explore phenomena (behavioral parenting programs, eye-witness testimony) from a common core (principles of learning). And just like engineers shape the physical world, so too would psychological engineers help shape the world of behavior.

In our opinion, the move toward such an integrated discipline of psychological engineering is highly desirable in light of the many problems that we currently face at the individual, societal, and species levels. Many of these problems are behavioral or the result of human behavior. Hence, applied learning psychologists have a vital role to play in solving them.

Box 5.2 Is Psychological Engineering Ethical or Moral?

For some, the term *psychological engineering* may have negative connotations (e.g., that we are secretly trying to manipulate individuals, groups, and societies to engage in certain practices). Yet it is foolish to assume that this is not already part and parcel of daily life. Politicians engineer their arguments in ways that increase their chances of pushing certain policies and winning elections. Advertisers and supermarkets engineer online and physical contexts to increase product purchase. Employers arrange their work environments to promote certain practices and minimize others. Many governments engineer consequences so that free speech and movement of peoples are promoted (through policies that promote tolerance and exposure) or undermined (e.g., through propaganda or coercion). We are increasingly plugged into a digital world in which "fake news" is engineered to reinforce one's pre-existing ideologies or push novel ones. Thus, psychological engineering is nothing new; it is simply a new name for a commonplace practice that continues to pervade and guide human behavior on large and small scales. The principles outlined in this book can help the reader identify when and how their behavior is being influenced, and equip them with the tools to respond to those influence attempts. Likewise, it also equips them with the tools to influence their own behavior and that of others—for the better. Like any technology, these principles can be used either to promote collective well-being (prosocial) or for selfish gain (antisocial). Thus psychological engineers need to be guided by ethical and societal values when manipulating the environment to produce behavioral change.

Think It Through 5.1: Do We Really Need the Functional Approach?

An anonymous reviewer of the book raised the following point:

The purpose and value of the functional approach is quite hard to understand.... Quite simply, throughout the book it is hard to see any examples of where this approach explains behavior. As far as I can see, everything that's described under this heading is simply a statement about the conditions of learning. No one would disagree that in order to develop explanations of behavior, we first need to clarify in some detail when learning does and doesn't take place, what the controlling variables are, etc. But what's the logic for turning this rather obvious point into such an overarching framework, and imbuing it with so much philosophical meaning? Put another way, what would be lost if the entire concept of the functional approach to learning was removed from the book, and it talked instead simply about the conditions of learning? ... Here's an analogy that might help to make this point, in case it's unclear. Chemists regard bonds as the cornerstone of their field and have standard theory about chemical bonds. Yet if one told a chemist that her theory was incomplete and needed to be supplemented by a functional theory characterizing the conditions (e.g., temperature, pressure) in which chemical reactions take place, she would (I submit) find this puzzling. It is chemical theory which explains why a given reaction depends on certain conditions being in place, not the other way around. Likewise, in learning, it is the

(continued)

Think It Through 5.1 (continued)

(cognitive?) theory which will eventually explain why learning depends on conditions X and Y, not the other way around.

What do you think? Now that you have come to the end of this book, do you think that the discussion of the functional approach added value to the book? Is cognitive theory, like chemical theory, the ultimate level of explanation?

Think It Through 5.2: Do We Really Need the Cognitive Approach?

Although none of the reviewers of this book questioned the merits of the cognitive approach, some functionally oriented researchers have argued that the cognitive approach is of little value to functional researchers, who are primarily interested in predicting and influencing real-world behavior (e.g., Barnes-Holmes & Hussey, 2016).

Now that you have read our book, what is your opinion on this matter? How useful has the cognitive approach been, both in terms of application and in terms of uncovering the mental processes that underlie learning?

Reflections on the "Think It Through" Questions

Think It Through 0.1: Are Other Definitions of Learning Possible?

It makes little sense to define learning as involving any change in behavior. The purpose of a concept such as *learning* is to distinguish in a meaningful way certain changes in behavior from others. We must therefore have a criterion that allows us to distinguish between changes in behavior that may or may not be instances of learning. Our criterion for making this distinction is the *cause* of the change in behavior. If this cause is a regularity in the environment, then we define the change in behavior as an instance of learning. But are there, in addition to the cause of the change, alternative criteria that can be used to determine whether learning has occurred?

A first alternative is a criterion in terms of the presence or absence of an objective characteristic of the environment and/or the change in behavior. Such a definition would be easy to apply because one only has to check whether the crucial objective characteristic is present. The question, however, is whether we can make a meaningful objective distinction between changes in behavior that can or cannot be seen as instances of learning.

Suppose that one would define learning as those changes in behavior that occur in the absence of changes in the physical characteristics of the organism (e.g., a change in behavior as a result of breaking one's leg). In this case, a change in behavior can be considered learning if one does not simultaneously see observable physical change in the organism. But this definition is problematic. What about physical changes that cannot be responsible for the change in behavior? For example, the fact that a baby's nose grows during same the period when its grip reflex disappears is probably irrelevant to the reflex's disappearance and therefore cannot be used to determine whether the change in the reflex is an example of learning. You could take into account only physical changes that indicate a possible explanation of the change in behavior (e.g., changes in neuronal connections that may indicate maturation), but then the final criterion is again related to what are only possible causes of the change of behavior, and this is complicated by the fact that causal relations cannot be observed directly. In sum, it is unlikely that a criterion that is based purely on physical changes can lead to a meaningful definition of learning.

Another possibility is to base the criterion for learning on the adaptive properties of the change in behavior (i.e., on the consequences of that behavior for the organism). For example, one could define learning as changes in behavior that lead to *better* adaptation to the environment. But once again, we see problems with such an approach. First, this definition is just as difficult to apply as the definition that refers to the causes of the change in behavior. A definition in terms of the consequences of the change of behavior also implies a causal attribution—in this case, a statement about whether the change in behavior is the cause of better adaptation. Second, a question arises with regard to changes in behavior that are caused by regularities in the environment but are not adaptive. If the degree to which a change in behavior improves one's interaction with the environment is presented as the ultimate criterion, this implies that maladaptive forms of learning are by definition impossible. This is an unacceptable restriction for us.

Finally, one could define learning as a hypothetical mental process that is responsible for knowledge acquisition. In such a definition, the change in behavior is not central, but rather a change in mental representations or processes. Although this definition is popular in cognitive psychology and also closely relates to how people in Western societies think about learning, in our view, it creates more problems than it solves and is less useful than a definition that refers to the environmental causes of changes in behavior. In contrast to changes in behavior, mental contents such as "knowledge" are not directly observable. Ultimately, one can derive knowledge only from the presence of certain behaviors. For instance, imagine that I want to find out if someone has learned how to get a soft drink from a vending machine. I cannot simply look into her head to see if she possesses that knowledge. I can only make assumptions about her mental content on the basis of her motor behavior (e.g., does she sometimes get a soft drink from a vending machine?), verbal behavior (e.g., can she tell me how to remove soft drinks from a vending machine?), and physiological or neurological behavior (e.g., does she show a certain physiological or neuronal reaction if I give a wrong explanation of how one gets soft drinks from a vending machine?). Even with a definition in terms of mental content, one can speak of learning only if a certain behavior or change in behavior is observed.

This type of definition of learning (in terms of mental processes) has also led to the important problem of distinguishing between learning (in the sense of knowledge acquisition) and performance. If you define learning as the mental process of knowledge acquisition, then it is possible to "learn" without having a change in behavior, as shown by the phenomenon of latent learning (see box 0.2). This definition thus implies that behavior is a less than perfect indicator of "learning": even if there is no change in behavior, there can be a lot of "learning." How then can we infer that learning has taken place? In the absence of a verifiable criterion for the presence of learning, it indeed becomes difficult to study learning. This is why the problem of the distinction between "learning" and performance has led to endless debates in cognitive learning psychology (e.g., Miller & Escobar, 2001).

Our functional definition of learning as an effect does not create a distinction between learning and performance and therefore avoids this potential problem (see also box 0.2). According to our definition, you can say that learning has occurred only *after* you have observed a change in behavior. The question of when knowledge has been acquired is distinct from the question of whether learning has occurred. This does not mean that questions about knowledge acquisition or mental processes become less important. On the contrary, the study of the mental processes can proceed more smoothly precisely because we make such a distinction between learning as an effect and the mental processes of knowledge acquisition (see section 0.3.3 and De Houwer et al., 2013).

Think It Through 0.2: The Interaction between Learning and Genetics

The interaction between genetic and environmental factors is often cited in arguing that it is impossible to arrive at a conclusive definition of learning. In our opinion, however, this is a false debate. Phenomena such as imprinting are clearly examples of learning: there is an influence of a regularity in the environment (hearing a species-specific vocal pattern) that leads to a change in behavior (after hearing the song pattern, the bird can also sing the pattern as well). That learning occurs only under strict (and perhaps genetically determined) conditions does not diminish the fact that this is still a change in behavior due to regularities in the environment. Learning is always subject to certain conditions. For example, the behavior of someone who is blind will not be influenced by regularities in the visual characteristics of the environment. In other words, in order to learn about the visual characteristics of objects in the environment, you must be able to see. So the *capacity* to learn in certain ways is in many cases genetically determined (Skinner, 1984). During their lives, simple organisms such as single-celled creatures are very limited in their capacity to adapt their behavior to regularities in the environment. The capacity to adapt one's behavior to environmental regularities probably expanded during the early evolution of different animal species because of the advantage it conferred (see Jablonka & Lamb, 2005, Hayes, Sanford, & Chin, 2017, and Skinner, 1984, for excellent discussions of the relation between genetics and learning). Organisms that can adapt their behavior to the environment during their lifetime are more likely to reproduce. That is why the capacity to learn will be transferred to the next generations genetically. Certain forms of learning (e.g., imprinting) may be more genetically determined than others, but all learning is based on the condition that certain genetic material is present.

Think It Through 0.3: What Is the Relation between Functional and Mental Process Explanations?

The first statement is wrong. You can explain a change in behavior in terms of environmental regularities without making assumptions about the mental processes responsible for the fact that this regularity results in a change in behavior. A functional explanation refers only to the aspects of the environment that are responsible for a particular behavior. The second statement is correct. A mental process statement explains why a certain regularity in the environment results in a change in behavior. Thus, by definition, it is based on the assumption that the change in behavior is due to that particular regularity in the environment, and therefore it always includes a functional statement (for more on this, see De Houwer & Moors, 2015).

Think It Through 0.4: What Is the Relation between Cognitive and Neural Explanations of Learning?

Both statements are concerned with mechanistic explanations of learning: the researcher seeks to identify which mechanism mediates the impact of regularities on behavior. However, the types of mechanism are different. With cognitive explanations, it is a mental mechanism that consists of links between steps of information processing. Neuronal explanations refer to a neuronal mechanism that consists of links between neuronal activities. Thus, both types of explanations have the same explanandum (that which must be explained: learning) but different explanans (that by which it is explained: information processing vs. brain activity). One could say that the explanans is not fundamentally different because information processing takes place in the brain. However, a distinction must be made between the carrier of information (vehicle) and the content of information processing (content). Because information is nonphysical (Wiener, 1961; see section 0.3.2.2), the same content can in principle be placed on different carriers (the brain, the hard disk of a computer, a USB stick, etc.). Therefore, it is difficult to read the content of information from the physical characteristics of the carrier (but see Bechtel, 2008). We cannot see information directly in the brain; we can only deduce it from functional knowledge about the brain. Therefore, at least for practical reasons, it remains better to distinguish cognitive explanations in learning psychology from neural explanations.

Take the example of connections (so-called dendrites) that are formed between neurons in the brain. Cognitive researchers sometimes see this as evidence for the cognitive theory that learning is mediated through the formation of associations between mental representations. However, you cannot simply equate neurons with mental representations, nor can you simply equate neuronal connections with associations. Neurons may be carriers of information, but it is not at all clear whether the neurons under investigation are carriers of the information contained in a certain mental representation according to a given cognitive model. Neural connections may play a role in the processing of information, but it is quite possible that that role is completely different from what is assumed in the cognitive models. One must therefore remain cautious when making conclusions about mental processes based on neuronal activity.

Think It Through 2.1: Conditions Necessary for Blocking

To conclude that blocking has taken place, one must be sure that the weakening of CR for X is due to the A-US relation. Therefore, the CR for X in the experimental condition (A+, AX+) is compared with the CR for X in the first control condition (only AX+): both conditions differ with respect to the A-US relation. However, the first control condition is not perfect because it differs from the experimental condition also with respect to the total number of USs being presented (there are in total fewer USs in the first control condition). This can in itself explain why the CR for X is weak in the experimental condition, because we know from other research (see the US pre-exposure effect discussed in section 2.2.5.2) that the mere pre-presentation of USs has a negative impact on conditioning effects. The second condition is equated to the experimental condition with regard to the number of USs presented. If the CR for X is weaker in the experimental condition than in the second control condition, this cannot be due to the number of US presentations. However, the second control condition is not perfect either, because it differs from the experimental condition not only with respect to the A-US relation but also with regard to the total number of stimuli (only A and X in the experimental conditions vs. A, B, and X in the second control condition). Although it is not entirely clear why this difference in procedure can lead to a difference in the CR toward X, it is still safe to include the first control condition in the design because it checks for that difference. The CR to X can also be compared with the CR to K when the following trials are presented: A+ followed by AX+ and KL+. This is a within-subjects control. K is identical to X (because both are always presented together with another CS and both are followed by the US the same number of times), with the exception that only X is presented together with a stimulus that was already followed by the US (namely, A is presented and followed by the US on the A+ trials; this is not the case for L).

Think It Through 2.2: Overshadowing and Conditional Contingencies

In an overshadowing situation, there are trials in which both A and X are present and trials in which no CS is present. It is therefore impossible to compare situations that differ only with respect to the presence of X. The conditional contingency cannot be determined. In the control condition in which there are X+ trials, however, one can compare situations that differ only with regard to the presence of X (namely, X+ trials and situations in which no CS is present). In the X+ condition, the contingency is therefore positive.

Think It Through 2.3: The CS Pre-exposure Effect and Habituation

You can see both as effects of noncontingent stimulus presentations. In habituation, the effect is a reduction in the intensity of the original response that is elicited by a stimulus. With CS pre-exposure, the effect is a delay in classical conditioning. The CS pre-exposure effect can thus be seen as an example of an interaction between the effects of noncontingent stimulus presentations (i.e., the repeated presentation of a CS) and the effects of relations between stimuli (i.e., the joint presentation of the CS and US; see also chapter 4). Note that a functional explanation of the CS pre-exposure effects in terms of a decrease in the salience of the CS implies that the CS-pre-exposure effect is an indirect consequence of habituation. The CS's salience can indeed be seen as the extent to which the CS elicits an orientation response. By repeatedly presenting the CS, the extent to which the CS elicits an orientation response decreases (i.e., a habituation effect), which in turn results in a weaker conditioning effect.

Think It Through 2.4: The Relation between Renewal and Occasion Setting

In renewal studies, the context that is present during extinction can be regarded as a negative occasion setter. It is a signal that the CS-US relation is no longer valid. With spontaneous recovery, time can be seen as a context. During an initial period, the CS is followed by the US. During a second time period, the CS is not followed by the US. The presence of the second time period is therefore a signal indicating that the CS is not followed by the US. When that time period has elapsed, the CS will again trigger a CR.

Think It Through 2.5: Rescorla-Wagner (Example 1)

Possible solution:

Y+, then AY-, then Y+, then AY-, then AX+

Trial 1:

$Vy = 0$

delta $Vy = .50 (10 - 0) = 5$

Trial2:

$Vy = 5$

$Va = 0$

$Vay = 5 + 0 = 5$

delta $Vy = .50 (0 - 5) = -2.5$

delta $Va = .50 (0 - 5) = -2.5$

Trial 3:

$Vy = 2.5$

delta $Vy = .50 (10 - 2.5) = 3.75$

Trial 4:

$Vy = 6.25$

$Va = -2.5$

$Vay = 3.75$

delta $Vy = .50 (0 - 3.75) = -1.875$

delta $Va = .50 (0 - 3.75) = -1.875$

Trial 5:

$Va = -4.275$

$Vx = 0$

$Vax = -4.275$

delta $Va = .50 (10 - (-4.275)) = 7.1875$

delta $Vx = .50 (10 - (-4.275)) = 7.1875$

After these trials, X has an associative strength of 7.1875.

If you have only one AX+ trial (and A is not inhibitory), $Vx = 5$ will result after that one AX+ because:

$Va = 0$

$Vx = 0$

$Vax = 0$

delta $Vx = .50 (10 - 0) = 5$

So: if X is associated with an inhibitor on a + trial, X will get extra associative strength (and thus be "super" conditioned).

Think It Through 2.6: Rescorla-Wagner (Example 2)

Possible solution:

Imagine you have the following trials:

US-only, X-US, US-only, X-US (where X is a discrete CS, e.g., a tone)

If you view the context as a CS (which we designate with the letter C), you can rewrite those trials as:

C-US, CX-US, C-US, CX-US (where C-US stands for: the context C is present and the US is present and CX-US stands for: the context C is present, the tone is present, and the US is present).

Trial 1: C-US

$Vc = 0$

delta $Vc = .50 \ (10{-}0) = 5$

Trial 2: CX-US

$Vc = 5$

$Vx = 0$

$Vcx = 5 + 0 = 5$

delta $Vc = .50 \ (10 - 5) = 2.5$

delta $Vx = .50 \ (10 - 5) = 2.5$

Trial 3: C-US

$Vc = 7.5$

delta $Vc = .50 \ (10 - 7.5) = 1.25$

Trial 4: CX-US

$Vc = 8.75$

$Vx = 2.50$

$Vcx = 11.25$

delta $Vc = 50 \ (10 - 11.25) = -0.625$

delta $Vx = .50 \ (10 - 11.25) = -0.625$ (Note: you actually have an "overforecast" here; the US is expected to be stronger than it actually is, and as a result, associative strength will decrease slightly)

Compare this to a condition in which you have only X-US trials that you should see as CX-US trials because the context is always present:

Trial 1: CX-US

$Vc = 0$

$Vx = 0$

$Vcx = 0 + 0 = 0$

delta Vc = .50 (10 − 0) = 5

delta Vx = .50 (10 − 0) = 5 (Note that C and X already reached their maximum associative strength after the first trial; this is normally not the case, but in our numerical examples it is, because alpha x beta is very high, namely .50)

Trial 2: CX-US

Vc = 5

Vx = 5

Vcx = 10

delta Vc = .50 (10 − 10) = 0

delta Vx = .50 (10 − 10) = 0

So after two X-US trials (or CX-US), the associative strength of X is higher than after two X-US (CX-US) trials that were intermixed with two US-only (C-US) trials.

Think It Through 3.1: Devaluation Effects

The finding of Colwill and Rescorla (1985) is equivalent to the phenomenon of US revaluation in classical conditioning. It shows that the representation of the Sr is involved in operant conditioning.

Think It Through 3.2: Extrapolate Mental Process Theories of Classical Conditioning

Compare your own considerations with the contents of section 3.3, especially the parts on the nature and evaluation of S-R, R-Sr, and Sd-Sr models.

Think It Through 3.3: Fear Extinction and Avoidance

Let's assume that the formation of the Sd-Sr association is determined by an associative process as described by Rescorla and Wagner (1972). During the first (escape) phase of the experiment, a strong Sd-Sr association arises. When the Sd is presented, this leads to a strong expectation of the Sr. If, however, the avoidance behavior is made, the Sr does not occur. So there is a large expectation discrepancy. However, you can also conceptualize that the R is a CS. That may sound strange, but making an exact distinction between a behavior and a stimulus is difficult, so let us just assume that we treat the R as a CS. The escape trials can then be coded as A+ trials, where A is the Sd and + stands for the presence of the negative Sr. You can code the avoidance trials as AX- trials, where A stands for Sd, X stands for the avoidance behavior, and - stands for the absence of the aversive Sr. Using the Rescorla-Wagner formula, you can see that on the AX trials, the strength of the Sd-Sr (or A-US) association will decrease but will never completely disappear. This is because a piece of the expectation discrepancy on the AX trials is converted into an inhibitory R-Sr (or X-US) relation. As long as only the Sd is present, it will continue to lead to the expectation of the Sr. As soon as R can be emitted after the Sd, however, it will be expected that the Sr no longer occurs. The presence of R on the trials in which Sr does not occur thus leads to a protection of the associative strength of the Sd-Sr relation. Studies by Solomon, Kamin, and Wynne (1953) and Starr and Mineka (1977) indeed show little or no fear on trials with the Sd if the avoidance response can be emitted. However, as soon as the test animal no longer can emit the avoidance behavior R (e.g., because the opening to the safe area is closed), the Sd presentation again leads to fear.

Think It Through 4.1: Create Your Own Intersecting Regularities Procedure

Operant contingencies typically involve an antecedent stimulus (Sd), a response (R), and an outcome stimulus (Sr; see discussion of the three-term contingency in section 3.1.1.1). Hence, if there are two operant contingencies, they can have one or more of these three elements in common. As such, there are many possible procedures with intersecting operant contingencies, especially if you take into account the fact that operant contingencies can intersect in indirect ways (i.e., they do not have elements in common but they do both share elements with a third operant contingency), that intersections can also involve similar elements rather than identical elements (which allows one to examine the effect of different kinds of similarity), and that elements can be relations or regularities. In another example, consider the first experiment of Hughes et al. (2016, Experiment 1). At the start of each trial, participants see the message "Press key F" or "Press key J." After pressing F, a positive image appears on some trials and a neutral brand name on other trials. After pressing J, a negative image appears on some trials and second neutral brand name appears on other trials. This procedure can be seen as involving four operant regularities in which the messages are the antecedent stimuli, pressing the keys are responses, and the images and brand names are the outcome.

Press key F: press F => positive image (Contingency 1)

Press key F: press F => Brand Name 1 (Contingency 2)

Press key J: press J => negative image (Contingency 3)

Press key J: press J => Brand Name 2 (Contingency 4)

The first two contingencies share their antecedent (i.e., message "Press key F") and the response (press F). The last two contingencies also share their antecedent (i.e., message "Press key J") and their response (press J). Hughes et al. (2016, Experiment 1) showed that after experiencing these contingencies, participants prefer the first brand name over the second one. This change in liking is due to the valence of the positive image transferring to the liking of Brand Name 1 and the valence of the negative image transferring to the liking of Brand Name 2.

Think It Through 4.2: Learning via Analogy

From the perspective of relational learning, one could view this procedure as involving a metaregularity consisting of two stimulus contingencies. In the first condition, the pairing of VEKTE and FLOWERS (Regularity 1) and the pairing of FULL and FULL (Regularity 2) are the two regularities that co-occur (i.e., a regularity in the presence of those two standard regularities). In the second condition, each pairing of VEKTE and FLOWERS (Regularity 1) co-occurs with a pairing of EMPTY and FULL (Regularity 2). One possible functional analysis of the observed change in liking is that the relational properties of Regularity 2 transfer to Regularity 1. More specifically, because the stimuli of Regularity 2 are identical in the first condition, participants may start to respond "as if" the stimuli of Regularity 1 are also identical. This implies that they respond as if VEKTE is identical to FLOWERS, which includes responding in positive ways to VEKTE (because FLOWERS is also positive). Vice versa, in Condition 2, participants start to respond "as if" VEKTE is opposite to FLOWERS because EMPTY is also opposite to FULL. From this perspective, Regularity 2 can be regarded as equivalent to a US, Regularity 1 as equivalent to a CS, responding in an identical (Condition 1) or opposite (Condition 2) way to the elements of Regularity 2 as the UR, and responding in an identical way (Condition 1) or opposite (Condition 2) way to the elements of Regularity 1 as the CR. In other words, this analysis implies that the effect is an instance of relational classical conditioning. Note, however, that in section 4.3, we present another functional analysis of this effect in terms of AARR. Regardless of the functional analysis one adheres to, this type of effect could be referred to as learning via analogy: people learn to respond as if VEKTE is to FLOWERS as FULL is to FULL (i.e., similar) or FULL is to EMPTY (i.e., opposite).

Think It Through 5.1: Do We Really Need the Functional Approach?

Much of what we said in the introductory chapter is relevant to this question. So let's reconsider several points from that chapter and use them to respond to the reviewer's arguments. First, let's evaluate the reviewer's suggestion that little would be lost "if the entire concept of the functional approach to learning was removed from the book." Naturally, we disagree. In the context of our book, discussing the functional approach and its relation to the cognitive approach contributes to the aim of providing an introduction to the psychology of learning.

The functional approach has generated and continues to generate important concepts and findings, some of which are not mentioned in cognitively oriented textbooks on learning (e.g., the idea of stimulus class and response class as defined by units, the notion of NAARR and AARR). Contrary to what some think, the functional approach is still very much alive today (see also box 0.3). Hence, a thorough understanding of learning and research on learning requires knowledge about the functional approach and the recent ideas to emerge from it. Removing all discussion of the functional approach from the book would impoverish it.

Second, we do agree with the reviewer that one can separate functional knowledge about learning (or knowledge about the conditions of learning, as the reviewer calls it) from cognitive knowledge about learning. Yet, research in the cognitive tradition rarely does so. Instead, functional and cognitive knowledge about learning are frequently confounded with one another. For instance, conditioning is seen as semisynonymous to the mental process of association formation. Distinctions between the concepts of reinforcer and reward are rare, leading to widespread misunderstandings and inaccuracies. Specific effects such as blocking and latent inhibition are often named according to the potential (but often incorrect) mental theories of those effects, thus further fostering misunderstandings that hamper progress at the mental level. In contrast, by acknowledging the nature and merits of the functional approach and its relation to the cognitive approach, the need for, and benefits of, a clear separation between functional knowledge (conditions of learning) and cognitive knowledge (mental processes underlying knowledge) is encouraged and facilitated.

This brings us to the question of whether functional explanations actually explain anything. It is important to realize that the answer to such a question is *prescientific*: it depends on the philosophical assumptions and values that scientists bring with them to the table (for a detailed treatment, see Hughes, 2018). For functional researchers, an explanatory concept is evaluated based on its ability to predict and influence the behavior of interest. For instance, if the frequency with which a rat presses a lever can be altered by manipulating the contingency between lever pressing and food, then one can say that the contingency between lever pressing and food "explains" lever pressing (i.e., it allows us to predict and influence future lever pressing). If the rate at which a child engages in self-harm reduces when their his or her caretaker starts paying less attention to the harm behavior and more attention to other behaviors, then one can say that the interaction between the child and the caretaker "explains" the self-harm behavior (i.e., it enables us to alter the frequency of future self-harm behavior; see section 5.3.1). If the intensity with which a romantic partner criticizes you decreases whenever you respond to that criticism with even greater aggression and anger, then one can say that the coercive contingency between his or her behavior and yours "explains" your antisocial behavior. For functional researchers, these are valid explanations because the analytic-abstractive concepts being appealed to (e.g., reinforcement and punishment) allow them to achieve their scientific goal (in the above cases, to predict and influence lever pressing, self-harm, and coercive behavior within romantic relationships).

Cognitive researchers, however, have a different scientific aim: they want to know the mental processes via which elements in the environment influence behavior. For them, it does not suffice to show that the contingency between lever pressing and food influences lever pressing. They also want to know how this happens (e.g., via the formation of associations). Just as there is no way to determine which scientific goals are best, there is no way to determine which type of explanation is best. When we look at the reviewer's comments that prompted this Think It Through question, it seems clear that the reviewer does not accept functional explanations as "real" explanations. For instance, he or she is correct in saying that "it is chemical theory which explains why a given reaction depends on certain conditions being in place, not the other way around. Likewise, in learning, it is the (cognitive?) theory which will eventually explain why learning depends on conditions X and Y, not the other way around." Functional explanations indeed do not explain why conditions in the environment are important. However, knowing that a chemical bond or behavior is a function of a certain environmental condition does allow us to predict and influence chemical bond or behavior, which is also a way of explaining the chemical bond or behavior. If the value of the functional approach is assessed exclusively in terms of the number of cognitive explanations it generates, then one is unlikely to see any merit in the functional approach, because it is not interested in generating cognitive explanations. If one recognizes the value of the functional approach in its ability to predict and influence behavior, then one will clearly see merit in the approach and its explanations (see chapter 5).[1]

Finally, it is worth noting that the analogy between chemical theories and cognitive theories is not perfect. Although both types of theories are mechanistic (i.e., they want to describe the mechanism via which elements in the environment produces a certain outcome), the building blocks of the mechanisms differ. Whereas chemical mechanisms consist of physical entities (e.g., molecules and atoms), cognitive mechanisms consist of mental entities (i.e., informational representations). Because of the nonphysical nature of mental mechanisms, it is difficult to make progress in identifying those mechanisms (see Think It Through 0.4, and De Houwer, 2011b, for a discussion). Hence, when the reviewer says that "in learning, it is the (cognitive?) theory which will eventually explain why learning depends on conditions X and Y," the word *eventually* is well chosen. At present, cognitive theories of learning are far from perfect, and progress is slow. Until we have better theories, it will be vital to clearly separate functional knowledge from cognitive theories. Moreover, efforts to predict and influence behavior (see chapter 5) should not await the formulation of adequate cognitive theories. Using our functional knowledge, we can already explain behavior and tackle many of the important problems that we humans face.

Think It Through 5.2: Do We Really Need the Cognitive Approach?

Taking several arguments from the introductory chapter will help us answer this question as well. First, if your prescientific goals and values orientate you toward understanding the *mental* mechanisms via which elements in the environment influence behavior, then there is no other option than to adopt a cognitive approach. Second, if you are a functional researcher, you can, in principle, do without knowing anything about the cognitive approach. Merely focusing on environment-behavior relations will allow one to predict and influence behavior, even if nothing is known about the mediating mental mechanisms. In this sense, the relation between functional and cognitive psychology is asymmetrical: there can be functional psychology without cognitive psychology but there cannot be cognitive psychology without functional psychology (at least in the sense of an effect-centric functional approach; see Hughes et al., 2016, and box 0.4). Nevertheless, we do believe that functional researchers can benefit from interacting with cognitive researchers. Most of our arguments for this view have been laid out in the introductory chapter (e.g., cognitive theories can lead to the prediction of new functional knowledge; also see De Houwer, 2018a).

Now that we have arrived at the end of our book, a few more thoughts could be added to this. We have indeed seen examples of the added value of cognitive theories (e.g., predictions that led to new functional knowledge about cue competition and extinction; see section 2.3). However, in chapter 5, we also noted that the cognitive approach in learning psychology has generated relatively few applications. It is impressive to see how cognitive psychologists have designed clever experiments to test the predictions of their theories, but often, the ramifications of their work do not seem to extend beyond the lab. As we noted in chapter 5, cognitive psychologists should not necessarily be worried by this, if their main aim is to uncover the mental mechanisms that mediate learning. But even then—has much progress been made on this front? In this book, we have discussed many elegant cognitive theories, but all of them are flawed or limited in important ways. Often, it is difficult to refute those theories or to distinguish between them empirically. So are we any closer to achieving the aim of uncovering the mental mechanisms that mediate learning? Perhaps we are being overly pessimistic about the achievements of the cognitive approach to the psychology of learning, but we do believe that after fifty years of cognitive learning research, it is time for critical reflection on the past and the future of this approach.

Glossary

ΔP (delta P): reflects the extent to which the presence or absence of the US is correlated with the presence or absence of the CS.

A-B-A-B design: experimental design often used in single-subject research. Involves a baseline phase (the first A), followed by a treatment phase (the first B). To test if the intervention was effective, treatment is withdrawn (the second A) and then reintroduced (the second B).

A-B-C contingency: the three elements of an operant contingency—namely, an antecedent (a), behavior (b), and consequence (c). Also known as the *three-term contingency* or the *ABCs of behavior*.

Abstinence reinforcement interventions: a class of interventions that utilize operant contingencies to reinforce an alternative behavior (e.g., drug abstinence) that is incompatible with a to-be-changed behavior (e.g., drug use).

Abstraction: the act of simplifying by focusing on specific features of an event. Certain properties of the situation, organism, and context are disregarded so that the researcher's focus is centered on one or a limited number of properties that apply across a wide variety of cases.

Abstract types of functional knowledge: knowledge created by identifying those core aspects of the relation between environment and behavior that apply across many different stimuli, contexts, and organisms. Behavioral principles (e.g., classical or operant conditioning) represent examples of abstract functional knowledge.

Adaptation: the impact of environmental regularities on behavior.

Adaptive: relating to the perceived utility of a behavior or mental mechanism for fulfilling the (survival) goals of the organism.

Analytic-abstractive functional approach: scientific approach to the study of behavior that aims to develop abstract knowledge or principles that explain many different behaviors with *precision* (apply to specific instances of behavior), *scope* (apply to many different behaviors), and *depth* (cohere with development at different levels of scientific analysis).

Analytic-abstractive functional level: level of scientific analysis. This level (a) is functional (focused on environment-behavior relations) and (b) generates or utilizes abstract functional terms and concepts when doing so (e.g., lever pressing is an *operant* behavior).

Appetitive stimulus: a stimulus that an organism will work to produce or approach.

Applied behavior analysis: the scientific study of behavior change that relies on the principles of learning to evoke or elicit targeted behavioral change.

Applied cognitive learning psychologists: scientists who study the mediating impact of mental processes on environment-behavior relations with the aim of achieving behavioral change in some applied domain.

Applied functional learning psychologists: scientists who focus on those environmental regularities and moderators that lead to real-world behavioral change.

A-process: see *opponent-process theory of Solomon*. Solomon argued that there are two components underlying the reaction to an emotional stimulus. Every emotional stimulus evokes a primary process that Solomon calls an *a-process*. The a-process is evoked by the stimulus and is unaffected by repeated stimulus presentations.

Associative models: a class of models at the mental level of analysis, united by the idea that the formation and activation of associations between representations in memory mediates learning.

Associative strength: the strength of the association between mental representations.

Autoshaping: as an effect refers to changes in voluntary behavior that result from the pairing of stimuli.

Aversion learning: an increase in the probability of an aversive response to a CS as a result of CS-US pairings (e.g., food-nausea pairings).

Aversive stimulus: a stimulus that an organism will work to escape or avoid.

Avoidance learning: an increase in the frequency of a behavior that is due to the fact that the behavior reduces the probability of a stimulus.

Avoidance response: a behavior that reduces the probability that a stimulus will occur.

B-process: see *opponent-process theory of Solomon*. Solomon argued that there are two components underlying the reaction to an emotional stimulus. The b-process is evoked by the a-process (or, in later versions of the model, by stimuli that co-occur with the b-process), strengthens as the result of repeated stimulus presentations, and starts more quickly as the result of repeated stimulus presentations. The b-process and a-process impact behavior in opposite directions.

Backward blocking: as an effect refers to a reduction in the impact of AX trials on the CR to X that is due to presenting A+ trials after the AX+ trials.

Behavior: a transition in state that is due to a stimulus.

Behavioral contract: a common element in ABA interventions. Involves documenting one's functional analysis so that (a) the targeted behavior can be observed and measured, (b) descriptions of that behavior can be read and understood by others, and (c) the behavior can be distinguished from other types of behavior. Also used in reference to an operant-inspired educational intervention delivered by teachers to influence student behavior.

Behavioral maintenance: a change in behavior that continues even when the contingencies that constitute the intervention have been removed.

Behavioral repertoire: the collection of all behaviors that can be exhibited at a given moment in time.

Behaviorism: an intellectual tradition whose advocates (i.e., behaviorists) have, over time, subscribed to different philosophical positions (e.g., mechanism, functionalism), which have in turn influenced the ways they approach the study of behavior (e.g., methodological behaviorism, radical behaviorism).

Behaviorist (radical): a scientist who operates at the functional level of analysis and is concerned with explaining changes in behavior in terms of the environment.

Blocking (forward): as an effect refers to a reduction in the impact of AX trials on the CR to X that is due to presenting A+ trials before the AX+ trials.

Bouton's model: mental model on extinction in the context of classical conditioning. Argues that extinction as a procedure does not lead to the unlearning or forgetting of an association, but to the acquisition of new knowledge about the CS-US relation ("inhibitory associations").

Bradley's theory: mental model of noncontingent stimulus presentation effects. Argues that stimuli can elicit an orientation response (OR), either on the basis of the extent to which they are novel or on the basis of their significance. Repeated stimulus presentations are assumed to have a bigger impact on novelty than on significance. Stimuli differ in the extent to which they are novel or significant. Responses differ in the extent to which they are influenced by the novelty and significance of the stimuli.

Classical conditioning: as an effect refers to the impact of stimulus pairings on behavior.

Cognitive approach: scientific approach to the study of behavior, the goal of which is to develop knowledge about the mental mechanisms that mediate the impact of the environment on behavior.

Comparator model: an associative mental model concerned with classical conditioning effects. Posits that cue competition effects are due to a comparison of the strength of multiple associations.

Conditional contingency: the contingency between two stimuli in situations in which a certain condition is met. The condition that must be met is that the situations that are compared in terms of the probability of the US differ only with regard to the presence of the CS.

Conditional response (CR): a change in behavior due to the pairing of stimuli.

Conditional stimulus (CS): a stimulus that is examined in terms of whether responses to it change as the result its pairing with another stimulus.

Conditioned suppression: a reduction in the rate of responding that occurs as the result of presenting a CS that was previously paired with a US.

Conditioning through instructions: a change in behavior that is due to a verbal stimulus—namely, instructions about environmental regularities (e.g., the verbal stimulus "When you hear a tone, an electric shock will immediately follow" leads to a change in fear responses toward the tone).

Context: situations (historical and current) in which (relations between) stimuli and responses are embedded.

Contiguous: when stimuli are presented together in time and space.

Contingency: a reliable statistical relation in the spatiotemporal presence of two stimuli; the probability that one stimulus is present depends on the presence of the other stimulus.

Contingency judgment: a judgment about the strength of the relation between the presence of a cue and the presence of an outcome.

Contingency management treatments: a class of interventions derived from applied behavior analysis that are often used to treat, among other things, substance abuse problems. These treatments view problematic behavior as an instance of operant behavior under stimulus control and utilize functional knowledge to exert influence over that behavior.

Contingent: see *contingency*.

Counterconditioning: as an effect refers to a change in a previously conditioned response that results from pairing the CS with a US that is opposite to the US with which the CS was originally paired. For example, conditioned salivation to a tone that results from tone-food pairings can be eliminated by subsequently pairing the tone with an aversive shock.

Covert behavior: behavior that (in principle) is observable only to the organism emitting that behavior (e.g., thoughts or feelings).

CS postexposure: involves presenting the CS alone after the pairing of that CS with a US. Leads to CS postexposure effects (i.e., a reduced CR), also known as *extinction*.

CS pre-exposure: involves a procedure wherein the CS alone is repeatedly presented before a relation is established between the CS and US. Leads to CS pre-exposure effects (i.e., a reduced CR), also known as *latent inhibition*.

Descriptive level: a level of scientific analysis that is limited to possible ways of describing the features of events, without making claims about the relation between events (functional level) or the mental processes that mediate environment-behavior relations (cognitive level).

Direct contingency management: see *contingency management treatments*.

Direct operant conditioning: impact of a response-outcome relation on a (typically autonomic) response that is not mediated by a change in another (typically voluntary) behavior. In contrast, in indirect operant conditioning of (autonomic) responses the response-outcome relation (e.g., increase in heartbeat leads to receipt of money) has an effect on (autonomous) behavior (e.g., increase in heart rate) only because of a change in voluntary behavior (e.g., walking up and down stairs).

Discrepancy model: model put forward by Sokolov that posits that organisms constantly build up a model of their environment. When a stimulus that is not part of this model is subsequently administered, an orientation reflex (OR) is triggered and this new stimulus is included in the model. After repeated presentations of the same stimulus in the same context, there is no longer a discrepancy between the input and the stimulus representation, and the OR mechanism is inhibited.

Discrete trials procedure: experimental design in which the researcher needs to intervene (e.g., by putting a rat at the start position of a maze) in order to progress from one trial to the next.

Discriminative stimulus: at the descriptive level refers to a stimulus that signals whether a response will be followed by a consequence. At the functional level refers to a stimulus that influences the frequency of an operant response because it signals whether the response is followed by a consequence.

Dishabituation: the finding that a habituated response to a first stimulus is restored after a second stimulus is presented.

Drives: concept introduced by Hull (1943) to explain why certain stimuli function as reinforcers or punishers to a greater extent than others. Assumes that each organism has certain "drives" or "needs" and will strive to achieve an optimal level of satisfaction of those needs.

Dual-process models: a class of mental models concerned with the mental mechanisms that mediate the impact of environment on behavior. Often take the form of one "simple" mechanism (e.g., association formation) and one "complex" mechanism (e.g., formation of propositions).

Dynamics of affect: refers to a situation wherein the repeated presentation of an emotional stimulus leads to a weakening of the reaction to that stimulus but a strengthening of the counterreaction to the stimulus. This is the phenomenon that Solomon's *opponent-process theory* aims to explain.

Early and intensive behavioral interventions (EIBIs): a "package" of applied behavior analytic procedures systematically applied to tackle developmental or intellectual deficits. Typically consists of a comprehensive, hierarchically arranged curriculum implemented across several years to improve a child's overall functioning.

Effect: a change in behavior due to an element in the environmental. A learning effect is that subclass of effects in which the change in behavior is due a regularity in the environment.

Effect-centric functional approach: scientific approach to the study of behavior, the goal of which is to describe the impact of environment on behavior in terms of topographical (i.e., superficial) features.

Environmental regularity: all states in the environment of the organism that entail more than the presence of a single stimulus or behavior at a single point in time.

Escape learning: as an effect, an increase in the probability of a behavior that occurs because the behavior leads to the termination of a stimulus.

Escape response: see *escape learning*.

Evaluative conditioning: as an effect refers to a change in evaluative responding due to stimulus pairings.

Excitatory associations: associations via which activation of one representation leads to the activation of another representation.

Excitatory conditioning: said to occur when a positive contingency is established (i.e., when $p(US/CS) > p(US/\sim CS)$). *Excitatory* refers to the finding that there is an excitation (i.e., an increase or intensification) of a certain behavior (e.g., an increase in anxiety).

Expectation discrepancy: the discrepancy between the degree to which a US is expected to be present and the actual presence or absence of the US. This is a core concept in the Rescorla-Wagner model of classical conditioning.

Explanandum: that which needs to be explained.

Explanans: that by which the explanandum is explained.

Extinction: as an effect refers to the weakening of a CR as the result of CS only presentations that follow CS-US pairings.

Eyeblink reflex: an involuntary blinking of the eyelids elicited by stimulation of the cornea. Often used in research on classical conditioning.

Fear conditioning: as an effect refers to changes in fear responding as the result of stimulus pairings.

Forward conditioning procedure: a classical conditioning procedure wherein, on each trial, the CS is presented prior to the US. The resulting change in behavior due to such a procedure is known as a *forward conditioning effect*.

Free-operant methods: experimental designs that allow the researcher to register operant responses without having to intervene in order to iniate each trial. The opposite of discrete trials methods, in which the researcher has to intervene to initiate each trial.

Function: used in this book in the mathematical sense of function ("X is dependent on Y") and not in the sense of functionality ("X is at the service of Y").

Functional analysis: the process of identifying and testing the functional relationships between those stimuli and responses that make up one's unit of analysis.

Functional approach: a scientific approach to the study of behavior. Can be carried out in two related ways: initial identification of the environmental events that moderate changes in specific behavior (see *effect-centric functional approach*), and then creation of more abstract concepts from those environment-behavior relations (see *analytic-abstractive functional approach*).

Functional-cognitive framework: a metatheoretical framework that distinguishes between two mutually supportive but distinct levels of explanation: a *functional level* concerned with the identification of environmental events that lead to changes in behavior and a *mental level* concerned with the identification of mental mechanisms that mediate the impact of environment on behavior.

Functional explanations: explanations of behavior in terms of environmental events. Functional knowledge about learning (i.e., knowledge about which environmental regularities influence behavior under which conditions) thus provides functional explanations of behavior.

Habituation: as an effect refers to a decrease in the intensity of a response due to the repeated presentation of a single stimulus.

Heuristic value: the extent to which a theory or concept allows one to organize in a coherent manner existing functional knowledge in a given domain.

Higher-order conditioning: either a procedure in which CS1 is first paired with a US, and subsequently paired with CS2, or, as an effect, a change in behavior toward CS2 as a result of prior CS1-US followed by CS1-CS2 pairings.

Indirect operant conditioning: impact of a response-outcome relation on a (typically autonomic) response (e.g., increase in heartbeat because this leads to receiving money) that is mediated by a change in another (typically voluntary) behavior (e.g., walking up and down stairs). Contrasted with direct operant conditioning of (autonomic) responses, in which the response-outcome relation (e.g., increase in heartbeat leads to stimulation of the pleasure center in the brain) has an effect on (autonomous) behavior (e.g., increase in heartrate) independent of changes in voluntary behavior (e.g., walking up and down stairs).

Indirect relations: regularities in the spatiotemporal presence of two stimuli that do not co-occur but that are both related to a third stimulus. In the case of second-order relations, the two indirectly related stimuli both co-occur with the third stimulus. In the case of higher-order (third, fourth, etc.) relations, the two indirectly related stimuli are indirectly related to the third stimulus (e.g., in the case of third-order relations, the two indirectly related stimuli co-occur with different stimuli that in turn, both co-occur with a fifth stimulus).

Inhibitory associations: links between mental representations via which the increase in activation of one representation results in a decrease of the activation of the associated representation.

Inhibitory conditioning: as an effect refers to an instance of classical conditioning in which a (typically negative) CS-US relation results in a decrease in the intensity or likelihood of a response to the CS. As a mental process refers to the formation of inhibitory associations.

Intrinsically motivated: loosely defined mental term for the source of motivation for a certain action. *Intrinsic* involves an assumption that the source of motivation lies inside the organism itself, as opposed to *external motivation*, where some external event or other organism is said to motivate behavior.

Intrinsic relation: see *intrinsic R-Sr relations* and *intrinsic Sd-R relations*.

Intrinsic R-Sr relations: pre-experimental properties of the R-Sr relation; that is, properties established before the implementation of the operant conditioning procedure. The impact of intrinsic R-Sr relations can be demonstrated by showing an impact of the interaction between the nature of the R and the nature of the Sr on operant conditioning. It is often assumed that this impact arises because of phylogenetic factors, but this is difficult to substantiate.

Intrinsic Sd-R relations: pre-experimental properties of the Sd-R relation; that is, properties established before the implementation of the operant conditioning procedure. The impact of intrinsic Sd-R relations can be demonstrated by showing an impact of the interaction between the nature of the Sd and the nature of the R on operant conditioning. It is often assumed that this impact arises because of phylogenetic factors, but this is difficult to substantiate.

Latent learning: a change in behavior at Time 2, which is a function of the regularities that an organism experienced at Time 1.

Law of effect: idea introduced by Thorndike (1911) that holds that behavior that has appetitive outcomes will increase in frequency, whereas behavior that results in aversive (negative) outcomes will decrease in frequency.

Learned helplessness: the detrimental impact of the absence of an R-Sr relation on later effects of the presence of a R-Sr relation.

Learning: a change in behavior due to regularities in the environment.

Learning effects: see *learning*.

Learning procedures: an experimental context in which a certain regularity is present and a certain behavior is observed. A procedure is a list of observable actions that the researcher carries out when conducting an experiment.

Learning psychologists: a subset of psychologists concerned with changes in behavior due to environmental regularities.

Maturation: changes in the physical constitution or behavior of an organism that occur independently of events in the environment of the organism.

Mediation of learning: a (part of a) mechanism is said to mediate learning when it is represents a necessary causal step between the environmental regularity and the observed change in behavior.

Mere exposure effect: a change in liking due to the repeated presentation of a single stimulus.

Metaregularities: regularities in the occurrence of regularities.

Methodological behaviorism: an approach within the wider tradition of behaviorism that argues that only overt behavior can be objectively observed and that covert behavior (thoughts and feelings), as well as unconscious mental processes should therefore be omitted from scientific study.

Moderated learning: a situation where the impact of one regularity on behavior depends on (or is "moderated by") the presence of other regularities in the environment.

Moderators of learning: an element of the environment that serves to moderate the impact of environmental regularities on behavior.

Multiple baseline designs: experimental designs often used in single-subject contexts, which involve (a) targeting two or more behaviors, settings, or individuals, and (b) collecting baseline data at the same time. There are three different types: multiple baselines across settings, across subjects, and across behaviors.

Myth of the cognitive revolution: common misconception that cognitive psychology and behaviorism are *competitors* for scientific legitimacy, with cognitive psychology typically seen as superior in scientific legitimacy to behaviorism, which is assumed to have become extinct.

Needs: see *drives*.

Negative contingency: a contingency between two events wherein the presence of one event (e.g., presentation of the US) is less likely in situations in which the other event is present (e.g., presentation of the CS) than in situations wherein the other event is absent.

Negative occasion setter: in classical conditioning research, a stimulus whose presence is indicative of the absence of a CS-US relation.

Negative reinforcement: increase in the frequency of a behavior due to the fact that the behavior results in the absence of a stimulus (i.e., because there is a negative contingency between the behavior and the stimulus).

Noncontingent stimulus presentations: a procedure in which a stimulus is presented in a manner that is not contingent on (i.e., related to) the presence or absence of other stimuli.

Observational conditioning: a change in the behavior of an observer toward a stimulus that is due to the pairing of that stimulus and the behavior of a model.

Occasional setting: the effect of occasion setters on CRs.

Occasion setter: an event that indicates when a relation between a CS and a US is either present or absent.

Ontogenetic adaptation: the impact of regularities in the environment of an organism on the behavior of that organism during its lifetime. We use the word "learning" as a synonym of ontogenetic adaptation.

Operant behavior: behavior under the control of a consequence.

Operant class: at the functional level, a set of behaviors that are under the control of a particular outcome.

Operant conditioning: at the procedural level, the presence of a relation between a behavior and certain consequences; at the effect level, changes in behavior that result from regularities in the presence of behavior and consequences.

Opponent-process theory of Solomon: theory about the effect of noncontingent stimulus presentations on the "dynamics of affect" (i.e., the interplay between reactions and counterreactions).

Orientation response (OR): a set of different reactions that seem to orient an organism toward a stimulus (also called the *investigatory reaction* or *what-is-it response*).

Overshadowing: at the procedural level, a procedure that compares two groups: Group 1, which is exposed to a CS(X) that is always followed by a US (X+), and Group 2, which is exposed to trials in which the CS(X) is always presented together with another CS(A), and both are followed by the US (AX+). At the effect level, overshadowing refers to the fact that the CR to X is weaker in Group 2 than in Group 1. It seems as if the presence of A in the second group "overshadows" the effect of the (perfectly contingent) X-US relation.

Overt behavior: in the behavioral tradition, behavior that is observable (in principle) to organisms other than the organism emitting that behavior.

Phylogenetic adaptation: changes in the behavior of a species across generations due to regularities in the environment of members of that species.

Positive contingency: a contingency between two events in which the presence of one event (e.g., presentation of the US) is more likely when the other event is present (e.g., presentation of the CS) than when it is not.

Positive occasion setter: in classical conditioning research, a stimulus whose presence is indicative of the presence of a CS-US relation.

Positive reinforcement: increase in frequency of a behavior due to the fact that the behavior results in the presence of a stimulus (i.e., because there is a positive contingency between the behavior and the stimulus).

Predictive coding: the idea that organisms build a mental model of their environment and, based on this model, make predictions about what should happen in the world. When there is a mismatch between a prediction and the actual situation in the environment, this will lead to an adjustment of the model.

Predictive value: the extent to which something (e.g., a theory) allows one to make new predictions about environment-behavior relations. In learning psychology, the ability to make novel predictions about the conditions under which learning will occur.

Premack principle: if performing behavior (A) creates the possibility of performing a higher frequency behavior (B), then the frequency of behavior (A) will increase.

Preparatory responses: responses that prepare the organism in a certain way for the arrival of a certain stimulus.

Primacy effect: in situations where environmental regularities change, a primacy effect occurs when behavior is influenced more by the initial regularity than by the subsequent regularity.

Propositional models: class of models at the mental level of analysis whose core assumption is that learning is mediated by the formation and evaluation of propositions about stimulus relations in the environment.

Propositions: concept at the mental level of analysis that refers to an informational unit defined by two characteristics: (a) it contains information about how stimuli are related (e.g., A predicts B, A causes B, A co-occurs with B, etc.), and (b) that information has a truth value (e.g., A predicts B can, at least in principle, be evaluated as true or false).

Punishment: a behavioral effect whereby the relation between an R and Sr leads to a decrease in the probability of behavior.

Radical behaviorism: an approach within the wider tradition of behaviorism, instigated by Skinner. Unlike methodological behaviorism, it focuses on environmental-behavior relations rather than (behavior-behavior) mechanisms and accepts covert behavior (thoughts and feelings) as a topic for scientific study. It avoids the study of mediating mechanisms (whether behavioral, mental, or physiological) because its ultimate aim is to predict and influence behavior, which requires functional knowledge about aspects in the environment that can be directly observed and manipulated.

Recency: see *primacy effect*. In situations where environmental regularities change, a recency effect occurs when behavior is influenced more by the later regularity than by the initial regularity.

Reinforcement: a behavioral effect whereby the relation between an R and Sr leads to an increase in the frequency of behavior.

Reinforcer: a stimulus that leads to an increase in the frequency of behavior when this behavior is linked to that stimulus.

Relational contextual cue: a stimulus that signals (cues) which relational response is reinforced in a given context.

Relational learning: changes in behavior that are due to regularities in which relations function as stimuli.

Renewal: typically studied in the context of classical conditioning. An organism is exposed to the pairing of a CS and US (i.e., CS+ trials) in one context. Across trials a CR emerges. The organism is transferred to another context where the CS is presented without the US (CS trials). This leads to the disappearance of the CR. If, however, the organism is returned to the first context or a new context, presenting the CS will immediately elicit a CR again. This phenomenon is known as a *renewal effect*.

Rescorla-Wagner model: often considered the prototypical example of S-S mental models used to explain classical conditioning effects. Its core assumption is that the extent to which CS-US associations are modified depends on the extent to which the presence or absence of a US is expected.

Response class: descriptive label applied to a set of behaviors that all meet a certain criterion (e.g., that the result in moving a lever 1 cm downward). This criterion is called the *unit of behavior*.

Response deprivation model: model originally introduced by Timberlake and Allison (1974) that argues that a behavior will increase in frequency if it results in the opportunity of emitting a behavior with a low situational frequency (i.e., a behavior that, within the present context, has a frequency lower than its natural frequency).

Response generalization: a situation wherein changes in the probability of a target operant response also leads to changes in other responses.

Reward: mental level concept that is often confused with a reinforcer. Whether something is called a reward depends not on the function of that stimulus but on some property of the stimulus that is thought to give rise to reinforcing function of the stimulus.

Second-order conditioning: see *higher-order conditioning*.

Sensitization: an increase in the intensity of a reaction as a result of noncontingent stimulus presentations.

Sensory preconditioning: at the procedural level, the procedure whereby in a first phase, two neutral stimuli (e.g., a tone and a light) are presented together; in a second phase, one of the two stimuli is followed by a US until a CR is established (e.g., the light stimulus); and in a third phase, the other neutral stimulus from the first phase also evokes a CR (e.g., the tone). This CR to the second CS is termed a *sensory preconditioning effect*.

Sensory reinforcement: the observation that the mere presentation of sensory stimuli can be reinforcing in itself.

Shaping: the emergence of new instances of operant behavior through reinforcement of successive approximations to the behavior.

Simultaneous conditioning: in classical conditioning, the procedure of simultaneous presentation of the CS and US.

Single-subject designs: research design wherein the organism, rather than the behavior of another organism or group, serves as its own control.

Skinner box: an apparatus used to study free-operant behavior.

Sokolov's theory: see *discrepancy model.*

Solomon's theory: see *opponent-process theory of Solomon.*

Sometimes opponent processes (SOP): mental model, introduced by Wagner (1981), which has as one of its core ideas that two types of S-S associations can be formed: excitatory associations and inhibitory associations.

Spontaneous recovery: finding that extinguished CRs can emerge again as the result of the mere passage of time.

Sr: at the descriptive level, every event that depends on a behavior; at the functional level, one speaks of an Sr when the stimulus influences the behavior because of the R-Sr relation.

Standard regularities: regularities made up of individual elements.

Stimulus class: a collection or class of stimuli. Defined topographically on the basis of a shared feature (e.g., the class of blue stimuli) or functionally on the basis of a shared function (e.g., the class of stimuli that function as an Sd in a certain context).

Stimulus generalization: as an effect, the finding that stimuli that share properties with a stimulus present during conditioning (either operant or classical) will also occasion similar responses as the conditioned stimulus.

Stimulus-response (S-R) models: class of mental models that assume that learning is based on the formation of associations between stimuli and responses.

Stimulus-stimulus (S-S) models: class of mental models that assume that learning is based on the formation of associations between stimuli.

Superconditioning: from the Rescorla-Wagner model, the finding that conditioning can be made extra strong by pairing a CS together with a CS that has a negative associative strength (i.e., the strength of the association between the CS and US has a negative value).

Three-term contingency: see *A-B-C contingency.*

Unconditional response (UR): the response to a US.

Unconditional stimulus (US): a stimulus that elicits a UR.

Unconscious learning: from a cognitive perspective, learning that occurs when the organism does not have conscious knowledge of the regularities that produced the change in behavior; from a functional perspective, learning without the organism being able to discriminate the regularities that produced the change in behavior.

US pre-exposure: procedure where the US is repeatedly presented on its own before the CS is paired with that US.

US revaluation: procedure where the appetitive or aversive nature of a US is changed.

Notes

Introduction

1. Skinner (1953) divided behavior into two categories (i.e., **overt and covert behavior**). Overt behavior refers to responses that are observable by third parties, whereas covert behavior refers to responses that can be observed only by the organism itself. One could have long philosophical discussions about whether conscious thoughts, perceptions, and feelings qualify as behavior. Skinner ignored discussions about the "true nature" of behavior and took a purely pragmatic position: it may be useful to "act as if" thoughts, perceptions, and feelings are all types of behavior. After all, acting as if thoughts, perceptions, and feelings are types of behavior entails that the learning principles that apply to behavior in general can be applied to thoughts, perceptions, and feelings as well (for more on this, see the section on relational frame theory in chapter 3).

2. We use the term *regularity* in the sense of something that is orderly, regardless of whether the orderly pattern is limited to one point in time or repeated across time. Even the co-occurrence of two stimuli at one point in time can be considered orderly and thus a regularity. We realize that the latter statement does not sit well with an alternative definition of *regularity* as something that is periodic (i.e., occurring at fixed intervals in time (see https://www.thefreedictionary.com/regularity), but we hope that readers are willing to set aside this alternative view in the context of this book.

3. There is no a priori reason why the presentation of two stimuli at a single point in time could not influence behavior at a later point in time. For instance, a single pairing of a tone and shock could increase fear responding toward the tone when it is encountered again at a later point in time. The presentation of one stimulus at two moments in time could also be seen as a regularity that has the potential to influence behavior. For instance, imagine that the reaction evoked by a loud noise is stronger the first time the noise is presented than the second time it is presented. This change in behavior would qualify as an instance of learning if it can be argued that the reduction in the reaction to the noise on its second representation is due to the regularity in the presentation of the noise—that is, to the fact that it is presented for a second time. It can, however, be difficult to separate learning from priming. In a typical priming procedure, on each trial there are two stimuli that occur together in time and space (e.g., the word DOCTOR and the word NURSE). Hence, priming procedures involve a regularity in the environment (e.g., two words that co-occur). There is also a change in behavior (e.g., the time taken to decide that NURSE is an existing word is shorter when NURSE is preceded by the word DOCTOR

than when it is preceded by an unrelated word). One could argue, however, that in priming effects, the change in behavior is not caused by a regularity (e.g., the singular co-occurrence of the two words) but by the presence of a prime stimulus (e.g., the word DOCTOR). According to this analysis, priming effects are not instances of learning because the cause of the change in behavior is a single stimulus at one point in time (i.e., the prime), rather than a regularity in the presence of stimuli (i.e., the pairing of the prime and target). The picture gets more blurred when we consider priming studies in which the prime and target are identical (i.e., repetition priming). This also leads to a change in behavior (i.e., responding to the target is faster when preceded by an identical prime), but it is unclear whether this change is due to the presentation of the prime (in which case, the change in behavior would not qualify as an instance of learning) or to the fact that the target stimulus was already presented before (in which case, it would qualify as an instance of learning). One the one hand, problems with distinguishing priming and learning again illustrate that claims about learning are at best hypotheses about the causes of changes in behavior rather than "real" facts to be discovered. On the other hand, one could argue that these problems reveal the limitations of our definition of learning. As we noted at the start of this chapter, definitions are rarely perfect. We also noted that our definition should be regarded as a working definition rather the "true" definition of learning. Its only aim is to facilitate research and application. We hope that the remainder of this book shows that our definition serves this aim well.

4. Some researchers use the term *classical conditioning* only when one of the two stimuli has a biological relevance (e.g., food, painful stimuli). Although historically such stimuli are often used in research on classical conditioning, we see no reason to limit research on classical conditioning to these kinds of stimuli. Moreover, it is often difficult to determine what counts as a biologically relevant stimulus (De Houwer, 2011b).

5. Likewise, a distinction must also be made between **adaptation** and **adaptive**. While *adaptation* implies only that behavior is influenced by regularities in the environment, *adaptive* refers to achieving a certain norm or end goal (e.g., reproduction). Adaptation therefore implies only a change in behavior as a result of regularities in the environment, whereas adaptive implies something more (i.e., that there is a certain direction in which the behavior changes).

6. Note that we make a distinction between *moderation of learning* and *moderated learning*. As proposed by De Houwer et al. (2013), moderated learning refers to situations in which the effect of regularities on behavior (i.e., learning) depends on another regularity (see section 0.2.2). This therefore concerns situations in which learning is moderated by one specific type of moderator: another regularity in the environment. When learning depends on other types of moderators (e.g., the nature of the stimulus), we do not talk about "moderated learning" but about "moderation of learning." We adhere to this position but add the requirement that moderated learning should always involve a change in behavior. Hence, we define moderated learning as a change in behavior that is the joint effect of multiple regularities. This definition implies that the change in behavior would not occur in that manner if one of the regularities would be absent. The additional requirement allows us to exclude situations in which a regularity in the environment eliminates learning (e.g., when presenting a stimulus on its own eliminates the impact of stimulus pairings on behavior), which cannot be instances of learning (in the way that we defined learning) because there is no change in behavior.

7. Throughout this handbook we will refer to the "functional approach" as a shorthand for the analytic-abstractive functional approach.

8. Another reason is to predict behavior. For many functional researchers, however, prediction is relevant only to the extent that it can aid influence on behavior (see Hayes & Brownstein, 1986).

9. Although less crucial in the present context, cognitive researchers also see Tolman's studies as proof of the mediating role of motivational factors. More specifically, for them, it shows that it is not enough to have a mental representation to set behavior in motion; motivation to deploy that representation is also needed (e.g., deploy knowledge about the maze only when it is useful for locating a desired food).

10. Some readers might be reminded of Marr's (1982) popular distinction between the computational, algorithmic, and implementational levels of analysis. One could, however, argue that Marr's levels of analysis are all situated at the cognitive level of explanation in that they are directed at understanding the way that mental processes mediate behavioral phenomena. More specifically, computational analyses specify the input and output of a mental process, algorithmic analyses reveal the information processing steps via which the input is transformed to the output, and implementational analyses uncover the way in which mental processes are realized at the physical level. From this perspective, even cognitive researchers who analyze mental processes at the computational level operate at a different level of explanation than functional researchers. Although functional researchers also describe input-output relations, they do so not to improve understanding of mental processes but to better predict and influence behavior (Hayes & Brownstein, 1986). Moreover, functional researchers consider only inputs and outputs that are part of the environment (i.e., mental inputs and outputs are not taken into account; see De Houwer & Moors, 2015).

Chapter 1

1. As pointed out by a reviewer, a related phenomenon can occur at the sensory level. For instance, if an organism is no longer able to sense certain stimuli (because of exhaustion or structural damage to sensory organs), then responses to the presence of those stimuli will also change. Again, one could argue that such changes in behavior are not instances of learning because they are not due to regularities in the presence of events. That is, like changes in the behavioral repertoire, changes in sensory abilities provide a potential alternative explanation for changes in behavior.

2. The first author of this book (Jan De Houwer) learned this statement from his mentor Paul Eelen, who had it written in large letters on the door of his office.

Chapter 2

1. Some readers might object to equating outcomes to USs because only the latter are biologically relevant. Note, however, that we are drawing on a broad definition of classical conditioning that concerns only the impact of stimulus pairings on behavior, regardless of the nature of the stimuli or behaviors that are involved.

2. Although the literature on evaluative conditioning is extensive, surprisingly little is said about what "liking" actually entails. Intuitively, most of us have a sense of what it means to like or dislike something, but it is more difficult to delineate which behaviors are evaluative in nature and what makes them evaluative.

3. Conditioning that involves changes in the UR could also be interpreted in terms of enhanced priming. Just as the prime *doctor* speeds up responses to the target *nurse* in a lexical decision task (see introduction, note 3), the presentation of a biologically relevant CS (e.g., fake female quail) could be said to change responding to the US (e.g., sexual contact with an actual female). It is possible that under certain conditions, these priming effects become stronger with repetition—that is, the more often the prime (or CS) precedes the target (or US). Interestingly, such enhanced-priming-by-repetition effects have also been observed in research on induced resistance in plants (e.g., Song & Ryu, 2018). From this perspective, CS-US trials do not directly change the UR but they change the extent to which the CS primes the UR.

4. Spontaneous recovery can be seen as an instance of renewal in which time rather than spatial location functions as the context that modulates responding. More specifically, the time period during the CS-US pairings (acquisition phase) can be seen as Context A, the time period during CS-only (extinction phase) as Context B, and the time period after the delay as a new Context C.

5. Often (and also originally), S-R associations were conceived of in physiological terms as involving neural connections between stimulus and response centers in the brain. Given our focus on the mental level of explanation in the psychology of learning, we conceptualize an S-R association in mental terms—that is, as a link between mental representations. Note that the two perspectives overlap if one assumes that stimulus and response centers in the brain are the physiological basis for mental representations of stimuli and responses.

6. Some have argued that complex networks of associations can encode relational information and thus assumptions about the state of events in the world (e.g., Gawronski & Bodenhausen, 2018). However, we do not know any current associative model that captures the intricacies of relational information processing. Moreover, there are good reasons to doubt that associative models could ever achieve this (Hummel, 2010). But if an associative model could be constructed that encodes truth-evaluable relational information, we would consider it to be a propositional model because for us, propositions are about the content of information, not about the structure that is used to store that information. Hence, any representational structure that encodes truth-evaluable relational information would qualify as a proposition (De Houwer, 2018c).

Chapter 3

1. Another way of putting this is that a descriptive Sd is an event whose presence or absence is correlated with the presence or absence of a regularity.

2. There are different notations to refer to Sds or Srs with different functions (see Michael, 2004, p. 77 for an overview). In the learning literature, a somewhat different notation is usually used—namely, S^D and S^R, with the D and R in capital letters and superscript. For the sake of simplicity, we use the notations Sd and Sr for all these functions.

3. Note that some R-Sr relations in the environment might have little effect on behavior simply because R is unlikely to occur in the learning context. Consider a situation in which lever pressing stops the delivery of a painful shock. Because the delivery of a shock typically induces freezing (i.e., the rat

becomes still), it is unlikely that the rat will ever press the lever during the delivery of the shock and thus that it will experience that pressing the lever is followed by the discontinuation of the shock. This example illustrates that a distinction needs to be made between the Sd: R-Sr regularities that a researcher creates in the environment and the Sd: R-Sr regularities that an organism is exposed to. Because the researcher does not have full control over the behavior of the organism, the two do not necessarily overlap. Importantly, learning involves only effects of the regularities that are experienced by the organism. If the behavior of the organism does not change because it does not experience the regularities that are set up by the researcher, then this is not a failure of learning but a lack of opportunity for learning to occur.

4. A reviewer of this book argued that, at least with humans, one could simply ask people what they like and dislike and predict the function of stimuli based on those self-reports. However, from the attitude literature, we know that there is often a large discrepancy between what people say that they like and dislike and what they actually do (e.g., Wicker, 1969).

5. Note that during the test, outcomes are no longer presented (i.e., it is a test during extinction). Hence, any behavior that is emitted during the test is due to the regularities that were present during the first phase. This impact of the regularities during the first phase on performance during the test phase is modulated by what happens in the second phase.

6. In other words, one should look not only at the unit of behavior used by the researcher (namely, whether a plural form is used) but also at other units of behavior that lead to a similar response class (e.g., speaking about jewels, which leads to the frequent use of plurals).

7. This link between behavior and reinforcement is not present in many other gambling games. With the lotto, for example, the chances of winning in a certain draw are the same regardless of the number of times that one has entered the lotto previously (Ophalvens, 1987).

8. As the result of pairing a stimulus with a reinforcer, the presentation of the stimulus thus can function both as a reinforcer and as an establishing operation (see section 3.2.4.2). In the first case, the frequency of behaviors that produce the stimulus will increase (e.g., after tone-food pairings, the frequency of lever pressing increases if pressing the lever produces the tone). In the second case, it strengthens the impact of the original reinforcer on behaviors that produce the reinforcer (e.g., after tone-food pairings, the relation between lever pressing and food has more impact on the frequency of lever pressing when the tone is present).

9. Catania (2013) correctly points out that the difference between discrimination and generalization can be understood in terms of the overlap between the response class as delineated by the unit of behavior and the class of all behaviors that change effectively as a result of an R-Sr relation. Perfect discrimination means that both classes overlap completely (only behavior that belongs to the response class changes). Generalization means that also behaviors that are not part of the response class are affected by the R-Sr relation.

10. Note that stimuli can always accidentally share similarities with one another. But by choosing stimuli at random, the chance of this occurring (i.e., that stimuli are systematically related to each other) is reduced.

11. However, there are also S-R models in which the Sr is not important for learning. For example, Guthrie (1946) suggested that the formation of S-R associations is merely the result of the simultaneous occurrence of the stimulus and the response (see Bouton, 2016, pp. 246–249, for more details).

Chapter 4

1. Note that this effect is similar to sensory preconditioning in the context of evaluative conditioning. The main difference is that, in the studies by Hughes et al. (2016), the common stimulus is presented only after the behavior has been emitted, and the positive and negative images are presented before the shared neutral stimulus.

2. In fact, contextual cues can have two functions (see Hayes et al., 2001). First, they can signal the nature of the relational response that is reinforced (e.g., same, opposite, smaller than, bigger than). Second, they can signal the stimulus features that need to be responded to (e.g., color, shape). In this book, we use the term "relational contextual cues" in a broad sense that encompasses both functions. Although these functions can be separated in theory, in practice they are closely intertwined because a specific type of relational responding always involves specific stimulus features. For instance, in the example depicted in figure 4.3, the contextual cues do not only signal whether shape (left side) or color (right side) need to be related but also that participants should pick the comparison stimulus with the same shape (left side) or color (right side) as the sample stimulus (rather than the comparison with a different shape or color).

3. As is the case for all types of relational contextual cues, the impact of the sharing of features can depend on other contextual cues (i.e., higher-order relational contextual cues). For instance, in some contexts it might function as a cue for opposition. The shared features principle allows for these changes in function but postulates that the sharing of features by default functions as a cue for equivalence— that is, in the absence of higher-order relational contextual cues signaling a different function.

Chapter 5

1. In chapter 5 we will typically refer to the principles of learning rather than specific types of regularities or their moderators (for a quick recap on learning principles, see the introduction). Doing so will help highlight that although the stimuli, responses, organisms, contexts, and other properties vary from one domain to another, the principles of learning are relevant across domains, and can be used to change human behavior in many ways.

2. It is worth noting that one specific regularity (i.e., between stimuli and responses) and the principle abstracted from it (operant conditioning) have attracted the vast majority of attention in the applied functional learning literature. This is because the idea at the core of operant conditioning ("selection by consequences") seems to drive change at the biological, behavioral, and group levels (e.g., Catania, 2013; Jablonka & Lamb, 2007; Skinner, 1981). At the biological level, selection by consequences involves the selection (or retention) of physical characteristics that increase reproductive success and the discarding of those that undermine that success. At the behavioral level, the probability that a behavior will

be selected or discarded depends on its consequences (i.e., the stimuli or responses it produces). At the group level, cultural practices (e.g., customs) are likely selected or discarded by consequences that operate on the interlocking behavior of groups rather than individuals (for examples, see Glenn, 2004; for similar ideas on cultural and symbolic inheritance, see Jablonka & Lamb, 2007; Wilson et al., 2014). The key point is that operant conditioning has attracted the greatest part of applied functional learning psychologists' attention because of its utility in achieving behavioral change.

3. Applied learning psychologists are not the only group of functional learning psychologists who study environment-behavior relations in order to predict and influence behavior (also see contextual behavioral science; Hayes, Barnes-Holmes, & Wilson, 2012). There are still other groups both in (e.g., health, developmental, and applied social psychologists) and outside of psychology (e.g., epidemiologists, public health, and prevention scientists) that have the same goal. Although this chapter purposefully focuses on the principles of learning as used by applied learning psychologists, it is important to appreciate that those same principles can be used by all of the aforementioned disciplines to help accelerate the prediction and influence of their target behavior of interest.

4. Note that abstinence reinforcement interventions are not the only treatment plans to emerge from the learning psychology literature. The community reinforcement approach, for example, uses social, recreational, familial, and vocational reinforcement contingencies to support a drug-free lifestyle. This approach is effective in the treatment of alcohol and drug addiction (Meyers, Roozen, & Smith, 2011).

5. Although they are useful, abstinence reinforcement interventions have two potential problems. The first is that many individuals begin an abstinence program (and fall under the control of the reinforcement contingencies), yet many others do not. The second is that although some individuals continue to avoid drugs after reinforcement is discontinued, many resume drug use at some point. These two issues point to potential boundary conditions of these interventions and suggest that certain conditions might need to be met before the treatment is effective for many individuals; for example an increase in reinforcer value and more immediate (continuous) instead of delayed (partial) schedules may need to be used, with a focus on single vs. multiple drug abstinence. Likewise, it may be that abstinence reinforcement interventions need to be combined with other interventions maintained over extended periods to maintain their effectiveness (see Silverman et al., 2011).

6. Note that there are instances where cognitive theories about phenomena other than learning (e.g., attention) have led to interventions designed to change real-world behavior (e.g., cognitive bias modification). Although these interventions certainly stem from cognitive theories, they were not the product of the cognitive *learning* theories covered in this book.

Reflections on the "Think It Through" Questions

1. But keep in mind that even though the functional approach is not directed at generating cognitive explanations, cognitive researchers can nevertheless exploit that approach to better achieve their own aim of generating cognitive explanations (e.g., by using the empirical and conceptual knowledge generated by functional researchers in order to test their theories and more clearly separate to-be-explained functional knowledge from explanatory mental processes).

References

Adams, C. D., & Dickinson, A. (1981). Instrumental responding following reinforcer devaluation. *Quarterly Journal of Experimental Psychology, 33B*, 109–121.

Adelman, B. E. (2018). On the conditioning of plants: A review of experimental evidence. *Perspectives on Behavior Science, 41*, 431–446.

Alavosius, M. P., Newsome, W. D., Houmanfar, R., & Biglan, A. (2016). A functional contextualist analysis of the behavior and organizational practices relevant to climate change. In R. D. Zettle, S. C. Hayes, D. Barnes-Holmes, & A. Biglan (Eds.), *Handbook of contextual behavioral science* (pp. 513–530). New York, NY: Wiley.

American Psychiatric Association. (2013). *Diagnostic and statistical manual of mental disorders* (5th ed.). Washington, DC: Author.

Anderson, B. (2011). There is no such thing as attention. *Frontiers in Psychology, 2*, Article 246.

Antony, M. M., & Roemer, L. (2011). *Theories of psychotherapy: Behavior therapy*. Washington, DC: American Psychological Association.

Arcediano, F., Ortega, N., & Mature, H. (1996). A behavioural preparation for the study of human Pavlovian conditioning. *Quarterly Journal of Experimental Psychology, 49B*, 270–283.

Azrin, N. H., & Holz, W. C. (1966). Punishment. In W. K. Honig (Ed.), *Operant behavior: Areas of research and application* (pp. 390–477). New York, NY: Appleton-Century-Crofts.

Baeyens, F., Crombez, G., Van den Bergh, O., & Eelen, P. (1988). Once in contact always in contact: Evaluative conditioning is resistant to extinction. *Advances in Behaviour Research and Therapy, 10*, 179–199.

Baeyens, F., Eelen, P., Crombez, G., & Van den Bergh, O. (1992). Human evaluative conditioning: Acquisition trials, presentation schedule, evaluative style, and contingency awareness. *Behaviour Research and Therapy, 30*, 133–142.

Baeyens, F., Eelen, P., & Van den Bergh, O. (1990). Contingency awareness in evaluative conditioning: A case for unaware affective-evaluative learning. *Cognition & Emotion, 4*, 3–18.

Balleine, B. (1992). Instrumental performance following a shift in primary motivation depends on incentive learning. *Journal of Experimental Psychology: Animal Behavior Processes, 18*, 236–250.

Barlow, D. H. (2016). Paradigm clashes and progress: A personal reflection on a 50-year association with ABCT. *Cognitive and Behavioral Practice, 23*, 415–419.

Barnes-Holmes, D., & Hussey, I. (2016). The functional-cognitive meta-theoretical framework: Reflections, possible clarifications, and how to move forward. *International Journal of Psychology, 51*, 50–57.

Barnes-Holmes, Y., Kavanagh, D., & Murphy, C. (2016). Relational frame theory: Implications for education and developmental disabilities. In S. Hayes, D. Barnes-Holmes, R. Zettle, & T. Biglan (Eds.), *Handbook of contextual behavioral science* (pp. 227–253). New York, NY: Wiley.

Barrish, H. H., Saunders, M., & Wolf, M. M. (1969). Good Behavior Game: Effects of individual contingencies for group consequences on disruptive behavior in a classroom 1. *Journal of Applied Behavior Analysis, 2*, 119–124.

Barron, A. B., Hebets, E. A., Cleland, T. A., Fitzpatrick, C. L., Hauber, M. E., & Stevens, J. R. (2015). Embracing multiple definitions of learning. *Trends in Neurosciences, 38*, 405–407.

Barry, R. J. (2006). Promise versus reality in relation to the unitary orienting reflex: A case study examining the role of theory in psychophysiology. *International Journal of Psychophysiology, 62*, 353–366.

Barry, R. J. (2009). Habituation of the orienting reflex and the development of preliminary process theory. *Neurobiology of Learning and Memory, 92*, 235–242.

Bashinski, H. S., Werner, J. S., & Rudy, J. W. (1985). Determinants of infant visual fixation: Evidence for a two-process theory. *Journal of Experimental Child Psychology, 39*, 580–598.

Bechtel, W. (2008). *Mental mechanisms: Philosophical perspectives on cognitive neuroscience*. London, UK: Routledge.

Beck, A. T., Rush, J. A., Shaw, B. F., & Emery, G. (1979). *Cognitive therapy of depression*. New York, NY: Guilford Press.

Beckers, T., & Kindt, M. (2017). Memory reconsolidation interference as an emerging treatment for emotional disorders: Strengths, limitations, challenges, and opportunities. *Annual Review of Clinical Psychology, 13*, 99–121.

Beckers, T., Miller, R. R., De Houwer, J., & Urushihara, K. (2006). Reasoning rats: Forward blocking in Pavlovian animal conditioning is sensitive to constraints of causal inference. *Journal of Experimental Psychology: General, 135*, 92–102.

Bernstein, A. S. (1981). The orienting response and stimulus significance: Further comments. *Biological Psychology, 12*, 171–185.

Bernstein, I. L., Webster, M. M., & Bernstein, I. D. (1982). Food aversions in children receiving chemotherapy for cancer. *Cancer, 50*, 2961–2963.

Biglan, A. (2009). Increasing psychological flexibility to influence cultural evolution. *Behavior and Social Issues, 18*, 15–24.

Biglan, A. (2015). *The nurture effect: How the science of human behavior can improve our lives and our world*. Oakland, CA: New Harbinger.

Biglan, A. (2016). The need for a more effective science of cultural practices. *Behavior Analyst, 39*, 97–107.

Biglan, A., Brennan, P. A., Foster, S. L., Holder, H. D., Miller, T. R., Cunningham, P., & Zucker, R. A. (2004). *Helping adolescents at risk: Prevention of multiple problem behaviors.* New York, NY: Guilford Press.

Biglan, A., & Embry, D. D. (2013). A framework for intentional cultural change. *Journal of Contextual Behavioral Science, 2*, 95–104.

Binder, C., & Watkins, C. L. (2013). Precision teaching and direct instruction: Measurably superior instructional technology in schools. *Performance Improvement Quarterly, 26*, 73–115.

Binnun, N. L., Golland, Y., Davidovitch, M., & Rolnick, A. (2010). The biofeedback odyssey: From Neal Miller to current and future models of regulation. *Biofeedback, 38*, 136–141.

Bitterman, M. E. (1996). Comparative analysis of learning in honeybees. *Animal Learning and Behavior, 24*, 123–141.

Bjorklund, D. F. (2018). Behavioral epigenetics: The last nail in the coffin of genetic determinism. *Human Development, 61*, 54–59.

Blaisdell, A. P., Sawa, K., Leising, K. J., & Waldmann, M. R. (2006). Causal reasoning in rats. *Science, 311*(5763), 1020–1022.

Boddez, Y., De Houwer, J., & Beckers, T. (2017). The inferential reasoning theory of causal learning: Towards a multi-process propositional account. In M. R. Waldman (Ed.), *The Oxford handbook of causal reasoning* (pp. 53–78). Oxford, UK: Oxford University Press.

Boisseau, R. P., Vogel, D., & Dussutour, A. (2016). Habituation in non-neural organisms: Evidence from slime moulds. *Proceedings of the Royal Society B: Biological Sciences, 283*(1829), Article 20160446.

Bolles, R. C. (1972). The avoidance learning problem. *Psychology of Learning and Motivation, 6*, 97–145.

Bonardi, C., Robinson, J., & Jennings, D. (2017). Can existing associative principles explain occasion setting? Some old ideas and some new data. *Behavioural Processes, 137*, 5–18.

Bonetti, F., & Turatto, M. (2019). Habituation of oculomotor capture by sudden onsets: Stimulus specificity, spontaneous recovery, and dishabituation. *Journal of Experimental Psychology: Human Perception and Performance, 45*, 264–284.

Bouton, M. E. (1993). Context, time, and memory retrieval in the interference paradigms of Pavlovian learning. *Psychological Bulletin, 114*, 80–99.

Bouton, M. E. (1998). The role of context in classical conditioning: Some implications for cognitive behavior therapy. In W. T. O'Donahue (Ed.), *Learning and behaviour therapy* (pp. 59–84). Needham Heights, MA: Allyn & Bacon.

Bouton, M. E. (2004). Context and behavioral processes in extinction. *Learning and Memory, 11*, 485–494.

Bouton, M. E. (2007). *Learning and behavior: A contemporary synthesis.* Sunderland, MA: Sinauer.

Bouton, M. E. (2016). *Learning and behavior: A contemporary synthesis* (2nd ed.). Sunderland, MA: Sinauer.

Bradley, M. M. (2009). Natural selective attention: Orienting and emotion. *Psychophysiology, 46*, 1–11.

Bradshaw, C. P., Mitchell, M. M., & Leaf, P. J. (2010). Examining the effects of schoolwide positive behavioral interventions and supports on student outcomes: Results from a randomized controlled effectiveness trial in elementary schools. *Journal of Positive Behavior Interventions, 12*, 133–148.

Breedlove, S. M., & Watson, N. V. (2016). *Behavioral neuroscience*. Sunderland, MA: Sinauer.

Brembs, B. (2003). Operant conditioning in invertebrates. *Current Opinion in Neurobiology, 13*, 710–717.

Bridgeman, B. (2013). Applications of predictive control in neuroscience. *Behavioral Brain Sciences, 36*, 208–208.

Brown, P. L., & Jenkins, H. M. (1968). Auto-shaping of the pigeon's key-peck. *Journal of the Experimental Analysis of Behavior, 11*, 1–8.

Burgos, J. E. (2018). Is a nervous system necessary for learning? *Perspectives on Behavior Science, 41*, 343–369.

Butler, A. C., Chapman, J. E., Forman, E. M., & Beck, A. T. (2006). The empirical status of cognitive-behavioral therapy: A review of meta-analyses. *Clinical Psychology Review, 26*, 17–31.

Byrne, R. W., & Bates, L. A. (2006). Why are animals cognitive? *Current Biology, 16*, R445–R448.

Byrom, N. C., Msetfi, R. M., & Murphy, R. A. (2018). Human latent inhibition: Problems with the stimulus exposure effect. *Psychonomic Bulletin & Review, 25*, 2102–2118.

Capaldi, D. M., Pears, K. C., & Kerr, D. C. R. (2012). The Oregon Youth Study three-generational study: Theory, design, and findings. *Bulletin of the International Society of the Study of Behavioural Development, 2*, 29–33.

Capaldi, D. M., Pears, K. C., Kerr, D. C., Owen, L. D., & Kim, H. K. (2012). Growth in externalizing and internalizing problems in childhood: A prospective study of psychopathology across three generations. *Child Development, 83*, 1945–1959.

Carter, R. M., Hofstötter, C., Tsuchiya, N., & Koch, C. (2003). Working memory and fear conditioning. *Proceedings of the National Academy of Sciences, 100*, 1399–1404.

Cartoni, E., Balleine, B., & Baldassarre, G. (2016). Appetitive Pavlovian-instrumental transfer: A review. *Neuroscience & Biobehavioral Reviews, 71*, 829–848.

Catania, A. C. (2013). *Learning*. Cornwall-on-Hudson, NY: Sloan.

Cheng, P. W., & Holyoak, K. J. (1995). Complex adaptive systems as intuitive statisticians: Causality, contingency, and prediction. In J.-A. Meyer & H. Roitblat (Eds.), *Comparative approaches to cognition* (pp. 271–302). Cambridge, MA: MIT Press.

Cheng, P. W., & Novick, L. R. (1990). A probabilistic contrast model of causal induction. *Journal of Personality and Social Psychology, 58*, 545–567.

Cheng, P. W., & Novick, L. R. (1992). Covariation in natural causal induction. *Psychological Review, 99*, 365–382.

Chiesa, M. (1992). Radical behaviorism and scientific frameworks: From mechanistic to relational accounts. *American Psychologist, 47*, 1287–1299.

Chiesa, M. (1994). *Radical behaviorism: The philosophy and the science.* Boston, MA: Authors Cooperative.

Chomsky, N. (1959). A review of B. F. Skinner's *Verbal Behavior. Language, 35*, 26–58.

Clark, A. (1990). Connectionism, competence, and explanation. *British Journal for the Philosophy of Science, 41*, 195–222.

Clark, A. (2013). Whatever next? Predictive brains, situated agents, and the future of cognitive science. *Behavioral and Brain Sciences, 36*, 181–204.

Clark, R. E., Manns, J. R., & Squire, L. R. (2002). Classical conditioning, awareness, and brain systems. *Trends in Cognitive Sciences, 6*, 524–531.

Collins, D. J., & Shanks, D. R. (2002). Momentary and integrative response strategies in causal judgment. *Memory & Cognition, 30*, 1138–1147.

Colombo, J., & Mitchell, D. W. (2009). Infant visual habituation. *Neurobiology of Learning and Memory, 92*, 225–234.

Colwill, R. M., & Rescorla, R. A. (1985). Postconditioning devaluation of a reinforcer affects instrumental responding. *Journal of Experimental Psychology: Animal Behavior Processes, 11*, 120–132.

Colwill, R. M., & Rescorla, R. A. (1988). Associations between the discriminative stimulus and the reinforcer in instrumental learning. *Journal of Experimental Psychology: Animal Behavior Processes, 14*, 155–164.

Cook, S. A., & Harris, R. E. (1937). The verbal conditioning of the galvanic skin reflex. *Journal of Experimental Psychology, 21*, 202–210.

Craske, M. G., Hermans, D. E., & Vansteenwegen, D. E. (2006). *Fear and learning: From basic processes to clinical implications.* Washington, DC: American Psychological Association.

Craske, M. G., Treanor, M., Conway, C. C., Zbozinek, T., & Vervliet, B. (2014). Maximizing exposure therapy: An inhibitory learning approach. *Behaviour Research and Therapy, 58*, 10–23.

Daar, J. H., & Dixon, M. R. (2015). Conceptual, experimental, and therapeutic approaches to problem gambling. In H. S. Roane, J. E. Ringdahl, & T. S. Falcomata (Eds.), *Clinical and organizational applications of applied behavior analysis* (pp. 353–394). New York, NY: Elsevier.

Dawson, M. E., & Schell, A. M. (1987). Human autonomic and skeletal classical conditioning: The role of conscious cognitive factors. In G. Davey (Ed.), *Cognitive processes and Pavlovian conditioning in humans* (pp. 27–56). Chichester, UK: Wiley.

Debiec, J., & Olsson, A. (2017). Social fear learning: From animal models to human function. *Trends in Cognitive Sciences, 21*, 546–555.

Deci, E. L. (1971). Effects of externally mediated rewards on intrinsic motivation. *Journal of Personality and Social Psychology, 18*, 105–115.

Deci, E. L., & Ryan, R. M. (2000). The "what" and "why" of goal pursuits: Human needs and the self-determination of behavior. *Psychological Inquiry, 11*, 227–268.

Declercq, M., & De Houwer, J. (2009). Evidence for a hierarchical structure underlying avoidance behavior. *Journal of Experimental Psychology: Animal Behavior Processes, 35*, 123–128.

De Houwer, J. (2007). A conceptual and theoretical analysis of evaluative conditioning. *Spanish Journal of Psychology, 10*, 230–241.

De Houwer, J. (2009). The propositional approach to associative learning as an alternative for association formation models. *Learning and Behavior, 37*, 1–20.

De Houwer, J. (2011a). Evaluative conditioning: Methodological considerations. In K. C. Klauer, C. Stahl, & A. Voss (Eds.), *Cognitive methods in social psychology* (pp. 124–147). New York, NY: Guilford Press.

De Houwer, J. (2011b). Why the cognitive approach in psychology would profit from a functional approach and vice versa. *Perspectives on Psychological Science, 6*, 202–209.

De Houwer, J. (2014). A propositional perspective on context effects in human associative learning. *Behavioural Processes, 104*, 20–25.

De Houwer, J. (2018a). A functional-cognitive framework for cooperation between functional and cognitive researchers in the context of stimulus relations research. *Perspectives on Behavior Science, 41*, 229–240.

De Houwer, J. (2018b). A functional-cognitive perspective on the relation between conditioning and placebo research. *International Review of Neurobiology, 138*, 95–111.

De Houwer, J. (2018c). Propositional models of evaluative conditioning. *Social Psychological Bulletin, 13*, Article e28046.

De Houwer, J., Barnes-Holmes, Y., & Barnes-Holmes, D. (2016). Riding the waves: A functional-cognitive perspective on the relations among behavior therapy, cognitive behavior therapy, and acceptance and commitment therapy. *International Journal of Psychology, 51*, 40–44.

De Houwer, J., Barnes-Holmes, D., & Moors, A. (2013). What is learning? On the nature and merits of a functional definition of learning. *Psychonomic Bulletin Review, 20*, 631–642.

De Houwer, J., & Beckers, T. (2002). A review of recent developments in research and theories on human contingency learning. *Quarterly Journal of Experimental Psychology, 55B*, 289–310.

De Houwer, J., Beckers, T., & Glautier, S. (2002). Outcome and cue properties modulate blocking. *Quarterly Journal of Experimental Psychology, 55A*, 965–985.

De Houwer, J., Crombez, G., & Baeyens, F. (2005). Avoidance behavior can function as a negative occasion setter. *Journal of Experimental Psychology: Animal Behavior Processes, 31*, 101–106.

De Houwer, J., & Hughes, S. (2016). Evaluative conditioning as a symbolic phenomenon: On the relation between evaluative conditioning, evaluative conditioning via instructions, and persuasion. *Social Cognition, 34*, 480–494.

De Houwer, J., & Hughes, S. (2017). Environmental regularities as a concept for carving up the realm of learning research: Implications for relational frame theory. *Journal of Contextual Behavioral Science, 6,* 343–346.

De Houwer, J., Hughes, S., & Barnes-Holmes, D. (2016). Associative learning as higher order cognition: Learning in human and nonhuman animals from the perspective of propositional theories and relational frame theory. *Journal of Comparative Psychology, 130,* 215–225.

De Houwer, J., Hughes, S., & Barnes-Holmes, D. (2017). Psychological engineering: A functional-cognitive perspective on applied psychology. *Journal of Applied Research in Memory and Cognition, 6,* 1–13.

De Houwer, J., & Moors, A. (2015). Levels of analysis in social psychology. In B. Gawronski & G. Bodenhausen (Eds.), *Theory and explanation in social psychology* (pp. 24–40). New York, NY: Guilford Press.

De Houwer, J., Tanaka, A., Moors, A., & Tibboel, H. (2018). Kicking the habit: Why evidence for habits in humans might be overestimated. *Motivation Science, 4,* 50–59.

De Houwer, J., Thomas, S., & Baeyens, F. (2001). Association learning of likes and dislikes: A review of 25 years of research on human evaluative conditioning. *Psychological Bulletin, 127,* 853–869.

De Paepe, A. L., Williams, A. C. de C., & Crombez, G. (2019). Habituation to pain: A motivational-ethological perspective. *Pain, 160,* 1693–1697.

de Villiers, P. (1977). Choice in concurrent schedules and a quantitative formulation of the law of effect. In W. Honig & J. Staddon (Eds.), *Handbook of operant behavior* (pp. 233–287). Englewood Cliffs, NJ: Prentice-Hall.

Dickinson, A. (1980). *Contemporary animal learning theory.* Cambridge, UK: Cambridge University Press.

Dickinson, A. (2012). Associative learning and animal cognition. *Philosophical Transactions of the Royal Society B: Biological Sciences, 367,* 2733–2742.

Dickinson, A., & Balleine, B. (1995). Motivational control of instrumental action. *Current Directions in Psychological Science, 4,* 162–167.

Dishion, T. J., & Dodge, K. A. (2005). Peer contagion in interventions for children and adolescents: Moving towards an understanding of the ecology and dynamics of change. *Journal of Abnormal Child Psychology, 33,* 395–400.

Dobson, D. J. G., & Dobson, K. S. (2017). *The evidence-based practice of cognitive-behavioral therapy* (2nd ed.). New York, NY: Guilford Press.

Domjan, M. (1993). *The principles of learning and behavior* (3rd ed.). Belmont, CA: Brooks/Cole.

Domjan, M. (2000). *The essentials of conditioning and learning.* Belmont, CA: Wadsworth/Thomson Learning.

Domjan, M. (2005). Pavlovian conditioning: A functional perspective. *Annual Review of Psychology, 56,* 179–206.

Domjan, M. (2015). The Garcia-Koelling selective association effect: A historical and personal perspective. *International Journal of Comparative Psychology, 28.* http://escholarship.org/uc/item/5sx993rm

Domjan, M., Cusato, B., & Krause, M. (2004). Learning with arbitrary versus ecological conditioned stimuli: Evidence from sexual conditioning. *Psychonomic Bulletin and Review, 11*, 232–246.

Domjan, M., & Gutiérrez, G. (2019). The behavior system for sexual learning. *Behavioural Processes, 162*, 184–196.

Drummond, D., Tiffany, S. T., Glautier, S. E., & Remington, B. E. (1995). *Addictive behaviour: Cue exposure theory and practice*. Chichester, UK: Wiley.

Dulany, D. E., Jr. (1961). Hypotheses and habits in verbal "operant conditioning." *Journal of Abnormal Social Psychology, 63*, 251–263.

Dunne, G., & Askew, C. (2018). Vicarious learning and reduction of fear in children via adult and child models. *Emotion, 18*, 528–534.

Eelen, P. (2018). Classical conditioning: Classical yet modern. *Psychologica Belgica, 58*, 196–211. (Originally published 1980)

Eisenberg, R., & Cameron, J. (1996). Detrimental effects of reward: Reality or myth? *American Psychologist, 51*, 1153–1166.

Embry, D. D. (2002). The Good Behavior Game: A best practice candidate as a universal behavioral vaccine. *Clinical Child and Family Psychology Review, 5*, 273–297.

Embry, D. D., & Biglan, A. (2008). Evidence-based kernels: Fundamental units of behavioral influence. *Clinical Child and Family Psychology Review, 11*, 75–113.

Emmott, S. (2013). *Ten billion*. New York, NY: Vintage Books.

Epstein, L. H., Robinson, J. L., Roemmich, J. N., & Marusewski, A. (2011). Slow rates of habituation predict greater zBMI gains over 12 months in lean children. *Eating Behaviors, 12*, 214–218.

Epstein, L. H., Temple, J. L., Roemmich, J. N., & Bouton, M. E. (2009). Habituation as a determinant of human food intake. *Psychological Review, 116*, 384–407.

Etscorn, F., & Stephens, R. (1973). Establishment of conditioned taste aversions with a 24-hour CS-US interval. *Physiological Psychology, 1*, 251–253.

Evans, J. G., & Hammond, G. R. (1983a). Differential generalization of habituation across contexts as a function of stimulus significance. *Animal Learning Behavioral, 11*, 431–434.

Evans, J. G., & Hammond, G. R. (1983b). Habituation and recovery of orienting in rats as a function of stimulus significance. *Animal Learning Behavioral, 11*, 424–430.

Fanselow, M. S. (1989). The adaptive function of conditioned defensive behavior: An ecological approach to Pavlovian stimulus-substitution theory. In R. J. Blanchard, P. F. Brain, D. C. Blanchard, & S. Parmigiani (Eds.), *Ethoexperimental approaches to the study of behavior* (pp. 151–166). Boston, MA: Kluwer.

Fantino, E., Preston, R. A., & Dunn, R. (1993). Delay reduction: Current status. *Journal of the Experimental Analysis of Behavior, 60*, 159–169.

Fechner, G. T. (1876). *Vorschule der aesthetik* (Vol. 1). Leipzig, Germany: Breitkopf & Härtel.

Ferster, C. B., & Skinner, B. F. (1957). *Schedules of reinforcement*. New York, NY: Appleton-Century-Crofts.

Fisher, W. W., Piazza, C. C., & Roane, H. S. (2011). *Handbook of applied behavior analysis*. New York, NY: Guilford Press.

Fisher, W. W., & Zangrillo, A. N. (2015). Applied behavior analytic assessment and treatment of autism spectrum disorder. In H. S. Roane, J. E. Ringdahl, T. S. Falcomata, H. S. Roane, J. E. Ringdahl, & T. S. Falcomata (Eds.), *Clinical and organizational applications of applied behavior analysis* (pp. 19–45). San Diego, CA: Elsevier.

Forehand, R., Jones, D. J., & Parent, J. (2013). Behavioral parenting interventions for child disruptive behaviors and anxiety: What's different and what's the same. *Clinical Psychology Review, 33*, 133–145.

Forgatch, M. S., & Patterson, G. R. (2010). Parent management training—Oregon model: An intervention for antisocial behavior in children and adolescents. In J. R. Weisz & A. E. Kazdin (Eds.), *Evidence-based psychotherapies for children and adolescents* (pp. 159–177). New York, NY: Guilford Press.

Foxall, G. R. (2016). Operant behavioral economics. *Managerial and Decision Economics, 37*, 215–223.

Foxx, R. M. (2008). Applied behavior analysis treatment of autism: The state of the art. *Child and Adolescent Psychiatric Clinics of North America, 17*, 821–834.

Freeman, K. B., & Riley, A. L. (2009). The origins of conditioned taste aversion learning: A historical analysis. In S. Reilly & T. T. Schachtman (Eds.), *Conditioned taste aversions: Behavioral and neural processes* (pp. 9–36). New York, NY: Oxford University Press.

Friedman, S., Edling, T., & Cheney, C. D. (2006). Concepts in behavior, section I: The natural science of behavior. *Clinical Avian Medicine, 1*, 46–59.

Friman, P. C., & Piazza, C. (2011). Behavioral pediatrics. In W. Fisher, C. Piazza, & H. S. Roane (Eds.), *Handbook of applied behavior analysis* (pp. 433–450). New York, NY: Guilford Press.

Friston, K. (2009). The free-energy principle: A rough guide to the brain? *Trends in Cognitive Sciences, 13*, 293–301.

Frith, U., & Happé, F. (2005). Autism spectrum disorder. *Current Biology, 15*, R786–R790.

Furman, T. M., & Lepper, T. L. (2018). Applied behavior analysis: Definitional difficulties. *Psychological Record, 68*, 103–105.

Gagliano, M., Renton, M., Depczynski, M., & Mancuso, S. (2014). Experience teaches plants to learn faster and forget slower in environments where it matters. *Oecologia, 175*, 63–72.

Gallistel, C. R., Craig, A. R., & Shahan, T. A. (2019). Contingency, contiguity, and causality in conditioning: Applying information theory and Weber's Law to the assignment of credit problem. *Psychological Review*. Advance online publication. http://dx.doi.org/10.1037/rev0000163

Garcia, J., & Koelling, R. A. (1966). Relation of cue to consequence in avoidance learning. *Psychonomic Science, 4*, 123–124.

Gati, I., & Ben-Shakhar, G. (1990). Novelty and significance in orientation and habituation: A feature-matching approach. *Journal of Experimental Psychology: General, 119*, 251–263.

Gatzke-Kopp, L. M. (2011). The canary in the coalmine: The sensitivity of mesolimbic dopamine to environmental adversity during development. *Neuroscience & Biobehavioral Reviews, 35,* 794–803.

Gaume, A., Vialatte, A., Mora-Sanchez, A., Ramdani, C., & Vialatte, F.-B. (2016). A psychoengineering paradigm for the neurocognitive mechanisms of biofeedback and neurofeedback. *Neuroscience & Biobehavioral Reviews, 68,* 891–910.

Gawronski, B., & Bodenhausen, G. V. (2018). Evaluative conditioning from the perspective of the associative-propositional evaluation model. *Social Psychological Bulletin, 13,* Article e28024.

Gawronski, B., Rydell, R. J., De Houwer, J., Brannon, S. M., Ye, Y., Vervliet, B., & Hu, X. (2018). Contextualized attitude change. *Advances in Experimental Social Psychology, 57,* 1–52.

Gemberling, G. A., & Domjan, M. (1982). Selective associations in one-day-old rats: Taste-toxicosis and texture-shock aversion learning. *Journal of Comparative and Physiological Psychology, 96,* 105–113.

Gershoff, E. T., Goodman, G. S., Miller-Perrin, C. L., Holden, G. W., Jackson, Y., & Kazdin, A. E. (2018). The strength of the causal evidence against physical punishment of children and its implications for parents, psychologists, and policymakers. *American Psychologist, 73,* 626–638.

Ghirlanda, S., & Ibadullayev, I. (2015). Solution of the comparator theory of associative learning. *Psychological Review, 122,* 242–259.

Glenn, S. S. (2004). Individual behavior, culture, and social change. *Behavior Analyst, 27,* 133–151.

Gluck, M. A., Mercado, E., & Myers, C. E. (2016). *Learning and memory.* New York, NY: Worth.

González-Pardo, H., & Álvarez, M. P. (2013). Epigenetics and its implications for psychology. *Psicothema, 25,* 3–12.

Gormezano, I., Kehoe, E. J., & Marshall, B. S. (1983). Twenty years of classical conditioning research with the rabbit. In J. M. Sprague & A. N. Epstein (Eds.), *Progress in psychobiology and physiological psychology* (Vol. 10, pp. 197–275). Cambridge, MA: Academic Press.

Greenspoon, J. (1955). The reinforcing effect of two spoken sounds on the frequency of two responses. *American Journal of Psychology, 68,* 409–416.

Greenwald, A. E., Roose, K., & Williams, L. (2015). Applied behavior analysis and behavioral medicine: History of the relationship and opportunities for renewed collaboration. *Behavior and Social Issues, 24,* 23–38.

Greenwald, A. G. (1970). Sensory feedback mechanisms in performance control: With special reference to the ideo-motor mechanism. *Psychological Review, 77,* 73–99.

Greenwald, A. G., & De Houwer, J. (2017). Unconscious conditioning: Demonstration of existence and difference from conscious conditioning. *Journal of Experimental Psychology: General, 146,* 1705–1721.

Groves, P. M., & Thompson, R. F. (1970). Habituation: A dual-process theory. *Psychological Review, 77,* 419–450.

Guthrie, E. R. (1946). Psychological facts and psychological theory. *Psychological Bulletin, 43,* 1–20.

Hackenberg, T. D. (2009). Token reinforcement: A review and analysis. *Journal of the Experimental Analysis of Behavior, 91*, 257–286.

Hagenaars, M. A., Oitzl, M., & Roelofs, K. (2014). Updating freeze: Aligning animal and human research. *Neuroscience & Biobehavioral Reviews, 47*, 165–176.

Hammerl, M., Bloch, M., & Silverthorne, C. P. (1997). Effects of US-alone presentations on human evaluative conditioning. *Learning and Motivation, 28*, 491–509.

Hammond, L. J. (1980). The effect of contingency upon the appetitive conditioning of free operant behavior. *Journal of Experimental Analysis of Behavior, 34*, 297–304.

Hansen, J., & Sato, M. (2011). *Storms of my grandchildren: The truth about the coming climate catastrophe and our last chance to save humanity*. London, UK: Bloomsbury.

Harris, J. A., Kwok, D. W. S., & Gottlieb, D. A. (2019). The partial reinforcement extinction effect depends on learning about nonreinforced trials rather than reinforcement rate. *Journal of Experimental Psychology: Animal Learning and Cognition*. Advance online publication. http://dx.doi.org/10.1037/xan0000220

Haselgrove, M. (2016). Overcoming associative learning. *Journal of Comparative Psychology, 130*, 226–240.

Hayes, S. C. (1995). *Acceptance and commitment therapy (ACT): A therapy manual for the treatment of emotional avoidance*. Reno, NV: Context Press.

Hayes, S. C. (2016). Acceptance and commitment therapy, relational frame theory, and the third wave of behavior therapy. *Behavior Therapy, 47*, 869–885.

Hayes, S. C., Barnes-Holmes, D., & Roche, B. (2001). *Relational frame theory: A post-Skinnerian account of human language and cognition*. New York, NY: Kluwer.

Hayes, S. C., Barnes-Holmes, D., & Wilson, K. G. (2012). Contextual behavioral science: Creating a science more adequate to the challenge of the human condition. *Journal of Contextual Behavioral Science, 1*, 1–16.

Hayes, S. C., & Brownstein, A. J. (1986). Mentalism, behavior-behavior relations, and a behavior-analytic view of the purposes of science. *Behavior Analyst, 9*, 175–190.

Hayes, S. C., Sanford, B. T., & Chin, F. T. (2017). Carrying the baton: Evolution science and a contextual behavioral analysis of language and cognition. *Journal of Contextual Behavioral Science, 6*, 314–328.

Hayes, S. C., Strosahl, K., & Wilson, K. G. (1999). *Acceptance and commitment therapy: An experiential approach to behavior change*. New York, NY: Guilford Press.

Hearst, E., & Jenkins, H. M. (1974). *Sign-tracking: The stimulus-reinforcer relation and directed action*. Austin, TX: Psychonomic Society.

Hebb, D. O. (1949). *The organization of behavior*. New York, NY: Wiley.

Herrnstein, R. J. (1970). On the law of effect. *Journal of the Experimental Analysis of Behavior, 13*, 243–266.

Heyes, C. M. (1994). Social learning in animals: Categories and mechanisms. *Biological Reviews, 69*, 207–231.

Higgins, S., Silverman, K., & Heil, S. (2008). *Contingency management in the treatment of substance use disorders: A science-based treatment innovation.* New York, NY: Guilford Press.

Hofmann, W., De Houwer, J., Perugini, M., Baeyens, F., & Crombez, G. (2010). Evaluative conditioning in humans: A meta-analysis. *Psychological Bulletin, 136,* 390–421.

Holland, P. C. (1992). Occasion setting in Pavlovian conditioning. *Psychology of Learning and Motivation, 28,* 69–125.

Holland, P. C., & Rescorla, R. A. (1975). The effect of two ways of devaluing the unconditioned stimulus after first- and second-order appetitive conditioning. *Journal of Experimental Psychology: Animal Behavior Processes, 1,* 355–363.

Hommel, B., Müsseler, J., Aschersleben, G., & Prinz, W. (2001). The theory of event coding (TEC): A framework for perception and action planning. *Behavioral Brain Sciences, 24,* 849–878.

Horner, R. H., Sugai, G., Smolkowski, K., Eber, L., Nakasato, J., Todd, A. W., & Esperanza, J. (2009). A randomized, wait-list controlled effectiveness trial assessing school-wide positive behavior support in elementary schools. *Journal of Positive Behavior Interventions, 11,* 133–144.

Houmanfar, R., Rodrigues, N. J., & Ward, T. A. (2010). Emergence & metacontingency: Points of contact and departure. *Behavior and Social Issues, 19,* 53–78.

Hughes, S. (2018). The philosophy of science as it applies to clinical psychology. In S. C. Hayes & S. G. Hofmann (Eds.), *Process-based CBT: The science and core clinical competencies of cognitive behavioral therapy* (pp. 23–44). Oakland, CA: Context Press.

Hughes, S., & Barnes-Holmes, D. (2014). Associative concept learning, stimulus equivalence, and relational frame theory: Working out the similarities and differences between human and non-human behavior. *Journal of the Experimental Analysis of Behavior, 101,* 156–160.

Hughes, S., & Barnes-Holmes, D. (2016). Relational frame theory: The basic account. In S. Hayes, D. Barnes-Holmes, R. Zettle, and T. Biglan (Eds.), *Handbook of contextual behavioral science* (pp. 129–178). New York, NY: Wiley.

Hughes, S., Barnes-Holmes, D., Van Dessel, P., de Almeida, J. H., Stewart, I., & De Houwer, J. (2018). On the symbolic generalization of likes and dislikes. *Journal of Experimental Social Psychology, 79,* 365–377.

Hughes, S., De Houwer, J., & Barnes-Holmes, D. (2016). The moderating impact of distal regularities on the effect of stimulus pairings: A novel perspective on evaluative conditioning. *Experimental Psychology, 63,* 20–44.

Hughes, S., De Houwer, J., Mattavelli, S., & Hussey, I. (in press). The shared features principle: If two objects share a feature, people assume those objects also share other features. *Journal of Experimental Psychology: General.*

Hughes, S., De Houwer, J., & Perugini, M. (2016). Expanding the boundaries of evaluative learning research: How intersecting regularities shape our likes and dislikes. *Journal of Experimental Psychology: General, 145,* 731–754.

Hughes, S., Ye, Y., & De Houwer, J. (2019). Evaluative conditioning effects are modulated by the nature of contextual pairings. *Cognition & Emotion, 33*, 871–884.

Hull, C. L. (1943). *Principles of behavior: An introduction to behavior theory.* New York, NY: Appleton-Century-Crofts.

Hull, C. L. (1952). *A behavior system: An introduction to behavior theory concerning the individual organism.* New Haven, CT: Yale University Press.

Hummel, J. E. (2010). Symbolic vs. associative learning. *Cognitive Science, 34*, 958–965.

Hütter, M., & Sweldens, S. (2018). Dissociating controllable and uncontrollable effects of affective stimuli on attitudes and consumption. *Journal of Consumer Research, 45*, 320–349.

Iacono, W. G., & Lykken, D. T. (1983). The effects of instructions on electrodermal habituation. *Psychophysiology, 20*, 71–80.

IPCC. (2007). *Climate change 2007: Synthesis report. Contribution of working groups I, II and III to the fourth assessment report of the Intergovernmental Panel on Climate Change.* Geneva, Switzerland: IPCC.

Izuma, K., Kennedy, K., Fitzjohn, A., Sedikides, C., & Shibata, K. (2018). Neural activity in the reward-related brain regions predicts implicit self-esteem: A novel validity test of psychological measures using neuroimaging. *Journal of Personality and Social Psychology, 114*, 343–357.

Jablonka, E., & Lamb, M. (2005). *Evolution in four dimensions: Genetic, epigenetic, behavioral, and symbolic variation in the history of life.* Cambridge, MA: MIT Press.

Jablonka, E., & Lamb, M. J. (2007). Précis of evolution in four dimensions. *Behavioral and Brain Sciences, 30*, 353–365.

Jacobson, N. S., Martell, C. R., & Dimidjian, S. (2001). Behavioral activation treatment for depression: Returning to contextual roots. *Clinical Psychology: Science and Practice, 8*, 255–270.

Jensen, R. (2006). Behaviorism, latent learning, and cognitive maps: Needed revisions in introductory psychology textbooks. *Behavior Analyst, 29*, 187–209.

Johanson, C. E., Balster, R. L., & Bonese, K. (1976). Self-administration of psychomotor stimulant drugs: The effects of unlimited access. *Pharmacology Biochemistry and Behavior, 4*, 45–51.

Jones, L. B., Whittingham, K., Coyne, L., & Lightcap, A. (2016). A contextual behavioral science approach to parenting intervention and research. In R. D. Zettle, S. C. Hayes, D. Barnes-Holmes, & A. Biglan (Eds.), *Handbook of contextual behavioral science* (pp. 398–421). New York, NY: Wiley.

Jozefowiez, J. (2018). Associative versus predictive processes in Pavlovian conditioning. *Behavioural Processes, 154*, 21–26.

Kaiser, S., & Sachser, N. (2005). The effects of prenatal social stress on behaviour: Mechanisms and function. *Neuroscience & Biobehavioral Reviews, 29*, 283–294.

Kamin, L. J. (1968). *"Attention-like" processes in classical conditioning.* Paper presented at the Miami Symposium on the Prediction of Behavior: Aversive Stimulation.

Kazdin, A. E. (2011). *Single-case research designs: Methods for clinical and applied settings* (2nd ed.). New York, NY: Oxford University Press.

Kellam, S. G., Brown, C. H., Poduska, J. M., Ialongo, N. S., Wang, W., Toyinbo, P., ... Wilcox, H. C. (2008). Effects of a universal classroom behavior management program in first and second grades on young adult behavioral, psychiatric, and social outcomes. *Drug and Alcohol Dependence, 95*, 5–28.

Kellam, S. G., Mayer, L. S., Rebok, G. W., & Hawkins, W. E. (1998). Effects of improving achievement on aggressive behavior and of improving aggressive behavior on achievement through two preventative interventions: An investigation of causal paths. In B. P. Dohrenwend (Ed.), *Adversity, stress, and psychopathology* (pp. 486–505). New York, NY: Oxford University Press.

Kirsch, I., Lynn, S. J., Vigorito, M., & Miller, R. R. (2004) The role of cognition in classical and operant conditioning. *Journal of Clinical Psychology, 60*, 369–392.

Kish, G. B. (1966). Studies of sensory reinforcement. In W. K. Honig (Ed.), *Operant behaviour* (pp. 109–159). New York, NY: Appleton-Century-Crofts.

Kohlenberg, R., & Tsai, M. (1991). *Functional analytic psychotherapy: Creating intense and curative therapeutic relationships*. New York, NY: Springer.

Kolbert, E. (2014). *The sixth extinction: An unnatural History*. New York, NY: Holt.

Konorski, J. (1967). *Integrative activity of the brain: An interdisciplinary approach*. Chicago, IL: University of Chicago Press.

Koob, G. F., & Le Moal, M. (2008). Addiction and the brain antireward system. *Annual Review of Psychology, 59*, 29–53.

Kumaran, D., & Maguire, E. A. (2009). Novelty signals: A window into hippocampal information processing. *Trends in Cognitive Sciences, 13*, 47–54.

Lachman, S. J. (1997). Learning is a process: Toward an improved definition of learning. *Journal of Psychology, 131*, 477–480.

Lagnado, D. A., Waldmann, M. R., Hagmayer, Y., & Sloman, S. A. (2007). Beyond covariation: Cues to causal structure. In A. Gopnik & L. Schulz (Eds.), *Causal learning: Psychology, philosophy, and computation* (pp. 154–72). Oxford, UK: Oxford University Press.

Lee, D., Seo, H., & Jung, M. W. (2012). Neural basis of reinforcement learning and decision making. *Annual Review of Neuroscience, 35*, 287–308.

Leflot, G., van Lier, P. A., Onghena, P., & Colpin, H. (2013). The role of children's on-task behavior in the prevention of aggressive behavior development and peer rejection: A randomized controlled study of the Good Behavior Game in Belgian elementary classrooms. *Journal of School Psychology, 51*, 187–199.

Lehman, P. K., & Geller, E. S. (2004). Behavior analysis and environmental protection: Accomplishments and potential for more. *Behavior and Social Issues, 13*, 13–32.

Leising, K. J., & Bonardi, C. (2017). Occasion setting. *Behavioural Processes, 137*, 1–4.

Le Pelley, M. E., Mitchell, C. J., Beesley, T., George, D. N., & Wills, A. J. (2016). Attention and associative learning in humans: An integrative review. *Psychological Bulletin, 142,* 1111–1140.

Levey, A. B., & Martin, I. (1975). Classical conditioning of human "evaluative" responses. *Behaviour Research Therapy, 13,* 221–226.

Liljeholm, M., & Balleine, B. W. (2009). Mediated conditioning versus retrospective revaluation in humans: The influence of physical and functional similarity of cues. *Quarterly Journal of Experimental Psychology, 62,* 470–482.

Linehan, M. M. (1993). Dialectical behavior therapy for treatment of borderline personality disorder: Implications for the treatment of substance abuse. *NIDA research monograph, 137,* 201–201.

Liu, R. T., Kleiman, E. M., Nestor, B. A., & Cheek, S. M. (2015). The hopelessness theory of depression: A quarter-century in review. *Clinical Psychology: Science and Practice, 22,* 345–365.

Logue, A. W. (1988). A comparison of taste aversion learning in humans and other vertebrates: Evolutionary pressures in common. In R. C. Bolles & M. D. Beecher (Eds.), *Evolution and learning* (pp. 23–42). Waco, TX: Baylor University Press.

Longmore, R. J., & Worrell, M. (2007). Do we need to challenge thoughts in cognitive behavior therapy? *Clinical Psychology Review, 27,* 173–187.

Lonsdorf, T. B., Menz, M. M., Andreatta, M., Fullana, M. A., Golkar, A., Haaker, J., ... Reviews, B. (2017). Don't fear "fear conditioning": Methodological considerations for the design and analysis of studies on human fear acquisition, extinction, and return of fear. *Neuroscience & Biobehavioral Reviews, 77,* 247–285.

Lorenz, K. Z. (1937). The companion in the bird's world. *The Auk, 54,* 245–273.

Lotze, R. (1852). *Medicinische psychologie oder die physiologie der seele.* Leipzig, Germany: Weidmannsche Buchhandlung.

Lovibond, P. F. (2006). Fear and avoidance: An integrated expectancy model. In M. G. Craske, D. Hermans, & D. Vansteenwegen (Eds.), *Fear and learning: Basic science to clinical application* (pp. 117–132). Washington, DC: American Psychological Association.

Lovibond, P. F., & Shanks, D. R. (2002). The role of awareness in Pavlovian conditioning: Empirical evidence and theoretical implications. *Journal of Experimental Psychology: Animal Behavior Processes, 28,* 3–26.

Ludwig, T. D. (2015). Organizational behavior management: An enabler of applied behavior analysis. In H. S. Roane, J. E. Ringdahl, T. S. Falcomata, H. S. Roane, J. E. Ringdahl, & T. S. Falcomata (Eds.), *Clinical and organizational applications of applied behavior analysis* (pp. 605–626). San Diego, CA: Elsevier.

Luiselli, J. K., & Reed, D. D. (2015). Applied behavior analysis and sports performance. In H. S. Roane, J. E. Ringdahl, T. S. Falcomata, H. S. Roane, J. E. Ringdahl, & T. S. Falcomata (Eds.), *Clinical and organizational applications of applied behavior analysis* (pp. 523–553). San Diego, CA: Elsevier.

Luke, M., & Alavosius, M. (2012). Impacting community sustainability through behavior change: A research framework. *Behavior and Social Issues, 21,* 54–79.

Maatsch, J. L. (1959). Learning and fixation after a single shock trial. *Journal of Comparative and Physiological Psychology, 52*, 408–410.

MacCorquodale, K. (1970). On Chomsky's review of Skinner's *Verbal Behavior. Journal of the Experimental Analysis of Behavior, 13*, 83–99.

MacCorquodale, K., & Meehl, P. E. (1948). On a distinction between hypothetical constructs and intervening variables. *Psychological Review, 55*, 95–107.

Macfarlane, D. A. (1930). The role of kinesthesis in maze learning. *University of California Publications in Psychology, 4*, 277–305.

Mackintosh, N. J. (1975). A theory of attention: Variations in the associability of stimuli with reinforcement. *Psychological Review, 82*, 276–298.

Mackintosh, N. J. (1983). *Conditioning and associative learning.* Oxford, UK: Oxford University Press.

Madden, G. J., Price, J., & Sosa, F. A. (2017). Behavioral economic approaches to influencing children's dietary decision making at school. *Policy Insights from the Behavioral and Brain Sciences, 4*, 41–48.

Maes, E., Vanderoost, E., D'Hooge, R., De Houwer, J., & Beckers, T. (2017). Individual difference factors in the learning and transfer of patterning discriminations. *Frontiers in Psychology, 8*, 1262.

Mahoney, M. J. (1974). *Cognition and behavior modification.* Oxford, UK: Ballinger.

Maier, S. F., & Jackson, R. L. (1979). Learned helplessness: All of us were right (and wrong): Inescapable shock has multiple effects. *Psychology of Learning and Motivation, 13*, 155–218.

Maier, S. F., & Seligman, M. E. (1976). Learned helplessness: Theory and evidence. *Journal of Experimental Psychology: General, 105*, 3–46.

Maier, S. F., & Seligman, M. E. (2016). Learned helplessness at fifty: Insights from neuroscience. *Psychological Review, 123*, 349–367.

Malott, M. E., & Glenn, S. S. (2006). Targets of intervention in cultural and behavioral change. *Behavior and Social Issues, 15*, 31–56.

Maple, T. L., & Segura, V. D. (2015). Advancing behavior analysis in zoos and aquariums. *Behavior Analyst, 38*, 77–91.

Marr, D. (1982). *Vision.* San Francisco, CA: W. H. Freeman.

Masterpasqua, F. (2009). Psychology and epigenetics. *Review of General Psychology, 13*, 194–201.

Matson, J. L., Turygin, N. C., Beighley, J., Rieske, R., Tureck, K., & Matson, M. L. (2012). Applied behavior analysis in autism spectrum disorders: Recent developments, strengths, and pitfalls. *Research in Autism Spectrum Disorders, 6*, 144–150.

Matute, H., Vegas, S., & De Marez, P.-J. (2002). Flexible use of recent information in causal and predictive judgments. *Journal of Experimental Psychology: Learning, Memory, and Cognition, 28*, 714–725.

Maughan, D. R., Christiansen, E., Jenson, W. R., Olympia, D., & Clark, E. (2005). Behavioral parent training as a treatment for externalizing behaviors and disruptive behavior disorders: A meta-analysis. *School Psychology Review, 34*, 267–287.

McKeel, A. N., Dixon, M. R., Daar, J. H., Rowsey, K. E., & Szekely, S. (2015). Evaluating the efficacy of the PEAK relational training system using a randomized controlled trial of children with autism. *Journal of Behavioral Education, 24(2)*, 230–241.

McKell Carter, R., Hofstötter, C., Tsuchiya, N., & Koch, C. (2003). Working memory and fear conditioning. *Proceedings of the National Academy of Sciences, 100*, 1399–1404.

McLaren, I. P., Forrest, C., McLaren, R., Jones, F., Aitken, M., & Mackintosh, N. (2014). Associations and propositions: The case for a dual-process account of learning in humans. *Neurobiology of Learning and Memory, 108*, 185–195.

Meichenbaum, D. (1977). Cognitive behaviour modification. *Cognitive Behaviour Therapy, 6*, 185–192.

Mertens, G., Boddez, Y., Sevenster, D., Engelhard, I. M., & De Houwer, J. (2018). A review on the effects of verbal instructions in human fear conditioning: Empirical findings, theoretical considerations, and future directions. *Biological Psychology, 137*, 49–64.

Mertens, G., & Engelhard, I. M. (2020). A systematic review and meta-analysis of the evidence for unaware fear conditioning. *Neuroscience & Biobehavioral Reviews, 108*, 254–268.

Messer, S. B., & Gurman, A. S. (2011). *Essential psychotherapies: Theory and practice.* New York, NY: Guilford Press.

Meulders, A., Vervliet, B., Vansteenwegen, D., Hermans, D., & Baeyens, F. (2011). A new tool for assessing context conditioning induced by US-unpredictability in humans: The Martians task restyled. *Learning and Motivation, 42*, 1–12.

Meyers, R. J., Roozen, H. G., & Smith, J. E. (2011). The community reinforcement approach: An update of the evidence. *Alcohol Research & Health, 33*, 380–388.

Michael, J. L. (2004). *Concepts and principles of behavior analysis.* Kalamazoo, MI: Association for Behavior Analysis International.

Michelson, D., Davenport, C., Dretzke, J., Barlow, J., & Day, C. (2013). Do evidence-based interventions work when tested in the "real world?" A systematic review and meta-analysis of parent management training for the treatment of child disruptive behavior. *Clinical Child and Family Psychology Review, 16*, 18–34.

Miller, N. E. (1969). Learning of visceral and glandular responses. *Science, 163*(3866), 434–445.

Miller, N. E., & Dicara, L. (1967). Instrumental learning of heart rate changes in curarized rats: Shaping, and specificity to discriminative stimulus. *Journal of Comparative and Physiological Psychology, 63*, 12–19.

Miller, R. R., Barnet, R. C., & Grahame, N. J. (1995). Assessment of the Rescorla-Wagner model. *Psychological Bulletin, 117*, 363–386.

Miller, R. R., & Escobar, M. (2001). Contrasting acquisition-focused and performance-focused models of acquired behavior. *Current Directions in Psychological Science, 10*, 141–145.

Miller, R. R., Hallam, S. C., & Grahame, N. J. (1990). Inflation of comparator stimuli following CS training. *Animal Learning & Behavior, 18*, 434–443.

Miller, R. R., & Matute, H. (1996). Biological significance in forward and backward blocking: Resolution of a discrepancy between animal conditioning and human causal judgment. *Journal of Experimental Psychology: General, 25*, 370–386.

Miller, R. R., & Matzel, L. D. (1988). The comparator hypothesis: A response rule for the expression of associations. *Psychology of Learning and Motivation, 22*, 51–92.

Miller, R. R., & Witnauer, J. E. (2016). Retrospective revaluation: The phenomenon and its theoretical implications. *Behavioural Processes, 123*, 15–25.

Mineka, S. (1987). A primate model of phobic fears. In H. Eysenck & I. Martin (Eds.), *Theoretical foundations of behavior therapy* (pp. 81–111). New York, NY: Plenum Press.

Ming, S., Moran, L., & Stewart, I. (2014). Derived relational responding and generative language: Applications and future directions for teaching individuals with autism spectrum disorders. *European Journal of Behavior Analysis, 15*, 199–224.

Ming, S., & Stewart, I. (2017). When things are not the same: A review of research into relations of difference. *Journal of Applied Behavior Analysis, 50*, 429–455.

Mitchell, C. J., De Houwer, J., & Lovibond, P. F. (2009). The propositional nature of human associative learning. *Behavioral and Brain Sciences, 32*, 183–198.

Mok, L. W., Estevez, A. F., & Overmier, J. B. (2010). Unique outcome expectations as a training and pedagogical tool. *Psychological Record, 60*, 227–247.

Moore, B. R. (1973). The role of directed Pavlovian reactions in simple instrumental learning in the pigeon. In R. A. Hinde & J. Stevenson-Hinde, *Constraints on learning: Limitations and predispositions* (pp. 159–188). London, UK: Academic Press.

Moran, D. J., & Malott, R. W. (2004). *Evidence-based educational methods*. San Diego, CA: Elsevier Academic Press.

Moreland, R. L., & Topolinski, S. (2010). The mere exposure phenomenon: A lingering melody by Robert Zajonc. *Emotion Review, 2*, 329–339.

Moscarello, J. M., & Hartley, C. A. (2017). Agency and the calibration of motivated behavior. *Trends in Cognitive Sciences, 21*, 725–735.

Mowrer, O. (1947). On the dual nature of learning: A re-interpretation of "conditioning" and "problem-solving." *Harvard Educational Review, 17*, 102–148.

Mowrer, O. (1960). *Learning theory and behavior*. Hoboken, NJ: Wiley.

Muscott, H. S., Mann, E. L., & LeBrun, M. R. (2008). Positive behavioral interventions and supports in New Hampshire: Effects of large-scale implementation of schoolwide positive behavior support on student discipline and academic achievement. *Journal of Positive Behavior Interventions, 10*, 190–205.

Nader, K., Schafe, G. E., & Le Doux, J. E. (2000). Fear memories require protein synthesis in the amygdala for reconsolidation after retrieval. *Nature, 406*(6797), 722–726.

Nathan, P. E., & Gorman, J. M. (2007). *A guide to treatments that work*. New York, NY: Oxford University Press.

Neisser, U. (1967). *Cognitive psychology*. New York, NY: Appleton-Century-Crofts.

Neumann, D. L., & Longbottom, P. L. (2008). The renewal of extinguished conditioned fear with fear-relevant and fear-irrelevant stimuli by a context change after extinction. *Behaviour Research and Therapy, 46*, 188–206.

Neuringer, A. (2002). Operant variability: Evidence, functions, and theory. *Psychonomic Bulletin and Review, 9*, 672–705.

O'Donohue, W. T., & Fisher, J. E. (Eds.) (2008). *General principles and empirically supported techniques of cognitive behavior therapy*. Hoboken, NJ: Wiley.

Öhman, A., Fredrikson, M., Hugdahl, K., & Rimmö, P.-A. (1976). The premise of equipotentiality in human classical conditioning: conditioned electrodermal responses to potentially phobic stimuli. *Journal of Experimental Psychology: General, 105*, 313–337.

Olsson, A., & Phelps, E. A. (2007). Social learning of fear. *Nature Neuroscience, 10*, 1095–1102.

Ophalvens, M. (1987). De gekke gokker. *Tijdschrift Klinische Psychologie, 17*, 92–111.

Otten, S. (2016). The minimal group paradigm and its maximal impact in research on social categorization. *Current Opinion in Psychology, 11*, 85–89.

Overmier, J. B., & LoLordo, V. M. (1998). Learned helplessness. In W. O'Donohue (Ed.), *Learning and behavior therapy* (pp. 352–373). Boston, MA: Allyn & Bacon.

Palmer, D. C. (2006). On Chomsky's appraisal of Skinner's *Verbal Behavior*: A half century of misunderstanding. *Behavior Analyst, 29*, 253–267.

Papini, M. R., & Bitterman, M. (1990). The role of contingency in classical conditioning. *Psychological Review, 97*, 396–403.

Patterson, G. (1982). *Coercive family process*. Eugene, OR: Castalia.

Patterson, G., DeBaryshe, B., & Ramsey, E. (1989). A developmental perspective on antisocial behavior. *American Psychologist, 44*, 329–335.

Pavlov, I. P. (1927). *Conditioned reflexes: An investigation of the physiological activity of the cerebral cortex*. London, UK: Oxford University Press.

Pearce, J. M. (2002). Evaluation and development of a connectionist theory of configural learning. *Animal Learning & Behavior, 30*, 73–95.

Pearce, J. M., & Bouton, M. E. (2001). Theories of associative learning in animals. *Annual Review of Psychology, 52*, 111–139.

Pearce, J. M., & Dickinson, A. (1975). Pavlovian counterconditioning: Changing the suppressive properties of shock by association with food. *Journal of Experimental Psychology: Animal Behavior Processes, 1*, 170–177.

Pearce, J. M., & Hall, G. (1980). A model for Pavlovian learning: Variations in the effectiveness of conditioned but not of unconditioned stimuli. *Psychological Review, 87*, 532–552.

Peckham, G. W., & Peckham, E. G. (1887). Some observations on the mental powers of spiders. *Journal of Morphology, 1*, 383–419.

Perez, W. F., de Almeida, J. H., & de Rose, J. C. (2015). Transformation of meaning through relations of sameness and opposition. *The Psychological Record, 65*, 679–689.

Perez, W. F., Kovac, R., Nico, Y. C., Caro, D. M., Fidalgo, A. P., Linares, I., de Almeida, J. H., & de Rose, J. C. (2017). The transfer of Crel contextual control (same, opposite, less than, more than) through equivalence relations. *Journal of Experimental Analysis of Behavior, 108*, 318–334.

Perruchet, P. (1985). A pitfall for the expectancy theory of human eyelid conditioning. *Pavlovian Journal of Biological Science, 20*, 163–170.

Perry, J. L., & Carroll, M. E. (2008). The role of impulsive behavior in drug abuse. *Psychopharmacology, 200*, 1–26.

Perugini, M., Costantini, G., Hughes, S., & De Houwer, J. (2016). A functional perspective on personality. *International Journal of Psychology, 51*, 33–39.

Peterson, N. (1960). Control of behavior by presentation of an imprinted stimulus. *Science, 132*(3437), 1395–1396.

Peters-Scheffer, N., Didden, R., Korzilius, H., & Sturmey, P. (2011). A meta-analytic study on the effectiveness of comprehensive ABA-based early intervention programs for children with autism spectrum disorders. *Research in Autism Spectrum Disorders, 5*, 60–69.

Pierce, W. D., & Cheney, C. D. (2008). *Behavior analysis and learning.* New York, NY: Psychology Press.

Pierce, W. D., & Cheney, C. D. (2018). *Behavior analysis and learning: A biobehavioral approach* (6th ed.). New York, NY: Routledge.

Poldrack, R. A., & Yarkoni, T. (2016). From brain maps to cognitive ontologies: Informatics and the search for mental structure. *Annual Review of Psychology, 67*, 587–612.

Poulton, R., & Menzies, R. G. (2002). Non-associative fear acquisition: A review of the evidence from retrospective and longitudinal research. *Behaviour Research and Therapy, 40*, 127–149.

Premack, D. (1962). Reversibility of the reinforcement relation. *Science, 136*(3512), 255–257.

Premack, D. (1971). Catching up with common sense or two sides of a generalization: Reinforcement and punishment. In R. Glaser (Ed.), *The nature of reinforcement* (pp. 121–150). New York, NY: Academic Press.

Prendergast, M., Podus, D., Finney, J., Greenwell, L., & Roll, J. (2006). Contingency management for treatment of substance use disorders: A meta-analysis. *Addiction, 101*, 1546–1560.

Prével, A., Rivière, V., Darcheville, J.-C., & Urcelay, G. P. (2016). Conditioned reinforcement and backward association. *Learning & Motivation, 56*, 38–47.

Prével, A., Rivière, V., Darcheville, J.-C., Urcelay, G. P., & Miller, R. R. (2019). Excitatory second-order conditioning using a backward first-order conditioned stimulus: A challenge for prediction error reduction. *Quarterly Journal of Experimental Psychology, 72*, 1453–1465.

Purtle, R. B. (1973). Peak shift: A review. *Psychological Bulletin, 80*, 408–421.

Rachlin, H., & Green, L. (1972). Commitment, choice and self-control. *Journal of the Experimental Analysis of Behavior, 17*, 15–22.

Rachman, S. (1977). The conditioning theory of fearacquisition: A critical examination. *Behaviour Research and Therapy, 15*, 375–387.

Ramsay, D. S., & Woods, S. C. (2014). Clarifying the roles of homeostasis and allostasis in physiological regulation. *Psychological Review, 121*, 225–247.

Randich, A., & LoLordo, V. M. (1979). Associative and nonassociative theories of the UCS preexposure phenomenon: Implications for Pavlovian conditioning. *Psychological Bulletin, 86*, 523–548.

Rankin, C. H., Abrams, T., Barry, R. J., Bhatnagar, S., Clayton, D. F., Colombo, J., ... Marsland, S. (2009). Habituation revisited: An updated and revised description of the behavioral characteristics of habituation. *Neurobiology of Learning and Memory, 92*, 135–138.

Reed, D. D., Niileksela, C. R., & Kaplan, B. A. (2013). Behavioral economics. *Behavior Analysis in Practice, 6*, 34–54.

Rehfeldt, R. A., & Barnes-Holmes, Y. (2009). *Derived relational responding: Applications for learners with autism and other developmental disabilities: A progressive guide to change*. Oakland, CA: New Harbinger.

Reichow, B., & Wolery, M. (2009). Comprehensive synthesis of early intensive behavioral interventions for young children with autism based on the UCLA young autism project model. *Journal of Autism and Developmental Disorders, 39*, 23–41.

Remington, B., Roberts, P., & Steven, G. (1997). The effect of drink familiarity on tolerance to alcohol. *Addictive Behaviors, 22*, 45–53.

Rescorla, R. A. (1966). Predictability and number of pairings in Pavlovian fear conditioning. *Psychonomic Science, 4*, 383–384.

Rescorla, R. A. (1982). Comments on a technique for assessing associative learning. *Quantitative Analysis of Behavior: Acquisition, 3*, 41–61.

Rescorla, R. A. (1987). Facilitation and inhibition. *Journal of Experimental Psychology: Animal Behavior Processes, 13*, 250–259.

Rescorla, R. A. (1988). Pavlovian conditioning: It's not what you think it is. *American Psychologist, 43*, 151–160.

Rescorla, R. A. (1991). Associative relations in instrumental learning: The eighteenth Bartlett memorial lecture. *Quarterly Journal of Experimental Psychology, 43B*, 1–23.

Rescorla, R. A., & Wagner, A. R. (1972). A theory of Pavlovian conditioning: Variations in the effectiveness of reinforcement and nonreinforcement. *Classical Conditioning II: Current Research and Theory, 2*, 64–99.

Roane, H. S., Ringdahl, J. E., & Falcomata, T. S. (2015). *Clinical and organizational applications of applied behavior analysis*. London, UK: Academic Press.

Robinson, T. E., & Berridge, K. C. (1993). The neural basis of drug craving: An incentive-sensitization theory of addiction. *Brain Research Reviews, 18*, 247–291.

Robinson, T. E., & Berridge, K. C. (2008). The incentive sensitization theory of addiction: Some current issues. *Philosophical Transactions of the Royal Society B: Biological Sciences, 363*(1507), 3137–3146.

Roche, B., & Barnes, D. (1997). The behavior of organisms? *Psychological Record, 47*, 597–618.

Rosas, J. M., García-Gutiérrez, A., & Callejas-Aguilera, J. E. (2006). Effects of context change upon retrieval of first and second-learned information in human predictive learning. *Psicologica: International Journal of Methodology and Experimental Psychology, 27*, 35–56.

Rumelhart, D. E., & McClelland, J. L. (1986). *Parallel distributed processing: Explorations in the microstructure of cognition: Vol. 1. Foundations*. Cambridge, MA: MIT Press.

Rung, J. M., & Madden, G. J. (2018). Experimental reductions of delay discounting and impulsive choice: A systematic review and meta-analysis. *Journal of Experimental Psychology: General, 147*, 1349–1381.

Schmajuk, N. A., & Holland, P. C. (1998). *Occasion setting: Associative learning and cognition in animals*. Washington, DC: American Psychological Association.

Schneider, S. M. (2012). *The science of consequences: How they affect genes, change the brain, and impact our world*. Amherst, NY: Prometheus Books.

Schull, J. (1979). A conditioned opponent theory of Pavlovian conditioning and habituation. *The Psychology of Learning and Motivation, 13*, 57–90.

Schwartz, B., Wasserman, E. A., & Robbins, S. J. (2002). *The psychology of learning and behavior*. New York, NY: Norton.

Schwartz, S. J., Lilienfeld, S. O., Meca, A., & Sauvigné, K. C. (2016). The role of neuroscience within psychology: A call for inclusiveness over exclusiveness. *American Psychologist, 71*, 52–70.

Schweitzer, J. B., & Sulzer-Azaroff, B. (1988). Self-control: Teaching tolerance for delay in impulsive children. *Journal of the Experimental Analysis of Behavior, 50*, 173–186.

Seidel, R. J. (1959). A review of sensory preconditioning. *Psychological Bulletin, 56,* 58–73.

Seligman, M. E. (1975). *Helplessness: On depression, development, and death. A series of books in psychology.* New York, NY: W. H. Freeman.

Seligman, M. E., & Hager, J. L. (1972). *Biological boundaries of learning.* East Norwalk, CT: Appleton-Century-Crofts.

Seligman, M. E., Maier, S. F., & Solomon, R. L. (1971). Unpredictable and uncontrollable aversive events. In F. R. Brush (Ed.), *Aversive conditioning and learning* (pp. 347–400). San Diego, CA: Academic Press.

Sevenster, P. (1973). Incompatibility of response and reward. In R. A. Hinde & J. Stevenson-Hinde (Eds.), *Constraints on learning: Limitations and predispositions* (pp. 265–283). Oxford, UK: Academic Press.

Shanks, D. R. (1990). On the cognitive theory of conditioning. *Biological Psychology, 30,* 171–179.

Shanks, D. R. (2010). Learning: From association to cognition. *Annual Review of Psychology, 61,* 273–301.

Shanks, D. R., & St. John, M. F. (1994). Characteristics of dissociable human learning systems. *Behavioral and Brain Sciences, 17,* 367–395.

Sidman, M. (2001). *Coercion and its fallout.* Boston, MA: Authors Cooperative.

Sidman, M. (2009). Equivalence relations and behavior: An introductory tutorial. *Analysis of Verbal Behavior, 25,* 5–17.

Siegel, S. (1975). Evidence from rats that morphine tolerance is a learned response. *Journal of Comparative and Physiological Psychology, 89,* 498–506.

Siegel, S. (1989). Pharmacological conditioning and drug effects. In A. J. Goudie & M. W. Emmett-Oglesby, *Contemporary neuroscience. Psychoactive drugs: Tolerance and sensitization* (pp. 115–180). Totowa, NJ: Humana Press.

Siegel, S. (2008). Learning and the wisdom of the body. *Learning & Behavior, 36,* 242–252.

Silverman, K., Kaminski, B. J., Higgins, S. T., & Brady, J. V. (2011). Behavior analysis and treatment of drug addiction. In W. W. Fisher, C. C. Piazza, & H. S. Roane (Eds.), *Handbook of applied behavior analysis* (pp. 451–471). New York, NY: Guilford Press.

Simmons, J. P., Nelson, L. D., & Simonsohn, U. (2011). False-positive psychology: Undisclosed flexibility in data collection and analysis allows presenting anything as significant. *Psychological Science, 22,* 1359–1366.

Skinner, B. F. (1938). *The behavior of organisms: An experimental analysis.* New York, NY: Appleton-Century-Crofts.

Skinner, B. F. (1953). *Science and human behavior.* New York, NY: Macmillan.

Skinner, B. F. (1957). *Verbal behavior.* New York, NY: Appleton-Century-Crofts.

Skinner, B. F. (1966). An operant analysis of problem solving. In B. Kleinmutz (Ed.), *Problem solving: Research, method and theory.* New York, NY: Wiley.

Skinner, B. F. (1969). *Contingencies of reinforcement: A theoretical analysis.* New York, NY: Appleton-Century-Crofts.

Skinner, B. F. (1981). Selection by consequences. *Science, 213*(4507), 501–504.

Skinner, B. F. (1984). The evolution of behavior. *Journal of the Experimental Analysis of Behavior, 41,* 217–221.

Skinner, B. F. (1987). Why we are not acting to save the world. In B. F Skinner (Ed.), *Upon further reflection* (pp. 1–14). Englewood Cliffs, NJ: Prentice-Hall.

Skinner, B. F. (1990). Can psychology be a science of mind? *American Psychologist, 45,* 1206–1210.

Sokolov, E. N. (1960). Neuronal models and the orienting reflex. In M. A. Brazier (Ed.), *The central nervous system and behavior* (pp. 187–276). New York, NY: Macy.

Sokolov, E. N. (1963). Higher nervous functions: The orienting reflex. *Annual Review of Physiology, 25,* 545–580.

Sokolov, E. N. (1975). The neuronal mechanisms of the orienting reflex. In E. N. Sokolov & O. S. Vinogradova (Eds.), *Neuronal mechanisms of the orienting reflex* (pp. 217–235). Hillsdale, NJ: Erlbaum.

Solomon, R. L. (1980). The opponent-process theory of acquired motivation: The costs of pleasure and the benefits of pain. *American Psychologist, 35,* 691–712.

Solomon, R. L., & Corbit, J. D. (1973). An opponent-process theory of motivation: II. Cigarette addiction. *Journal of Abnormal Psychology, 81,* 158–171.

Solomon, R. L., & Corbit, J. D. (1974). An opponent-process theory of motivation: I. Temporal dynamics of affect. *Psychological Review, 81,* 119–145.

Solomon, R. L., Kamin, L. J., & Wynne, L. C. (1953). Traumatic avoidance learning: The outcomes of several extinction procedures with dogs. *Journal of Abnormal and Social Psychology, 48,* 291–302.

Song, G. C., & Ryu, C. M. (2018). Evidence for volatile memory in plants: Boosting defence priming through the recurrent application of plant volatiles. *Molecules and Cells, 41,* 724–732.

Sosa, R., & Ramírez, M. N. (2019). Conditioned inhibition: Historical critiques and controversies in the light of recent advances. *Journal of Experimental Psychology: Animal Learning and Cognition, 45,* 17–42.

Spiegler, M. D., & Guevremont, D. C. (2010). *Contemporary behavior therapy* (5th ed.). Belmont, CA: Wadsworth.

Starr, M. D., & Mineka, S. (1977). Determinants of fear over the course of avoidance learning. *Learning & Motivation, 8,* 332–350.

St. Claire-Smith, R. S. (1979). The overshadowing and blocking of punishment. *Quarterly Journal of Experimental Psychology, 31,* 51–61.

Stitzer, M., & Petry, N. (2006). Contingency management for treatment of substance abuse. *Annual Review of Clinical Psychology, 2,* 411–434.

Stockard, J., Wood, T. W., Coughlin, C., & Rasplica Khoury, C. (2018). The effectiveness of direct instruction curricula: A meta-analysis of a half century of research. *Review of Educational Research, 88,* 479–507.

Stout, S. C., & Miller, R. R. (2007). Sometimes-competing retrieval (SOCR): A formalization of the comparator hypothesis. *Psychological Review, 114,* 759–783.

Strack, F., & Deutsch, R. (2004). Reflective and impulsive determinants of social behavior. *Personality and Social Psychology Review, 8,* 220–247.

Sugai, G., Horner, R., & Algozzine, B. (2011, April 19). Reducing the effectiveness of bullying behavior in schools. Positive Behavioral Interventions & Supports. https://www.pbis.org/resource/reducing-the-effectiveness-of-bullying-behavior-in-schools

Surwit, R. S. (1972). *The anticipatory modifications of the conditioning of a fear response in humans.* (Unpublished doctoral dissertation). McGill University.

Sutton, R. S., & Barto, A. G. (1998). *Reinforcement learning: An introduction.* Cambridge, MA: MIT Press.

Tate, R. L., Perdices, M., Rosenkoetter, U., Shadish, W., Vohra, S., Barlow, D. H., & McDonald, S. (2016). The single-case reporting guideline in behavioural interventions (SCRIBE) 2016 statement. *Aphasiology, 30,* 862–876.

Taub, E. (2010). What psychology as a science owes Neal Miller: The example of his biofeedback research. *Biofeedback, 38,* 108–117.

Testa, T. J. (1974). Causal relationships and the acquisition of avoidance responses. *Psychological Review, 81,* 491–505.

Thaler, R. H., & Sunstein, C. R. (2008). *Nudge: Improving decisions about health, wealth, and happiness.* New Haven, CT: Yale University Press.

Theios, J. (1963). Simple conditioning as two-stage all-or-none learning. *Psychological Review, 70,* 403–417.

Thome, J., Hauschild, S., Koppe, G., Liebke, L., Rausch, S., Herzog, J. I., & Hermans, D. (2017). Generalisation of fear in PTSD related to prolonged childhood maltreatment: An experimental study. *Psychological Medicine, 48,* 2223–2234.

Thompson, L. G. (2010). Climate change: The evidence and our options. *Behavior Analyst, 33,* 153–170.

Thompson, R. F. (2009). Habituation: A history. *Neurobiology of Learning Memory, 92,* 127–134.

Thompson, R. F., & Steinmetz, J. (2009). The role of the cerebellum in classical conditioning of discrete behavioral responses. *Neuroscience, 162,* 732–755.

Thorndike, E. L. (1911). *Animal intelligence: Experimental studies.* New York, NY: Macmillan.

Thorndike, E. L. (1932). Reward and punishment in animal learning. *Comparative Psychology Monographs, 8,* 4, 65.

Tibboel, H., De Houwer, J., & Van Bockstaele, B. (2015). Implicit measures of "wanting" and "liking" in humans. *Neuroscience & Biobehavioral Reviews, 57,* 350–364.

Timberlake, W. (1984). Behavior regulation and learned performance: Some misapprehensions and disagreements. *Journal of the Experimental Analysis of Behavior, 41*, 355–375.

Timberlake, W., & Allison, J. (1974). Response deprivation: An empirical approach to instrumental performance. *Psychological Review, 81*, 146–164.

Timberlake, W., & Farmer-Dougan, V. A. (1991). Reinforcement in applied settings: Figuring out ahead of time what will work. *Psychological Bulletin, 110*, 379–391.

Todes, D. P. (2014). *Ivan Pavlov: A Russian Life in Science.* Oxford, UK: Oxford University Press.

Tolman, E. C. (1938). The determiners of behavior at a choice point. *Psychological Review, 45*, 1–41.

Tolman, E. C., & Honzik, C. H. (1930). Introduction and removal of reward, and maze performance in rats. *University of California Publications in Psychology, 4*, 257–275.

Törneke, N. (2010). *Learning RFT: An introduction to relational frame theory and its clinical application.* Oakland, CA: New Harbinger.

Trask, S., Thrailkill, E. A., & Bouton, M. E. (2017). Occasion setting, inhibition, and the contextual control of extinction in Pavlovian and instrumental (operant) learning. *Behavioural Processes, 137*, 64–72.

Tryon, W. W. (2005). Possible mechanisms for why desensitization and exposure therapy work. *Clinical Psychology Review, 25*, 67–95.

Unkelbach, C., Fiedler, K., Bayer, M., Stegmüller, M., & Danner, D. (2008). Why positive information is processed faster: The density hypothesis. *Journal of Personality and Social Psychology, 95*, 36–49.

Vadillo, M. A., Konstantinidis, E., & Shanks, D. R. (2016). Underpowered samples, false negatives, and unconscious learning. *Psychonomic Bulletin Review, 23*, 87–102.

Vahey, N., & Whelan, R. (2016). The functional-cognitive framework as a tool for accelerating progress in cognitive neuroscience: On the benefits of bridging rather than reducing levels of analyses. *International Journal of Psychology, 51*, 45–49.

Van Dessel, P., De Houwer, J., Gast, A., & Smith, C.T. (2015). Instruction-based approach-avoidance effects: Changing stimulus evaluation via the mere instruction to approach or avoid stimuli. *Experimental Psychology, 62*, 161–169.

Van Dessel, P., Mertens, G., Smith, C. T., & De Houwer, J. (2017). The mere exposure instruction effect: Mere exposure instructions influence liking. *Experimental Psychology, 64*, 299–314.

Van Gucht, D., Vansteenwegen, D., Beckers, T., Hermans, D., Baeyens, F., & Van den Bergh, O. (2008). Repeated cue exposure effects on subjective and physiological indices of chocolate craving. *Appetite, 50*, 19–24.

Van Horik, J., Clayton, N., & Emery, N. J. (2012). Convergent evolution of cognition in corvids, apes, and other animals. In J. Vonk & T. K. Shackelford (Eds.), *Oxford handbook of comparative evolutionary psychology* (pp. 80–101). New York, NY: Oxford University Press.

Van Osselaer, S. M. (2008). Associative learning and consumer decisions. In C. P. Haugtvedt, P. Herr, & F. R. Kardes, *Handbook of consumer psychology* (pp. 699–729). Mahwah, NJ: Erlbaum.

Vervliet, B., Craske, M. G., & Hermans, D. (2013). Fear extinction and relapse: State of the art. *Annual Review of Clinical Psychology, 9*, 215–248.

Virués-Ortega, J. (2010). Applied behavior analytic intervention for autism in early childhood: Meta-analysis, meta-regression and dose-response meta-analysis of multiple outcomes. *Clinical Psychology Review, 30*, 387–399.

Vogel, E. H., Ponce, F. P., & Wagner, A. R. (2019). The development and present status of the SOP model of associative learning. *Quarterly Journal of Experimental Psychology, 72*, 346–374.

Vollmayr, B., & Gass, P. (2013). Learned helplessness: Unique features and translational value of a cognitive depression model. *Cell and Tissue Research, 354*, 171–178.

Wagenaar, A. C., & Burris, S. C. (2013). *Public health law research: Theory and methods.* New York, NY: Wiley.

Wagner, A. R. (1981). SOP: A model of automatic memory processing in animal behavior. In N. E. Spears & R. R. Miller (Eds.), *Information processing in animals: Memory mechanisms* (pp. 5–47). Hillsdale, NJ: Erlbaum.

Wagner, A. R., & Brandon, S. E. (2001). A componential theory of Pavlovian conditioning. In R. R. Mowrer, & S. B. Klein (Eds.), *Handbook of contemporary learning theories* (pp. 23–64). Mahwah, NJ: Erlbaum.

Waldmann, M. R., & Holyoak, K. J. (1992). Predictive and diagnostic learning within causal models: Asymmetries in cue competition. *Journal of Experimental Psychology: General, 121*, 222–236.

Ward-Robinson, J., & Hall, G. (1996). Backward sensory preconditioning. *Journal of Experimental Psychology: Animal Behavior Processes, 22*, 395–404.

Warren, Z., McPheeters, M. L., Sathe, N., Foss-Feig, J. H., Glasser, A., & Veenstra-VanderWeele, J. (2011). A systematic review of early intensive intervention for autism spectrum disorders. *Pediatrics, 127*, e1303–e1311.

Watanabe, S., Sakamoto, J., & Wakita, M. (1995). Pigeons' discrimination of painting by Monet and Picasso. *Journal of the Experimental Analysis of Behavior, 63*, 165–174.

Watrin, J. P., & Darwich, R. (2012). On behaviorism in the cognitive revolution: Myth and reactions. *Review of General Psychology, 16*, 269–282.

Watson, J. B. (1913). Psychology as the behaviorist views it. *Psychological Review, 20*, 158–177.

Watson, J. S. (1967). Memory and "contingency analysis" in infant learning. *Merrill-Palmer Quarterly of Behavior and Development, 13*, 55–76.

Watson, J. S. (1971). Cognitive-perceptual development in infancy: Setting for the seventies. *Merrill-Palmer Quarterly of Behavior and Development, 17*, 139–152.

Weaver, I. C., Cervoni, N., Champagne, F. A., D'Alessio, A. C., Sharma, S., Seckl, J. R., … Meaney, M. J. (2004). Epigenetic programming by maternal behavior. *Nature Neuroscience, 7*, 847–854.

Weidemann, G., McAndrew, A., Livesey, E. J., & McLaren, I. P. (2016). Evidence for multiple processes contributing to the Perruchet effect: Response priming and associative learning. *Journal of Experimental Psychology: Animal Learning and Cognition, 42*, 366–379.

Weiss, M. J. (2001). Expanding ABA intervention in intensive programs for children with autism: The inclusion of natural environment training and fluency based instruction. *Behavior Analyst Today, 2,* 182–186.

Wendel, S. (2014). *Designing for behavioral change: Applying psychology and behavioral economics.* Sebastopol, CA: O'Reilly.

Wicker, A. W. (1969). Attitudes versus actions: The relationship of verbal and overt behavioral responses to attitude objects. *Journal of Social Issues, 25,* 41–78.

Wiener, N. (1961). *Cybernetics, or control and communication in animal and machine* (2nd ed.). Cambridge, MA: MIT Press.

Wilson, D. S., Hayes, S. C., Biglan, A., & Embry, D. D. (2014). Evolving the future: Toward a science of intentional change. *Behavioral and Brain Sciences, 37,* 395–416.

Witnauer, J. E., Urcelay, G. P., & Miller, R. R. (2014). The error in total error reduction. *Neurobiology of Learning and Memory, 108,* 119–135.

Wittgenstein, L. (1958). *Philosophical investigations.* New York, NY: Macmillan.

Wood, W., & Rünger, D. (2016). Psychology of habit. *Annual Review of Psychology, 67,* 289–314.

Yin, X., Guven, N., & Dietis, N. (2016). Stress-based animal models of depression: Do we actually know what we are doing? *Brain Research, 1652,* 30–42.

Young, J. E., Klosko, J. S., & Weishaar, M. E. (2003). *Schema therapy: A practitioner's guide.* New York, NY: Guilford Press.

Zajonc, R. B. (1968). Attitudinal effects of mere exposure. *Journal of Personality Social Psychology, 9*(2, pt. 2), 1–27.

Zettle, R. D., Barnes-Holmes, D., Hayes, S. C., & Biglan, A. (2016). *Handbook of contextual behavioral science.* New York, NY: Wiley.

Zimbardo, P. G. (1992). Psychology and life. New York: Harper/Collins.

Index